THE LITTLE
BLACK BOOK OF

PARIS

*The Essential Guide to the
City of Light*

VESNA NESKOW

MAPS BY DAVID LINDROTH, INC.

ILLUSTRATED BY
KERREN BARBAS STECKLER

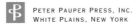

PETER PAUPER PRESS, INC.
WHITE PLAINS, NEW YORK

FOR TANYA AND PETE,
WHO FIRST GAVE ME THE
GIFT OF TRAVEL

Editor: Mara Conlon
Proofreader: JCommunications, LLC

Designed by Heather Zschock

Illustrations copyright © 2011 Kerren Barbas
Paris Métro Map © 2011 Régie Autonome des Transports
Parisiens (RATP). Used with permission.
Neighborhood maps © 2011 David Lindroth Inc.

Copyright © 2011
Peter Pauper Press, Inc.
202 Mamaroneck Avenue
White Plains, NY 10601
All rights reserved
ISBN 978-1-4413-0346-2
Printed in Hong Kong
7 6 5 4 3 2

Visit us at www.peterpauper.com

THE LITTLE
BLACK BOOK OF
PARIS

CONTENTS

INTRODUCTION

Paris conjures visions of sophistication, drama, and romance. The clichés abound, yet there's no denying the allure and beauty of the City of Light. Flamboyant and mysterious, Gothic and modern, refined and bawdy—Paris is all these, with room for both grandeur and coziness. It is a city imbued with history, a center of art, culture, and fashion, a cauldron of the intellectual avant-garde. But it is also a city of well-tended gardens, of cafés highly suited to people-watching, a feast of grand architectural splendors and small delights around every corner. And speaking of feasts, the food's not bad, either!

Paris is best seen on foot, walking up and down narrow passages and wide boulevards. With map in hand, it's hard to get lost. But what a treat it is to meander through the streets, taking in unexpected pleasures at nearly every step.

We encourage you to do just that: wander the streets as you visit the sites in this guidebook. There are so many extraordinary places in Paris that we've kept to our favorites, those exemplifying Paris as a center of style and re-invention, both historically and today. By exploring the city you'll discover what you love most.

Paris is divided into numbered sectors called *arrondissements*, postal codes by which Parisians identify locations. However, we've arranged this guidebook by clusters of neighborhoods, or quarters. (You will find that we have included the *arrondissements* within the specific addresses of sites.) The first seven chapters cover such clusters in central Paris, each with its own map. The eighth chapter highlights places on the city's outskirts, and the ninth chapter includes short excursions to spots near Paris. We've also included an overview map of the entire city inside the front cover and a public transportation map in the back.

Once you've explored Paris and been enchanted by its beauty and spirit, you can quote Humphrey Bogart when, in the movie *Casablanca*, he tells Ingrid Bergman, "We'll always have Paris."

GREAT VIEWS

For the best—and it's free!—sightseeing tour, walk along the Seine River. The views are spectacular. Be sure to look down at the walkways bordering the water: you'll see lovers kissing beneath the trees, students poring over books, fishermen patiently holding a line in the water, and the occasional beret-topped *grand-père* calmly feeding the pigeons.

You'll find other great views from atop the Eiffel Tower, the steps and terraces of Sacré-Coeur, the Georges restaurant on the roof of Beaubourg (Centre Georges Pompidou), the roof of the Institute of the Arab World, and, following in the footsteps of Quasimodo, the North Tower of Notre Dame.

For a river view, ride a tourist boat *(bateau-mouche)* along the Seine. **Bateaux-Mouches** depart from the Alma Bridge *(T. 01-42.25.96.10, www.bateaux-mouches.fr)*. **Bateaux Parisiens** depart from Port de la Bourdonnais, near the Eiffel Tower *(T. 01-76.64.14.45, www.bateaux parisiens.com)*. **Vedettes du Pont-Neuf** *(Square du Vert Galant, Paris 1st, T. 01-46.33.98.38, www.vedettes dupontneuf.com)* are open boats. Or catch the **Batobus** *(T. 08-25.05.01.01, www.batobus.com)*, public transportation on the river, at any of its eight stops between the Eiffel Tower and the Jardin des Plantes.

HOW TO USE THIS GUIDE

We have included a map for each neighborhood with color-coded numbers corresponding to the places mentioned in the text. **Red** symbols indicate **Places to See** (landmarks and arts & entertainment). **Blue** symbols indicate **Places to Eat & Drink** (restaurants, cafés, bars, and nightlife). **Orange** symbols indicate **Where to Shop**. **Green** symbols indicate **Where to Stay**. Some restaurants and shops are closed in August, so check before going.

Here are our keys for restaurant and hotel costs:

Restaurants

Cost of an appetizer and main course without drinks

(€)	Up to 25€
(€€)	25€-50€
(€€€)	50€-75€
(€€€€)	75€ and up

Hotels
Cost per night

(€)	Up to 150€
(€€)	150€-250€
(€€€)	250€-400€
(€€€€)	400€ and up

Abbreviations
M métro (subway) station

ALL ABOUT MONEY

Money changing

The currency in France is the euro (€). ATMs abound and most places take credit cards. Visa is commonly called "Carte Bleue." MasterCard is often referred to as "Eurocard." Exchange rates for cash or travelers' checks are best in banks, but some offer the service for clients only. Avoid changing money in airports, train stations, hotels, restaurants, and shops. You can try these places:

AMERICAN EXPRESS: 11 rue Scribe, 9th *(M: Opéra, exit rue Scribe, T. 01-47.77.70.00)*

CITIBANK: 1-5 rue Paul Cézanne, 8th *(M: St-Philippe-du-Roule, T. 01-70.75.50.00)*

COMPTOIR DE CHANGE OPÉRA: 9 rue Scribe, 9th *(M: Opéra, T. 01-47.42.20.96)*

MULTICHANGE: 7 rue de Castiglione, 1st (and other locations) *(M: Tuileries, T. 01-40.15.61.16, www.multi-change.com)*

Tipping

A 15% service charge is added to all hotel and restaurant bills in France. But sometimes an additional tip is appropriate. A few extra euro-cents in a bar or café is fine; up to 10% in a restaurant if the waiter was particularly good. In hotels, tip 1€/bag for bellboys, 1€ for room service, 1€/day for housekeeping. For taxi drivers, tip 10%–15% on meter fares. In hair salons, give 10%–15% for any service.

Got cents?

Decimal points and commas are reversed from the U.S. system. So euros are separated from euro-cents *(centimes)* by a comma, and hundreds are separated from thousands by a period. On price tags, a € sign often replaces the decimal point (8,50€ = 8€50).

PUBLIC TRANSPORTATION

Getting to and from the Airport

Paris's two major airports are Roissy/Charles de Gaulle (CDG) and Orly. Flights from the U.S. generally go to CDG. Free shuttle buses marked "ADP" (Aéroports de Paris) connect the terminals and go to the Roissy RER (regional rapid-transit train/subway) station. The airport RER costs about 9€ one way.

Taxis into town cost about 50€ during off-hours, more at peak hours. Car and van services require reservations (17€–27€ per person). Aéroport Limousine Service *(T. 01-40.71.84.62)* is a fixed-fare car service. Airport

Connection *(T. 01-43.65.55.55, www.airport-connection. com)* is a door-to-door minibus service. Airport Shuttle is another van service *(toll-free: 0-800-699-699).*

Non-reservation buses include the Air France Bus, about 15€ *(T. 01-41.56.89.00, recording in French and English),* and RoissyBus, the RATP city bus, about 9€ *(T. 01-42.66.56.56).*

More information on getting into the city is available at:
www.parisnet.com/info_airplane.html
www.parisnet.com/airport_shuttle.html
www.paris.org/Accueil/Airport
www.worldairportguide.co.uk/airports/cdg/cdg.asp
www.paris-cdg.com

Métro, RER, SNCF, and Travel Passes

"Le Métro" is the subway. Individual métro/bus tickets cost 1€60, and a book of 10 tickets *(carnet)* costs 11€60. Visitors' passes are also sold at métro stations and online. Métro lines are identified by different numbers and colors. There is a fold-out Paris métro map in the back of this book. The métro runs daily from 5:30AM to 12:40AM.

The **RER** is a system of commuter trains that transports people from the outskirts of Paris into the central city. Many of the stations overlap with the métro stations and can be used interchangeably (tickets and passes are valid for both within the city). There are five different lines (A, B, C, D, and E), each with a different color. These are indicated on the map in the back of the book with slightly thicker lines than the métro lines. In some cases, it might be quicker to use an RER train to get from one destination to another because there will be fewer stops in between than on the métro train. The RER trains run daily from 5:30AM to 1:00AM.

There are five **SNCF** *(reservations & information: from U.S. 011-33-8-92.35.35.35, in France 08-90.36.10.10, open daily 7AM–10PM, www.sncf.com)* rail train stations that travel much further out of the city. These can be used for long-distance destinations and excursions. The station names appear in boldface type in the map at the back of the book, and the lines are a light gray color. You would use these for destinations featured in Chapter 9.

Paris Visite is a pass for 1, 2, 3, or 5 consecutive days of unlimited travel on the métro or buses *(www.paris visite.com/en/index.php)*. Some passes are for Paris only; others include outskirts.

PHONE NUMBER, S'IL VOUS PLAÎT?

When calling Paris direct from the U.S., dial 011-33 then drop the initial 0 in the number. When dialing within France or within Paris, dial the number as it appears (with the initial 0).

SHOPPING

Opening hours: We have included specific store hours wherever possible in this guide. As a general rule, Paris shops are usually open Monday through Saturday from 10AM to 7PM. But there are exceptions. Some shops are open on Sundays. Markets and neighborhood stores may be closed on Mondays. Boutiques often close for lunch, and small shops close for vacation, usually in August.

Sales: By law, sales *(soldes)* are held twice a year in France, in January and July. In Paris they last a month. At other times of year, good deals are marked in stores as *promotions*.

Tax refunds: If you spend a minimum of 175€ in one store, you can get a tax refund *(détaxe)*. You must show your passport and fill out a form in the store. On leaving at the airport, go to the *bureau de détaxe* to get your forms stamped. Do this before going through passport control or baggage check-in: you may have to show your purchases. Back home, return the pink copy in the envelope provided; keep the other for your records. If traveling to other EU countries, get your forms stamped in the airport customs office of the last EU country you leave. It takes about three months to get the refund.

Duty-free shops: Best at airports. The duty-free shops around Opéra and Palais Royal aren't much of a deal.

Chain and discount stores: Fnac is a chain store great for books, CDs, and electronics. Paris's main discount chain stores are Prisunic and Monoprix.

SAY IT IN FRENCH

Although it's best to carry a phrase book, here are a few basic words and phrases to get you started.

Bonjour *(bohn-zhOOR)* Hello; good morning/day

Bon soir *(bohn sWAH)* Good evening

Au revoir *(oh-vwAR)* Good-bye

S'il vous plaît *(sill voo plEH)* Please

Je voudrais... *(zhuh voo-DRAY)* I would like …

Merci *(mare-sEE)* Thank you

Oui *(wEE)* Yes

Non *(nOH)* No

Où est... *(oo ay...)* Where is …

le métro *(luh meh-tRO)* subway

un carnet *(un car-nAY)* packet of 10 subway tickets

un billet *(un bee-yAY)* ticket

la rue *(lah rOO)* street

l'hôtel *(low-tEL)* hotel; house/mansion

le magasin *(magazEHN)* store

le grand magasin *(gran magazEHN)* department store

le restaurant *(restorON)* restaurant

Parlez-vous anglais? *(par-lay voo ohng-LAY)*
  Do you speak English?

Où sont les toilettes? *(oo sohn les twalET?)*
  Where is the bathroom?

Ça coûte combien? *(Sah koot kombee-EN?)*
  How much does that cost?

Madame *(mah-dAHM)* Ma'am; Mrs.

Mademoiselle *(mahd-mwa-zEL)* Miss

Monsieur *(muss-YUH)* Sir; Mr.

ETIQUETTE TIP

Whether it's "Bonjour," "Au revoir," "Merci," or "S'il vous plaît," it's rude to address someone without saying "Madame" or "Monsieur" after the address. On entering a shop, always first say, "Bonjour, Madame/Monsieur." If you enter a store with a man and a woman clerk, greet both with, "Bonjour, Madame, Monsieur." Even the surliest Parisian waiter will say hello! Just don't call him "garçon"—it means both "waiter" and "boy" and is considered rude. Better to say, "S'il vous plaît, Monsieur."

BOOKING TICKETS

You can buy theatre and concert tickets at any **Fnac** (*one branch is at 74 ave. des Champs-Élysées, 8th, M: George V, T. 08-25.02.00.20, wwwfnac.com; hours: M–Sa 10AM–12AM, Su 12PM–12AM*) or **Virgin Megastore** (*52–60 ave. des Champs-Élysées, 8th, M: Franklin D. Roosevelt, T. 01-49.53.50.00; hours: M–Sa 10AM–12AM, Su 12PM–12AM*), and also at **Carrousel du Louvre** (*99 rue de Rivoli, 1st, M: Concorde, T. 01-43.16.47.10; hours: M–Su 10AM–8PM*). Same-day, half-price tickets (commercial fare) sell at **Kiosque de la Madeleine** (*15 pl. de la Madeleine, 8th, M: Madeleine or Concorde; hours: Tu–Sa 12:30PM–8PM, Sun 12:30PM–4PM*). Most theaters are closed on Mondays. Magazines with local listings for arts and entertainment are available at newsstands—in French, every Wednesday: *Pariscope*, *L'Officiel des Spectacles*, and *Zurban*; in English: *Paris Free Voice* and *The City* (quarterly).

Paris Museum is a pass for 1, 3, or 5 consecutive days of unlimited visits to museums (permanent collections) and monuments. Kids under 18 enter most museums free; those 18 to 25 years old at reduced rates. See the following Web sites for more information:

www.museums-of-paris.com/museum-pass.php
www.conciergerie.com
www.discoverfrance.net

SEASONAL EVENTS

Winter-Spring:

Africolor, mid-Dec., African music festival *(various venues in St-Denis, M: Basilique de St-Denis, T. 01-47.97. 69.99, www.africolor.com)*

Printemps des Poètes, Mar., national poetry festival *(various venues, 6 rue du Tage, 13th, T. 01-53.80.08.00, www.printempsdespoetes.com)*

Summer:

French Tennis Open, May-June *(Stade Roland Garros, 2 ave. Gordon-Bennett, 16th, M: Porte d'Auteuil, T. 01-47.43.48.00, www.frenchopen.org)*

Quinzaine des Réalisateurs, May-June, films from the Cannes Festival *(Forum des Images, Porte St-Eustache, Forum des Halles, 1st, M: Les Halles, T. 01-44.89.99.99, www.quinzaine-realisateurs.com)*

Paris Jazz Festival, June-July *(Parc Floral de Paris, Bois de Vincennes, 12th, M: Château de Vincennes, T. 08-20. 00.75.75, 01-49.57.24.84, www.parcfloraldeparis.com)*

Gay Pride March, last Sat. in June *(Centre Gai et Lesbien, 11th, T. 01-43.57.21.47, www.inter-lgbt.org)*

Bastille Day, July 14, celebration of French Revolution, dancing at pl. de la Bastille on eve, parade in morning, fireworks at Champ de Mars at night

Paris-Plage, mid-July to mid-Aug., sandy beach along the Seine *(T. 08-20.00.75.75, www.paris.fr)*

Tour de France, July, ends at Champs-Élysées *(T. 01-41. 33.15.00, www.letour.fr)*

Autumn:

Villette Jazz Festival, early Sep. *(Parc de la Villette, 211 ave. Jean-Jaurès, 19th, M: Porte de Pantin, T. 01-40.03. 75.75, www.jazzalavillette.com)*

Nuit Blanche ("All-Nighter"), early Oct., galleries, museums, bars, clubs open all night *(www.paris.fr)*

FIAC, end Oct., international art fair *(Louvre, Grand Palais, and other venues, T. 01-47.56.64.21, www.fiac. com/?eq=en)*

Fête du Beaujolais Nouveau, 3rd Thurs. in Nov., new vintage, wine tastings throughout the city *(www.beaujolais gourmand.com)*

Festival d'Automne, mid-Sep–late Dec, festival of contemporary theater, dance, and opera *(various venues, T. 01-53.45.17.00, www.festival-automne.com)*

PARIS'S TOP PICKS

Paris offers an abundance of one-of-a-kind attractions for visitors. Here are 11 of the top picks not to be missed!

chapter 1

INVALIDES

CHAILLOT

CHAMPS-ÉLYSÉES

INVALIDES
CHAILLOT
CHAMPS-ÉLYSÉES

Places to See:

Places to Eat & Drink:

Where to Shop:

★ *Top Picks*

If you are lucky enough to have lived in Paris as a young man, then wherever you go for the rest of your life, it stays with you, for Paris is a moveable feast.

—*Ernest Hemingway*

INVALIDES

8 **13** to Invalides; **12** to Assemblée Nationale;
13 to Varenne; **8** to École Militaire;
6 to Bir Hakeim (Tour Eiffel)

• SNAPSHOT •

Over its colorful history, Invalides has been refuge to torn and tattered soldiers, a tool of rebellious crowds, and home to Napoleon's Tomb. From monuments to government buildings to 18th-century aristocratic town houses, the Invalides area exudes *hauteur* and beauty on a grand scale. It is the Left (southern) Bank's equivalent of Right (northern) Bank grandeur. It's home to the renowned Eiffel Tower, the magnificent Rodin Museum, and other "not-to-be-missed" sites.

PLACES TO SEE
Landmarks:

The Art Nouveau lamps of the ornate, exuberant **Pont Alexandre III (1)** *(off ave. du Maréchal-Gallieni, 8th)* create an elegant curve bridging the Seine River. The gilded statuary—cherubs, nymphs, and winged horses —of this flamboyant bridge leads directly to the **Hôtel des Invalides (2)** *(Esplanade des Invalides, 7th, 01-44.42.37.72, www.invalides.org; hours: Oct–Mar 10AM–5PM; Apr–Sep 10AM–6PM; closed 1st M of month, Jan 1, May 1, Nov 1, Dec 25)* on the Left Bank. Commissioned by Louis XIV as a hospital for French soldiers, Invalides now houses several military museums, notably the **Musée de l'Armée** and **Napoleon's Tomb** (under the gilded Baroque dome). East of Invalides, along the Seine, is the **Assemblée Nationale (3)**, or Palais Bourbon *(33 quai d'Orsay, 7th, 01-40.63.60.00, www.assemblee-nationale.fr)*, the lower body of the French parliament. The Prime Minister resides at the **Hôtel Matignon (4)** *(57 rue de Varenne, 7th, closed to public)*.

On the other (west) side of Invalides is the **École Militaire** with its vast training ground, the **Champ de Mars** (great for jogging). At the far end of this park, bordering the Seine, is Paris's most renowned sight, the cast-iron ★**EIFFEL TOWER (5)** *(Champ de Mars, 7th, 01-44.11.23.23, www.tour-eiffel.fr; hours: Jan–Jun 12, Sep–Dec 9:30AM–11:45PM; Jun 13–Aug 9AM–12:45AM)*. Built for the 1889 World's Fair and the centennial of the French Revolution, the *Tour Eiffel* was condemned in its time as an eyesore, called both a "belfry skeleton" and a "truly tragic street lamp." Guy de Maupassant said it was a "high and skinny pyramid of iron ladders...which just peters out into a ridiculous thin shape like a factory chimney." Some claimed they lunched there to avoid looking at it. Still, two million people visited the tower in 1889; less than a century later, it had become perhaps the most beloved symbol of Paris. Observation platforms at all three

TOP PICK!

levels provide spectacular views, next to souvenir shops, cafés, and exhibitions. The stunning night view of Paris from the Eiffel Tower may leave you breathless; and for ten minutes every hour a dazzling 20,000-bulb light show makes the ironwork seem magical.

Arts & Entertainment:

The **Rodin Museum (6)** *(79 rue de Varenne, 7th, 01-44.18.61.10, www.musee-rodin.fr; hours: 10AM–5:45PM; closed M)* is one of the best in Paris, with Auguste Rodin's great sculptures on display both inside and in the garden outside. Don't miss *The Kiss, The Thinker, Balzac, The Gates of Hell,* and *The Burghers of Calais.* For a unique underground museum, pop into the **Sewers (7)** *(Égouts de Paris, opposite 93 quai d'Orsay, off the Alma Bridge, 7th, 01-53. 68.27.81, www.egouts.tenebres.eu; hours: Oct–Apr Sa–W 11AM–4PM; May–Sep Sa–W 11AM–5PM).* If you're in the mood for a non-mainstream film, **La Pagode (8)** *(57 bis, rue de Babylone, 7th, 01-45.55.48.48; call for show times)* shows international independent films.

PLACES TO EAT & DRINK

Lunch at the cozy *crêperie* **Aux Ducs de Bourgogne (9)** *(€)* *(30 rue de Bourgogne, 7th, 01-45.51.32.48, lunch only)* or order take-outs. The intimate **Bistrot le P'tit Troquet (10)** *(€–€€)* *(28 rue de l'Exposition, 7th, 01-47.05.80.39, lepetittroquet.abemadi.com; M–Sa 12PM–2:30PM, 7:30PM–10:30PM)* serves traditional French food. The food and the views at **Jules Verne (11)** (€€€€) *(Eiffel Tower, Level 2, 7th, 01-45.55. 61.44, www.lejulesverne-paris.com; hours: 12:15PM–1:30PM, 7PM–9:30PM, book ahead)* are fabulous, but the less expensive Eiffel Tower (5) cafés have the same vista. Chef Christian Constant boasts three restaurants in the area: **Café Constant (12)** (€€) *(139 rue St-Dominique, 7th, 01-47.53.73.34, www.leviolondingres.com; hours: Tu–Su, 8:30AM breakfast, 12PM–2:30PM, 7PM–10:30PM, drinks all day)*, **Les Fables de la Fontaine (13)** (€€) *(131 rue St-Dominique, 7th, 01-44.18.37.55, www.leviolondingres.com; hours: 12PM–2:30PM, 7:15PM–11PM)* for seafood, and the exquisite **Le Violon d'Ingres (14)** (€€) *(135 rue St-Dominique, 7th, 01-45.55.15.05, www.leviolondingres.com; hours: Tu–Sa 12PM–2:30PM, 7PM–10:30PM)*. Hugely hip **Les Cocottes (15)** (€-€€) *(135 rue Saint-Dominique, 7th, no reservations, www.leviolondingres.com; M–Sa 12PM–2:30PM, 7:15PM–10:30PM)* is the French answer to the American diner.

WHERE TO SHOP

At Maison Poujauran (16) *(18-20 rue Jean-Nicot, 7th, 01-47.05.80.88)*, a tiny old-fashioned *boulangerie*, you'll find wonderful *baguettes* and biscuits *(sablés)*; it's the official bread supplier to the Élysée Palace, the presidential residence—credentials well-earned. Populus Alba (44) *(10 rue Portalis, 8th, 01-42.93.60.32, call for appt)* showcases furniture designs, sculpture, and drawings by Christian Astuguevieille.

WHERE TO STAY

Practical, minimalist rooms make **Grand Hôtel Lévêque** **(17)** (€) *(29 rue Cler, 7th, 01-47.05.49.15, www.hotel-leveque.com)* a low-budget favorite. For elegance and luxury in the diplomatic neighborhood around parliament, **Bourgogne & Montana (18)** (€€-€€€) *(3 rue de Bourgogne, 7th, 01-45.51.20.22, www.bourgogne-montana.com)* exudes tradition for a classy clientele. Quiet and hospitable, **Hôtel de Londres Eiffel (19)** (€€) *(1 rue Augereau, 7th, 01-45.51.63.02, www.londres-eiffel.com)* is tastefully outfitted.

6 **9** *to Trocadéro;* **9** *to Iéna or Alma-Marceau;*
2 *to Victor Hugo;* **1** **2** **6** *to Ch. de Gaulle-Étoile*

• SNAPSHOT •

"Opulent" and "staid" best describe the exclusive
Chaillot quarter. The village of Chaillot was annexed
into Paris and underwent surgery during the moderniza-
tions of Baron Haussmann, under Napoleon III, to
become a neighborhood of grandeur for the *haute bourgeoisie*. It is arguably one of the best places in Paris to
catch phenomenal views of the city and its treasures.

PLACES TO SEE
Landmarks:

Facing the Eiffel Tower, across the Seine past the Iéna
Bridge, is the monumental **Palais de Chaillot (20)** *(17 pl.
du Trocadéro, 16th)*. Its two curved neoclassical wings,
harsh and cumbersome, provide great photo
ops from the central terrace: a magnificent view
of the river and the Eiffel Tower. The **Trocadéro
Gardens (21)** *(16th)* sweep down from the terrace, around a long central pool of fountains
bordered by statues.

Arts & Entertainment:

The **Palais de Chaillot (20)** *(see also above)* houses
several museums: for architecture, the **Cité de
l'Architecture et du Patrimoine** *(1 pl. du Trocadéro,*

16th, 01-58.51.52.00, *www.citechaillot.fr; hours: M, W, F–Su 11AM–7PM, Th 11AM–9PM)*; for anthropology and archaeology, the **Musée de l'Homme** *(17 Parvis des Libertés et des Droits de l'Homme, 16th, 01-44.05.72.72, www.museedelhomme.fr; hours: W–M 9:45AM–5:15PM)*; and for French maritime history, the **Musée de la Marine** *(17 pl. du Trocadéro, 16th, 01-53.65.69.69, www.musee-marine.fr; hours: W–M 10AM–6PM)*. For the history of winemaking (and tastings), visit the **Musée du Vin (22)** *(rue des Eaux, 16th, 01-45.25.63.26, www.museeduvin paris.com; hours: Tu–Su 10AM–6PM)*. The **Théâtre National de Chaillot** *(1 pl. du Trocadéro, 16th, 01-53.65.30.00, www.theatre-chaillot.fr)* in the **Palais de Chaillot (20)** *(see also page 28)* stages classics and some musicals. Nearby is the **Musée Guimet (23)** *(6 pl. d'Iéna, 16th, 01-56.52.53.00, www.museeguimet.fr; hours: W–M 10AM–6PM)*, one of the world's major museums of Asian art. The Neoclassical **Palais de Tokyo (24)** *(13 ave. du Président-Wilson, 16th, 01-47.23.54.01, www.palaisde tokyo.com; hours: Tu–Su 12PM–12AM)* is notable for its stunningly redesigned interior. It houses the **Museum of Modern Art** in the east wing and the **Site de Création Contemporaine** in the west wing. Versatile, dynamic, and imaginative, the space morphs for each exhibit's needs. The café terrace affords a great view of the Seine. Paris fashion shows are by invitation only, but the **Palais Galliéra Fashion Museum (25)** *(Musée de la Mode et du Costume, Palais Galliéra, 10 ave. Pierre 1er de Serbie, 16th, 01-56.52.86.00; hours: W–M 10AM–6PM)* holds two or three French fashion exhibits per year. Free concerts at **Maison de Radio-France (26)** *(116 ave. du Président-*

Kennedy, 16th, 01-45.20.63.14, www.radiofrance.fr; call for concert times) feature classical music and well-known popular musicians.

PLACES TO EAT & DRINK
Where to Eat:

Celebrity chef Pascal Barbot's culinary creations at **L'Astrance (27)** **(€€€)** *(4 rue Beethoven, 16th, 01-40.50.84.40; hours: Tu–F 12:15PM–1:30PM, 8:15PM–9PM)* are superb; it's tiny, so book months in advance. Equally *magnifique* is **La Table de Joël Robuchon (28)** **(€€€)** *(16 ave. Bugeaud, 16th, 01-56.28.16.16, www.joel-robuchon.com; hours: 12PM–2:30PM, 7PM–11PM)*. For a trip into surreal fantasy, the Philippe Starck-designed **Cristal Room (29)** **(€€€€)** *(11 pl. des États-Unis, 16th, 01-40.22.11.10, www.baccarat.fr; hours: M–Sa 12:15PM–2:15PM, 7:15PM–10:30PM, reserve 1 month ahead)* is very hot. The décor reflects the eccentricity of the mansion's former owner, Marie-Laure de Noailles, friend of Cocteau, Dalí, Man Ray, and Buñuel. Or opt for a sandwich at one of the many elegant cafés on the Place du Trocadéro. The postmodern **Tokyo Eat (30)** **(€€)** *(Palais de Tokyo, 13 ave. du Président-Wilson, 16th, 01-47.20.00.29; hours: Tu-Su 12PM–12AM)*, the restaurant at the **Palais de Tokyo (24)** *(see also page 29)*, is as much an artistic and aesthetically pleasing experience as it is a culinary one.

Bars & Nightlife:

This staid neighborhood isn't known for nightlife. But there's a cultural night scene at the **Palais de Tokyo (24)** *(see also page 29)*, where fabulous exhibits of international art are open until midnight.

WHERE TO SHOP

A host of fashion designers display their work in boutiques along **Avenue Victor Hugo (31)**, among them **Apostrophe** *(No. 5)*. The style strength of this particular avenue can best be described in two words: conservative and classic.

WHERE TO STAY

This area is not very exciting for tourists; it is well suited for business travelers. For casual French chic, **Au Palais de Chaillot Hôtel (32)** (€) *(35 ave. Raymond Poincaré, 16th, 01-53.70.09.09, www.hotelpalaisdechaillot.com)* offers bang for the buck. The rooms at **Hôtel du Rond-Point de Longchamp (33)** (€€€) *(86 rue de Longchamp, at pl. de Mexico, 16th, 01-45.05.13.63),* vary in décor from Louis XIV to efficiently modern.

CHAMPS-ÉLYSÉES

① ❷ ❻ *to Ch. de Gaulle-Étoile;*
① *to George V or FDR;* ❾ *to Alma Marceau;*
① ⑬ *to Champs-Élysées-Clemenceau;*
① ⑧ ⑫ *to Concorde*

• SNAPSHOT •

The Champs-Élysées district and the Place Charles-de-Gaulle (or Place de l'Étoile) epitomize the spirit of the *grands boulevards*. Twelve wide avenues radiate from the rotary of l'Étoile ("star"), cutting a grandiose swath through majestic *fin-de-siècle* residences. Despite the infiltration of commercialism on Champs-Élysées Avenue, the quarter is among the city's most aristocratic—and among the most popular for tourists who wish to take in perhaps the most famous avenue of the city. But the area is not just a tourist spot—it hosts numerous events and spectacular displays of national pride on days such as Bastille Day and New Year's Eve.

PLACES TO SEE
Landmarks:

TOP PICK!

In the center of Étoile, an island in a sea of moving vehicles, towers the ★**ARC DE TRIOMPHE (35)** *(pl. Charles-de-Gaulle/Étoile, 8th, 01-55.37.73.77, www.arcdetriomphe paris.com; hours: Apr–Sep 10AM–11PM, Oct–Mar 10AM–10:30PM).* Commissioned by Napoleon, the enormous, 164-foot-tall structure was to be a triumphal gateway for the emperor's returning armies. Instead, in 1840, four years after the building's completion, Napoleon's ashes passed beneath the arch on the way to his tomb in Les Invalides. Victorious French soldiers finally marched through the arch at the end of WWI. Beneath it lies the Tomb of the Unknown Soldier. Once the focus of fashionable society, the **Avenue des Champs-Élysées** has lost much of its aristocratic cachet but remains Paris's most famous street. The **Grand Palais (36)** *(Porte A, 3 ave. Général-Eisenhower, 8th, 01-44.13.17.17, www.grand palais.fr, www.grandpalaisparis.com; hours: W 10AM– 10PM, Th–M 10AM–8PM)*, an imposing exhibition hall with a magnificent glass-roofed central atrium, mixes classical stonework with Art Nouveau ironwork, topped with galloping bronze horses. Architecturally similar, the **Petit Palais (37)** *(ave. Winston Churchill, 8th, 01-53.43.40.00, www.petitpalais.paris.fr; hours: Tu–Su 10AM–6PM)* exhibits the city's collection of French and Renaissance art. Its dome mirrors the Invalides cupola directly across the river. North of the Champs-Élysées, the beautiful **Élysée Palace (38)** *(55 rue du Faubourg-St-Honoré, 8th, closed to the public),* with its English gardens, is the official residence of the president of the Republic. At the eastern end of the Champs-Élysées, the **★PLACE DE LA CONCORDE (39)** *(8th),* with its beautiful fountains, was built in 1750 with a grand statue of Louis XV in the center. During the French

TOP PICK!

Revolution, the statue was dismantled and a guillotine set up in its place: Louis XVI, Marie-Antoinette, Robespierre, Danton, along with more than 1,000 others, all lost their heads here. Concorde, Paris's largest square, is a focal point for surrounding major landmarks: the **Arc de Triomphe (35)** (west) *(see also page 32)*, the **Madeleine church** (north), the **National Assembly** (south), and the **Tuileries Gardens** and **Louvre** (east). At the center of the square is a wonderful gift from Egypt—a 75-foot-tall **obelisk**, covered in hieroglyphics, from the temple of Luxor.

Arts & Entertainment:

Besides the museums mentioned earlier, it's fun to visit the **Atelier Renault (40)** *(53 ave. des Champs-Élysées, 8th, 08-11.88.28.11, www.atelier-renault.com; hours: Su–Th 10:30AM–12:30AM, F–Sa 10:30AM–2:30AM)*, where cars aren't only on the showroom floor, they're on the walls, too. The top classical music and opera concert venue is the **Théâtre des Champs-Élysées (41)** *(15 ave. Montaigne, 8th, 01-49.52.50.50, www.theatrechampselysees.fr; call for show times)*. Or take a cooking class at **L'Atelier des Chefs (42)** *(10 rue de Penthièvre, 8th, 01-53.30.05.82, www. latelierdeschefs.fr; call for course times)* in a glass-roofed loft. **Musée Jacquemart-André (43)** *(158 bd. Haussmann, 8th, 01-45.62.11.59, www.musee-jacquemart-andre.com; hours: 10AM–6PM)*, once the home of banker Édouard André and portraitist Nélie Jacquemart, is an extravagant jewel containing an extraordinary collection of paintings, tapestries, and furniture.

PLACES TO EAT & DRINK
Where to Eat:

Fish is the centerpiece at **La Marée (70)** (€€) *(258 rue du Faubourg St-Honoré at 1 rue Daru, 8th, 01-43.80.20.00, www.lamaree.fr; hours: M–F 12:30PM–2:30PM, 7:30PM–10:30PM, Sa–Su 7:30PM–10:30PM)*. Drugstore Publicis (59) (€€) *(133 ave. des Champs-Élysées, 8th, 01-44.43.77.64, www.publicisdrugstore.com; hours: M–F 8AM–2AM, Sa–Su 10AM–2AM)*, good for a quick bite, is a stylish general store with restaurants and a pharmacy. The **Atelier Renault Café/Bar (45)** (€–€€) *(53 ave. des Champs-Élysées, 8th, 08-11.88.28.11, www.atelier-renault.com; hours: Su–Th 10:30AM–12:30AM, F–Sa 10:30AM–2:30AM) (see also page 34)* is a perfect people-watching place. An avant-garde, extravagant food experience for gourmets, **Pierre Gagnaire (46)** (€€€€) *(Hôtel Balzac, 6 rue Balzac, 8th, 01-58.36.12.50, www.pierre-gagnaire.com; hours: M–F 12PM–1:30PM, 7:30PM–10PM, Su 7:30PM–10PM, closed first 2 wks Aug)* dazzles as it delights. **Restaurant Guy Savoy (47)** (€€€€) *(18 rue Troyon, 17th, 01-43.80.40.61, www.guysavoy.com; hours: Tu–F 12PM–2PM, 7PM–10:30PM, Sa 7PM–10:30PM)* combines country inn hospitality with sensuous gastronomy. The cafeteria-style self-service at **Monte Carlo Restaurant Buffet (48)** (€) *(9 ave. de Wagram, 17th, 01-43.80.02.20/21; call for hours)* is a great bargain for the area. It has many dishes to choose from and even comes with wine. Celebrity chef Alain Ducasse does gourmet sandwiches in his deli/bread shop **BE Boulangépicier (49)** (€) *(73 bd. de Courcelles, 8th, 01-46.22.20.20, www.boulangepicier.com; hours: M–Sa 7AM–8PM)*.

Bars & Nightlife:

With a wide selection of wines to sample, along with seasonal French dishes, **L'Écluse François-1er (50)** *(64 rue François 1er, 8th, 01-47.20.77.09, www.lecluse baravin.com; hours: 8:30AM–1AM)* is a trendy wine bar. There's a line to get into the hip club **Nirvana (51)** *(3 ave. Matignon, 8th, 01-53.89.18.91; hours: M–Su 8AM–2AM)*, but it's friendly, and the dance floor rocks (the restaurant is expensive).

WHERE TO SHOP

In and around the triangle of **avenues George V**, **Champs-Élysées**, and **Montaigne** is an embarrassment of riches, overflowing with designer fashion houses. You'll find women's wear at **Inès de la Fressange (53)** *(31 ave. Franklin D. Roosevelt, 8th, 01-56.88.34.00)* (she's the official face of France, traditionally called "Marianne"), and French linens at **D. Porthault (54)** *(50 ave. Montaigne, 8th, 01-47.20.75.25, www.dporthault.com)*. For specialty foodstuffs, **Fouquet (55)** *(22 rue François 1er, 8th, 01-47.23.30.36, www.fouquet.fr)* is a dream.

Men's shirts and neckties are the focus at **Alain Figaret (57)** *(14 bis rue Marbeuf, 8th, 01-47.23.35.49 www.alain-figaret.com; hours: M–Sa 10AM–7PM)*. Classic French high fashion can't get much finer than at **Hermès (58)** *(42 ave. George V, 8th, 01-47.20.48.51)*. There's everything from toys to books to shampoo at **Drugstore Publicis (59)** *(133 ave. des Champs-Élysées, 8th, 01-44.43.75.07, www.publicisdrugstore.com; hours: M–F 8AM–2AM, Sa–Su 10AM–2AM)*. The chain store **Monoprix (60)** *(branch at 52 ave. des Champs-Élysées, 8th, 01-53.77.65.65, www.monoprix.fr; hours: M–Sa 9AM–12AM)* has a variety of good inexpensive items. Next door the **Virgin Megastore (61)** *(52-60 ave. des Champs-Élysées, 8th, 01-49.53. 50.00, www.virginmegastore.fr; hours: M–Sa 10AM–12AM, Su 12PM–12AM)* sells CDs, books, and electronics.

Expensive art and antiques galleries line **Avenue Matignon**, as well as a stamp and postcard collectors' market. Artcurial (62) *(7 rond-point des Champs-Élysées, 8th, 01-42.99.20.20, www.artcurial.com; hours: M–Sa 10:30AM–7PM)* boasts one of the largest collections of

art books in Paris. The **rue du Faubourg St-Honoré** (and its continuation rue St-Honoré) is Paris's most famous street for shopping. *Prêt-à-porter* designer shops abound, along with places such as the Anne Sémonin (63) *(Hôtel Le Bristol, 108 rue du Faubourg St-Honoré, 8th, 01-42.66.24.22, www. annesemonin.com, www.hotel-bristol.com; hours: M–Sa 11AM–8PM, Su on request)* day spa and Anna Lowe (65) *(104 rue du Faubourg St-Honoré, 8th, 01-40.06.02.42, www.annalowe.com)*, which offers savings of about 40% on off-the-runway women's designer clothes.

Down the street, legendary Roger Vivier (64) *(29 rue du Faubourg-St-Honoré, 8th, 01-53.43.85.50, www.rogervivier.com)* shoes are like foot sculpture from the inventor of stiletto heels.

WHERE TO STAY

Luxurious Hôtel Plaza Athénée (67) (€€€€) *(25 ave. Montaigne, 8th, 01-53.67.66.65, www.plaza-athenee-paris.com)* is a legend, drawing fashionistas, honeymooners, and aristocracy alike. The near-antiques at Hôtel Résidence Lord Byron (68) (€-€€) *(5 rue*

Chateaubriand, 8th, 01-43.59.89.98, www.hotel-lord byron.fr) lend a warm ambience while the courtyard soothes the senses. **Galileo Hôtel (69)** (€€) *(54 rue Galilée, 8th, 01-47.20.66.06, www.galileohotel.com)* is elegant and sophisticated, modest and quiet. Luxurious yet minimalist, **L'Hôtel de Sers (34)** (€€€€) *(41 ave. Pierre 1er de Serbie, 8th, 01-53.23.75.75, www. hoteldesers.com)* was once a nobleman's *pied-à-terre.*

chapter 2

MADELEINE/OPÉRA

TUILERIES/LOUVRE/
PALAIS ROYAL

MADELEINE/OPÉRA TUILERIES/LOUVRE/ PALAIS ROYAL

Places to See:

1. Madeleine
2. OPÉRA GARNIER ★
4. Musée Gustave Moreau
27. Tuileries Gardens
28. Arc de Triomphe du Carrousel
29. LOUVRE MUSEUM ★
30. Louvre Pyramid
31. Place Vendôme
32. Palais Royal
33. Galerie Vivienne
34. Galerie Colbert
35. Place des Victoires
36. Jeu de Paume
37. Orangerie
38. Museum of Decorative Arts
39. Comédie Française
40. National Library-Richelieu Branch
41. Legrand Filles et Fils

Places to Eat & Drink:

3. Café de la Paix
5. Fauchon
6. Hédiard
7. Senderens
8. Farnesina
9. Ladurée
10. Cojean
11. Chez Jean
12. La Patata
13. Harry's New York Bar
42. L'Ardoise
43. Ferdi
44. Le Soufflé
45. Lescure
47. L'Écume St-Honoré
48. Le Pain Quotidien
50. Le Carré des Feuillants
51. Angelina
52. Café Marly
53. Le Grand Véfour
54. L'Épi d'Or
56. A Priori Thé
57. Chez Georges
58. Café Moderne
59. Aux Lyonnais
60. Bar Hemingway
61. Le Café des Initiés
62. Le Fumoir

Where to Shop:

14. Maille
15. Jadis et Gourmande

★ *Top Picks*

Where to Stay:

①⑧⑫ *to Concorde;* ⑧⑫⑭ *to Madeleine;*
③⑦⑧ *to Opéra;* ⑦⑨ *to Chaussée d'Antin*

• SNAPSHOT •

In the 19th century Baron Haussmann transformed Paris from a medieval fortress village into a modern city. With extraordinary vision he created wide, open boulevards that gave the city its aura of splendor and assured its place as one of the most beautiful cities of the world. Besides increasing ventilation and integrating the newly extended water and sewer systems, the avenues had the advantage of making it harder for rebellious citizens to erect barricades—a lesson learned from the revolutions which took place between 1789 and 1848. Nowhere is his extraordinary urban planning as visible as in the areas around Madeleine and the Opéra. The opulent use of space, in boulevards as well as buildings, has made it a prestigious location for the headquarters of major banks, while its bustling streets attract tourists, fashionistas, and people-watchers.

PLACES TO SEE
Landmarks:

North of the **Place de la Concorde** at the other end of rue Royale is the Neoclassical church known as Madeleine (1) *(pl. de la Madeleine, 8th, 01-44.51.69.00, www. eglise-lamadeleine.com; hours: 9AM–7PM)*. With its 52 Corinthian columns, it looks like a Greek temple. It faces what could be its mirror-image, the **National Assembly**, straight across Concorde and over the river. **Place de la Madeleine** is known for luxury food shops, but it was also home to luminaries: No. 9, for example, was Marcel Proust's childhood house. Follow the majestic Boulevard des Capucines, and you'll arrive at the ★OPÉRA GARNIER (2) *(pl. de l'Opéra, 9th, 08-92.89.90.90, from U.S. 011-33-1-71.25.24.23, www.operadeparis.fr; box office hours: M–Sa 10:30AM–6:30PM)*. Tons of gilt and marble went into building the **Paris Opéra**. Its mix of styles, ranging from Classical to Baroque, features gold busts, winged angels, rearing horses, and ornate columns. The façade sculpture *La Danse* by Jean Baptiste Carpeaux was deemed so shockingly suggestive it was once splashed with ink. Inside, the auditorium has a false ceiling created by Marc Chagall in 1964. Named after its architect, Charles Garnier, the opera house is emblematic of Second Empire grandeur and excess. Garnier also built the sumptuous **Café de la Paix (3)** *(see also page 45)* on the corner of the Place de l'Opéra and Boulevard des Capucines.

TOP PICK!

Arts & Entertainment:

The **ballet company** of the Opéra Garnier (2) *(pl. de l'Opéra, 9th, 08-92.89.90.90, www.operadeparis.fr; box office hours: M–Sa 10:30AM–6:30PM)* performs classical and contemporary pieces. The Opéra also hosts modern dance companies from around the world. The wonderful **Musée Gustave Moreau (4)** *(14 rue de la Rochefoucauld, 9th, 01-48.74.38.50, www.musee-moreau.fr; hours: W–M 10AM–5:15PM)* is devoted to this Symbolist painter's art, life, and obsessions.

PLACES TO EAT & DRINK
Where to Eat:

Place de la Madeleine is a cornucopia of restaurants and luxury groceries.

Fauchon (5) (€€) *(24-26 pl. de la Madeleine, 8th, 01-70.39.38.00, www. fauchon.com; hours: café M–Sa 8AM–6PM, deli M–Sa 8AM–9PM)* is famous for its fabulous delicacies, as is **Hédiard (6)** (€€€) *(21 pl. de la Madeleine, 8th, 01-43.12.88.99, www.hediard.fr; hours: M–F 8:30AM–10PM, Sa 12PM–10:30PM)*; eat there or take it home. **Senderens (7)** (€€€-€€€€) *(9 pl. de la Madeleine, 8th, 01-42.65.22.90, www.senderens.fr; hours: 12PM–2:45PM, 7:30PM–11:15PM, book ahead)*, in its Art Nouveau décor, serves divine dishes; the prix-fixe lunch will burn a smaller hole in your pocket. Isabelle Adjani and Inès de la Fressange swear by the fantastic Italian fare at **Farnesina (8)** (€€-€€€) *(9 rue Boissy d'Anglas, 8th, 01-42.66.65.57; hours: M–F 12PM–2:30PM, 7:30PM–10:30PM, Sa 7:30PM–10:30PM)*. One of the most classic tearooms in Paris, **Ladurée (9)** (€-€€) *(16 rue Royale, 8th, 01-42.60.21.79, www.laduree.fr; hours: M–Th 8:30AM–7:30PM, F–Sa 8:30AM–8PM, Su 10AM–7PM)* began as a bakery and sweet shop in 1862. Healthy soups, salads, and sandwiches at **Cojean (10)** (€) *(4-6 rue de Sèze, 9th, 01-40.06.08.80, www.cojean.fr; hours: M–F 8:30AM–6PM, Sa 10AM–7PM)* feature the freshest produce.

If you're at the Opéra, the **Café de la Paix (3)** (€€€-€€€€) *(Grand Hôtel Inter-Continental, 12 bd. des Capucines,*

9th, 01-40.07.36.36, www.cafedelapaix.fr; hours: 12PM–3PM, 6PM–11:30PM, terrace 9AM–11:30PM) is an experience, if not for a meal, then at least a *café exprès* and a sandwich on the terrace. The saying goes that if you sit there long enough, you'll see all the world go by. **Chez Jean (11) (€€)** *(8 rue St-Lazare, 9th, 01-48.78.62.73, www.restaurantjean.fr; hours: M–F 12PM–2:30PM, 8PM–10:30PM)*, with the fresh seasonal creations of its capable chef, is a bargain for nouvelle cuisine. For a cheap eat, **La Patata (12) (€)** *(25 bd. des Italiens, 2nd, 01-42.68.16.66, www.patatacafe.com; hours: 12PM–12AM)* offers salads and baked potatoes with a variety of toppings.

Bars & Nightlife:
Café de la Paix (3) *(see also "Places to Eat & Drink," open to 1AM)*, is great for a relaxed people-watching evening. Ever classic, **Harry's New York Bar (13)** *(5 rue Daunou, 2nd, 01-42.61.71.14, www.harrys-bar.fr; hours: cocktail bar 10AM–4PM, piano bar M–Th 10PM–2PM, F–Sa 10PM–3PM)* is still popular with American ex-pats in Paris.

WHERE TO SHOP
Place de la Madeleine is known for luxury foodstuffs: **Fauchon (5)** and **Hédiard (6)** *(see also page 45)* are practically unbeatable. On the opposite side of the square, Maille (14) *(6 pl. de la Madeleine, 8th, 01-40.15.06.00, www.maille. com)*, the famous mustard maker, sells divine mustards, vinegars, and olive oil. The specialty shop Jadis et Gourmande (15) *(27 rue Boissy d'Anglas, 8th, 01-42.65.23.23, www.jadiset gourmande.fr; hours: M 12PM–7PM, Tu–Sa*

10AM–7PM) is known for the *tresse*, a chocolate with nuts and candied orange peel. Or, to satisfy the craving for the perfect, small piece of oh-so-slightly bitter chocolate, head for La Maison du Chocolat (16) *(8 bd. de la Madeleine, 9th, 01-47.42.86.52, www.lamaisonduchocolat.com; hours: M–Sa 10AM–7:30PM)*. Treat yourself to some pampering at the beauty salon Institut Carita (18) *(11 rue du Faubourg-St-Honoré, 8th, 01-44.94.11.11, www.carita. fr; Tu–Sa 10AM–6:30PM)*. Eyeglasses have been the specialty of Lafont et Fils (19) *(2 rue Duphot, 1st, 01-42.60.01.02, www.lafont-paris.com; hours: M 10:30AM–1:30PM, 2:30PM–7PM, Tu–F 10:30AM–7PM, Sa 11AM–7PM)* for three generations—conservative or eccentric, they make a fashion statement.

The **Place de l'Opéra** is encircled by specialty boutiques, like Lancel (20) *(8 pl. de l'Opera, 9th, 01-47.42.37.29, www.lancel.com; hours: M–F 10AM–7:30PM, Sa 10AM–8PM)* for leather goods and **Clerc** jewelers. Behind the Opéra on **Blvd. Haussmann** are two of Paris's most renowned department stores: Galeries Lafayette (21) *(40 bd. Haussmann, 9th, 01-42.82.34.56, www.galerieslafayette. com; hours: M–Sa 9:30AM–8PM, Th to 9PM)* and Au Printemps (22) *(64 bd. Haussmann, 9th, 01-42.82.57.87, www.printemps.com; hours: M–Sa 9:35AM–8PM, Th to 10PM)*, which carry designer ready-to-wear, among other things. Several streets north, L'Atelier du Chocolat de Bayonne (23) *(107-109 rue St-Lazare, Passage du Havre, 9th, 01-40.16.09.13, www.atelierduchocolat.fr; hours:*

M–Sa 10AM–7:30PM, *Th to* 8:30PM) is famous for its chocolate bouquets. Adorn yourself with some jewelry from **Cartier (25)** *(13 rue de la Paix, 2nd, 01-58.18.23.00, www.cartier.com)*. **Thierry Mugler (17)** *(49 ave. de l'Opéra, 2nd, 01-53.05.25.80, www.thierrymugler.com)* is a fashion boutique.

WHERE TO STAY

A feng shui expert helped design the Zen-inspired **Hôtel de Noailles (24)** (€€€) *(9 rue de la Michodière, 2nd, 01-47.42.92.90, www.hotelnoailles.com)*. Luxury in a modern setting makes **Park Hyatt Paris-Vendôme (26)** (€€€€) *(5 rue de la Paix, 2nd, 01-58.71.12.34, www.paris.vendome.hyatt.com)* the destination for elegant but trendy travelers with deep pockets; the glass conservatory-dining room, with its potted orchids and displays of works by contemporary artists such as Ed Paschke and Llyn Foulkes, is especially pleasing.

1 **8** **12** *to Concorde;* **1** *to Tuileries, Palais Royal (Musée du Louvre), or Louvre/Rivoli;* **3** *to Bourse*

• SNAPSHOT •

The Louvre, the geographic center of Paris, was built as a fortress against the English in 1190. Around 1360 it was transformed into a royal residence, undergoing alterations by successive rulers over the centuries. In 1793 after the French Revolution it was turned into a museum with the royal collection on public display. It remains one of the major museums in the world, with a vast collection of art and antiquities. Stretching between the Louvre and Concorde, the Tuileries Gardens are an extension of the Louvre, with pavilions on either side housing other museums. Together with the opulent Place Vendôme and elegant Palais Royal to the north, this quarter affords a glimpse into the extravagant life of the French rulers and the power and riches of the *ancien régime*.

PLACES TO SEE
Landmarks:

Terraces, alleys, slopes, stairways, and stone pools were carefully planned for the royal **Tuileries Gardens (27)** *(rue de Rivoli/Quai François Mitterrand, 1st, 01-40.20.90.43; hours: 7:30AM–7PM)* situated along the Seine on the eastern border of Concorde. Statues by

19th- and 20th-century artists complete the architectural whole with magnificent vistas in every direction. The **Arc de Triomphe du Carrousel (28)**—built to celebrate Napoleon's 1805 victories—stands between the Tuileries and the Louvre. Stand beneath the arch for a fantastic view of Paris, stretching in a straight line from the Louvre through the Tuileries, past Concorde, along the Champs-Élysées, through the Arc de Triomphe, across to the Grand Arch at La Défense, just beyond Paris—an axis covering half the city. With nearly a third of a million works of art, the **★LOUVRE MUSEUM (29)** *(rue de Rivoli, 1st, 01-42.60.61.61, www.louvre.fr; hours: Th, Sa–M 9AM–6PM, W, F 9AM–10PM)* boasts one of the greatest art collections in the world. Formerly a medieval fortress and Renaissance royal palace, the Louvre became a museum after the Revolution. Its treasures include masterpieces of Egyptian, Etruscan, Greek, Roman, and Oriental art, as well as more modern European works. Some of the most famous pieces are Leonardo da Vinci's *Mona Lisa*, the *Greek Winged Victory of Samothrace, Venus de Milo*, and the Assyrian *Winged Bull with Human Head*. A modern counterpoint to the museum's historic architectural splendor, I. M. Pei's striking 1989 glass **Louvre Pyramid (30)** *(courtyard)*, serves as the museum's main entrance. The

 surrounding reflecting pools create a dizzying mirror image of the glass and steel structure while small pyramids echo the larger one's effect. The riverfront views are spectacular. Bordering the Tuileries and the Louvre to the north, **rue de Rivoli**, with its long row of arches, is home to expensive hotels, boutiques, and bookshops.

From rue de Rivoli, take rue de Castiglione and you'll arrive at one of Paris's most majestic squares, **Place Vendôme (31)** *(connecting to the Opéra via rue de la Paix)*. Built by Versailles architect Mansart, the octagonal square is an elegant example of harmonious, graceful 17th-century architecture. Many of the mansions were homes of bankers; one of them, No. 15, is now the **Hôtel Ritz (90)** *(see also page 59)*, where Coco Chanel lived, not far from her *salon de couture*. No. 12 was the house in which Chopin died in 1849. Today, under the arches encircling the square at ground level, **Place Vendôme (31)** is home to the haute jewelers of the world.

Just north of the Louvre is **Palais Royal (32)** *(pl. du Palais-Royal, 1st; hours: gardens 7:30AM–8:30PM)*, which has been through many phases—once Cardinal Richelieu's palace, then the childhood home of Louis XIV, and later the scene of elaborate and lavish gatherings as well as gambling and indulgent, rowdy celebrations. Today its arched courtyard bustles with boutiques and restaurants. Not to be missed are the stunning early 19th-century shopping arcades (*passages* or *galeries*), with their high vaulted roofs of glass and iron. From the far (north) end of Palais Royal, take rue Vivienne then turn right onto rue des Petits Champs. To the left you'll find **Galerie Vivienne (33)** and **Galerie Colbert (34)**—

wander into any *galerie*, but be sure to check out these two. Rue des Petits Champs turns into La Feuillade before reaching the elegant fashion mecca, **Place des Victoires (35)** *(rue la Feuillade, 1st/2nd)*, built around a statue of Louis XIV.

Arts & Entertainment:

Museums abound: the **Louvre (29)** *(see also page 50)* for arts and antiquities, the **Jeu de Paume (36)** *(Jardin des Tuileries, pl. de la Concorde, 8th, 01-47.03.12.50, www. jeudepaume.org; hours: Tu 12PM–9PM, W–F 12PM–7PM, Sa–Su 10AM–7PM)* for contemporary art, the **Orangerie (37)** *(pl. de la Concorde, 1st, 01-44.77. 80.07, www.musee-orangerie.fr; hours: W–M 9AM–6PM)* for great Impressionist works, and the **Museum of Decorative Arts (38)** *(Palais de Louvre, 107 rue de Rivoli, 1st, 01-44.55.57.50, www.lesartsdecoratifs.fr; hours: Tu–Su 11AM–6, Th to 9PM)* for art and design and its Art Nouveau and Art Deco collections. Near the Palais Royal entrance, France's finest classical theater is staged at the **Comédie Française (39)** *(2 rue de Richelieu, 1st, 08-25.10.16.80, www.comedie-francaise.fr; box office hours: 11AM–6PM)*. The **National Library-Richelieu Branch (40)** *(58 rue de Richelieu, 2nd, 01-53.79.59.59, www.bnf.fr; hours: M–Sa 9AM–5PM)*, north of Palais Royal, became an exhibition space once its books were moved to the Mitterand branch. For a change of pace, **Legrand Filles et Fils (41)** *(1 rue de la Banque, 2nd, 01-42.60.07.12, www.caves-legrand.com; hours: M 11AM–7PM, Tu–F 10AM–7:30PM, Sa 10AM–7PM)* offers wine courses focusing on a region or producer.

PLACES TO EAT & DRINK
Where to Eat:

The area bordered by Tuileries, Concorde, Place Vendôme, and Palais Royal is replete with cozy restaurants. Though Place Vendôme is one of the priciest spots in town, the nearby **L'Ardoise (42) (€€)** *(28 rue du Mont-Thabor, 1st, 01-42.96.28.18, www.lardoise-paris.com; hours: Tu–Sa 12PM–2:30PM, 6:30PM–11PM, Su 6:30PM–11PM)* is reasonably priced for good New Bistro fare. A few doors down, fashionistas feast on great burgers at lunch and tapas for dinner at **Ferdi (43) (€€)** *(32 rue du Mont-Thabor, 1st, 01-42.60.82.52; hours: Tu–Sa lunch & dinner)*; you might spot Penélope Cruz there. Two doors away, **Le Soufflé (44) (€-€€)** *(36 rue du Mont-Thabor, 1st, 01-42.60.27.19, www.lesouffle.fr; hours: 12PM–2:30PM, 7PM–10PM, closed 3 wks Aug)*, an American favorite, offers a large variety of sweet and savory soufflés. Two streets down, quantity is the key word at **Lescure (45) (€€)** *(7 rue de Mondovi, 1st, 01-42.60.18.91; hours: M–F 12PM–10:15PM)*, where the tables are so close together you can rub shoulders with your neighbor.

At **L'Écume St-Honoré (47) (€)** *(6 rue du Marché-St-Honoré, 1st, 01-42.61.93.87; hours: Tu–F 8:30AM–2PM, 4PM–7:30PM, F until 10PM, Sa 8:30AM–10PM)*, you'll feel like you're in Brittany eating fresh oysters at a seaside shack. Communal wooden tables make brunch a rustic affair at **Le Pain Quotidien (48) (€€)** *(18 pl. du*

Marché-St-Honoré, 1st, 01-42.96.31.70, www.lepainquotidien.com; hours: 8AM–10PM). Splurge at **Le Carré des Feuillants (50)** (€€€€) *(14 rue de Castiglione, 1st, 01-42.86.82.82, www.carredesfeuillants.fr; hours: M–F 12PM–2PM, 7:30PM–10PM)*, where the haute cuisine is fantastic and the service is superb. At least once, try the decadent desserts and rich hot chocolate at the old-world tea salon **Angelina (51)** (€) *(226 rue de Rivoli, 1st, 01-42.96.47.10; hours: M–F 9:30AM–6:45PM, Sa–Su 9AM–7PM)*.

One goes to **Café Marly (52)** (€€) *(93 rue de Rivoli, 1st, 01-49.26.06.60; hours: 8AM–1AM)*, facing I. M. Pei's pyramid, for its amazing setting and to see and be seen. The famous **Le Grand Véfour (53)** (€€€€) *(17 rue de Beaujolais, 1st, 01-42.96.56.27, www.grand-vefour.com; hours: M–Th 12:30PM–1:30PM, 8PM–9:30PM, F 12:30PM–2PM, closed 1 wk Apr, during Aug, & Dec 24-31)*, bordering the gardens of Palais Royal, is one of the most beautiful restaurants of Paris. Mirrors reflect the Napoleonic splendor of elegant ceiling and wall paintings, sculpted cornices, and hanging light fixtures. It was frequented by Colette, Jean Cocteau, Victor Hugo, and Napoleon. To avoid paying an arm and a leg, try the prix-fixe lunch. For good value and a brasserie that seems like it hasn't changed in decades, **L'Épi d'Or (54)** (€-€€) *(25 rue Jean-Jacques Rousseau, 1st, 01-42.36.38.12; hours: open M–Sa 12PM–2:30PM, 7:30PM–10:30PM)* has "French" stamped all over it; best to reserve for dinner and be on time.

In the lavish Galerie Vivienne (33) near Place des Victoires (35) *(see also page 52)*, an indoor terrace with glass arcade gives warmth to the upscale tea salon **A Priori Thé (56)** (€€) *(35-37 Galerie Vivienne, 2nd, 01-42.97.48.75; hours: M–Th 12:15PM–6PM, F–Su 12:15PM–6:30PM)*; it also serves weekend brunch. On the other side of Place des Victoires (35), the trendy crowd flocks to the famous Parisian bistro **Chez Georges (57)** (€€€) *(1 rue du Mail, 2nd, 01-42.60.07.11; hours: M–F 12PM–2PM, 7PM–10PM, closed Aug)* for an authentic experience of classic French food. Further north, across from the Bourse (old stock market), **Café Moderne (58)** (€€) *(40 rue Notre-Dame-des-Victoires, 2nd, 01-53.40.84.10, www.cafe moderne.fr; hours: M–F breakfast, lunch, dinner; Sa dinner only)*—stylish, chic, yet cozy—boasts an eclectic menu with international flavors. Nearby, the draw at **Aux Lyonnais (59)** (€€-€€€) *(32 rue St-Marc, 2nd, 01-42.96.65.04, www.alain-ducasse.com; hours: Tu–F 12PM–2PM, 7:30PM–11PM, Sa 7:30PM–11PM)*, besides vintage bistro décor, is its owner, Alain Ducasse; the prices are very reasonable for Lyonnais cooking from this celebrated chef.

Bars & Nightlife:

Bar Hemingway (60) *(Hôtel Ritz, 15 pl. Vendôme, 1st, 01-43.16.33.65, www.ritzparis.com; hours: 10:30AM–2AM)*, made famous by its most illustrious client Papa H, might be a cliché but the wood and leather luxury exudes charm. **Le Café des Initiés (61)** *(3 pl. des Deux-Ecus, 1st, 01-42.33.78.29, www.lecafedesinities.com; hours: M–F 7:30AM–2AM, Sa–Su 9AM–2AM)* is a trendy *apéritif* hangout with friendly staff. For more elegance and a slightly colonial air, try **Le Fumoir (62)** *(6 rue de l'Amiral-de-Coligny, 1st, 01-42.92.00.24, www.lefumoir. com; hours: 11AM–2AM).*

WHERE TO SHOP

The boutique of designer **Loulou de la Falaise (49)** *(21 rue Cambon, 1st, 01-42. 60.02.66)* is awash in vibrantly colored, imaginative clothes and accessories. Walk through the arches of the rue de Rivoli, where boutiques and bookstores will catch your eye, including **WH Smith (64)** *(248 rue de Rivoli, 1st, 01-44.77.88.99, www.whsmith.fr; hours: M–Sa 9AM–7PM, Su 12:30PM–7PM),* the renowned English bookseller. Across the rue de Rivoli from the Louvre, the **Louvre des Antiquaires (65)** *(2 pl. du Palais-Royal, 1st, 01-42.97.27.27, www.louvre-antiquaires.com; Tu–Su 11AM–7PM, closed Su in Jul–Aug)* houses 250 reputable dealers of high-quality antiques.

Fine jewels are the theme at **Place Vendôme (31)** *(see also page 51)*, where the great names of jewelry design sparkle with their gems: among them, **Mauboussin (66)** *(20 pl. Vendôme, 1st, 01-44.55.10.10, www.mauboussin.com),* **Van Cleef & Arpels (67)** *(22 pl. Vendôme, 1st, 01-53.45.35.50, www.vancleef-arpels.com),* **Boucheron (68)** *(26 pl. Vendôme, 1st, 01-42.61.58.16, www.boucheron. com),* and **Chanel (69)** *(18 pl. Vendôme, 1st, 01-*

55.35.50.05, *www.chanel.com*). For gems of another sort, take a whiff of jewelry designer Joel Rosenthal's exclusive perfumes at JAR (72) *(14 rue de Castiglione, 1st, 01-40.20.47.20)*. At the same address, sexy stilettos by Rodolphe Ménudier (73) *(14 rue de Castiglione, 1st, www.rodolphemenudier. com)* are sure to turn heads. For classic men's shirts and pajamas, Charvet (74) *(28 pl. Vendôme, 1st, 01-42.60.30.70)* has been shirtmaker to royalty and bourgeoisie since 1838.

Rue St-Honoré, just south of **Place Vendôme (31)** *(see also page 51)*, is one of the most famous shopping streets of Paris. To the west it's called rue du Faubourg-St-Honoré. As you walk eastward the shops go from extremely expensive couturiers to more moderate designer boutiques to the humbler shops of Les Halles. A few blocks east of Place Vendôme is an original Paris concept store, Colette (75) *(213 rue St-Honoré, 1st, 01-55.35.33.90, www.colette.fr; hours: M–Sa 11AM–7PM)*, a design emporium of clothing, art objects, and electronics, with a photo gallery, bookshop, and exhibition space. Jacques Le Corre (76) *(193 rue St-Honoré, 1st, 01-42.96.97.40, www.jacqueslecorre.com)* designs stylish but practical hats, bags, and shoes.

In the Palais Royal courtyard be sure to visit Italian costume jewelry designer Donatella Pellini's shop Pellini France (77) *(20 gal. de Montpensier, Jardins du Palais Royal, 1st, 01-42.96.18.68)*; her whimsical, elegant designs use stones and resins in cascades of colors and intriguing shapes. The destination for vintage haute couture is **Didier Ludot (78)** *(20-24 gal. de Montpensier, Jardins du Palais Royal, 1st, 01-42.96.06.56, www.didierludot.com)*. Alongside the Palais Royal, **Martin Margiela (79)** *(25 bis, rue de Montpensier, 1st, 01-40.15.07.55, www.maisonmartinmargiela.com)*, protégé of Jean Paul Gaultier, has opened his own boutique of inventive clothing and accessories. At **Galerie Vivienne (33)** *(see also pages 51–52)* you'll find stylish boutiques, such as **Jean Paul Gaultier (80)** *(No. 6, Galerie Vivienne, 1st, 01-42.86.05.05, www.jeanpaulgaultier.com)*. For the little black beret, little black suit, little black cardigan, head to **Claudie Pierlot (81)** *(1 rue du 29 Juillet, 1st, 01-42.60.05.67, www.claudiepierlot.com)*. The 1940s look is the thing at **Corinne Sarrut (55)** *(4 rue du 29 Juillet, 1st, 01-42.60.20.01, www.corinnesarrut.fr)*, who designed Audrey Tautou's costumes for the film *Amélie*. **Galerie Véro-Dodat (82)** *(rue du Bouloi/Jean-Jacques Rousseau, 1st)* is another passage of antiquaries, vintage shops, and furniture designers.

Place des Victoires (35) *(see also page 52)* is the locus of major fashion boutiques, including **Kenzo (84)** *(3 pl. des Victoires, 1st, 01-40.39.72.03, www.kenzo.com)*. You'll find apparel and accessory wonders at **Lucien Pellat-Finet (85)** *(231 rue St-Honoré, 1st, www.lucienpellat-finet.com)*. **Sandrine Philippe (86)** *(6 rue Hérold, 1st, 01-40.26.21.78, sandrinephilippe.com)* designs sophisticated, romantic fashions with a way of making you feel like you're part of a story behind her clothes. The signature cuts and finishes of Yohji Yamamoto (87) *(4 rue Cambon, 1st, 01-40.20.00.71, www.yohji yamamoto.co.jp)*, are inspired by the kimono.

WHERE TO STAY

Clean and comfortable, Hôtel Vivienne (70) (€) *(40 rue Vivienne, 2nd, 01-42.33.13.26)* is a good budget hotel. The best rooms at Hôtel Brighton (88) (€€-€€€) *(218 rue de Rivoli, 1st, 01-47.03.61.61, www.esprit-de-france.com)* have great views. Overlooking the Tuileries Gardens, the very expensive Hôtel Meurice (89) (€€€€) *(228 rue de Rivoli, 1st, 01-44.58.10.10, www.hotelmeurice.com)* boasts a discerning clientele—including actor Rupert Everett— and its spa is divine. Pure, unabashed luxury reigns at the Hôtel Ritz (90) (€€€€) *(15 pl. Vendôme, 1st, 01-43.16.30.30, www.ritzparis.com)*. If you don't like flamboyance, Hôtel Costes (91) (€€€€) *(239 rue St-Honoré, 1st, 01-42.44.50.00, www.hotelcostes.com)* isn't for you. More intimate, with painted beams and picturesque furnishings, is Le Relais St-Honoré (92) (€€-€€€) *(308 rue St-Honoré, 1st, 01-42.96.06.06, www.relaissainthonore. com)*—you might think you've been transported to a charming country manor. And within walking distance from Palais Royal, Hôtel Thérèse (93) (€€-€€€) *(5-7 rue Thérèse, 1st, 01-42.96.10.01, www.hoteltherese.com)* offers subdued luxury.

chapter 3

LES HALLES/ MONTORGUEIL

HÔTEL DE VILLE/ BEAUBOURG

MARAIS

LES HALLES/MONTORGUEIL
HÔTEL DE VILLE/BEAUBOURG
MARAIS

Places to See:

1. Forum des Halles
2. Halles Garden
3. Fontaine des Innocents
4. Pavillon des Arts
5. St-Eustache
6. Bourse de Commerce
7. Tour Jean Sans Peur
8. Théâtre du Châtelet
49. Place du Châtelet
50. Théâtre de la Ville
51. Tour St-Jacques
52. Hôtel de Ville
53. St. Gervais-St. Protais
54. Cloître des Billettes
55. St-Merri
56. CENTRE GEORGES POMPIDOU ★
57. Fontaine de Stravinsky
58. Rue Quincampoix
59. 51 rue de Montmorency
60. IRCAM
61. Musée de la Poupée
62. Musée d'Art et d'Histoire du Judaïsme
63. L'Atelier de Fred
64. Musée des Arts et Métiers
84. Hôtel de Sens
85. Shoah Memorial
87. Hôtel de Sully
88. Place des Vosges
89. Victor Hugo House
90. Musée Carnavalet
91. Musée Cognacq-Jay
92. Picasso Museum
93. Hôtel de Rohan
94. Hôtel de Soubise
95. Rue Vieille-du-Temple
96. Rue Ste-Croix-de-la-Bretonnerie
97. Museum of Magic
98. Maison Européenne de la Photographie
99. La Galerie d'Architecture

Places to Eat & Drink:

9. Au Pied de Cochon
11. Chez Denise—La Tour de Montlhéry
12. Le Père Fouettard
13. Au Chien qui Fume
14. Le Louchebem
15. Le Pas-Sage Obligé
16. Les Embruns
17. La Potée des Halles
18. Le Cochon à l'Oreille

★ *Top Pick*

Where to Shop:

Where to Stay:

4 to Les Halles; **1 4 7 11 14** to Châtelet;
7 to Pont Neuf; **1** to Louvre-Rivoli;
4 to Étienne Marcel;
3 to Sentier; **3 4** to Réaumur-Sébastopol;
4 8 9 to Strasbourg-St-Denis

• SNAPSHOT •

Les Halles was once the farmers' market of Paris, sheltered beneath beautiful glass and cast-iron pavilions. When Émile Zola dubbed it "the belly of Paris," he was referring to the food market, but the description applied equally to the unsavory and "alternate" characters who inhabited the area. The pavilions were demolished in 1969 and were later replaced by the Forum des Halles, an underground mall and transportation hub. A mixed mass of humanity still crowds the streets, and rue St-Denis has long been a red-light district, but there are plenty of remarkable spots in Les Halles. More picturesque, however, is the hip Montorgueil area, directly north of the Forum. The small streets around rue Tiquetonne and rue Étienne Marcel turn up funky

corners and trendy finds. All-night bistros thrive in Les Halles, while Montorgueil is crammed with romantic cafés as well as food and wine merchants slightly reminiscent of the old Halles.

PLACES TO SEE
Landmarks:

The **Forum des Halles (1)** *(rues Rambuteau/Pierre Lescot/Berger, 1st)* is a three-level mall with shops, cinemas, and a pool. Despite its open central courtyard, it's rather gloomy. The surrounding landscape, the **Halles Garden (2)** *(west of Forum des Halles, 1st)*, is as devoid of charm as the Forum. Architecture and city planning buffs are challenged by this bad 1970s attempt at urban renewal. Kitty-cornered (SE) from the Forum is the **Fontaine des Innocents (3)** *(rue Berger/rue Pierre Lescot, 1st)*, a Renaissance fountain erected on the site of the Innocents Cemetery, from which vast numbers of corpses were moved in 1785 to the Catacombs *(see Chapter 6, page 162)*. In the diametrically opposite corner of the Forum is a mushroom-shaped glass-and-steel structure, the **Pavillon des Arts (4)** *(101 rue Rambuteau, 1st, 01-42.33.82.50; hours: Tu–Su 11:30AM–6:30PM, call for shows)*, an exhibition space.

Among this mishmash of futuristic bad taste is one of Paris's most magnificent churches, **St-Eustache (5)** *(rue du Jour, 1st, 01-42.36.31.05, www.st-eustache.org; hours: M–F 9:30AM–7PM, Sa 10AM–7PM, Su 9AM–7PM)*, north of the **Halles Garden (2)** *(see also above)*. Modeled on Notre-Dame, with its flying buttresses, its plan is Gothic, but the decoration is sumptuously Renaissance. Historic figures are affiliated with this church, where Cardinal Richelieu and the Marquise de Pompadour (Louis XV's official mistress) were baptized. Another interesting building is nearby: at the east end of the **Halles Garden (2)**, the **Bourse de Commerce (6)**

(2 rue de Viarmes, 1st, 01-42.33.06.67; hours: by appt M–F 9AM–6PM) provides group tours of this commodities market.

St-Eustache (5) *(see also page 65)* marks the beginning of a more soulful area north of Les Halles. Stroll along the narrow **rue Montorgueil** and take in the flavors of the fruit and vegetable vendors, the wine and cheese merchants, and the ubiquitous cafés. The **Tour Jean Sans Peur (7)** *(20 rue Étienne Marcel, 2nd, 01-40.26.20.28, www.tourjeansanspeur.com; hours: Apr–Nov W–Su 1:30PM–6PM, Nov–Mar W, Sa–Su 1:30PM–6PM)* was the Duke of Burgundy's attempt to protect himself from reprisals after he assassinated his rival, the Duke of Orleans, which was believed to have ignited the Hundred Years' War. Burgundian symbols—oak, hawthorn, and hops—are carved into the turret. Rues Montorgueil, Tiquetonne, and Étienne Marcel are fun, funky places to explore around the Forum and are a bit more appealing to the eyes.

Arts & Entertainment:

The **Pavillon des Arts (4)** *(see also page 65)* exhibits unusual works, often showcasing unique objects or themes, from French as well as foreign museums. The free recitals at **St-Eustache (5)** *(Su 5:30PM), (see also page 65)* feature its 8,000-pipe organ. **Théâtre du Châtelet (8)** *(1 pl. du Châtelet, 1st, west side of the square, info 01-40.28.28. 00, booking 01-40.28.28.40, www.chatelet-theatre.com)* is one of Paris's main venues for classical music, opera, and dance; its annual *Bleu sur Scène* blues festival brings major artists, like Herbie Hancock and Ornette Coleman.

PLACES TO EAT & DRINK
Where to Eat:

Though fast-food joints glut Les Halles, you can still eat well at a number of restaurants and cafés. A stone's throw from the Bourse de Commerce (6) *(see also page 66)* is a brasserie once frequented by market workers: **Au Pied de Cochon (9)** (€€-€€€) *(6 rue Coquillière, 1st, 01-40.13.77.00, www.pieddecochon.com; hours: open 24/7)* serves such classics as onion soup and oysters, but its specialty is grilled pig's feet in béarnaise sauce. Several restaurants just south of Halles offer good deals. Fun, friendly, and open all night, **Chez Denise—La Tour de Montlhéry (11)** (€€-€€€) *(5 rue des Prouvaires, 1st, 01-42.36.21.82; hours: 12PM–3PM, 7:30PM–5AM)* serves excellent classics and is frequented by artists, writers, and professional business "suits" alike. Inexpensive and relaxing, **Le Père Fouettard (12)** (€) *(9 rue Pierre Lescot, 1st, 01-42.33.74.17; hours: 7:30AM–2AM)* has a year-round terrace. **Au Chien qui Fume (13)** (€€) *(33 rue du Pont-Neuf, 1st, 01-42.36.07.42, www.auchienquifume.com; hours: 12PM–2AM)* serves delicious brasserie classics, including braised rabbit; the décor's motif is dogs dressed as people—the place is, after all, "The Smoking Dog." **Le Louchebem (14)** (€-€€) *(31 rue Berger, 1st, 01-42.33.12.99, www.le-louchebem.fr; hours: M–Sa open to 11:30PM)* is a steak lover's haven and another Halles original. Excellent fresh fish is the specialty at **Les Embruns (16)** (€€-€€€) *(4 rue Sauval, 1st, 01-40.26.08.07; hours: Tu–Sa 12PM–1:30PM, 7PM–8:30PM)*.

In the Montorgueil area, **La Potée des Halles (17)** (€–€€) *(3 rue Étienne Marcel, 1st, 01-45.08.50.11; hours: M, W–F 12PM–2:30PM, 7PM–11:30PM, Tu 12PM–2:30PM, Sa–Su 7PM–11:30PM, closed Aug)* is steamy with beans, cabbage, pork, and veal. Classified a national monument, its tiled walls depict hand-painted beer and coffee goddesses. The original chairs display the names of Halles workers who were regulars; some of them still are, at 70 or 80. Another authentic working-class haunt, **Le Cochon à l'Oreille (18)** (€) *(15 rue Montmartre, 1st, 01-42.36.07.56; hours: Tu–Sa 12PM–2:30PM, 7PM–10:30PM)* serves huge, hearty portions to a mostly French clientele. In the lively food market street, rue Montorgueil, from which the area gets its name, **Foody's Brunch Café (19)** (€) *(26 rue Montorgueil, 1st, 01-40.13.02.53; hours: M–Sa 11:30AM–5PM, closed first 3 wks Aug)* is a self-service vegetarian restaurant with soups, salads, fresh juice, and bakery goods at great prices. Artistry and imagination are bywords at gay restaurant **Aux Trois Petits Cochons (20)** (€€) *(31 rue Tiquetonne, 2nd, 01-42.33.39.69, www.auxtroispetits cochons.fr, dinner only, from 8PM)*, where the food is noteworthy and the presentation carefully arranged. The owners' success led to a second restaurant a street away: more informal, **Pig'z (21)** (€€) *(5 rue Marie Stuart, 2nd, 01-42.33.05.89, www.pigz.fr, dinner only; hours: Tu–Sa open from 8PM)* is just as popular, so reserve a table. You'll get a shot of local neighbors and artists at both places. The oldest *pâtisserie* in

Paris, classified as a historical monument, **Stohrer (22)** (€) *(51 rue Montorgueil, 2nd, 01-42.33.38.20, www.stohrer.fr; hours: 7:30AM–8:30PM)* was opened in 1730 by Marie Antoinette's personal baker.

Now we know why she said, "Let them eat cake!" Around the corner, at the classic, old-style bistro **Aux Crus de Bourgogne (23)** (€€) *(3 rue Bachaumont, 2nd, 01-42.33.48.24; hours: M–F 12PM–2:30PM, 7PM–11PM)* nostalgia is served up with the house specialty, fresh lobster. **La Crêpe Dentelle (30)** (€) *(10 rue Léopold Bellan, 2nd, 01-40.41.04.23; hours: M–F 12PM–3:30PM, 7PM–11PM)* is a family-run *crêperie* serving an array of delicious crêpes and indulgent desserts.

Bars & Nightlife:

Kong (24) *(1 rue du Pont-Neuf, 1st, 01-40.39.09.00, www.kong.fr; hours: happy hour 6PM–8PM, music bar 10:30PM–2AM, restaurant 10:30AM–2AM)* is one of the city's hot spots designed by hotshot Philippe Starck and featured on *Sex and the City*—the too-too-cool staff is part of the heavy-on-style, light-on-substance ambience. One of the most famous jazz clubs in Europe is **Le Slow Club (25)** *(130 rue de Rivoli, 1st, 01-42.33.84.30; hours: Tu–Th 10PM–3AM, F–Sa 10PM–4AM)*, with big band and R&B rocking the tiny space.

Rue des Lombards in Les Halles is known for live jazz. Among the notable clubs of the street are **Au Duc des Lombards (26)** *(42 rue des Lombards, 1st, 01-42.33.22.88, www.ducdeslombards. com; hours: M–Sa, call for hours)*, and **Baiser Salé (27)** *(58 rue des Lombards, 1st, 01-42.33.37.71, www.lebaisersale. com; call for hours)*. Included in the list is also **Le Sunset/Le Sunside (28)** *(60 rue des Lombards, 1st, 01-40.26.21.25/01-40.26.46.60, www.sunset-sunside.com; call for hours)*, where artists from both sides of the Atlantic play (electric in the former; acoustic, the latter). Lively **Bistrot d'Eustache (29) (€-€€)** *(37 rue Berger, 1st, 09-54.89.23.20; call for hours)*, a charming throwback to the jazz age of the 1930s and 1940s, serves traditional French food; the jazz is live, with gypsy guitar jazz on Thursday nights.

WHERE TO SHOP

La Grande Boutique de l'Artisan Parfumeur (31) *(2 rue l'Amiral Coligny, 1st, 01-44.88.27.50, www.laboutiquedelartisan parfumeur.com)* is the flagship store of the grand perfume specialist. Besides selling fragrances, candles, and creams, the place gives evening lectures on the art and history of perfumery. If you must take home an enamel Parisian street sign, go to **Plaques et Pots (33)** *(12 rue de la Ferronnerie, 1st, 01-42.36.21.72, www.plaquesetpots.com).*

Hop to the other side of Les Halles for all manner of kitchen utensils and tableware at the famous **E. Dehillerin (34)** *(18 rue Coquillière, 1st, 01-42.36.53.13, www.e-dehillerin.fr; hours: M 9AM–12:30PM, 2PM–6PM, Tu–Sa 9AM–6PM).* The competition is equally famous: **A. Simon (35)** *(48 rue Montmartre, 2nd, 01-42.33.71.65, www.a-simon.fr)* and **Mora (36)** *(13 rue Montmartre, 1st, 01-45.08.19.24, www.mora.fr; hours: M–F 9AM–6:15PM, Sa 10AM–1PM, 1:45PM–6:30PM).* For all manner of beads, ribbon, buttons, yarn, and trim, visit **La Droguerie (37)** *(9-11 rue du Jour, 1st, 01-45.08.93.27, www.ladroguerie.com; hours: M 2PM–6:45PM, Tu–Sa 10:30AM–6:45PM).* Rue du Jour has spawned a small **Agnès b (38)** *(2, 3, 4, 6, 19 rue du Jour, 1st, women 01-45.08.56.56, men 01-42.33.04.13, travel 01-40.13.91.27,*

children 01-40.39.96.88, infants 01-42.33.27.34, www. agnesb.com) empire, where black is the staple wardrobe color and some bright patterns are mixed in for fun.

When the walking gets to you, enter the medieval stone walls of Spa Nuxe (40) *(32 rue Montorgueil, 1st, 01-55.80.71.40, www.nuxe.com)* for an exotic serene experience of their treatments, or just pick up a few beauty products. Conversely, try the hammam (Turkish bath) at Aux Bains Montorgueil (41) *(55 rue Montorgueil, 2nd, 01-44.88.01.78)* for a steam bath, an exfoliation, and a massage. If sewing and crafts are your passion, don't miss Declercq Passementiers (42) *(15 rue Étienne Marcel, 1st, 01-44.76.90.70, www.declercqpassementiers.fr)* for fantastic trimmings and tassels. Walk along the trendy **rue Étienne Marcel**, lined with hip names in fashion—Yohji Yamamoto, Joseph, and Diesel, among others. In the Montorgueil quarter, **rue Tiquetonne** is a trendsetter. It's full of workshops, restaurants, and boutiques, including Killiwatch (43) *(64 rue Tiquetonne, 2nd, 01-42.21. 17.37)*, a designer and secondhand clothing store. Increasingly popular, it sells used fashions by the kilo. Next door, the elegant, sexy, and feminine shoes at Patrick Cox (44) *(62 rue Tiquetonne, 2nd, 01-40. 26.66.55, www.patrickcox.com)* practically strut off the catwalk. One street up, between rue St-Denis and rue Dussoubs, is the Passage du Grand Cerf (45) *(St-Denis/rue Dussoubs, www.passagedugrandcerf.com; hours: M–Sa 8:30AM–8PM)*, with its Belle Époque ironwork and funky, fashionable purveyors of clothing, accessories, lighting, and art objects; prominent shops include **As'Art** *(No. 3)*, for unique African and ethnic gifts, **MX Sylvie Branellec** *(No. 6)*, with jewelry focused on pearls, and **PM CO Style** *(No. 5)*, for a variety of fascinating design objects from the far corners of Earth. Barbara Bui (46) *(23 rue Etienne Marcel, 1st, 01-40.26.43.65, www.barbarabui.com)* reflects her French and Vietnamese roots with refined and graceful designer clothes. Gourmet cookbooks, old and new, abound at Librairie Gourmande (86) *(92-96 rue Montmartre, 2nd, 01-43.54.37.27, www.librairie-gourmande.fr; hours: M–Sa 11AM–7PM)*: they include French, American, and English editions.

WHERE TO STAY

Les Halles isn't the best place to stay, but the Montorgueil area affords some bargains. Ambience is missing at the **Tiquetonne Hotel (47)** (€) *(6 rue Tiquetonne, 2nd, 01-42.36.94.58),* but it's cheap, clean, and very, very basic (with chenille bedspreads). **Hôtel du Cygne (48)** (€-€€) *(3 rue du Cygne, 1st, 01-42.60.14.16, www.hotelducygne.fr)* is reliable, appealing, and livable, with rooms decorated in Laura Ashley style.

HÔTEL DE VILLE/BEAUBOURG

1 4 7 11 14 *to Châtelet;*
1 11 *to Hôtel de Ville;* **11** *to Rambuteau;*
3 11 *to Arts et Métiers;*
3 4 *to Réaumur-Sébastopol;*
4 8 9 *to Strasbourg-St-Denis*

• SNAPSHOT •

Dominated by the Hôtel de Ville (town hall) and the Centre Georges Pompidou (colloquially referred to as "Beaubourg"), this district is jam-packed with interesting landmarks, museums, bars, and shops. Two aesthetics coexist: the ornate marble—replete with turrets and statues—of the Hôtel de Ville corresponds to the pomp and circumstance of its stature; a few streets away the "inside-out" structure of Beaubourg—with color-coded pipes, scaffolding, and ducts—puts the functional works of the building on public display. The district is exciting and vibrant, attracting a crowd eager for street spectacles —and there are plenty of those in the Hôtel de Ville/ Beaubourg quarter.

PLACES TO SEE
Landmarks:

Start at **Place du Châtelet (49)** *(at bd. De Sébastopol, 4th)*. Once a fortress defending the city from the north, it is now a major métro hub. Above ground, in the center of the square, is a fountain—yet another monument to Napoleon's victories. On either side of **Place du Châtelet**

(49) are the twin theaters **Théâtre du Châtelet (8)** *(west side; see page 66)* and **Théâtre de la Ville (50)** *(east side; 2 pl. du Châtelet, 4th, 01-42.74.22.77, www.theatredelaville-paris.com)*. In the northeast corner, the **Tour St-Jacques (51)** *(Sq. de la Tour St-Jacques, 4th)* seems to oversee the area. Flamboyantly Gothic, the tower is what is left standing of a church that served as the meeting point for pilgrims before venturing out on voyages. The tower was a favorite of the Surrealists, perhaps because of the plethora of gargoyles or because of their incongruity with the figure at the base of the tower, a statue of Blaise Pascal, who conducted barometrical experiments at the site in the 17th century.

As you walk along the *quai* (embankment) of the Seine eastward, gaze along the river at the fabulous views. Across the Seine, you'll see the old **Conciergerie** prison *(see Chapter 5, page 125)*; further to the left, the cathedral of **Notre-Dame** *(see Chapter 5, page 126)*; and in the distance to the right, the **Eiffel Tower** *(see Chapter 1, page 24)*. Great photo ops! Continuing along the *quai*, you'll arrive at the **Hôtel de Ville (52)** *(pl. de l'Hôtel de Ville, 29 rue de Rivoli, 4th, 01-42.76.40.40; hours: M–Sa 10AM–7PM)*, which serves as town hall, city council premises, and official residence of the mayor of Paris. It is also the venue for receptions honoring foreign dignitaries. With its elaborate, sculpted exterior and the impressive interior adorned with chandeliers, statues, caryatids, and a majestic staircase, the **Hôtel de Ville (52)** exudes power, pomp, and ceremony. The square facing the building has had its share of power-filled days: it was once the main site for public executions.

East of the **Hôtel de Ville (52)** is the 6th-century church **St. Gervais-St. Protais (53)** *(pl. St-Gervais, 4th, 01.48.87.32. 02; hours: M–F 6AM–9PM, Sa–Su 7AM–9PM)*, the façade of which is made up of three levels of columns—Doric, Ionic, and Corinthian. This beautiful church is famous for its lovely religious music. Walk around the back, up the picturesque **rue des Barres** where artists set up their easels and small cafés cover the terraced sidewalk with tables and chairs. A few streets northwestward is the 7th-century church of **St-Merri (55)** *(76 rue de la Verrerie, 4th, 01-42.71.93.93; hours: 3PM–5PM)*, decidedly Gothic.

Follow the rue St-Martin two streets north and you'll come to the ★**CENTRE GEORGES POMPIDOU (56)**, or "Beaubourg" *(pl. Georges Pompidou/rue Beaubourg, 4th, 01-44.78.12.33, www. centrepompidou.fr; hours: W–M 11AM–9PM)*. Opened in 1977, it was an immediate success and has remained so; its inside-out structure makes it one of the most unique examples of modern architecture. The workings of the building—air ducts, water shafts, utility pipes, elevators, escalators, and structural steel struts—are all on the out-side, color-coded to distinguish their functions, while the glass and steel walls give a sense of interior-exterior permeability. This leaves the entire interior space with the flexibility to adapt to the center's activities and needs. The museum boasts a collection of more than 50,000 works, covering painting, sculpture, drawing, photography, architecture, design, cinema, video, and audio-visual archives in addition to a library, screening rooms, and performance and exhibition spaces.

Outside Beaubourg, on the large esplanade, pavement artists and street performers do their thing to crowds of willing onlookers. South of Beaubourg, the **Fontaine de Stravinsky (57)** *(pl. Igor Stravinsky, rue Brismiche, 4th)*, created by artists Niki de St-Phalle and Jean Tinguely, is an intermingling orchestra of delightfully colorful and fanciful creature sculptures, each contributing to the waterworks extravaganza. Along **rue Quincampoix (58)** *(rue des Lombards/rue Rambuteau, 4th)*, a bevy of galleries, cafés, and bars animate the cobblestone street and its restored 18th-century residences. A block past its northern end is the (probably) oldest house in Paris: **51 rue de Montmorency (59)** *(rue Beaubourg/rue St-Martin, 3rd; closed to public)* built in 1407.

Arts & Entertainment:

Théâtre de la Ville (50) *(see also page 76)* is a must-stop for modern dance fans, where many important choreographers, such as Maguy Marin and Jean-Claude Gallotta, have showcased their talents. The modern art exhibits, audio-visual screenings, and performance art at **Centre Georges Pompidou (56)** *(see also page 77)* are not to be missed. By the southern flank of Centre Pompidou, **IRCAM (60)** *(1 pl. Igor Stravinsky, 4th, 01-44.78.48.43, www.ircam.fr; call for show hours),* dedicated to musical experimentation and research, offers contemporary music concerts; Pierre Boulez has been actively involved in IRCAM since its conception. A street north of Beaubourg, the **Musée de la Poupée (61)** *(impasse Berthaud, 3rd, 01-42.72.73.11, www.museedelapoupeeparis.com; hours: Tu–Su 10AM–6PM)* exhibits dolls from around the world, has a doll hospital, and offers doll-making classes for adults and children. The **Musée d'Art et d'Histoire du Judaïsme (62)** *(Hôtel de St-Aignan, 71 rue du Temple, 3rd, 01-53.01.86.53, www.mahj.org; hours: M–F 11AM–6PM, Su 10AM–6PM)* is dedicated to French Jewish culture from the Middle Ages to the present. Take cooking classes (small groups) at **L'Atelier de Fred (63)** *(Passage de l'Ancre, 223 rue St-Martin, 3rd, 01-40.29.46.04, www.latelierdefred.com)* to impress your friends back home with an authentic, homemade Parisian meal. The **Musée des Arts et Métiers (64)** (Museum of Science and Industry) *(60 rue Réaumur, 3rd, 01-53.01.82.00, www.arts-et-metiers.net; hours: Tu–W, F–Su 10AM–6PM, Th 10AM–9:30PM)* hosts conferences ranging from cloud computing to how to anticipate natural disasters; among other inventive objects, the mechanical figures and prototype machines are amusing.

PLACES TO EAT & DRINK
Where to Eat:

Take in the sights, from the fashion-model wait staff to the Parisian rooftops and major gems of the city, at **Georges (67)** (€€€) *(Centre Pompidou, 19 rue Beaubourg, 4th, 01-44.78.47.99, www.centrepompidou.fr; hours: W–M 11AM–1AM)*, the ultra-chic café-restaurant on the terrace of Beaubourg; the food's good and the view is superlative. Best for drinks, light fare, and brunch, **Café Beaubourg (68)** (€€) *(100 rue St-Martin, 4th, 01-48.87.63.96; hours: Su–W 8AM–12AM, Th–Sa 8AM–1AM)* faces the esplanade of Beaubourg—and offers its fashion-

able patrons a great place from which to people watch. For classic French dishes that are simple but surprising, **Le Hangar (69)** (€€) *(12 impasse Berthaud, 3rd, 01-42.74.55.44, cash only; hours: Tu–Sa 12PM–2:30PM, 7:30PM–11PM, closed Aug)*, a cozy bistro by the doll museum, is one of the best values in Paris. Around the corner is another great find: good food and friendly staff are served up at **Le Petit Marcel (70)** (€) *(65 rue Rambuteau, 4th, 01-48.87.10.20; hours: 8AM–1AM)*. **Le 404 (71)** (€€) *(69 rue des Gravilliers, 3rd, 01-42.74.57.81; hours: M–F 12PM–2:30PM, 8PM–2AM, Sa–Su 12PM–4PM brunch, 8PM–2AM)* is a fabulous Moroccan restaurant that's funky, sexy, and noisy; get down with the table-dancing crowd. Tiny but popular and friendly, **Le Potager du Marais (74)** (€) *(22 rue Rambuteau, 4th, 01-42.74.24.66; hours 12PM–12AM)* has great vegetarian food.

Bars & Nightlife:

Andy Wahloo (73) *(69 rue Gravilliers, 3rd, 01-42.71. 20.38; hours: Tu–Sa 4PM–2AM)*, a North African bar next door to **Le 404 (71)** *(see page 80)*, has an industrial décor and amicable staff ready to serve beer, cocktails, and hookahs.

WHERE TO SHOP

Contemporary interior decorations at **Sentou Galerie (75)** *(29 rue François-Miron, 4th, 01-42.78.50.60; hours: Tu–Sa 10AM–7PM)* have become the new classics; you'll find cutting-edge French design here. The designers and artists showcased at **FR66 (76)** *(25 rue du Renard, 4th, 01-44.54.35.36, www.fr66.com; hours: M–Sa 10AM–7PM, closed 2–3 wks Aug)*, a shop that sometimes seems more like a gallery, create unique items for the home.

MARAIS

7 to Pont Marie; **1** to St. Paul;
8 to Chemin Vert or St-Sébastien-Froissart

• SNAPSHOT •

Likely the most fascinating quarter of Paris, the Marais is also one of the most beautiful. Its exquisite character comes partially from a successful combination of diverse cultures and styles. Old elegance is embodied in the 17th-century mansions, expertly restored in the 1960s. These coexist harmoniously with boutiques displaying contemporary art, fashion, and culture. At the same time, small artisans and shopkeepers have held their own against the tide of gentrification, as have the old Jewish quarter and other ethnic neighborhoods. The entry of a vibrant gay culture has brought with it renewal and its own fashion and culture. Galleries, original new designers, bookshops, boutiques, and exhibition spaces line streets such as rue Vieille-du-Temple, rue Debelleyme, rue Charlot, rue des Rosiers, and rue du Roi-de-Sicile. The café culture too is strong. The historical landmarks, superb architecture, and romantic narrow streets garnished with coach lamps and ironwork add to the magic of the scene.

PLACES TO SEE
Landmarks:

Just past the **Pont-Marie** and one street in from the river, Hôtel de Sens (84) *(1 rue du Figuier, 4th, 01-42.78. 14.60; hours: Tu–Sa 1PM–7PM)*, now home to the Forney fine arts library, is a rare medieval building built between 1475-1507, its turrets and arches evocative of a time when Bourbons, Guises, and Cardinal de Pellevé occupied the premises. Just westward, at the border of the Jewish quarter, the Shoah Memorial (85) *(17 rue Geoffroy-l'Asnier, 4th, 01-42.77.44.72 www.memorial delashoah.org; hours: Su–W, F 10AM–6PM, Th 10AM–10PM)*, with its Memorial to the Unknown Jewish Martyr, is a memorial, study center, and museum dedicated to the Holocaust. **Rue des Rosiers,** a once colorful area, is fast being taken over by chain stores, and its old Jewish character is fading. The Hôtel de Sully (87) *(62 rue St-Antoine, 4th, 01-42.74.47.75; hours: Tu–F 12PM–7PM, Sa–Su 10AM–7PM)*, a beautiful late-Renaissance mansion, houses the Center for National Monuments.

A step away is the heart of the Marais, the Place des Vosges (88) *(rue des Francs Bourgeois, 4th).* Perhaps the most lovely and aesthetically pleasing square in the world, it's perfectly symmetrical: 36 houses, equally placed on four sides, stand gracefully over rows of arcades. Red brick and stone facades with slate blue roofs and dormer windows lend a simple yet regal elegance to the large square, where jousts, tournaments, and historic events took place. Literati, such as Madame de Sévigné, held salons here. The **Victor Hugo House (89)** *(6 pl. des Vosges, 4th, 01-42.72.10.16, www.musee-hugo.paris.fr; hours: Tu–Su 10AM–6PM)* is where the writer lived and where *Les Misérables* was created. Stroll under the arcades to find a variety of shops, galleries, and cafés—it's where Inspector Maigret of the Simenon detective novels likes to sip a *café-au-lait*.

Explore the many stunning small streets in the area as you make your way northward toward the **Musée Carnavalet (90)** *(23 rue de Sévigné, 3rd, 01-44.59.58.58, www.carnavalet.paris.fr; hours: Tu–Su 10AM–6PM)*, a mansion dedicated to the history of Paris *(see also page 86)*. One street westward, you have the opportunity to enter an old Marais home: the **Musée Cognacq-Jay (91)** *(Hôtel de Donon, 8 rue Elzévir, 3rd, 01-40.27.07.21; hours: Tu–Su 10AM–6PM)* was once the residence of a prominent businessman and art collector. A short walk

away, the **Picasso Museum (92)** *(Hôtel Salé, 5 rue de Thorigny, 3rd, 01-42.71.25.21, www.musee-picasso. fr; hours: Oct–Mar W–M 9:30AM–5:30PM, Apr–Sep W–M 9:30AM–6PM)* is housed in a grand Marais mansion. Picasso admirers are treated to masterpieces in paintings, etchings, and sculptures. Kitty-corner, the **National Archives** are housed in the Hôtel de Rohan (93) *(87 rue Vieille-*

du-Temple, 3rd, 01-40.27.60.96; hours: Tu–Su 12PM–6PM) and around the corner in the Hôtel de Soubise (94) *(60 rue des Francs-Bourgeois, 3rd, 01-40.27.60.96; hours: M, W–F 10AM–12:30PM, 2PM–5:30PM, Sa–Su 2PM–5:30PM)*; both buildings are marvelous examples of 18th-century architecture. Cloître des Billettes (54) *(24 rue des Archives, 4th, 01-40.72.38. 79; hours: 11AM–7PM)*, the oldest medieval cloister in Paris, was built in 1427 for the Brothers of Charity. The courtyard, with its Gothic galleries, colonnaded arches, and arcades topped by graceful vaults, is especially appealing. The cloister presents work by emerging artists; exhibits change twice a month and are usually free. Be sure to stroll along the rue Vieille-du-Temple (95) *(rue de Rivoli/rue de Poitou, 3rd/4th)*—its charm comes not only from the 13th-century medieval houses but also from the street's many luxury shops. Further to the west, around rue Ste-Croix-de-la-Bretonnerie (96) *(rue de Temple/rue Vieille-du-Temple, 4th)*, is the **gay district** ("pink triangle"), a vibrant, stylish scene replete with hotels, bars, clubs, and restaurants.

Arts & Entertainment:

Magicians ply their trade outside the wonderful Museum of Magic (97) *(11 rue St-Paul, 4th, 01-42.72.13.26, www.museedelamagie.com; hours: W, Sa–Su 2PM–7PM)*; inside, they demonstrate with museum pieces. In a magnificent mansion, the Maison Européenne de la Photographie (98) *(5-7 rue de Fourcy, 4th, 01-44.78.75.00, www.mep-fr.org; hours: W–Su 11AM–8PM)* houses more than 15,000 works of contemporary photography; and its café is super-chic. The 140-room **Musée Carnavalet (90)** *(see also page 84)* covers the history of Paris, through paintings, sculptures, documents, objects, and memorabilia. Some samplings of what is on view are: a piece of the Bastille prison, lithographs, porcelain vases, and Proust's reconstructed cork-lined bedroom (where he wrote most of *À la recherche du temps perdu, Remembrance of Things Past*). On a more human scale, the refined **Musée Cognacq-Jay (91)** *(see also page 84)* is home to a once private collection of 18th-century art and furniture. The **Picasso Museum (92)** *(see also page 84)* has an astonishing collection of work from all periods of the artist's long and diverse career. **La Galerie d'Architecture (99)** *(11 rue des Blancs-Manteaux, 4th, 01-49.96.64.00, www.galerie-architecture.fr; hours: Tu–Sa 11AM–7PM)* shows the work of contemporary architects against a clean, crisp, white backdrop.

PLACES TO EAT & DRINK
Where to Eat:
Le Pas-Sage Obligé (15) (€) *(27-31 rue du Bourg-Tibourg, 4th, 01-40.41.95.03, www.lepassageoblige.com; hours: M–Sa 9AM–6PM)* ranges from vegetarian dishes to steaks and cheeseburgers. Supposedly the first wine bar in Paris, **Le Coude Fou (65) (€–€€)** *(12 rue du Bourg-Tibourg, 4th, 01-42.77.15.16, www.lecoudefou.com; hours: 12PM–2AM)* is friendly and intimate with food better than the usual wine bar fare. The best afternoon tea outside London is to be had at **Mariage Frères (66) (€–€€)** *(30 rue du Bourg-Tibourg, 4th, 01-42.72.28.11,*

www.mariagefreres.com; hours: 12PM–7PM, tea counters & museums 10:30AM–7:30PM). A gem of haute cuisine, **L'Ambroisie (100) (€€€€)** *(9 pl. des Vosges, 4th, 01-42.78.51.45, www.ambroisie-placedesvosges.com; hours: Tu–Sa 12PM–1:45PM, 8PM–9:45PM, closed Feb & end Jul–end Aug)* is said to be one of the most beautiful restaurants in Paris. The food is spectacular while the décor is ornate and Versailles-like; the unique experience is worth the steep price. For a less refined evening, **L'Auberge de Jarente (101) (€–€€)** *(7 rue Jarente, 4th, 01-42.77.49.35; hours: Tu–Sa 12PM–2:30PM, 7:30PM–10:30PM)* is casual, friendly, and serves hearty Basque food. At **Au Bourguignon du Marais (102) (€€)** *(52 rue François-Miron, 4th, 01-48.87.15.40; hours: M–Sa 12PM–11PM)* the excellent selection of burgundy goes with its classic bistro fare. Best for cakes and tea, **Le Loir dans la Théière (105) (€)** *(3 rue des Rosiers, 4th, 01-42.72.90.61; hours: M–F 11:30AM–7PM, Sa–Su 10AM–7PM)* is funky and cool; inspired by *Alice in Wonderland*, its name means "The Dormouse in the Teapot." While the Jewish character of **rue des Rosiers** may be on the wane, the African soul of nearby **rue Elzévir** is flourishing. Senegalese and African dishes and delicacies are on the menu at **Le Petit Dakar (106) (€)** *(6 rue Elzévir, 3rd, 01-44.59.34.74, www.petit-dakar. abcsalles.com; hours: M–Sa 12PM–2:30PM, 7:30PM–10:30PM, closed Aug)*; try the silky palm hearts and sweet-and-sour chicken and lemon stew. For arguably the best couscous in Paris, try

Chez Omar (108) (€€) *(47 rue de Bretagne, 3rd, 01-42.72.36.26; hours: M–Sa 12PM–2:30PM, 7PM–10:30PM, Su 7PM–10:30PM)*, a North African favorite among the cognoscenti. The combination Maghreb-French cuisine is worth the wait in line.

Bars & Nightlife:

You might expect Edith Piaf to saunter into **Le Connétable (72)** *(55 rue des Archives, 3rd, 01-42.77.41.40; hours: M–Sa 11AM–3PM, 7PM–3AM)*: it's a typical Parisian bar, chatty regulars and all. Vibrant sounds in music—from cabaret to jazz to fusion—emanate from **Les 7 Lézards (109)** *(10 rue des Rosiers, 4th, 01-48.87.08.97, www.7lezards.com; hours: opens 6PM, jazz sets begin 9PM)*. **Le Jokko (110)** *(5 rue Elzévir, 3rd, 06-16.36.07.27, www.le-jokko.abcsalles.com; call for hours)* is an African-themed bar and exhibition space featuring live music. At the literary wine bar **La Belle Hortense (111)** *(31 rue Vieille-du-Temple, 4th, 01-48.04.74.60, www.cafeine.com; hours: 5PM–2AM)*, sip a glass of red wine and peruse a book from the window ledges. For some, wine's a game; at **L'Apparemment Café (112)** *(18 rue des Coutures-St-Gervais, 3rd, 01-48.87.12.22; hours: 12PM–2AM)* wine goes with the game: you can play cards or a board game while sipping your *verre de rouge*. Further south in the **gay district**, (also known as the "pink triangle"), **L'Open Café (113)** *(17 rue des Archives, 4th, 01-42.72.26.18, www.opencafe.fr; hours: Su–Th 11AM–2AM, F–Sa 11AM–4AM)* is a favorite gay café and a happening night spot. Mixed gay-straight techno-lovers crowd the floor of **Le Mixer (114)** *(23 rue Ste-*

Croix-de-la-Bretonnerie, 4th, 01-48.87.55.44, hours: 5PM–2AM). Straight-friendly gay locale **Amnésia Café (115)** *(42 rue Vieille-du-Temple, 4th, 01-42.72.16.94; hours: Su–Th 11AM–2AM, F–Sa 11AM–3AM)* gets rowdy at night; they serve drinks, sandwiches, and brunch. Nearby, long-standing **Le Central (116)** *(33 rue Vieille-du-Temple, 4th, 01-48.87.56.08, www.hotelcentral marais.com; hours: M–F 4PM–2AM, Sa–Su 2PM–2AM)* is a cozy spot for natives and travelers alike.

WHERE TO SHOP

Julian Schnabel's art adorns the walls of the showroom loft of Tunisian-born Azzedine Alaïa **(77)** *(7 rue de Moussy, 4th, 01-42.72.19.19),* emphasizing that the sexy, form-fitting clothes are wearable art; check out the discounted styles at the nearby outlet *(81 rue de la Verrerie, 4th).* Colorful tweeds and woolens, Audrey Hepburn-style, make Blancs Manteaux **(78)** *(42 rue des Blancs Manteaux, 4th, 01-42.71.70.00, www.blancsmanteaux.com)* a find; its wares are mostly shipped, so the shop is more of a depot. Stroll through the 60 or so shops of antiques and bric-a-brac dealers at Village St-Paul **(117)** *(along rue St-Paul, near rue Charlemagne, 4th; hours: Th–M 11AM–7PM).* Senteurs de Fée **(120)** *(10 rue de Sévigné, 4th, 01-44.54.97.27; hours: Su–M 2PM–7:30PM, Tu–Th 11AM–7:30PM, F–Sa 12PM–8PM)* stocks incense.

Rue des Francs-Bourgeois is a great shopping street. Fabulous white linen and stretchy laces are elegant and comfortable at Anne Fontaine (122) *(12 rue des Francs-Bourgeois, 3rd, 01-44.59.81.59, www.annefontaine.com)*. Enter Ali Baba's cave, full of fabulous Tunisian homeware, at 2 Mille et 1 Nuits (123) *(13 rue des Francs-Bourgeois, 4th, 01-48.87.07.07, 2001nuits.free.fr)*. Zadig & Voltaire (125) *(42 rue des Francs-Bourgeois, 3rd, 01-44.54.00.60, www.zadig-et-voltaire.com)*, with branches around the city, is popular for its casual, urban wardrobe offerings. Issey Miyake's innovative textile design is evident at A-poc (126) *(47 rue des Francs-Bourgeois, 4th, 01-44.54.07.05)*; the name is derived from "a piece of cloth," the concept being to design wearable art from one piece of fabric.

Painted chests and armoires abound among the refurbished 18th- and 19th-century furniture at Meubles Peints (127) *(32 rue Sévigné, 4th, 01-42.77.54.60, www.meublespeints.com)*. Photo buffs will flock to fashion photography bookshop Comptoir de l'Image (128) *(44 rue de Sévigné, 3rd, 01-42.72.09.17)* and Galerie Chez Valentin (129) *(9 rue St-Gilles, 3rd, 01-48.87.42.55, www.galeriechezvalentin.com; hours: Tu–Sa 11AM–1PM, 2PM–7PM)*, which exhibits experimental video, photography, and installations.

African art and crafts are on display at La Boutique de la CSAO (130) *(9 rue Elzévir, 3rd, 01-42.71.33.17, www.csao.fr; hours: M–Sa 11AM–1PM, 2PM–*

7PM), and contemporary African art at La Galerie 3A (131) *(9 rue Elzévir, 3rd, 01-42.77.66.42, www.csao.fr; hours: M–Sa 11AM–1PM, 2–7PM)*. Wispy fabrics, inventive details, and incredible use of color have given the Japanese fashion designer Tsumori Chisato (132) *(20 rue Barbette, 3rd, 01-42.78.18.88)* a dedicated fan base in Paris. The Bains du Marais (133) *(31-33 rue des Blancs-Manteaux, 4th, 01-44.61.02.02, www.lesbainsdumarais.com)* offers a break from the wear and tear of sightseeing and shopping. Open to women Monday through Wednesday *(M 11AM–8PM, Tu 10AM–11PM, W 10AM–7PM)*; open to men Thursday and Friday *(Th 10AM–11PM, F 10AM–8PM)*; and open to both on Wednesday evenings and weekends *(W 7PM–11PM, Sa 10AM–8PM, Su 10AM–11PM, closed Aug)*, the spa gives divine hamman treatments. Or you can combine a facial with manicure, pedicure, haircut, or another salon offering.

Rue Vieille-du-Temple (95) is another treasure trove for shopping. Limited-edition designer tableware gives new meaning to glassware and crockery at Chône (135) *(60 rue Vieille-du-Temple, 3rd, 01-44.78.90.00)*. Chocolates and pastries reign at Cacao et Chocolat (136) *(36 rue Vieille-du-Temple, 4th, 01-42.71.50.06)*.

For carefully crafted books on international architecture, art, and design, try Archibooks (138) *(18-20 rue de la Perle, 3rd, 01-42.25.15.58, www.archibooks.com)*.

With clothing by up-and-coming avant-garde design ers, graffiti-filled walls, and photo exhibits, Surface to Air Boutique (32) *(108 rue Vieille-du-Temple, 3rd, 01-44.61.76.27, www.surfacetoair.com; hours: M–Sa 11:30AM–7:30PM, Su 12PM–6PM)* is the cat's meow in concept stores. Hunt for great discounts at L'Habilleur (140) *(44 rue de Poitou, 3rd, 01-48.87.77.12)*: end-of-line designer pieces and hot-off-the-runway creations are 50%-70% off. Rue Charlot (141) *(beginning at rue de Quatre Fils, 3rd)* has been inventively redone, harboring galleries, bookshops, cafés, and shops, such as **Passage de Retz** *(No. 9)* and **Moon Young Hee** *(No. 62)*.

WHERE TO STAY

Hôtel Bourg Tibourg (81) (€€-€€€) *(19 rue du Bourg-Tibourg, 4th, 01-42.78.47.39, www.bourgtibourg. com)*—part of the Costes Brothers' empire—is dramatic, sensual, and intimate; silk and taffeta, fringes and tassels, the hotel is a tasteful combination of styles, textures, and colors reminiscent of the private inner chambers of a princely retreat. A revamped 17th-century town house, Hôtel de la Bretonnerie (82) (€-€€) *(22 rue Ste-Croix-de-la-Bretonnerie, 4th, 01-48.87.77.63, www.bretonnerie. com)* is comfortable, tasteful, and a good value. In the budget category, Hôtel de Nice (83) (€) *(42 bis, rue de Rivoli, 4th, 01-42.78.55.29, www.hoteldenice.com)* is filled with "busy" patterns and textiles and has its space challenges, but is a good bargain and is well located.

Near the Jewish quarter at the Hôtel Caron de Beaumarchais (142) (€-€€) *(12 rue Vieille-du-Temple, 4th, 01-42.72.34.12, www.carondebeaumarchais.com)* the service is impeccable; small rooms with 18th-century décor are prepared with great attention to detail. A good find at a reasonable price (especially for the neighborhood), **Grand Hôtel Malher (143)** (€-€€) *(5 rue Malher, 4th, 01-42.72.60.92, www.grandhotelmalher.com)* is comfortable and well run. Simple and unassuming, **Hôtel Jeanne d'Arc (144)** (€) *(3 rue Jarente, 4th, 01-48.87.62.11, www.parishotels.com)* is a great budget hotel. Modern and medieval, the luxury hotel **Pavillon de la Reine (145)** (€€€-€€€€) *(28 pl. des Vosges, 3rd, 01-40.29.19.19, www.pavillon-de-la-reine.com)* has breathtaking views. Small is beautiful at **Hôtel de la Place des Vosges (146)** (€-€€) *(12 rue de Birague, 4th, 01-42.72.60.46, www.hotelplacedesvosges.com),* and accommodations are well maintained; the remodeled rooms have hardwood floors, wooden beams, and exposed stone walls (ask for the "discovery rate" for roughly a 25% discount on the new rooms). Close by, **Hôtel Turenne Le Marais (147)** (€-€€) *(6 rue de Turenne, 4th, 01-42.78.43.25, www.turennemarais.com)* is part of a hotel chain; rooms are color coordinated and charming. Nearer the **Musée Carnavalet (90)** and **Picasso Museum (92)**, **Hôtel des Chevaliers (148)** (€-€€) *(30 rue de Turenne, 3rd, 01-42.72.73.47, www.chevaliers-paris-hotel.com)* has small but comfortable rooms. If you love Christian Lacroix clothes, you'll love the profusion of color in his room designs at **Hôtel du Petit Moulin (149)** (€€-€€€) *(29/31 rue de Poitou, 3rd, 01-42.74.10.10, www.hotelpetitmoulinparis.com).*

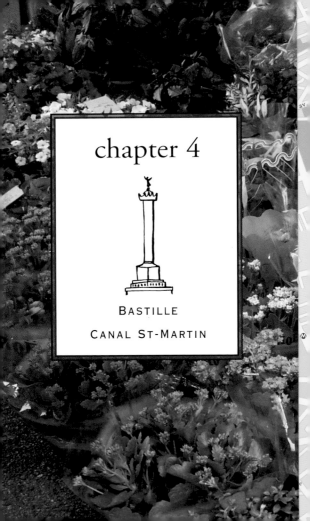

chapter 4

BASTILLE

CANAL ST-MARTIN

20,000+Words
Spelled and Divided for Quick Reference

Ninth Edition

Charles E. Zoubek
Mary Margaret Hosler

GLENCOE
Macmillan/McGraw-Hill

Lake Forest, Illinois
Columbus, Ohio
Mission Hills, California
Peoria, Illinois

Library of Congress Cataloging-in-Publication Data

Zoubek, Charles E., 1913-
    20,000+ words: spelled and divided for quick reference. — 9th ed./
Charles E. Zoubek, Mary Margaret Hosler.
        p.   cm.
    1. Spellers.   I. Hosler, Mary Margaret.   II. Title.
PE1146.L4 1991
428.1—dc20

20,000+ WORDS, Ninth Edition

Send all inquiries to:
Glencoe Division, Macmillan/McGraw-Hill
936 Eastwind Drive
Westerville, OH 43081

ISBN: 0-02-820050-0 (hardcover edition)
            0-02-820051-9 (spiral-bound edition)

1 2 3 4 5 6 7 8 9 10 11 12 A-KPA-KP 00 99 98 97 96 95 94 93 92 91

A Quick Guide to
20,000+Words

**Abbreviations of States
and Territories of the
Unites States, Inside
Back Cover**

Foreword

When the first edition of *20,000 Words* was published in 1934, a lengthy explanation of its purpose was necessary. Since that time, thousands of administrative assistants, document processing operators, students, teachers, and writers have come to rely on *20,000 Words*—now entitled *20,000+ Words*—as one of their most valued desk reference books.

The book's originator, Dr. Louis A. Leslie, carried *20,000 Words* through seven editions, keeping pace with the changing language of business and society. The ninth edition continues to keep the book current and useful for anyone who communicates in written form.

The word list in *20,000+ Words* is a dictionary without definitions. Since most references to a standard dictionary are to verify spelling or to determine an acceptable point for word division, the absence of definitions dramatically increases the speed and ease with which a given word may be found.

In general, the word list of *20,000+ Words* is in agreement with *Webster's Ninth New Collegiate Dictionary,* 1989.

New Features in Ninth Edition

Five new features of *20,000+ Words, Ninth Edition,* will make the book even more helpful to the writer in correct spelling and ease of locating a needed word.

1. Guide letters and guide words. The addition of guide letters and guide words to each page increases the speed with which a user can locate a needed reference. Positioned at the top outside corner of the page, the guides add a popular tool to the array of reference sources in *20,000+ Words.*

2. Bolded words. Words most commonly misspelled in business writing are set in bold-face print. Displaying these 500 most frequently misspelled words in bold-face print makes them easy to locate in the word list. The bold print may also make the correct spelling easier to remember.

3. Derivatives. A third new feature is the inclusion of many derivatives along with base words. Derivatives often cause spelling questions: for example, when to double a consonant in forming a past tense or when to drop a final *e* before adding *-ing.* These and many other troublesome spellings that arise when using derivatives can now be found in the word list. Many irregularly formed plurals are also included.

4. Updated word list. The word list has been extensively revised and updated. Words no longer in common use have been deleted, while words now in current use have been added. As a result, the ninth edition contains an up-to-date listing of words used frequently in today's writing.

5. Electronic workplace terms. The ninth edition also includes terms frequently used when writing in or about the electronic workplace. These terms are now listed alphabetically within the word list, making them convenient to locate.

Improved Features

1. Often-confused pairs and groups of words. Sometimes a writer faces the challenge of choosing from two or more often-confused words—words such as *affect* and *effect*; *cite, sight,* and *site*; or *morning* and *mourning.* Entries for confusing pairs and groups include both simple definitions and cross-references. An example is the entry for the word *main*: "main (chief; cf. *mane*)." First, the writer finds the word itself—*main*. Then, a brief definition appears—*chief*. Finally, the *cf.* notation (meaning "compare with") and the word or words easily confused with the entry word—*mane*. The writer can easily confirm a correct choice or can reference other possibilities.

2. One Word, Two Words, or Hyphenated? A major problem for the writer and the keyboarder is to determine whether a compound word or term is written as one word, as two words, or with a hyphen. The English language has so many inconsistencies that analogy is of no help. For example, the *ice age* was a time of widespread glaciation that left many areas *icebound* and *ice-cold*.

Many expressions go through an evolutionary process of first being written as two separate words, then as a hyphenated word, and finally as one word. The word list shows a number of terms that may be written in all three ways depending on their use in context. A quick check can help a writer use the appropriate compound for each writing need.

3. Revised Appendix. The purpose of the Appendix is to provide additional information that one may need in writing. The Appendix covers spelling tips, numbers style, common abbreviations and acronyms, and a list of troublesome place names. A helpful reference feature on the inside back cover is the list of abbreviations for states and territories of the United States.

Clear, concise rule statements followed by an increased number of examples make the reference task as easy as possible. Users needing more comprehensive rule statements should consult *The Gregg Reference Manual, Sixth Edition,* by William A. Sabin.

The Word List

The alphabetic word listing in *20,000+ Words* serves two primary purposes: first, it is a quick reference for checking spelling; and second, it is an indicator of appropriate word division in writing. The ninth edition of *20,000+ Words* follows the syllabication and the rationale as shown in *Webster's Ninth New Collegiate Dictionary*, 1989.

Checking Spelling

The word list in *20,000+ Words* is a dictionary without definitions. The number of entries on each page and absence of definitions make scanning a column or a page for a certain word very easy. Guide letters and guide words—a new feature in the ninth edition—make use of the book even easier. The guide letters—the bold letters at the top outside corner of each page—help locate the right section of the book. The pair of guide words on each page assists in finding the needed page quickly.

Word Division

Correct syllabication and appropriate word division in writing may not be the same. Word divisions shown in the following word list are acceptable points for breaking a word at the end of a line of print or writing. The word list in *20,000+ Words* shows these points with a dot (sometimes called a bullet).

For example, the noun *re·frig·er·a·tor* may be ended on one line at any of the following points: *re-*, *refrig-*, *refriger-*, or *refrigera-*. The hyphen after the word part shows that the word is incomplete; that is, part of the word appears at the beginning of the next line.

Words should not be divided after a single initial letter or before a single terminal letter. Therefore, dots are not

1

shown in those positions even though a single beginning or ending letter may be a separate syllable. For example, the noun *idea* is shown without division marks.

The writer should keep in mind that excessive word division is distracting to the reader. In general, avoid dividing words at the ends of more than two consecutive lines or at the end of a page.

If a writer must divide a word, certain points of division are preferable to others. In a hyphenated word such as *self-employed* the best division point is at the hyphen. In a solid or closed compound such as *timetable* the best division point is between the words that make up the compound (*time·table*). Other preferable points for word division include after prefixes (*super·natural*), before suffixes (*advertise·ment*), and after single-vowel syllables (*consoli·date* rather than *consol·idate*).

In the word list, word division points are indicated by centered dots, sometimes called bullets:

sab·bat·i·cal   ad·ver·tise·ment

Hyphenated words appear in the word list just as they should be written or typed, with hyphens between words that make up the compound. The hyphen should be included in these expressions whether the word is used in the middle or at the end of a line.

loose-leaf   one-sided   corn-fed

Certain expressions written as two or more separate words also appear in the word list. These terms are included because the combinations occur often enough to make people think they may be written as solid or hyphenated compounds rather than as separate words. A writer should not use a hyphen to divide these expressions between the words of the open compound.

ad hoc   front matter   oil slick

Certain words may be spelled, punctuated, or divided differently depending on their part of speech. In such situations, variations appear with part-of-speech designations (*n* for *noun*, *v* for *verb*, *adj* for *adjective*, and *adv* for *adverb*). Indications of acceptable word division may vary in such pairs or groups of entries.

ash can (n)   ash·can (adj)

Cross-reference

Many pairs or groups of words cause problems for writers because of similarities in spelling or pronunciation. Cross-references between these confusing pairs of words can help the writer not only spell and divide the word correctly but also to make sure of choosing the right word for the intended meaning. A parenthetical notation indicating a brief definition for the entry word and a cross-reference to easily confused words follows the entry.

aid (help; cf. *aide*)   aide (assistant; cf. *aid*)

Derivatives

An entry may include both a base word and one or more derivatives. Derivatives appear below and slightly indented from the base word. If a hyphen precedes a derivative, the user must look at both the base word and the derivative to find the spelling. As much of the base word is shown as is necessary to understand the correct spelling of the derivative. When multiple derivatives appear for a single base word, the same part of the base word is shown for each derivative.

ca·ble
    -bled, -bling

The abbreviation (*pl*) following an entry indicates the plural form when there may be confusion in identifying the entry.

    daugh·ter-in-law
      daugh·ters-in-law (pl)

aba·cus
ab·a·lo·ne
aban·don
  -don·er, -don·ment
aban·doned
abase
  abased, abas·ing,
  abase·ment
abash
abate
  abat·ed, abat·ing,
  abat·er
abate·ment
ab·bé
ab·bess
ab·bey
  -beys
ab·bot
ab·bre·vi·ate
  -at·ed, -at·ing,
  -a·tor
ab·bre·vi·a·tion
ab·di·cate
  -cat·ed, -cat·ing,
  -ca·tion, -ca·tor
ab·do·men
  -dom·i·nal,
  -dom·i·nal·ly
ab·duct

-duc·tor
ab·duc·tion
ab·er·rant
ab·er·rat·ed
ab·er·ra·tion
abet
  abet·ted,
  abet·ting,
  abet·ment
abey·ance
ab·hor
  -horred, -hor·ring
ab·hor·rence
ab·hor·rent
abide
  abode or abid·ed,
  abid·ing, abid·er
abil·i·ty
  -ties
ab·ject
  -ject·ly, -ject·ness
ab·jec·tion
ab·jure
  -jured, -jur·ing,
  -jur·er
ablaze
able
able-bod·ied
ab·lu·tion

ably
ab·ne·gate
  -gat·ed, -gat·ing,
  -ga·tor
ab·ne·ga·tion
ab·nor·mal
  -mal·ly
ab·nor·mal·i·ty
  -ties
aboard
abode
abol·ish
  -ish·able, -ish·er,
  -ish·ment
ab·o·li·tion
ab·o·li·tion·ism
  -tion·ist
A-bomb
abom·i·na·ble
  -bly
abom·i·nate
  -nat·ed, -nat·ing,
  -na·tor
abom·i·na·tion
ab·orig·i·nal
  -nal·ly
ab·orig·i·ne
abort
abor·tion

abor·tion·ist
abor·tive
abound
about
about-face
above
above all
above·board
above·ground
ab·ra·ca·dab·ra
abrade
abra·sion
abra·sive
 -sive·ly, -sive·ness
ab·re·ac·tion
 -re·act
abreast
abridge
 abridged,
 abridg·ing
 abridg·er
abridg·ment
abroad
ab·ro·gate
 -gat·ed, -gat·ing,
 -ga·tion
abrupt
 abrupt·ly,
 abrupt·ness
ab·scess
 -scess·es, -scessed
ab·scond
 -scond·er
ab·sence

ab·sent
ab·sen·tee
ab·sen·tee·ism
ab·sent·mind·ed
 -ed·ly, -ed·ness
ab·so·lute
ab·so·lute·ly
ab·so·lu·tion
ab·so·lut·ism
ab·solve
 -solved, -solv·ing,
 -solv·er
ab·sorb
 -sorb·abil·i·ty,
 -sorb·able, -sorb·er
ab·sor·bance
ab·sor·ben·cy
 -cies
ab·sor·bent
ab·sorb·ing
ab·sorp·tion
ab·stain
 -stain·er
ab·ste·mi·ous
ab·sten·tion
ab·sti·nence
ab·sti·nent
ab·stract
 -stract·ness
ab·stract·ed
ab·strac·tion
ab·strac·tion·ism
ab·surd
 -surd·ness

ab·sur·di·ty
abun·dance
abun·dant
abuse
 abused, abus·ing,
 abus·er
abu·sive
 -sive·ly, -sive·ness
abut
 abut·ted, abut·ting
abut·ment
abys·mal
 -mal·ly
abyss
aca·cia
ac·a·deme
ac·a·de·mia
ac·a·dem·ic
 -dem·i·cal·ly
ac·a·de·mi·cian
acad·e·my
 -mies
a cap·pel·la
ac·cede (agree; cf.
 exceed)
 -ced·ed, -ced·ing
ac·cel·er·ate
 -at·ed, -at·ing,
 -at·ing·ly
ac·cel·er·a·tion
ac·cel·er·a·tor
ac·cent
ac·cen·tu·ate
 -tu·a·tion

ac·cept (take; cf.
  except)
ac·cept·able
  -able·ness, -ably,
  -abil·i·ty
ac·cep·tance
ac·cep·ta·tion
ac·cept·ed
ac·cess
  (admittance; cf.
  excess)
ac·ces·si·ble
  -si·ble·ness,
  -si·bly, -si·bil·i·ty
ac·ces·sion
ac·ces·so·rize
  -rized, -riz·ing
ac·ces·so·ry
  -ries
ac·ci·dence
ac·ci·dent
ac·ci·den·tal
  -tal·ly, -tal·ness
ac·claim
ac·cla·ma·tion
ac·cli·mate
  -mat·ed, -mat·ing
ac·cli·ma·tize
ac·co·lade
ac·com·mo·date
  -dat·ed, -dat·ing
ac·com·mo·da·tion
ac·com·pa·ni·ment
ac·com·pa·nist

ac·com·pa·ny
  -nied, -ny·ing
ac·com·plice
ac·com·plish
  -plish·able,
  -plish·er
ac·com·plished
ac·com·plish·ment
ac·cord
ac·cor·dance
ac·cord·ing·ly
ac·cor·di·on
ac·cost
ac·count
ac·count·able
  -able·ness, -ably,
  -abil·i·ty
ac·coun·tan·cy
ac·coun·tant
ac·count·ing
ac·cou·ter·ment
ac·cred·it
  -cred·i·table,
  -cred·i·ta·tion
ac·cre·tion
ac·cru·al
ac·crue
  -crued, -cru·ing,
  -cru·able
ac·cu·mu·late
  -lat·ed, -lat·ing
ac·cu·mu·la·tion
ac·cu·mu·la·tive
ac·cu·mu·la·tor

ac·cu·ra·cy
  -cies
ac·cu·rate
  -rate·ly,
  -rate·ness
ac·cursed
ac·cu·sa·tion
ac·cu·sa·tive
ac·cu·sa·to·ry
ac·cuse
  -cused, -cus·ing,
  -cus·er
ac·cus·tom
ac·cus·tomed
ac·er·bate
  -bat·ed, -bat·ing
ac·e·tate
ace·tic
ac·e·tone
acet·y·lene
ache
  ached, ach·ing
achieve
  achieved,
  achiev·ing,
  achiev·able,
  achiev·er
achieve·ment
ach·ro·mat·ic
ac·id
acid·ic
acid·i·fy
  -fied, -fying,
  -fi·ca·tion

acid·i·ty
  -ties
acid·u·lous
ac·knowl·edge
  -edged, -edg·ing,
  -edge·able
ac·knowl·edg·ment
ac·me (highest
  point; cf. *acne*)
ac·ne (skin disorder;
  cf. *acme*)
ac·o·lyte
acorn
acous·tic
acous·tics
ac·quaint
ac·quain·tance
ac·qui·esce
  -esced, -esc·ing
ac·qui·es·cence
ac·qui·es·cent
  -cent·ly
ac·quir·able
ac·quire
  -quired, -quir·ing
ac·quire·ment
ac·qui·si·tion
ac·quis·i·tive
  -tive·ly, -tive·ness
ac·quit
  -quit·ted,
  -quit·ting,
  -quit·ter
ac·quit·tal

acre
acre·age
ac·rid
ac·ri·mo·ni·ous
  -ous·ness
ac·ri·mo·ny
ac·ro·bat
  -bat·ic, -bat·i·cal·ly
ac·ro·nym
across
across-the-board
acros·tic
acryl·ic
act·ing
ac·tion
ac·tion·able
ac·tion·less
ac·ti·vate
  -vat·ed, -va·ting,
  -va·tion
ac·tive
  -tive·ly, -tive·ness
ac·tiv·ism
  -tiv·ist
ac·tiv·i·ty
ac·tiv·i·ties
ac·tor
ac·tress
ac·tu·al
ac·tu·al·i·ty
ac·tu·al·ly
ac·tu·ar·i·al
ac·tu·ary
  -ar·ies

ac·tu·ate
  -at·ed, -at·ing
ac·tu·a·tor
acu·ity
acu·men
acu·punc·ture
  -tur·ist
acute
  acute·ly,
  acute·ness
ad (advertisement;
  cf. *add*)
ad·age
ada·gio
ad·a·mant
adapt (adjust; cf.
  adept, adopt)
adapt·able
  -abil·i·ty
ad·ap·ta·tion
adapt·er
add (plus; cf. *ad*)
ad·den·da (pl)
  -den·dum (sing)
ad·dict
ad·dic·tive
ad·dic·tion
ad·dic·tive
ad·di·tion
  (increase; cf.
  edition)
ad·di·tion·al
  -al·ly
ad·di·tive

8

add-on
ad·dress
ad·dress·able
ad·dress·ee
ad·dress·ees
ad·dress·ing
ad·duce
ad·e·noid
ad·e·noi·dal
ad·ept (skillful; cf. *adapt, adopt*)
ad·e·qua·cy
  -cies
ad·e·quate
  -quate·ly,
  -quate·ness
ad·here
  -hered, -her·ing
ad·her·ence
ad·her·ent
ad·he·sion
ad·he·sive
  -sive·ly, -sive·ness
ad hoc
adieu
  adieus (pl)
adi·os
ad·i·pose
ad·ja·cen·cy
  -cies
ad·ja·cent
ad·jec·tive
ad·join (be next to; cf. *adjourn*)

ad·journ (suspend; cf. *adjoin*)
ad·journ·ment
ad·ju·di·cate
  -cat·ed, -cat·ing,
  -ca·tor
ad·ju·di·ca·tion
ad·junct
ad·ju·ra·tion
ad·jure
  -jured, -jur·ing
ad·just
  -just·abil·i·ty,
  -just·able
ad·just·ed
ad·just·er
ad·just·ment
ad·ju·tant
ad lib (adv)
ad-lib (v, n, adj)
  ad-libbed,
  ad-lib·bing
ad·mass
ad·min·is·ter
  -tered, -ter·ing
ad·min·is·tra·tion
ad·min·is·tra·tive
ad·min·is·tra·tor
ad·min·is·tra·trix
ad·mi·ra·ble
ad·mi·ral
ad·mi·ral·ty
ad·mi·ra·tion
ad·mire

-mired, -mir·ing,
  -mir·er
ad·mis·si·ble
  -bil·i·ty
ad·mis·sion
ad·mit
  -mit·ted, -mit·ting,
  -mit·ted·ly
ad·mit·tance
ad·mix·ture
ad·mon·ish
  -ish·er, -ish·ing·ly,
  -ish·ment
ad·mo·ni·tion
ad·mon·i·to·ry
ad nau·se·am
ado·be
ad·o·les·cence
ad·o·les·cent
adopt (accept; cf. *adapt, adept*)
  adopt·abil·i·ty,
  adopt·able,
  adopt·er
adop·tion
adop·tive
ador·able
ad·o·ra·tion
adore
  adored, ador·ing,
  ador·er
adorn
adorn·ment
ad·re·nal

adren·a·line
adrift
adroit
adsorb
ad·sor·bent
ad·sorp·tion
ad·u·late
  -lat·ed, -lat·ing,
  -la·tion
adult
adul·ter·ate
  -at·ed, -at·ing
adul·tery
ad·um·brate
  -brat·ed, -brat·ing,
  -bra·tion
ad va·lo·rem
ad·vance
  -vanced, -vanc·ing
ad·vance·ment
ad·van·tage
  -taged, -tag·ing
ad·van·ta·geous
  -geous·ly,
  -geous·ness
ad·vent
ad·ven·ti·tious
ad·ven·ture
  -tured, -tur·ing
ad·ven·tur·er
ad·ven·ture·some
ad·ven·tur·ous
ad·verb
ad·ver·bi·al

ad·ver·sar·i·al
ad·ver·sary
  -sar·ies
ad·verse
  (unfavorable; cf.
  averse)
ad·ver·si·ty
ad·vert
ad·ver·tise
  -tised, -tis·ing,
  -tis·er
ad·ver·tise·ment
ad·vice (n)(counsel;
  cf. *advise*)
ad·vis·able
  -abil·i·ty
ad·vise (v)(give
  counsel; cf.
  advice)
  -vised, -vis·ing,
  -vis·er
ad·vis·ee
ad·vise·ment
ad·vi·so·ry
  -ries
ad·vo·ca·cy
ad·vo·cate
  -cat·ed, -cat·ing,
  -ca·tion
ae·gis
ae·on
aer·ate
  -at·ed, -at·ing,
  -a·tion

ae·ri·al (adj)
aer·i·al (n)
ae·ri·al·ist
aer·o·bat·ics
aer·o·bic
aero·dy·nam·ics
  -nam·i·cal·ly
aero·nau·tics
  -ti·cal, -ti·cal·ly
aero·sol
aero·space
aes·thet·ic
  -thet·i·cal·ly
aes·thet·ics
afar
af·fa·ble
af·fair
af·fect (influence; cf.
  effect)
af·fec·ta·tion
af·fect·ed
af·fect·ing
af·fec·tion
af·fec·tion·ate
  -ate·ly
af·fec·tive
  -tive·ly, -tiv·i·ty
af·fi·ance
af·fi·da·vit
af·fil·i·ate
  -at·ed, -at·ing,
  -a·tion
af·fin·i·ty
  -ties

af·firm
af·fir·ma·tion
af·fir·ma·tive
af·fix
af·flict
af·flic·tion
af·flu·ence
af·flu·en·cy
   -cies
af·flu·ent (well-to-
   do; cf. *effluent*)
af·ford
af·fray
af·fright
af·front
af·ghan
afield
afire
afloat
afoot
afore
afore·men·tioned
afore·said
afore·thought
afraid
afresh
Af·ri·can
Af·ro-Amer·i·can
af·ter
af·ter·care
af·ter·ef·fect
af·ter·glow
af·ter·hours
af·ter·life

af·ter·math
af·ter·noon
af·ter·taste
af·ter·tax
af·ter·thought
af·ter·ward
again
against
ag·ate
age
   aged, ag·ing
age-group
ageless
agen·cy
agen·cies
age-old
agen·da
ag·glom·er·ate
ag·gran·dize
   -dized, -dizing,
   -dize·ment
ag·gra·vate
   -vat·ed, -vat·ing
ag·gra·va·tion
ag·gre·gate
   -gat·ed, -gat·ing
ag·gre·ga·tion
ag·gres·sion
ag·gres·sive
   -sive·ly, -sive·ness
ag·gres·sor
ag·grieve
   -grieved,
   -griev·ing

aghast
ag·ile
agil·i·ty
   -ties
ag·i·tate
   -tat·ed, -tat·ing,
   -ta·tion
ag·i·ta·tor
aglitter
aglow
ag·nos·tic
ago
ag·o·nize
   -nized, -niz·ing
ag·o·ny
   -nies
ag·o·ra·pho·bia
agrar·i·an
agree
   agreed, agree·ing
agree·able
agree·ment
ag·ri·busi·ness
ag·ri·cul·tur·al
ag·ri·cul·ture
agron·o·my
aground
ahead
ahoy
aid (v)(help; cf. *aide*)
aide (n)(assistant; cf.
   aid)
aide-de-camp
AIDS

ail (be ill; cf. *ale*)
ai·le·ron
ail·ment
aim
  aim·less,
  aim·less·ness
air (atmosphere; cf.
  heir)
air bag
air base
air·borne
air brake
air·brush
air coach
air-con·di·tion
  -tion·er, -tion·ing
air-cool
  air-cooled
air·craft
air-drop (v)
air-drop (n)
air-dry (adj)
Aire·dale terrier
Air Ex·press
air·fare
air·field
air·flow
air·foil
air force
air·freight
air gun
air hole
air·ing
air lane

air letter
air·lift
air·line
air·lin·er
air lock
air·mail
air·man
air mass
air mile
air piracy
air·plane
air pock·et
air·port
air pump
air raid
air·ship
air·sick
air·space
air·speed
air·stream
air·strip
air·tight
air·time
air-to-air
air·wave
air·way
air·wor·thy
  -thi·ness
airy
aisle (passageway;
  cf. *isle*)
akim·bo
al·a·bas·ter
a la carte

alac·ri·ty
a la king
a la mode
alarm
alarm·ism
  -ist
alas
al·ba·tross
  -tross·es (pl)
al·be·it
al·bi·no
  -nos
al·bum
al·bu·men
al·co·hol
al·co·hol·ic
al·co·hol·ism
al·cove
al·der·man
al·der·wom·an
ale (beer; cf. *ail*)
alex·ia
al·fal·fa
al·fres·co
al·ga
  al·gae (pl)
al·ge·bra
al·ge·bra·ic
  -bra·i·cal·ly
al·go·rithm
alias
al·i·bi
  -bied, -bi·ing
alien

alien·able
alien·ate
  -at·ed, -at·ing
alien·ation
align
align·ment
alike
al·i·mo·ny
  -nies
al·ka·li
  -lies
al·ka·line
al·ka·loid
all (wholly; cf. *awl*)
all-Amer·i·can
all-around
al·lay (v)(soothe; cf.
  alley, ally)
al·le·ga·tion
al·lege
  -leged, -leg·ing
al·leged
  -leg·ed·ly
al·le·giance
al·le·gor·i·cal
al·le·go·ry
  -ries
al·le·gret·to
al·le·gro
al·le·lu·ia
al·le·mande
al·ler·gic
al·ler·gy
  -gies

al·le·vi·ate
  -at·ed, -at·ing,
  -a·tion
al·ley (n)(passage;
  cf. *allay, ally*)
al·leys
al·ley·way
al·li·ance
al·lied
al·li·ga·tor
all-im·por·tant
all-in·clu·sive
al·lit·er·ate
  -at·ed, -at·ing
al·lit·er·a·tion
al·lit·er·a·tive
al·lo·ca·ble
al·lo·cate
  -cat·ed, -cat·ing,
  -ca·tion
al·lo·cu·tion
al·lot
  -lot·ted, -lot·ting
al·lot·ment
al·low
al·low·able
al·low·ance
al·lowed
al·low·ed·ly
al·loy
all right
al·lude (refer to; cf.
  elude)
  -lud·ed, -lud·ing

al·lure
  -lured, -lur·ing,
  -lure·ment
al·lu·sion
  -lu·sive·ly,
  -lu·sive·ness
al·lu·vi·al
al·ly (n, v)(associate;
  cf. *allay, alley*)
  -lies, -lied, -ly·ing
al·ma ma·ter
al·ma·nac
al·mighty
al·mond
al·most
alms (charity; cf.
  arms)
aloft
alo·ha
alone
along
aloud (adv)(audibly;
  cf. *allowed*)
al·paca
al·pha·bet
al·pha·bet·ic
  -bet·i·cal·ly
al·pha·bet·ize
  -ized, -izing
al·pha·nu·mer·ic
  -mer·ics
al·pine
al·ready
al·so

al·tar (n)(for
  worship; cf. *alter*)
al·tar·piece
al·ter (v)(change; cf.
  altar)
  -tered, -ter·ing
al·ter·a·tion
al·ter·cate
  -cat·ed, -cat·ing
al·ter·ca·tion
al·ter·nate
  -nat·ed, -nat·ing
al·ter·na·tion
al·ter·na·tive
al·ter·na·tor
al·though
al·tim·e·ter
al·ti·tude
al·to
  al·tos
al·to·geth·er
al·tru·ism
  -ist, -is·tic,
  -is·ti·cal·ly
al·um
alu·mi·nize
  -nized, -niz·ing
alu·mi·num
alum·na (fem sing)
  alum·nae (fem pl)
alum·nus (sing)
  alum·ni (pl)
al·ways
alys·sum

Alz·hei·mer's
amal·gam
amal·gam·ate
  -at·ed, -at·ing
amal·gam·ation
aman·u·en·sis
  -en·ses (pl)
am·a·ryl·lis
am·a·teur
  -teur·ish,
  -teur·ism
amaze
  amazed, amaz·ing,
  amaz·ing·ly
amaze·ment
am·bas·sa·dor
am·ber
am·bi·dex·trous
am·bi·ence
am·bi·ent
am·bi·gu·ity
  -ities
am·big·u·ous
am·bi·tion
am·bi·tious
am·biv·a·lence
am·ble
  -bled, -bling
am·bro·sia
am·bu·lance
am·bu·late
  -lat·ed, -lat·ing,
  -la·tion
am·bu·la·to·ry

am·bush
ame·lio·rate
  -lio·rat·ed,
  -lior·a·tion
amen
ame·na·ble
amend (to change;
  cf. *emend*)
amend·ment
ame·ni·ty
  -ties
Am·er·asian
Amer·i·can
Amer·i·ca·na
Amer·i·can·ism
Amer·i·can·iza·tion
am·e·thyst
ami·a·ble
  -ble·ness, -bly,
  -bil·i·ty
am·i·ca·ble
  -ble·ness, -bly,
  -bil·i·ty
amid
amid·ships
ami·go
  -gos
ami·no acid
Amish
am·i·ty
  -ties
am·me·ter
am·mo·nia
am·mu·ni·tion

am·ne·sia
am·nes·ty
am·nio·cen·te·sis
amoe·ba
 -bas
among
amor·al
am·o·rous
amor·phous
am·or·ti·za·tion
am·or·tize
 -tized, -tiz·ing,
 -tiz·able
amount
am·per·age
am·pere
am·per·sand
am·phib·i·an
am·phib·i·ous
am·phi·the·ater
am·ple
 -ple·ness, -ply
am·pli·fi·ca·tion
am·pli·fi·er
am·pli·fy
 -fied, -fy·ing
am·pli·tude
am·pu·tate
 -tat·ed, -tat·ing,
 -ta·tion
am·pu·tee
am·u·let
amuse
 amused, amus·ing

amuse·ment
amus·ing
 -ing·ness
anach·ro·nism
 -nis·tic,
 -nis·ti·cal·ly
an·a·con·da
an·aer·o·bic
 -bi·cal·ly
ana·gram
 -grammed,
 -gram·ming
an·al·ge·sia
an·a·log
an·a·log·i·cal
anal·o·gous
anal·o·gy
 -gies
anal·y·sis
 -y·ses (pl)
an·a·lyst (one who
 analyzes; cf.
 annalist)
an·a·lyt·ic
an·a·lyt·i·cal
 -cal·ly
an·a·lyze
 -lyzed, -lyz·ing,
 -lyz·er
an·ar·chic
an·ar·chism
an·ar·chist
an·ar·chy
anath·e·ma

anat·o·mist
anat·o·mize
 -mized, -miz·ing
anat·o·my
 -mies
an·a·tom·ic
 -tom·i·cal,
 -tom·i·cal·ly
an·ces·tor
an·ces·tral
 -tral·ly
an·ces·try
an·chor
 -chored, -chor·ing
an·chor·age
an·chor·man
an·chor·peo·ple
an·chor·per·son
an·chor·wom·an
an·cho·vy
 -vies
an·cient
an·cil·lary
an·dan·te
and·iron
and/or
an·ec·dot·al
an·ec·dote
ane·mia
 ane·mic
an·e·mom·e·ter
anem·o·ne
an·er·oid
an·es·the·sia

an·es·the·si·ol·o·gist
an·es·thet·ic
anes·the·tist
anes·the·tize
  -tized, -tiz·ing
an·eu·rysm
anew
an·gel (spiritual
  being; cf. *angle*)
an·gel·fish
an·ger
  -gered, -ger·ing
an·gi·na
an·gle (in geometry;
  cf. *angel*)
  -gled, -gling
an·gle iron
an·gler
an·gle·worm
An·gli·can
an·gli·cism
an·gli·cize
  -cized, -ciz·ing
an·gling
An·glo·phile
An·glo·phobe
An·glo-Sax·on
an·go·ra
an·gry
  -gri·er, -gri·est,
  -gri·ly
an·guish
an·gu·lar
an·gu·lar·i·ty

an·i·line
an·i·mad·ver·sion
an·i·mal
an·i·mate
  -mat·ed, -mat·ing,
  -mate·ly
an·i·ma·tion
an·i·mos·i·ty
  -ties
an·i·mus
an·ise
ani·seed
an·kle
an·kle·bone
an·klet
an·nal·ist (writer of
  annals; cf.
  analyst)
an·nals
an·neal
an·nex
  -nex·ation,
  -nex·ation·ist
an·ni·hi·late
  -lat·ing, -la·tion,
  -la·tor
an·ni·ver·sa·ry
  -ries
an·no·tate
  -tat·ed, -tat·ing
an·no·ta·tion
an·nounce
  -nounced,
  -nounc·ing

an·nounce·ment
an·nounc·er
an·noy
an·noy·ance
an·noy·ing
an·nu·al
  -al·ly
an·nu·al·ize
  -ized, -iz·ing
an·nu·itant
an·nu·ity
  -ties
an·nul
  -nulled, -nul·ling
an·nu·lar
an·nul·ment
an·nun·ci·a·tion
an·nun·ci·a·tor
an·ode
an·od·ize
  -ized, -iz·ing
an·o·dyne
anoint
anom·a·lous
anom·a·ly
  -ies
an·o·nym·i·ty
anon·y·mous
an·orex·ia
an·orex·ic
an·oth·er
an·swer
  -swered, -swer·ing
an·swer·able

ant (insect; cf. *aunt*)
ant·ac·id
an·tag·o·nism
an·tag·o·nist
an·tag·o·nis·tic
an·tag·o·nize
  -nized, -niz·ing
ant·arc·tic
ant·eat·er
an·te·bel·lum
an·te·ced·ent
an·te·cham·ber
an·te·date
an·te·di·lu·vi·an
an·te·lope
  -lope (pl)
an·te me·ri·di·em
an·te·na·tal
  -tal·ly
an·ten·na
  -nae (pl)
an·te·pe·nult
  -pen·ul·ti·mate
an·te·ri·or
an·te·room
an·them
ant·hill
an·thol·o·gy
  -gies
an·thra·cite
an·thrax
an·thro·poid
an·thro·pol·o·gy
  -gist

an·thro·po·mor·phic
  -phi·cal·ly
an·ti·bi·ot·ic
an·ti·body
an·ti·busi·ness
an·tic
an·tic·i·pate
  -pat·ed, -pat·ing
an·tic·i·pa·tion
an·tic·i·pa·to·ry
an·ti·cli·mac·tic
an·ti·cli·max
an·ti·dote
an·ti·freeze
an·ti·gen
an·ti·knock
an·ti·log·a·rithm
an·ti·ma·cas·sar
an·ti·mag·net·ic
an·ti·mo·ny
an·ti·node
an·ti·nu·cle·ar
an·ti·pa·thet·ic
  -thet·i·cal·ly
an·tip·a·thy
  -thies
an·ti·per·son·nel
an·ti·per·spi·rant
an·ti·phon
an·ti·quar·i·an
an·ti·quate
  -quat·ed,
  -quat·ing
an·tique

-tiqued, -tiqu·ing
an·tiq·ui·ty
an·ti-Sem·i·tism
an·ti·sep·tic
  -sep·ti·cal·ly
an·ti·so·cial
an·tith·e·sis
  -e·ses (pl)
an·ti·tox·in
an·ti·trust
ant·ler
  -lered
ant·onym
an·vil
anx·i·ety
  -eties
anx·ious
  -ious·ness
any
any·body
any·how
any·more
any·one
any·place
any·thing
any·time
any·way
any·where
aor·ta
  -tas
aor·tic
apace
apart
apart·heid

apart·ment
ap·a·thet·ic
ap·a·thy
aper·i·tif
ap·er·ture
apex
  apex·es
apha·sia
  -si·ac
aphid
aph·o·rism
api·ary (for bees; cf.
  aviary)
  -ar·ies
apiece
aplomb
apoc·a·lypse
apoc·a·lyp·tic
apo·gee
apo·lit·i·cal
Apol·lo
apol·o·get·ic
  -get·i·cal·ly
apol·o·gize
  -gized, -giz·ing
apol·o·gy
  -gies
ap·o·plec·tic
ap·o·plexy
apos·ta·sy
  -sies
apos·tate
a pos·te·ri·o·ri
apos·tle

apos·to·late
ap·os·tol·ic
apos·tro·phe
apoth·e·cary
  -car·ies
Ap·pa·la·chian
ap·pall
  -palled, -pall·ing
Ap·pa·loo·sa
ap·pa·ra·tus
  -tus·es (pl)
ap·par·el
  -eled, -el·ing
ap·par·ent
  -ent·ly
ap·pa·ri·tion
ap·peal
  -peal·abil·i·ty,
  -peal·able
ap·peal·ing
ap·pear
ap·pear·ance
ap·pease
  -peas·ing,
  -peas·able,
  -pease·ment
ap·pel·lant
ap·pel·late
ap·pel·lee
ap·pend
ap·pend·age
ap·pen·dec·to·my
  -mies
ap·pen·di·ci·tis

ap·pen·dix
  -dix·es or -di·ces
  (pl)
ap·per·ceive
  -ceived, -ceiv·ing
ap·per·cep·tion
ap·per·tain
ap·pe·tite
ap·pe·tiz·er
ap·pe·tiz·ing
ap·plaud
ap·plause
ap·ple
ap·ple·jack
ap·pli·ance
ap·pli·ca·ble
  -bil·i·ty
ap·pli·cant
ap·pli·ca·tion
ap·pli·ca·tive
ap·pli·ca·tor
ap·plied
ap·pli·qué
ap·ply
  -ply·ing
ap·point
ap·poin·tee
ap·point·ive
ap·point·ment
ap·por·tion
ap·por·tion·ment
ap·po·site
ap·po·si·tion
ap·prais·al

ap·praise (value; cf. *apprise*)
  -praised,
  -prais·ing
ap·prais·er
ap·pre·cia·ble
ap·pre·ci·ate
  -at·ed, -at·ing
ap·pre·ci·a·tion
ap·pre·cia·tive
ap·pre·hend
ap·pre·hen·si·ble
ap·pre·hen·sion
ap·pre·hen·sive
ap·pren·tice
  -ticed, -tic·ing,
  -tice·ship
ap·prise (inform; cf. *appraise*)
  -prised, -pris·ing
ap·proach
ap·proach·able
ap·pro·bate
  -bat·ed, -bat·ing,
  -ba·to·ry
ap·pro·ba·tion
ap·pro·pri·ate (v)
  -at·ed, -at·ing
ap·pro·pri·ate (adj)
  -ate·ly, -ate·ness
ap·pro·pri·a·tion
ap·prov·al
ap·prove
  -proved, -prov·ing

ap·prox·i·mate (v, adj)
  -mat·ed, -mat·ing
ap·prox·i·mate·ly
ap·prox·i·ma·tion
ap·pur·te·nance
ap·pur·te·nant
apri·cot
April
a pri·o·ri
apron
ap·ro·pos
apt
  apt·ly, apt·ness
ap·ti·tude
aqua·cul·ture
aqua·ma·rine
aqua·naut
aquar·i·um
Aquar·i·us
aquat·ic
aq·ue·duct
aque·ous
aqui·fer
aq·ui·line
ar·a·besque
Ar·a·bic
ar·a·ble
arach·noid
ar·bi·ter
ar·bi·tra·ble
ar·bi·trage
  -traged, -trag·ing
ar·bit·ra·ment

ar·bi·trary
  -trari·ly,
  -trari·ness
ar·bi·trate
  -trat·ed, -trat·ing,
  -tra·tive
ar·bi·tra·tion
ar·bi·tra·tor
ar·bor
ar·bo·re·al
ar·bo·re·tum
ar·bor·vi·tae
ar·bu·tus
arc (curved line; cf. *ark*)
ar·cade
ar·chae·ol·o·gy
  -o·log·i·cal,
  -o·log·i·cal·ly,
  -ol·o·gist
ar·cha·ic
arch·an·gel
arch·bish·op
arch·dea·con
arch·di·o·cese
arch·duch·ess
arch·duchy
arch·duke
arch·en·e·my
  -mies
ar·cher
ar·chery
ar·che·type
arch·fiend

ar·chi·epis·co·pal
ar·chi·pel·a·go
   -goes
ar·chi·tect
ar·chi·tec·tur·al
ar·chi·tec·ture
ar·chiv·al
ar·chive
   -chived, -chiv·ing
ar·chi·vist
arch·way
arc·tic
ar·dent
ar·dor
ar·du·ous
ar·ea (space; cf.
   aria)
area·way
are·na
ar·gon
ar·go·sy
   -sies
ar·got
ar·gu·able
ar·gue
   -gued, -gu·ing
ar·gu·ment
ar·gu·men·ta·tion
ar·gu·men·ta·tive
ar·gyle
aria (melody; cf.
   area)
ar·id
   arid·i·ty,

ar·id·ness
ari·o·so
   -sos
ar·is·toc·ra·cy
   -cies
aris·to·crat
aris·to·crat·ic
Ar·is·to·te·lian
arith·me·tic
   -met·i·cal,
   -met·i·cal·ly,
   -me·ti·cian
ark (refuge; cf. *arc*)
ar·ma·da
ar·ma·dil·lo
   -los
ar·ma·ment
ar·ma·ture
arm·chair
arm·ful
   -fuls
arm·hole
ar·mi·stice
arm·let
ar·mor
ar·mor·er
ar·mo·ri·al
ar·mory
   -mor·ies
arm·pit
arm·rest
arms (weapons; cf.
   alms)
ar·my

-mies
ar·ni·ca
aro·ma
ar·o·mat·ic
around
around-the-clock
arouse
   aroused, arous·ing
ar·peg·gio
   -gios
ar·raign
   -raign·ment
ar·range
   -ranged, -rang·ing,
   -rang·er
ar·range·ment
ar·rant
ar·ras
   ar·ras (pl)
ar·ray
ar·rear
ar·rear·age
ar·rest
ar·riv·al
ar·rive
   -rived, -riv·ing
ar·ro·gance
ar·ro·gant
ar·ro·gate
ar·row
ar·row·head
ar·row·root
ar·royo
   -royos

ar·se·nal
ar·se·nic
ar·son
  -son·ist, -son·ous
ar·te·ri·al
ar·te·rio·scle·ro·sis
ar·tery
  -ter·ies
art·ful
ar·thri·tis
  -thrit·i·des (pl)
ar·ti·choke
ar·ti·cle
  -cled, -cling
ar·tic·u·late
  -lat·ed, -lat·ing
ar·tic·u·la·tion
ar·ti·fact
ar·ti·fice
ar·ti·fi·cer
ar·ti·fi·cial
  -ci·al·i·ty, -cial·ly,
  -cial·ness
ar·til·lery
ar·ti·san
art·ist
ar·tiste
ar·tis·tic
art·ist·ry
art·less
art·work
Ary·an
as·bes·tos
as·cend

as·cen·dan·cy
as·cen·dant
as·cend·ing
as·cen·sion
as·cent (motion
  upward; cf. *assent*)
as·cer·tain
  -tain·able,
  -tain·ment
as·cet·ic
  -cet·i·cal·ly,
  -cet·i·cism
as·cribe
  -cribed, -crib·ing
asep·sis
asep·tic
  -ti·cal·ly
ashamed
ash can (n)
ash·can (adj)
ash·en
ashore
ash·tray
ashy
Asian
Asi·at·ic
aside
as·i·nine
ask
  asked, ask·ing
askance
askew
asleep
as·par·a·gus

as·pect
as·pen
as·per·i·ty
  -ties
as·perse
  -persed, -pers·ing
as·per·sion
as·phalt
as·phyx·ia
as·phyx·i·ate
  -at·ed, -at·ing,
  -a·tion
as·pic
as·pi·rant
as·pi·rate
as·pi·ra·tion
as·pi·ra·tor
as·pire
  -pired, -pir·ing
as·pi·rin
  as·pi·rin (pl)
as·sail
  -sail·able, -sail·ant
as·sas·sin
as·sas·si·nate
  -nat·ed, -nat·ing,
  -na·tion
as·sault
as·say (analyze; cf.
  essay)
as·sem·blage
as·sem·ble
  -bled, -bling,
  -bler

as·sem·bly
 -blies
as·sem·bly·man
as·sem·bly·wom·an
as·sent (consent; cf.
 ascent)
as·sert
as·ser·tion
as·ser·tive
as·sess
 -sess·able
as·sess·ment
as·ses·sor
as·set
as·sev·er·ate
 -ated, -at·ing,
 -a·tion
as·si·du·i·ty
 -ities
as·sid·u·ous
as·sign
as·sig·na·tion
as·sign·ee
as·sign·ment
as·sim·i·la·ble
as·sim·i·late
 -lat·ed, -lat·ing,
 -la·tor
as·sim·i·la·tion
as·sim·i·la·tive
as·sim·i·la·to·ry
as·sist
as·sis·tance (help;
 cf. *assistants*)

as·sis·tant
 -tants (helpers; cf.
 assistance)
as·sis·tant·ship
as·so·ci·ate
 -at·ing
as·so·ci·at·ed
as·so·ci·a·tion
as·so·cia·tive
as·so·nance
as·sort
as·sort·ment
as·suage
 -suaged,
 -suag·ing,
 -suage·ment
as·sume
 -sumed, -sum·ing,
 -sum·able
as·sump·tion
as·sur·ance
as·sure
 -sured, -sur·ing
as·ter
as·ter·isk
as·ter·oid
asth·ma
as·tig·mat·ic
astig·ma·tism
as·ton·ish
as·ton·ish·ment
as·tound
as·tral
astray

astride
as·trin·gent
 -gen·cy, -gent·ly
as·tro·dome
as·trol·o·ger
as·trol·o·gy
as·tro·naut
as·tro·nau·tics
as·tron·o·mer
as·tro·nom·i·cal
as·tron·o·my
 -mies
as·tute
 -tute·ly,
 -tute·ness
asun·der
asy·lum
asym·met·ric
asyn·chro·nous
at·a·rac·tic
at·a·vism
ate·lier
athe·ism
athe·ist
 -is·tic
ath·e·nae·um
ath·lete
ath·let·ic
ath·let·ics
athwart
At·lan·tic
at·las
at·mo·sphere
at·mo·spher·ic

at·om
atom·ic
at·om·ize
at·om·iz·er
aton·al
atone
 atoned, aton·ing
atone·ment
atri·um
 atria (pl)
atro·cious
atroc·i·ty
 -ties
at·ro·phy
 -phies
at·tach
at·ta·ché
at·ta·ché case
at·tached
at·tach·ment
at·tack
at·tain
 -tain·abil·i·ty,
 -tain·able
at·tain·der
at·tain·ment
at·tar
at·tempt
at·tend
at·ten·dance
at·ten·dant
at·ten·tion
at·ten·tive
at·ten·u·ate

 -at·ed, -at·ing,
 -a·tion
at·test
at·tic
at·tire
 -tired, -tir·ing
at·ti·tude
at·ti·tu·di·nal
at·tor·ney
 -neys
at·tor·ney-at-law
 at·tor·neys-at-law
 (pl)
at·tract
at·trac·tion
at·trac·tive
at·tri·bute (n)
at·trib·ute (v)
 -ut·ed, -ut·ing,
 -ut·able
at·tri·bu·tion
at·trib·u·tive
at·tri·tion
at·tune
atyp·i·cal
au·burn
au cou·rant
auc·tion
auc·tion·eer
au·da·cious
au·dac·i·ty
 -ties
au·di·ble
 -bly, -bil·i·ty

au·di·ence
au·dio
au·di·ol·o·gy
au·dio·phile
au·dio·vi·su·al
au·dit
au·di·tion
 -tioned, -tion·ing
au·di·tor
au·di·to·ri·um
 -riums (pl)
au·di·to·ry
auf Wie·der·seh·en
au·ger (tool; cf.
 augur)
aught (slightest
 thing; cf. *ought*)
aug·ment
aug·men·ta·tion
aug·men·ta·tive
au gra·tin
au·gur (predict; cf.
 auger)
au·gu·ry
 -ries
au·gust (majestic)
Au·gust (month)
au jus
auk
auld lang syne
au na·tu·rel
aunt (relative; cf.
 ant)
au·ra

au·ral (heard; cf. *oral*)
  -ral·ly
au·re·ate
au·re·ole
Au·reo·my·cin
au·ri·cle
au·ric·u·lar
au·rif·er·ous
au·ro·ra bo·re·al·is
aus·pice
  -pic·es (pl)
aus·pi·cious
  -cious·ly,
  -cious·ness
aus·tere
  -tere·ly, -tere·ness
aus·ter·i·ty
  -ties
Aus·tra·lian
au·then·tic
  -ti·cal·ly, -tic·i·ty
au·then·ti·cate
  -cat·ed, -cat·ing,
  -ca·tion
au·thor
au·thor·i·tar·i·an
au·thor·i·ta·tive
au·thor·i·ty
  -ties
au·tho·ri·za·tion
au·tho·rize
  -riz·ing
au·tho·rized
au·thor·ship

au·tism
  -tis·tic, -tis·ti·cal·ly
au·to·bahn
au·to·bio·graph·i·cal
au·to·bi·og·ra·phy
au·toch·tho·nous
au·toc·ra·cy
  -cies
au·to·crat
au·to·crat·ic
au·to·graph
au·to·graph·ic
au·to·in·fec·tion
au·to·in·tox·i·ca·tion
au·to·mate
  -mat·ed, -mat·ing
au·to·mat·ic
  -mat·i·cal·ly
au·to·ma·tion
au·tom·a·tism
au·tom·a·ti·za·tion
au·tom·a·tize
  -tized, -tiz·ing
au·tom·a·ton
  -atons
au·to·mo·bile
au·to·mo·tive
au·ton·o·mous
au·ton·o·my
  -mies
au·top·sy
  -sies
au·to·sug·ges·tion
au·tumn

-tum·nal,
  -tum·nal·ly
aux·il·ia·ry
  -ries
avail
avail·abil·i·ty
  -ties
avail·able
av·a·lanche
avant-garde
av·a·rice
av·a·ri·cious
avenge
  avenged,
  aveng·ing,
  aveng·er
av·e·nue
aver
  averred, aver·ring
av·er·age
averse (disinclined;
  cf. *adverse*)
aver·sion
avert
avi·ary (for birds; cf.
  apiary)
  -ar·ies
avi·a·tion
avi·a·tor
avi·a·trix
avi·cul·ture
av·id
avid·i·ty
avi·on·ics

av·o·ca·do
  -dos
av·o·ca·tion (hobby;
  cf. *vocation*)
avoid
  avoid·able,
  avoid·ably
avoid·ance
av·oir·du·pois
avow
avow·al
avun·cu·lar
await
awake
awak·en
  -ened, -en·ing

award
aware
  aware·ness
awash
away (absent; cf.
  aweigh)
aweigh (of anchor;
  cf. *away*)
awe·some
aw·ful
awhile
awk·ward
awl (tool; cf. *all*)
aw·ning
awoke
awry

ax
ax·i·al
ax·i·om
ax·i·om·at·ic
ax·is
  ax·es (pl)
ax·le
ax·le·tree
aye
ayes
aza·lea
az·i·muth
Az·tec
azure

B

baa
bab·bitt met·al
bab·ble (chatter; cf.
  bauble, bubble)
  -bled, -bling
ba·boon
ba·bush·ka
ba·by
  -bies, -bied,
  -by·hood
baby boom
  boom·er

ba·by-sit
  ba·by-sat, ba·by-
  sit·ting, ba·by-
  sit·ter
bac·ca·lau·re·ate
bac·ca·rat
bach·e·lor
  -lor·hood, -lor·ette
ba·cil·lus
  -li (pl)
back·ache
back·bite

  -bit, -biting, -bit·er
back·board
back·bone
back·break·ing
back door (n)
back·door (adj)
back·drop
back·er
back·field
back·fire
back·gam·mon
back·ground

back·hand
  -hand·ed
back·hoe
back·lash
back·log
back off
back·pack
back·rest
back room
back·scat·ter
back·seat
back·slide
  -slid, -slid·ing,
  -slid·er
back·stage
back·stairs
back·stitch
back·stop
back·stretch
back·stroke
back talk
back-to-back
back·track
back up (v)
back·up (n)
back·ward
  -ward·ly,
  -ward·ness
back·wash
back·wa·ter
back·woods
  -woods·man
back·yard
ba·con

bac·te·ria (pl)
  -ri·um (sing)
bac·te·ri·al
  -al·ly
bac·te·ri·cid·al
  -cid·al·ly
bac·te·ri·cide
bac·te·ri·ol·o·gy
  -o·log·ic,
  -o·log·i·cal·ly,
  -ol·o·gist
bad (not good; cf.
  bade)
bade (commanded;
  cf. *bad*)
badge
bad·ger
  -gered,
  -ger·ing
ba·di·nage
bad·land
bad·min·ton
baf·fle
  -fled, -fling,
  -fle·ment
bag
  bagged, bag·ging,
  bag·ger
ba·gel
bag·gage
bag·gy
  -gi·er, -gi·est,
  -gi·ness
bag·pipe

bail (release; cf. *bale*)
  bailed (set free; cf.
  baled)
bail·ee
bai·liff
bai·li·wick
bail·ment
bail·or
bait (a lure; cf. *bate*)
bake
  baked, bak·ing,
  bak·er
Ba·ke·lite
bak·er's doz·en
bal·ance
  -anced,
  -anc·ing
bal·co·ny
  -nies
bald (hairless; cf.
  balled, bawled)
  bald·ish, bald·ly,
  bald·ness
bal·der·dash
bale (package; cf.
  bail)
  baled (packaged;
  cf. *bailed*) bal·ing,
  bal·er
bale·ful
balk
bal·kan·ize
  -ized, -iz·ing,
  -iza·tion

26

balky
  balk·i·er,
  balk·i·est,
  balk·i·ness
bal·lad
bal·lad·eer
bal·lad·ry
bal·last
ball bear·ing
balled (made a ball;
  cf. *bald, bawled*)
bal·le·ri·na
bal·let
bal·lis·tic
bal·lis·tics
bal·loon
bal·loon·ist
bal·lot
ball·park
ball·point
ball·room
bal·ly·hoo
  -hoos (pl)
balm
bal·mor·al
balmy
  balm·i·er,
  balm·i·est,
  balm·i·ness
ba·lo·ney
bal·sa
bal·sam
Bal·tic
bal·us·trade

bam·boo
bam·boo·zle
  -zled, -zling
ba·nal
ba·nana
band (narrow strip;
  cf. *banned*)
  bands (pl. of *band*;
  cf. *banns, bans*)
ban·dage
  -daged, -dag·ing
ban·dan·na
band·box
ban·deau
  -deaux (pl)
ban·dit
band·mas·ter
ban·do·lier
band saw
band shell
band·stand
band·wag·on
ban·dy
  -died, -dy·ing
bane·ful
ban·gle
ban·ish
  -ish·er,
  -ish·ment
ban·is·ter
ban·jo
  -jos (pl), -jo·ist
bank·book
bank·card

bank dis·count
bank·er
bank mon·ey
bank note
bank rate
bank·roll
bank·rupt
bank·rupt·cy
  -cies
banned (prohibited;
  cf. *band*)
ban·ner
banns (of marriage;
  cf. *bands, bans*)
ban·quet
ban·quette
bans (forbids; cf.
  bands, banns)
ban·shee
ban·tam
ban·ter
ban·yan
ban·zai
bap·tism
bap·tist
bap·tize
  -tized, -tiz·ing,
  -tiz·er
bar
  barred (kept from;
  cf. *bard*), bar·ring
bar·bar·i·an
bar·bar·ic
bar·ba·rism

27

bar·bar·i·ty
  -ties
bar·ba·rize
  -rized, -riz·ing
bar·ba·rous
bar·be·cue
bar·bell
bar·ber
  -bered, -ber·ing
bar·ber·shop
bar·bi·tu·rate
bar chart
bar code
bard (poet; cf.
  barred)
bare (uncover; cf.
  bear), bar·er,
  bar·est, bare·ness,
  bared, bar·ing
bare·back
bare·faced
bare·foot
bare·hand·ed
bare·head·ed
bare·ly
bar·gain
barge·man
bari·tone
bar·i·um
bar·keep·er
bark·er
bar·ley
bar·ley·corn
bar·maid

bar·na·cle
barn·storm
  -storm·er
barn·yard
baro·graph
ba·rom·e·ter
baro·met·ric
  -ri·cal·ly
bar·on (nobleman;
  cf. *barren*)
bar·on·age
bar·on·ess
bar·on·et
bar·on·et·cy
ba·ro·ni·al
bar·ony
  -on·ies
ba·roque
ba·rouche
bar·rack
bar·ra·cu·da
  -da (pl)
bar·rage
  -raged, -rag·ing
barred (shut out; cf.
  bard)
bar·rel
bar·ren (sterile; cf.
  baron)
bar·rette
bar·ri·cade
  -cad·ed, -cad·ing
bar·ri·er
bar·ring

bar·rio
  -rios (pl)
bar·ris·ter
bar·room
bar·row
bar·tend·er
bar·ter
bas·al
ba·salt
base (foundation; cf.
  bass)
bas·es (pl)
base·ball
base·board
base·line
base·ment
base pay
bash·ful
ba·sic
  -si·cal·ly, -sic·i·ty
ba·sil
ba·sil·i·ca
bas·i·lisk
ba·sin
bas·i·net (helmet; cf.
  bassinet)
ba·sis (foundation;
  cf. *bases*)
ba·ses (pl)
bas·ket
  -ket·ful
bas·ket·ball
bas·ket·work
bas-re·lief

bass (deep voice; cf.
  base)
  bass (pl)
bas·si·net (cradle;
  cf. *basinet*)
bas·soon
bass·wood
bas·tion
batch
bate (moderate; cf.
  bait)
  bat·ed, bat·ing
ba·teau
  ba·teaux (pl)
bath (n)
  baths
bathe (v)
  bathed, bath·ing
bath·house
bath mat
ba·thom·e·ter
ba·thos
bath·robe
bath·room
bath·tub
bathy·scaphe
bathy·sphere
ba·tiste
ba·ton
bat·tal·ion
bat·ten
  -tened, -ten·ing
bat·ter
bat·tery

-ter·ies
bat·tle
  -tled, -tling, -tler
bat·tle-ax
bat·tle cruis·er
bat·tle cry
bat·tle·field
bat·tle·ground
bat·tle group
bat·tle·ment
bat·tle-scarred
bat·tle·ship
bau·ble (trifle; cf.
  babble, bubble)
baud
baux·ite
Ba·var·i·an
bawl
  bawled (cried; cf.
  bald, balled)
bay·ber·ry
bay·o·net
bay·ou
bay rum
ba·zaar (market; cf.
  bizarre)
ba·zoo·ka
beach (shore; cf.
  beech)
beach·comb·er
beach·head
bea·con
bea·dle
bead·work

beady
bea·gle
bear (n)(animal;
  cf. *bare*) bears
bear (v)(hold; cf. *bare*)
  bore, borne,
  bear·ing
bear·able
beard
  beard·ed,
  beard·less
bear·er
bear·skin
beat (flog; cf. *beet*)
be·atif·ic
be·at·i·fi·ca·tion
be·at·i·fy
  -fied, -fy·ing
be·at·i·tude
beat·nik
beau (suitor; cf. *bow*)
  beaux (pl)
beau·te·ous
beau·ti·cian
beau·ti·ful
  -ful·ly, -ful·ness
beau·ti·fy
  -fied, -fying,
  -fi·ca·tion
beau·ty
  -ties
bea·ver
  -vers
be·calm

be·cause
beck·on
  -oned, -on·ing
be·cloud
be·come
  -came, -com·ing,
  -com·ing·ly
be·daz·zle
bed board
bed·bug
bed·clothes
bed·ding
be·deck
be·dev·il
bed·fast
bed·fel·low
bed·lam
bed·ou·in
  bed·ou·in (pl)
bed·post
be·drag·gled
bed·rid·den
bed·rock
bed·room
bed·side
bed·sore
bed·spread
bed·stead
bed·time
beech (tree; cf. *beach*)
  beech·es (pl)
beech·nut
beef·eat·er
beef·steak

bee·hive
bee·keep·er
bee·line
been
beer (liquor; cf. *bier*)
bees·wax
beet (vegetable; cf.
  beat)
bee·tle
be·fall
be·fit
  -fit·ted, -fit·ting
be·fore
be·fore·hand
be·fore·time
be·friend
be·fud·dle
beg·gar
  -gared, -gar·ing
beg·gar·ly
  -gar·li·ness
beg·gary
  -gar·ies
be·gin
be·gin·ning
be·go·nia
be·grudge
be·guile
  -guiled, -guil·ing,
  -guile·ment
be·half
be·have
  -haved, -hav·ing,
  -hav·er

be·hav·ior
  -ior·al, -ior·al·ly
be·hav·ior·ism
be·head
be·he·moth
be·hest
be·hind
be·hind-the-scenes
be·hold
be·hoove
  -hooved, -hoov·ing
beige
be·ing
be·la·bor
be·lat·ed
  -ed·ly, -ed·ness
be·lay
bel can·to
be·lea·guer
  -guered, -guer·ing
bel·fry
  -fries
Bel·gian
be·lie
  -lied, -ly·ing, -li·er
be·lief
be·liev·able
  -ably, -abil·ity
be·lieve
  -lieved, -liev·ing,
  -liev·er
be·lit·tle
  -tled, -tling,
  -tle·ment

bell (that rings; cf. *belle*)
bel·la·don·na
bell·boy
belle (girl; cf. *bell*)
belles let·tres
bell·hop
bel·li·cose
bel·lig·er·ence
bel·lig·er·ent
bell jar
bel·lows
bell·pull
bell tow·er
bell·weth·er
bel·ly
  -lies
bel·ly·ache
belly button
be·long
be·loved
be·low
belt·ing
be·moan
bench mark
bench war·rant
bend
  bent, bend·ing
be·neath
ben·e·dict
bene·dic·tion
bene·dic·to·ry
bene·fac·tion
bene·fac·tor

be·nef·i·cence
be·nef·i·cent
  -cent·ly
ben·e·fi·cial
ben·e·fi·cia·ry
  -ries
ben·e·fit
  -fit·ed, -fit·ing,
  -fit·er
be·nev·o·lence
be·nev·o·lent
be·night·ed
be·nign
ben·zene
be·queath
be·quest
be·rate
be·reave
  -reaved, -reav·ing
be·reave·ment
beri·beri
ber·ry (fruit; cf. *bury*)
  -ries
ber·serk
berth (place; cf. *birth*)
ber·yl
be·ryl·li·um
be·seech
be·set·ting
be·side
be·sides
be·siege
  -sieged, -sieg·ing,
  -sieg·er

be·smear
be·smirch
be·speak
  -spoke, -spo·ken,
  -speak·ing
bes·tial
bes·ti·al·i·ty
  -ties
best man
be·stow
best-sell·er
  best-sell·ing
bet
  bet·ted, bet·ting
be·tide
be·to·ken
  -kened, -ken·ing
be·tray
  -tray·al, -tray·er
be·troth
be·troth·al
bet·ter (good; cf. *bettor*)
bet·ter·ment
bet·tor (one who wagers; cf. *better*)
be·tween
be·tween·times
be·twixt
bev·el
  -eled, -el·ing
bev·er·age
bevy
  bev·ies

be·wail
be·ware
be·wil·der
  -dered, -der·ing,
  -der·ing·ly
be·wil·der·ment
be·witch
be·yond
be·zel
bi·an·nu·al (twice
  yearly; cf.
  biennial)
  -al·ly
bi·as
  -as·ness, -ased,
  -as·ing
bi·be·lot
bi·ble
bib·li·cal
  -cal·ly
bib·li·og·ra·pher
bib·li·og·ra·phy
  -phies
bib·lio·graph·ic
  -graph·i·cal·ly
bib·lio·phile
bib·u·lous
bi·cam·er·al
bi·car·bon·ate
bi·cen·te·na·ry
bi·cen·ten·ni·al
bi·ceps
  bi·ceps (pl)
bi·chlo·ride

bi·chro·mate
bi·cus·pid
bi·cy·cle
  -cled, -cling, -cler
bi·cy·clist
bid
  bade, bid·den,
  bid·der
bi·di·rec·tion·al
bi·en·ni·al (once in
  two years; cf.
  biannual)
  -al·ly
bi·en·ni·um
  -ni·ums
bier (for funeral; cf.
  beer)
bi·fo·cal
bi·fur·cate
  -cat·ed, -cat·ing
big
  big·ger, big·gest,
  big·ness
big·a·mous
big·a·my
  -mist
Big Ben
big game
big·head
  -head·ed
big·heart·ed
big·horn
  -horn (pl)
bight

big·ot
  -ot·ed, -ot·ed·ly
big·ot·ry
  -ries
bi·jou
bi·ki·ni
bi·lat·er·al
bile
bi·lev·el
bi·lin·gual
  -gual·ly
bi·lin·gual·ism
bilk
bill·board
billed (charged; cf.
  build)
bil·let-doux
  bil·lets-doux (pl)
bill·fold
bil·liards
bill·ing
bil·lion
  bil·lionth
bil·lion·aire
bill of fare
bill of lad·ing
bil·low
  -lowy
bil·ly goat
bi·me·tal·lic
bi·met·al·lism
bi·met·al·list
  -lis·tic
bi·month·ly

bi·na·ry
  -ries
bind
  bound, bind·ing
bind·er
bind·ery
  -er·ies
bin·go
bin·na·cle
bin·oc·u·lar
bi·no·mi·al
bio·chem·i·cal
  -cal·ly
bio·chem·is·try
  -chem·ist
bio·de·grad·able
  -abil·ty
bio·de·grade
  -deg·ra·da·tion
bio·feed·back
bi·og·ra·pher
bio·graph·i·cal
bi·og·ra·phy
  -phies
bi·o·log·i·cal
bi·ol·o·gy
  -gist
bi·on·ics
bi·op·sy
bio·sci·ence
bi·par·ti·san
  -san·ism,
  -san·ship
bi·par·tite

bi·ped
bi·plane
bi·po·lar
bi·ra·cial
bird·bath
bird·call
bird-dog (v)
  bird-dog·ging
bird·house
bird·ie
bird·lime
bird·man
bird·seed
bird's-eye
birth (born; cf. *berth*)
birth·day
birth·mark
birth·place
birth·rate
birth·right
birth·stone
bis·cuit
bi·sect
bi·sex·u·al
bish·op
bish·op·ric
bis·muth
bi·son
  bi·son (pl)
bisque
bite
  bit, bit·ten,
  bit·ing
bit·stock

bit·ter
  -ter·ish
bit·tern
bit·ter·ness
bit·ter·root
bit·ter·sweet
bit·ter·weed
bi·tu·men
bi·tu·mi·nous
bi·valve
biv·ouac
  -ouack·ed,
  -ouack·ing
bi·week·ly
bi·zarre (odd; cf.
  bazaar)
  -zarre·ly,
  -zarre·ness
bi·zon·al
black·ball
black·ber·ry
black·board
black·en
  -ened,
  -en·ing,
  -en·er
black·head
black·jack
black light
black·list
black·mail
black out (v)
black·out (n)
black sheep

black·smith
black·top
blad·der
blade
blam·able
blame
 blamed,
 blam·ing,
 blame·less
blame·ful
blame·wor·thy
 -thi·ness
blanch
blan·dish
 -dish·ment
blan·ket
blar·ney
bla·sé
blas·pheme
 -phemed,
 -phem·ing,
 -phem·er
blas·phe·mous
 -mous·ly
blas·phe·my
 -mies
blast off (v)
blast-off (n)
bla·tan·cy
 -cies
bla·tant
 -tant·ly
blaze
 blazed, blaz·ing

blaz·er
bla·zon
 -zoned, -zon·ing,
 -zon·er
bleach
 bleach·able
bleach·er
 -er·ite
blem·ish
blend
 blend·ed, blend·ing
bless
 blessed, bless·ing
blew (air; cf. *blue*)
blind
 blind·ness
blind·er
blind·fold
blink·er
blin·tze
bliss·ful
 -ful·ly, -ful·ness
blis·ter
 -tered, -ter·ing
blithe
 blith·er, blith·est,
 blithe·ly
blithe·some
blitz·krieg
bliz·zard
bloat
bloc (political; cf.
 block)
block (of wood; cf.

 bloc)
block·ade
 -ad·ed, -ad·ing,
 -ad·er
block·bust·er
block·head
blond
blood
blood·cur·dling
blood·ed
blood·less
blood·let·ting
blood·mo·bile
blood·root
blood·shed
blood·shot
blood·stain
blood·suck·er
blood·thirsty
blood ves·sel
bloody
 blood·i·er,
 blood·i·est,
 blood·i·ly
blos·som
blotch
blot·ter
blouse
 blous·es
blow-dry
blow·er
blow·fly
blow·gun
blow out (v)

blow·out (n)
blow over
blow·pipe
blow·torch
blub·ber
  -bered, -ber·ing
blub·bery
blud·geon
blue (color; cf. *blew*)
  blu·er, blu·est,
  blue·ness
blue·bell
blue·ber·ry
blue·bird
blue·bon·net
blue book
blue-col·lar
blue·fish
blue flu
blue·grass
blue·jack·et
blue jay
blue jeans
blue law
blue moon
blue-pen·cil
blue·print
blues
blu·et
bluff
blu·ing
blu·ish
blun·der
  -dered, -der·ing,

-der·er
blun·der·buss
blunt
  blunt·ness
blur
  blurred, blur·ring
blurb
blurt
blus·ter
  -tered, -ter·ing,
  -ter·er
boa
boar (animal; cf. *bore*)
board (wood; cf.
  bored)
board foot
board·ing·house
board·ing school
board·room
board·walk
boast
boast·ful
  -ful·ly, -ful·ness
boat·house
boat·load
boat people
boat·swain
bob
  bobbed, bob·bing
bob·bin
bob·cat
bob·o·link
bob·sled
bob·tail

bob·white
bod·ice
bodi·less
bodi·ly
bod·kin
body
  bod·ies, bod·ied
Boer
bo·gey
  -geys (pl)
bo·gey·man
bog·gle
  -gled, -gling
bo·gus
Bo·he·mi·an
boil·er
boil·er·plate
bois·ter·ous
bold
  bold·er (stronger;
  cf. *boulder*)
bold·face
bold-faced
bole (trunk of tree;
  cf. *boll, bowl*)
bo·le·ro
  -ros (pl)
bo·li·var
boll (of cotton; cf.
  bole, bowl)
boll wee·vil
bol·ster
  -stered, -ster·ing,
  -ster·er

bolt·er
bolt·rope
bo·lus
bomb
bom·bard
  -bard·ment
bom·bar·dier
bom·bast
bom·bas·tic
bom·ba·zine
bomb·shell
bomb·sight
bo·na fide
bo·nan·za
bon·bon
bond·age
bond·hold·er
bonds·man
bone
  boned, bon·ing
bone·meal
bon·fire
bon mot
  bons mots (pl)
bon·net
bon·ny
  -ni·er, -ni·est,
  -ni·ly
bo·nus
bon vi·vant
  bons vivants (pl)
bon voy·age
bony
  bon·i·er, bon·i·est

boo
boo·dle
book
book·bind·er
  -bind·ery
book·bind·ing
book·case
book club
book·end
book·ie
book·ish
book·keep·er
  -keep·ing
book·let
book·mak·er
  -mak·ing
book·man
book·mark
book·mo·bile
book·plate
book·sell·er
book·shelf
book·store
book val·ue
book·worm
boo·mer·ang
boon·dog·gle
boor·ish
  -ish·ly, -ish·ness
boost·er
boot·black
boot·ed
boo·tee
booth

booths
boot·jack
boot·leg
boo·ty
  -ties
booze
  boozed, booz·ing,
  booz·er
bo·rate
bo·rax
Bor·deaux
  Bor·deaux (pl)
bor·der (edge)
  -dered, -der·ing
bor·der·line
bore (weary; cf. *boar*)
  bored (tired; cf.
  board), bor·ing
bo·re·al
Bo·re·as
bore·dom
born-again
bo·ron
bor·ough (division
  of city; cf. *burro,
  burrow*)
bor·row
bo·som
bossy
  boss·i·er, boss·i·est
bo·tan·i·cal
bot·a·nist
bot·a·ny
botch

both
both·er
  -ered, -er·ing
both·er·some
bot·tle
  -tled, -tling, -tler
bot·tle·neck
bot·tom
bot·tom·less
bot·u·lism
bou·doir
bouf·fant
bough (of tree; cf.
  bow)
bought
bouil·la·baisse
bouil·lon (soup; cf.
  bullion)
boul·der (rock; cf.
  bolder)
bou·le·vard
bounce
  bounced,
  bounc·ing
bounc·er
bound
bound·ary
  -aries
bound·er
bound·less
boun·te·ous
boun·ti·ful
boun·ty
  -ties

bou·quet
bour·bon
bour·geois (adj, n)
  bour·geois (pl)
bour·geoi·sie
bou·tique
bou·ton·niere
bo·vine
bow (knot; cf. *beau*)
bow (salutation; cf.
  bough)
bowd·ler·ize
  -ized, -iz·ing,
  -iz·er
bow·el
bow·er
bow·ery
  -er·ies
bow·knot
bowl (dish; cf. *bole*,
  boll)
bowl·er
bow·line
bowl·ing
bow·man
bow·sprit
bow·string
bow tie
box·car
box·er
box·ing
box kite
box lunch
box of·fice

box score
box spring
box·wood
boy (youth; cf. *buoy*)
boy·cott
boy·sen·ber·ry
brace·let
brac·er
brack·et
brack·ish
brag
  bragged,
  brag·ging,
  brag·ger
brag·ga·do·cio
brag·gart
braille
brain·child
brain·less
brain·pow·er
brain·storm
brain trust
brain·wash·ing
brain wave
brainy
  brain·i·er,
  brain·i·est,
  brain·i·ness
braise (cook slowly;
  cf. *braze*)
  braised, brais·ing
brake (on a car; cf.
  break)
  braked, brak·ing

brake·man
bram·ble
brand
bran·dish
brand-new
bran·dy
  -dies, -died,
  -dy·ing
brass·bound
bras·siere
bra·va·do
brav·ery
  -er·ies
bra·vo
  -vos (pl), -vo·ing,
  -voed
bra·vu·ra
brawl
brawny
  brawn·i·er,
  brawn·i·est,
  brawn·i·ness
braze (solder; cf.
  braise)
  brazed, braz·ing,
  braz·er
bra·zen
  -zened, -zen·ing
bra·zier
bra·zil·wood
breach (violation; cf.
  breech)
bread (food; cf. *bred*)
bread·fruit

bread·stuff
breadth (size; cf.
  breath)
bread·win·ner
break (shatter; cf.
  brake) break·ing,
  broke, bro·ken
break·able
break·age
break down (v)
break·down (n)
break·er
break-even
break·fast
break·neck
break out (v)
break·out (n)
break through (v)
break·through (n)
break·wa·ter
breast
breast·bone
breast·stroke
breath (n)(of air; cf.
  breadth)
Breath·a·ly·zer
breathe (v)
  breathed,
  breath·ing
breath·er
breath·less
breath·tak·ing
breech (rear; cf.
  breach)

breech·load·er
  breech·load·ing
breed
  bred (produced;
  cf. *bread*),
  breed·ing
breeze
breeze·way
breezy
  breez·i·er,
  breez·i·ly,
  breez·i·ness
breth·ren
bre·vet
  -vet·ted, -vet·ting
bre·via·ry
  -ries
brev·i·ty
  -ties
brew
  brew·ing
brew·ery
  -er·ies
brews (ferments; cf.
  bruise)
bribe
  bribed, brib·ing,
  brib·er
brib·ery
  -er·ies
bric-a-brac
  bric-a-brac (pl)
brick
  bricks

brick·bat
brick·lay·er
brick red
brick·work
brick·yard
brid·al (wedding; cf. *bridle*)
bride
bride·groom
brides·maid
bridge
  bridged, bridg·ing
bridge·work
bri·dle (harness; cf. *bridal*)
  -dled, -dling
brief
brief·case
brief·less
bri·er
brig
bri·gade
  -gad·ed, -gad·ing
brig·a·dier
brig·and
bright
bright·en
  -ened, -en·ing, -en·er
bright·ness
bright·work
bril·liance
bril·lian·cy
  -cies

bril·liant
bril·lian·tine
brim
  brimmed, brim·ming
brim·ful
brim·mer
brim·stone
brin·dle
bring
  brought, bring·ing
brink
brink·man·ship
briny
  brin·i·er, brin·i·est, brin·i·ness
bri·quette
brisk
bris·ket
bris·tle
  -tled, -tling
bris·tol (cardboard)
Britain (nation; cf. *Briton*)
Bri·tan·nic
Brit·ish
Brit·ish·er
Brit·on (person; cf. *Britain*)
brit·tle
  -tler, -tlest, -tle·ness
broach (open; cf.

brooch)
broad
  broad·ly, broad·ness
broad·ax
broad·cast
  -cast·ed, -cast·ing, -cast·er
broad·cloth
broad·en
  -ened, -en·ing
broad jump
broad-leaved (adj)
broad-mind·ed
  -ed·ness, -ed·ly
broad·side
broad·sword
broad·tail
bro·cade
broc·co·li
bro·chette
bro·chure
brogue
broil
broil·er
broke
bro·ken
bro·ken·heart·ed
bro·ker
bro·ker·age
bro·mate
bro·mide
bro·mine
bron·chi·al

bron·chi·tis
bron·cho·scope
bron·co
  -cos
bronze
  bronzed,
  bronz·ing,
  bronz·er
brooch (pin; cf.
  broach)
brood
brood·er
brook
broom·stick
broth
  broths
broth·er
  broth·ers
broth·er·hood
broth·er-in-law
  broth·ers-in-law (pl)
broth·er·ly
brougham
brought
brow
brow·beat
  -beat·en
brown bread
brown·out
brown·stone
brown sug·ar
browse
  browsed,
  brows·ing,

browser
bru·in
bruise (crush; cf.
  brews)
  bruised, bruis·ing
bruis·er
bru·net or
  bru·nette
brunt
brush
brush-off (n)
brush up (v)
brush·up (n)
brush·wood
brush·work
brusque
bru·tal
bru·tal·i·ty
  -ties
bru·tal·ize
  -ized, -iz·ing,
  -iza·tion
brute
brut·ish
bub·ble (soap; cf.
  babble, bauble)
bub·bly
  -bli·er, -bli·est
buc·ca·neer
buck·board
buck·et
buck·eye
buck·le
  -led, -ling

buck·ram
buck·saw
buck·shot
buck·skin
buck·wheat
bu·col·ic
Bud·dha
Bud·dhism
bud·ding
bud·get
buf·fa·lo (sing)
  buf·fa·lo or
  buf·fa·loes (pl)
buff·er
  -ered, -er·ing
buf·fet
buf·foon
buf·foon·ery
bug·bear
bu·gle
  -gled, -gling
build (construct; cf.
  billed)
  built, build·ing
build·er
build up (v)
build·up (n)
built-in
built-up
bul·bous
Bul·gar·i·an
bulge
  bulged, bulg·ing
bulk·head

bulky
 bulk·i·er,
 bulk·i·est,
 bulk·i·ness
bull·dog
bull·doze
bull·doz·er
bul·let
bul·le·tin
bul·let·proof
bu·lim·ia
bull·fight
bull·finch
bull·frog
bull·head
bul·lion (gold or
 silver; cf. *bouillon*)
bull·ock
bull pen
bull's-eye
 bull's-eyes (pl)
bull·ter·ri·er
bull·whip
bul·ly
 -lies, -lied, -ly·ing
bul·rush
bul·wark
bum·ble·bee
bump·er
bump·kin
bumpy
 bump·i·er,
 bump·i·ly,
 bump·i·ness

bunch
bun·dle
 -dled, -dling, -dler
bun·ga·low
bun·gle
 -gled, -gling, -gler
bun·ion
bunk
bunk beds
bun·ker
 -kered, -ker·ing
bun·kum or
 bun·combe
bun·ting
buoy (signal; cf. *boy*)
buoy·an·cy
buoy·ant
bur·den
 -dened, -den·ing
bur·den·some
bur·dock
bu·reau
 -reaus (pl)
bu·reau·cra·cy
 -cies
bur·reau·crat
bu·reau·crat·ic
bur·geon
bur·gher
bur·glar
bur·glar·ize
 -ized, -iz·ing
bur·glar·proof
bur·glary

-glar·ies
bur·go·mas·ter
bur·gun·dy
 -dies
buri·al
bur·lap
bur·lesque
 -lesqued,
 -lesqu·ing
bur·ly
 -li·er, -li·est,
 -li·ness
Bur·mese
burn
 burned, burn·ing
burn·er
bur·nish
bur·noose
burn·sides
burr
bur·ro (donkey; cf.
 borough, burrow)
 bur·ros (pl)
bur·row (dig; cf.
 borough, burro)
bur·sar
bur·sa·ry
 -ries
bur·si·tis
burst
bury (conceal; cf.
 berry)
 bur·ied, bury·ing
bus·boy

41

bush·el
-eled, -el·ing, -el·er

busi·ness (enter-
prise; cf. *busyness*)

busi·ness·like

busi·ness·man

busi·ness·peo·ple

busi·ness·wom·an

bus·ing

bus·tle
-tled, -tling

busy
bus·i·er, bus·i·est,
bus·ied

busy· ness (busy
state; cf. *business*)

busy·work

but (conjunction; cf.
butt)

butch·er
-ered, -er·ing

butch·ery
-er·ies

but·ler

butt (end; cf. *but*)

butte

but·ter

but·ter·fat

but·ter·fly
-flies

but·ter·milk

but·ter·nut

but·ter·scotch

but·ter·weed

but·tery
-ter·ies

but·tock

but·ton
-toned, -ton·er,
-ton·ing

but·ton·hole

but·ton·hook

but·tress

bux·om

buy (acquire; cf. *by,
bye*)
buy·ing, buy·er,
bought

buzz

buz·zard

buzz·er

buzz saw

buzz·word

by (near, farewell; cf.
buy, bye)

by and large

bye (tournament; cf.
buy, by)

by-elec·tion

by·gone

by·law

by·line

by·pass

by·play

by-prod·uct

by·stand·er

byte

by·way

by·word

Byz·an·tine

C

ca·bal
-balled, -bal·ling

ca·bana

cab·a·ret

cab·bage

cab·driv·er

cab·in

cab·i·net

cab·i·net·mak·er

cab·i·net·work

ca·ble
-bled, -bling

ca·ble·gram
ca·boose
cab·ri·ole
cab·stand
ca·cao
cac·cia·to·re
cache
  cached, cach·ing
ca·chet
cach·in·nate
  -nat·ed, -nat·ing,
  -na·tion
ca·cique
cack·le
  -led, -ling, -ler
ca·coph·o·ny
  -nies
cac·tus
  cacti (pl)
ca·dav·er
ca·dav·er·ous
cad·die
  -dies
ca·dence
ca·den·za
ca·det
cad·mi·um
cad·re
ca·du·ceus
Cae·sar
cae·su·ra
  -su·ras (pl)
ca·fé
caf·e·te·ria

caf·feine
cairn·gorm
cais·son
cai·tiff
ca·jole
  -joled, -jol·ing,
  -jol·ery
Ca·jun
cake
  caked, cak·ing
cal·a·bash
cal·a·boose
ca·lam·i·tous
ca·lam·i·ty
  -ties
cal·car·e·ous
cal·cif·er·ous
cal·ci·fy
  -fied, -fy·ing,
  -fi·ca·tion
cal·ci·mine
cal·ci·na·tion
cal·cine
  -cined, -cin·ing
cal·ci·um
cal·cu·la·ble
cal·cu·late
  -lat·ed, -lat·ing
cal·cu·la·tion
cal·cu·la·tor
cal·cu·lus
  -li (pl)
cal·dron
cal·en·dar (for

dates; cf. *calender,*
colander)
-dared, -dar·ing
cal·en·der (ma-
  chine; cf.
  calendar,
  colander)
-dered, -der·ing,
  -der·er
calf
  calves (pl)
calf·skin
cal·i·ber
cal·i·brate
  -brat·ed, -brat·ing,
  -bra·tor
cal·i·bra·tion
cal·i·co
  -coes (pl)
cal·i·per
  -pered, -per·ing
ca·liph
cal·is·then·ics
calk
call·able
cal·lig·ra·pher
cal·lig·ra·phy
call·ing
cal·li·ope
cal·lous (hardened;
  cf. *callus*)
cal·low
cal·lus (hardened
  surface; cf. *callous*)

calm
  calm·ly, calm·ness
ca·lo·ric
cal·o·rie
  -ries
cal·o·rim·e·ter
ca·lum·ni·ate
  -at·ed, -at·ing,
  -a·tion
ca·lum·ni·ous
cal·um·ny
  -nies
cal·va·ry
  -ries
Cal·vin·ism
ca·lyp·so
  -sos (pl)
ca·lyx
  -lyx·es (pl)
ca·ma·ra·de·rie
cam·ber
  -bered, -ber·ing
cam·bi·um
  -bi·ums
Cam·bo·di·an
cam·bric
cam·el
ca·mel·lia
Cam·e·lot
Cam·em·bert
cam·eo
  -eos
cam·era
cam·i·sole

cam·ou·flage
  -flaged, -flag·ing,
  -flage·able
cam·paign
camp·er
cam·pe·si·no
  -nos
camp·ground
cam·phor
cam·pus
cam·shaft
cam wheel
can
  canned, can·ning
Ca·na·di·an
ca·nal
can·a·li·za·tion
can·a·pé
ca·nard
ca·nary
  -nar·ies
ca·nas·ta
can·cel
  -celed, -cel·ing,
  -cel·able
can·cel·la·tion
can·cer
  -ous, -ous·ly
can·de·la·bra
can·des·cent
can·did
  -ly, -ness
can·di·da·cy
  -cies

can·di·date
can·died
can·dle
  -dled, -dling, -dler
can·dle·light
can·dle·mas
can·dle·pow·er
can·dle·snuff·er
can·dle·stick
can·dle·wood
can·dor
can·dy
  -dies, -died,
  -dy·ing
ca·nine
can·is·ter
can·ker
  -ker·ous, -kered,
  -ker·ing
can·ker sore
can·ker·worm
can·na
can·na·bis
can·nery
  -ner·ies
can·ni·bal
can·ni·bal·ism
  -is·tic
can·ni·bal·ize
  -ized, -iz·ing,
  -iza·tion
can·no·li
can·non (gun; cf.
  canon, canyon)

can·non·ball
can·non·eer
can·not
can·ny
  -ni·er, -ni·est,
  -ni·ness
ca·noe
  -noed, -noe·ing,
  -noe·ist
can·on (rule; cf.
  cannon, canyon)
ca·non·i·cal
can·on·ize
  -ized, -iz·ing,
  -i·za·tion
can·o·py
  -pies
can·ta·loupe
can·tan·ker·ous
can·ta·ta
can·ta·trice
can·teen
can·ter
can·ti·cle
can·ti·le·ver
can·ti·na
can·to
  -tos
can·ton
  -ton·al
Can·ton·ese
  Can·ton·ese (pl)
can·ton·ment
can·tor

can·vas (n)(cloth; cf.
  canvass)
can·vass (v)(solicit;
  cf. *canvas*)
  -vased, -vas·ing,
  -vass·er
can·yon (ravine; cf.
  cannon, canon)
ca·pa·bil·i·ty
ca·pa·bil·i·ties
ca·pa·ble
  -bly
ca·pa·cious
ca·pac·i·tate
  -tat·ed, -tat·ing
ca·pac·i·tor
ca·pac·i·ty
  -ties
ca·par·i·son
ca·per
  -pered, -per·ing
cap·il·lar·i·ty
  -ties
cap·il·lary
  -lar·ies
cap·i·tal (city,
  property; cf.
  capitol)
cap·i·tal·ism
cap·i·tal·ist
  -is·tic, -is·ti·cal·ly
cap·i·tal·iza·tion
cap·i·tal·ize
  -ized, -iz·ing

cap·i·tate
cap·i·tol (building;
  cf. *capital*)
ca·pit·u·late
  -lat·ed, -lat·ing
ca·pit·u·la·tion
cap·puc·ci·no
ca·price
ca·pri·cious
cap·size
  -sized, -siz·ing
cap·stan
cap·stone
cap·sule
  -suled, -sul·ing
cap·tain
cap·tion
  -tioned, -tion·ing,
  -tion·less
cap·tious
  -tious·ly,
  -tious·ness
cap·ti·vate
  -va·tion, -vat·ed,
  -vat·ing
cap·tive
cap·tiv·i·ty
cap·tor
cap·ture
  -tured, -tur·ing
ca·rafe
car·a·mel
car·a·mel·ize
  -ized, -iz·ing

car·at or kar·at
   (weight; cf. *caret*,
   carrot)
car·a·van
   -vanned,
   -van·ning
car·a·way
car·bide
car·bine
car·bo·hy·drate
car·bol·ic
car·bon
   -bon·less
car·bo·na·ceous
car·bon·ate
   -at·ed, -at·ing,
   -ation
car·bon dating (n)
   car·bon-date (v)
car·bon·ic
car·bon·if·er·ous
car·bon·ize
   -ized, -iz·ing
Car·bo·run·dum
car·box·yl
   -yl·ic
car·bun·cle
   -cled, -cu·lar
car·bu·re·tor
car·cass
car·cin·o·gen
   -gen·ic, -ge·nic·i·ty
car·ci·no·ma
   -mas, -ma·tous

card·board
card cat·a·log
card·hold·er
car·di·ac
car·di·gan
car·di·nal
   -nal·ly
car·dio·gram
car·dio·graph
   -dio·graph·ic,
   -di·og·ra·phy
car·di·ol·o·gy
   -ol·o·gist,
   -o·log·i·cal
car·dio·vas·cu·lar
ca·reen
ca·reer
care·ful
   -ful·ler, -ful·lest,
   -ful·ly
care·less
   -less·ly, -less·ness
ca·ress
   -res·sive,
   -res·sive·ly,
   -ress·er
car·et (a symbol; cf.
   carat, carrot)
care·worn
car·fare
car·go (sing)
   -goes (pl)
car·hop
Ca·rib·be·an

car·i·bou
   car·i·bou (pl)
car·i·ca·ture
   -tur·al, -tur·ist,
   -tured
car·ies
   car·ies (pl)
car·il·lon
ca·ri·o·ca
car·load
car·mine
car·nage
car·nal
   -nal·ity, -nal·ly
car·na·tion
car·ne·lian
car·ni·val
car·niv·o·rous
   -rous·ness
car·ol
   -oled, -o·ling,
   -ol·er
car·om
ca·rot·id
ca·rous·al
ca·rouse
   -roused, -rous·ing,
   -rous·er
car·ou·sel
car·pen·ter
   -tered, -ter·ing
car·pen·try
car·pet
car·pet·bag·ger

car·pet·ing
car pool
car·port
car·riage
car·ri·er
car·ri·on
car·rot (vegetable;
    cf. *carat, caret*)
car·rou·sel (var. of
    carousel)
car·ry
    -ry·ing
car·ries
    -ried
car·ry·all
car·ry·over (n)
cart·age
carte blanche
car·tel
car·ti·lage
car·tog·ra·pher
car·tog·ra·phy
car·ton (box; cf.
    cartoon)
car·toon (picture; cf.
    carton)
    -toon·ing,
    -toon·ish, -toon·ist
car·tridge
carve
    carved, carv·ing,
    carv·er
ca·sa·ba
cas·cade

-cad·ed, -cad·ing
case hard·en
    case-hard·ened
ca·sein
case·ment
case·work
cash-and-car·ry
cash·book
ca·shew
cash·ier (n)
ca·shier (v)
cash·mere
ca·si·no
    -nos
cas·ket
casque
cas·se·role
cas·sette
cas·sia
cas·sock
cast (throw; cf. *caste*)
    cast·ing
cas·ta·net
cast·away
caste (social class;
    cf. *cast*)
cas·tel·lat·ed
cas·ti·gate
    -gat·ed, -gat·ing,
    -ga·tor
Cas·til·ian
cast iron (n)
cast-iron (adj)
cas·tle

-tled, -tling
cast-off (adj)
cast·off (n)
cas·tor
ca·su·al
    -al·ly, -al·ness
ca·su·al·ty
ca·su·ist
    -is·tic, -is·ti·cal
ca·su·ist·ry
    -ries
cat·a·clysm
    -clys·mal,
    -clys·mic,
    -clys·mi·cal·ly
cat·a·comb
cat·a·falque
Cat·a·lan
cat·a·lep·sy
    -lep·sies, -lep·tic,
    -lep·ti·cally
cat·a·log
    -loged, -log·ing
ca·tal·pa
ca·tal·y·sis
    -y·ses (pl)
cat·a·lyst
cat·a·lyt·ic
cat·a·ma·ran
cat·a·mount
cat·a·pult
cat·a·ract
ca·tas·tro·phe
    cat·a·stroph·ic

Ca·taw·ba
  -ba or -bas (pl)
cat·bird
cat·boat
cat·call
catch·all
catch·er
catch-22
  catch-22's or
  catch-22s (pl)
catch·word
cat·e·che·sis
  -che·ses (pl),
  -chet·i·cal
cat·e·chism
  -chis·mal, -chis·tic
cat·e·chist
cat·e·chu·men
cat·e·gor·i·cal
  -cal·ly
cat·e·go·rize
  -rized, -riz·ing,
  -ri·za·tion
cat·e·go·ry
  -ries
ca·ter
  -ter·er
cat·er·pil·lar
cat·er·waul
cat·fish
cat·gut
ca·thar·sis
  -thar·ses (pl)
ca·thar·tic

ca·the·dral
cath·e·ter
cath·ode
  cath·od·al,
  ca·thod·ic,
  ca·thod·i·cal·ly
cath·ode-ray tube
cath·o·lic
  ca·thol·i·cal·ly,
  ca·thol·i·cize
Ca·thol·i·cism
cath·o·lic·i·ty
cat·like
cat·nip
cat-o'-nine-tails
  cat-o'-nine-tails
  (pl)
cat·sup
cat·tail
cat·tle
cat·walk
Cau·ca·sian
cau·cus
cau·dal
cau·li·flow·er
caulk
  caulk·er,
  caulk·ing
caus·al
  -al·ly
cau·sal·i·ty
cau·sa·tion
caus·ative
cause

caused, caus·ing,
  caus·er
cause·way
caus·tic
  -ti·cal·ly, -tic·i·ty
cau·ter·ize
  -ized, -iz·ing,
  -iza·tion
cau·tery (effect of
  burning tissue; cf.
  coterie)
  -ter·ies
cau·tion
  -tioned, -tion·ing
cau·tion·ary
cau·tious
  -tious·ness
cav·al·cade
cav·a·lier
  -lier·ism
cav·al·ry
  -ries
ca·ve·at emp·tor
cav·ern
cav·ern·ous
cav·i·ar
cav·il
  -iled, -il·ing, -il·er
cav·i·ty
  -ties
ca·vort
cease
  ceased, ceas·ing
cease-fire

cease·less
ce·dar
cede (yield; cf. *seed*)
  ced·ed, ced·ing,
  ced·er
ce·dil·la
ceil
ceil·ing (limit,
  overhead wall; cf.
  sealing)
  -inged
cel·e·brant
cel·e·brate
  -brat·ed, -brat·ing,
  -bra·tion
ce·leb·ri·ty
  -ties
ce·ler·i·ty
cel·ery
  -er·ies
ce·les·tial
cel·i·ba·cy
cel·i·bate
cel·lar (underground
  storeroom; cf.
  seller)
cel·lo
  -los, -list
cel·lo·phane
cel·lu·lar
  -lar·i·ty
cel·lu·lite
cel·lu·loid
cel·lu·lose

Cel·sius
ce·ment
ce·men·ta·tion
cem·e·tery
  -ter·ies
ceno·taph
Ce·no·zo·ic
cen·ser (for incense;
  cf. *censor, sensor*)
cen·sor (supervisor
  of morals; cf.
  censer, sensor)
  -sored, -sor·ing
cen·so·ri·ous
cen·sor·ship
cen·sur·able
cen·sure
  -sured, -sur·ing
cen·sus (count; cf.
  senses)
cent (penny; cf.
  scent, sent)
cen·taur
cen·ta·vo
  -vos
cen·te·na·ry
cen·ten·ni·al
cen·ter·board
cen·ter·piece
cen·ti·grade
cen·ti·gram
cen·ti·li·ter
cen·time
cen·ti·me·ter

cen·ti·pede
cen·tral
cen·tral·ize
  -ized, -iz·ing,
  -iza·tion
cen·tral
  pro·cess·ing unit
cen·trif·u·gal
  -gal·ly
cen·tri·fuge
  -fuged, -fug·ing
cen·trip·e·tal
cen·trist
cen·tu·ry
  -ries
ce·phal·ic
ce·ram·ic
ce·re·al (grain; cf.
  serial)
cer·e·bel·lum
  -bel·lums
ce·re·bral
ce·re·bral pal·sy
ce·re·bro·spi·nal
ce·re·brum
  -brums
cer·e·mo·ni·al
cer·e·mo·ni·ous
cer·e·mo·ny
  -nies
ce·rise
ce·ri·um
cer·tain
cer·tain·ly

cer·tain·ty
-ties
cer·tif·i·cate
-cat·ed, -cat·ing,
-ca·to·ry
cer·ti·fi·ca·tions
cer·ti·fy
-fied, -fy·ing,
-fi·able
cer·ti·tude
ce·ru·le·an
cer·vi·cal
cer·vix
-vi·ces (pl)
ce·si·um
ces·sa·tion
ces·sion (yielding;
cf. *session*)
cess·pool
Chab·lis
chafe (irritate; cf.
chaff)
chafed, chaf·ing
chaff (banter; cf.
chafe)
cha·grin
-grined, -grin·ing
chain gang
chain mail
chain saw
chain-smoke
chain-smok·er
chain stitch
chair·man

-maned, -man·ing
chair·per·son
chair·wom·an
chaise longue
chaise longues
chal·ce·do·ny
-nies
cha·let
chal·ice
chalk
chalky
chal·lenge
-lenged, -leng·ing
chal·lis
-lises (pl)
cham·ber
-bered, -ber·ing
cham·ber·lain
cham·ber·maid
cha·me·leon
cham·ois
cham·pagne (wine;
cf. *champaign*)
cham·paign (plain;
cf. *champagne*)
cham·per·ty
-per·tous
cham·pi·on
cham·pi·on·ship
chan·cel
chan·cel·lery
-ler·ies
chan·cel·lor
chan·cery

-cer·ies
chan·de·lier
chan·dler
change
changed,
chang·ing
change·able
-able·ness, -ably,
-abil·i·ty
change·less
change·over
chan·nel
-neled, -nel·ing
chan·teuse
chan·ti·cleer
cha·os
cha·ot·ic
chap·ar·ral
chap·book
cha·peau
-peaus (pl)
cha·pel
chap·er·on
-oned, -on·ing,
-on·age
chap·fall·en
chap·lain
-lain·cy
chap·let
-let·ed
chap·ter
char·ac·ter
char·ac·ter·is·tic
char·ac·ter·iza·tion

char·ac·ter·ize
-ized, -iz·ing
char·ac·ter print·er
cha·rade
char·coal
charge
charged,
charg·ing
charge·able
charge ac·count
char·gé d'af·faires
chargés d'affaires
(pl)
char·i·ot
cha·ris·ma
char·i·ta·ble
-ta·bly
char·i·ty
-ties
char·la·tan
-tan·ism, -tan·ry
char·ley horse
char·nel
char·ter
char·treuse
char·wom·an
chase (pursue)
chased (past tense
of *chase*; cf.
chaste), chas·ing
chasm
chas·sis
chas·sis (pl)
chaste (virtuous; cf.

chased)
chast·er, chast·est,
chaste·ness
chas·ten
-tened, -ten·ing
chas·tise
-tised, -tis·ing,
-tise·ment
chas·ti·ty
cha·su·ble
châ·teau
-teaus (pl)
chat·tel
chat·ter
chat·ter·box
chauf·feur
-feured, -feur·ing
chau·vin·ism
cheap·en
-ened, -en·ing
cheap·skate
check·book
check·er
check·er·board
check in (v)
check-in (n)
check·list
check mark
check·mate
check off (v)
check·off (n)
check out (v)
check·out (n)
check·point

check·rein
check·room
check up (v)
check·up (n)
cheek·bone
cheer·ful
-ful·ly, -ful·ness
cheer·less
cheery
cheer·i·er,
cheer·i·est,
cheer·i·ly
cheese·burg·er
cheese·cake
cheese·cloth
chef
chef d'oeu·vre
chefs d'oeu·vre (pl)
chem·i·cal
-cal·ly
che·mise
chem·ist
chem·is·try
-tries
che·mo·ther·a·py
che·nille
cher·ish
Cher·o·kee
Cher·o·kee (pl)
cher·ry
-ries
cher·ub
cher·u·bim or
cher·ubs (pl)

chess
  chess·board,
  chess·man
ches·ter·field
chest·nut
che·va·lier
chev·ron
Chey·enne
  Chey·enne (pl)
Chi·an·ti
chiar·oscu·ro
chi·ca·nery
  -ner·ies
Chi·ca·no
  -nos (pl)
chick·a·dee
chick·en
  -ened, -en·ing
chick·en·heart·ed
chick·en pox
chick-pea
chic·o·ry
  -ries
chide
chief·ly
chief·tain
chif·fon
chig·ger
chi·gnon
Chi·hua·hua
chil·blain
child
  chil·dren (pl),
  child·less,

child·less·ness
child·birth
child·hood
child·ish
  -ish·ly, -ish·ness
child·like
child·proof
chill
  chill·ing·ly,
  chill·ness
chilly
  chill·i·er,
  chill·i·est,
  chill·i·ness
chi·me·ra
chi·me·ri·cal
chim·ney
  -neys
chim·pan·zee
chi·na·ber·ry
Chi·na·town
chi·na·ware
chin·chil·la
Chi·nese
  Chi·nese (pl)
Chi·no (of China; cf.
  chino)
chi·no (cloth; cf.
  Chino)
Chi·nook
  Chi·nook (pl)
chintz
chip
  chipped,

chip·ping
chip·munk
chi·rop·o·dy
  -dist
chi·ro·prac·tic
  -prac·tor
chis·el
  -eled, -eling, -el·er
chit·chat
chiv·al·rous
  -rous·ness
chiv·al·ry
  -ries
chlo·ral
chlo·rate
chlor·dane or
  chlor·dan
chlo·ride
chlo·ri·nate
  -nat·ed, -nat·ing,
  -na·tion
chlo·rine
chlo·rite
  -rit·ic
chlo·ro·form
chlo·ro·phyll
chlo·rous
chock-full
choc·o·late
Choc·taw
  Choc·taw (pl)
choice
  choic·er, choic·est,
  choice·ness

choir (singers; cf.
  quire)
choke·cher·ry
chok·er
cho·ler
chol·era
cho·ler·ic
cho·les·ter·ol
choose (select; cf.
  chose)
  chose, cho·sen,
  choos·ing
chop·per
chop·stick
chop su·ey
  chop su·eys (pl)
cho·ral (of a chorus;
  cf. *chorale, coral,*
  corral)
cho·rale (sacred
  song; cf. *choral,*
  coral, corral)
chord (music; cf.
  cord)
chore
cho·rea
cho·re·og·ra·phy
  -phies
cho·ris·ter
chor·tle
  -tled, -tling
cho·rus
chose (selected; cf.
  choose)

chow·der
chow mein
chrism
chris·ten
  -tened, -ten·ing
Chris·ten·dom
Chris·tian
Chris·tian·i·ty
Chris·tian·ize
  -ized, -iz·ing
Christ·mas
Christ·mas·tide
chro·mate
chro·mat·ic
chro·ma·tog·ra·phy
chrome
chro·mite
chro·mi·um
chro·mo·some
chron·ic
chron·i·cle
  -cled, -cling, -cler
chro·no·graph
chro·no·log·i·cal
  -cal·ly
chro·nol·o·gy
  -gies
chro·nom·e·ter
chro·no·met·ric
chry·san·the·mum
chuck·le
  -led, -ling,
  -le·some
chum

  chummed,
  chum·ming
chum·my
  -mi·er, -mi·est,
  -mi·ness
chunk
church·go·er
church·yard
churl
churl·ish
  -ish·ly, -ish·ness
churn
chute (slide; cf.
  shoot)
chut·ney
  -neys (pl)
chutz·pah
ci·bo·ri·um
  -ria (pl)
ci·ca·da
  -das (pl)
ci·ca·trix
  -tri·ces (pl)
ci·der
ci·gar
cig·a·rette
cinc·ture
cin·der
Cin·der·el·la
cin·e·ma
cin·e·mat·o·graph
cin·e·ma·tog·ra·pher
cin·na·bar
cin·na·mon

53

cinque·foil

ci·pher
  -phered, -pher·ing

cir·cle
  -cled, -cling

cir·clet

cir·cuit

cir·cu·itous
  -itous·ness

cir·cuit·ry
  -ries

cir·cu·lar
  -lar·ity, -lar·ly

cir·cu·lar·ize
  -ized, -iz·ing,
  -iza·tion

cir·cu·late
  -lated, -lat·ing,
  -lat·able

cir·cu·la·to·ry

cir·cum·cise
  -cised, -cis·ing,
  -cis·er

cir·cum·ci·sion

cir·cum·fer·ence
  -fer·en·tial

cir·cum·flex

cir·cum·lo·cu·tion

cir·cum·nav·i·gate

cir·cum·scribe

cir·cum·spect
  -spec·tion,
  -spect·ly

cir·cum·stance

cir·cum·stan·tial
  -ti·al·i·ty, -tial·ly

cir·cum·stan·ti·ate
  -at·ed, -at·ing

cir·cum·vent
  -ven·tion

cir·cus

cir·rho·sis
  -rho·ses (pl)

cir·ro·cu·mu·lus

cir·ro·stra·tus

cis·tern

cit·a·del

ci·ta·tion

cite (quote; cf. *sight,
  site*)
  cit·ed, cit·ing,
  cit·able

cit·i·zen

cit·i·zen·ry
  -ries

cit·i·zen·ship

ci·trate

cit·ron

cit·ro·nel·la

cit·rus
  cit·rus (pl)

city
  cit·ies

civ·ic
  civ·i·cal·ly

civ·il

ci·vil·ian

ci·vil·i·ty

-ties

civ·i·li·za·tion

civ·i·lize
  -lized, -liz·ing

civ·il·ly

claim
  claim·er,
  claim·able

claim·ant

clair·voy·ance

clair·voy·ant

cla·mant

clam·bake

clam·ber (climb; cf.
  clamor)
  -bered, -ber·ing

clam·my
  -mi·er, -mi·est,
  -mi·ness

clam·or (outcry; cf.
  clamber)
  -ored, -or·ing

clam·or·ous

clam·shell

clan·des·tine
  -tine·ly, -tine·ness

clang

clan·nish
  -nish·ness

clans·man

clap·board

clap·per

claque

clar·et

clar·i·fy
 -fied, -fy·ing,
 -fi·ca·tion
clar·i·net
 -net·ist
clar·i·on
clar·i·ty
clas·sic
clas·si·cal
clas·si·cism
clas·si·cist
clas·si·fi·ca·tion
clas·si·fy
 -fied, -fy·ing,
 -fi·able
class·ism
class·mate
class·room
clat·ter
 -ter·er, -ter·ing·ly
clause (grammati-
 cal; cf. *claws*)
claus·tro·pho·bia
 -phobe
clav·i·cle
claw
 claws (sharp toes;
 cf. *clause*)
clean
 clean·ness
clean-cut
clean·er
clean·hand·ed
clean·ly

-li·er, -li·est,
 -li·ness
cleanse
 cleansed,
 cleans·ing
cleans·er
clear·ance
clear-cut
clear-eyed
clear·head·ed
 -head·ed·ly,
 -head·ed·ness
clear·ing·house
clear-sight·ed
cleav·age
cleav·er
cle·ma·tis
clem·en·cy
 -cies
clem·ent
cler·gy
 -gies
cler·gy·man
cler·gy·wom·an
cler·ic
cler·i·cal
cler·i·cal·ism
clev·er
 -er·ish, -er·ly,
 -er·ness
clew or clue
 clewed or clued,
 clew·ing or
 clue·ing

cli·ché
cli·ent
cli·en·tele
cliff-hang·er
cli·mac·tic (of a
 climax; cf. *climatic*)
cli·mate
cli·ma·tic (of
 climate; cf.
 climactic)
cli·ma·tol·o·gy
 -tol·o·gist,
 -to·log·i·cal,
 -to·log·i·cal·ly
cli·max
cling·stone
clin·ic
clin·i·cal
cli·ni·cian
clin·ker
clip
 clipped, clip·ping
clique
 cliqu·ish,
 clique·ish·ness
cloak-and-dag·ger
clob·ber
 -bered, -ber·ing
clock-watch·er
clock·wise
clock·work
clod·hop·per
clog
 clogged, clog·ging

clois·ter
-tered, -ter·ing
clone
cloned, clon·ing
closed-end
closed
closed-cap·tioned
close-fist·ed
close-hauled
clos·ing
close-knit
close·ness
close-out
clos·et
-et·ful
close up (adv)
close-up (n)
clo·sure
cloth (n)
cloths
clothe (v)
clothed, cloth·ing
clothes·pin
cloth·ier
clo·ture
cloud·burst
cloudy
cloud·i·er,
cloud·i·est,
cloud·i·ness
clout
cloven foot
clo·ver
clo·ver·leaf

club
clubbed,
club·bing
club chair
club·foot
-foot·ed
club·house
club steak
clum·sy
-si·er, -si·ly,
-si·ness
clus·ter
-tered, -ter·ing
clutch
clut·ter
coach·man
co·ad·ju·tor
co·ag·u·late
-lated, -lat·ing,
-la·tion
co·alesce
co·alesced,
co·alesc·ing,
co·ales·cent
coal gas
co·ali·tion
coal tar
coarse (rough; cf.
corse, course)
coars·er, coars·est,
coarse·ly
coars·en
coars·ened,
coars·en·ing

coast
coast·al
coast·er
coast guard
coast·line
coast-to-coast
coat·tail
coax
co·ax·i·al
co·balt
cob·bler
cob·ble·stone
CO·BOL
co·bra
cob·web
-webbed
co·caine
coc·cyx
coc·cy·ges or
coc·cyx·es (pl)
co·chair
co·chair·man
co·chi·neal
cock·a·too
-toos
cock·boat
cock·crow
cock·le
cock·le·bur
cock·le·shell
cock·ney
cock·neys (pl)
cock·pit
cock·roach

cock·sure
cock·tail
co·coa
co·co·nut
co·coon
code
  cod·ed, cod·ing
co·de·fen·dant
co·deine
co·dex
  co·di·ces (pl)
cod·fish
cod·i·cil
cod·i·fy
  -fied, -fy·ing,
  -fi·ca·tion
co·ed
co·ed·i·tor
  co·ed·it
co·ed·u·ca·tion
co·ef·fi·cient
coel·acanth
co·erce
  -erced, -erc·ing,
  -erc·ible
co·er·cion
co·er·cive
co·eval
co·ex·ist
  -is·tence, -is·tent
cof·fee
cof·fee·house
cof·fee·pot
cof·fee shop

cof·fee ta·ble
cof·fer
cof·fin
co·gen·cy
co·gent
cog·i·tate
  -tat·ed, -tat·ing
cog·i·ta·tion
cog·i·ta·tive
co·gnac
cog·nate
  -nate·ly
cog·ni·zance
cog·ni·zant
cog·wheel
co·hab·it
co·heir
co·here
  -hered, -her·ing
co·her·ence
co·her·en·cy
  -cies
co·her·ent
  -ent·ly
co·he·sion
co·he·sive
  -sive·ly
co·hort
coif·feur (person; cf.
  coiffure)
coif·fure (style; cf.
  coiffeur)
coin
coin·age

co·in·cide
  -cid·ed, -cid·ing
co·in·ci·dence
co·in·ci·dent
co·in·ci·den·tal
co·in·sur·ance
co·in·sure
co·ition
coke
  coked, cok·ing
col·an·der (perfo-
  rated utensil; cf.
  calendar,
  calender)
cold-blood·ed
cold chis·el
cold cream
cold cuts
cold frame
cold front
cold sore
cold sweat
cold war
cold wave
co·le·op·tera
  -tera (pl), -ter·ous
cole·slaw
col·ic
col·ic·root
col·i·se·um
co·li·tis
col·lab·o·rate
  -rat·ed, -rat·ing,
  -ra·tion

57

col·lage
col·lapse
  -lapsed, -laps·ing,
  -laps·ible
col·lar
col·lar·bone
col·late
  -lat·ed, -lat·ing,
  -la·tor
col·lat·er·al
col·la·tion
col·league
col·lect
  -lect·ible
col·lect·ed
  -lect·ed·ness
col·lec·tion
col·lec·tive
  -tive·ly
col·lec·tiv·ism
col·lec·tor
col·lege
col·le·gial
col·le·gi·al·i·ty
col·le·gian
col·le·giate
col·le·gi·um
  -gia or -gi·ums (pl)
col·lide
  -lid·ed, -lid·ing
col·lie (dog; cf.
  coolie, coolly)
col·lier
col·liery

-lier·ies
col·li·sion (crash; cf.
  collusion)
col·lo·ca·tion
col·loid
col·lo·qui·al
  -qui·al·ly
col·lo·qui·al·ism
col·lo·qui·um
  -qui·ums or -quia
  (pl)
col·lo·quy
  -quies (pl)
col·lu·sion (secret
  agreement; cf.
  collision)
  -sive
co·logne
  -logned
co·lon
  colons or co·la (pl)
col·o·nel (officer; cf.
  kernel)
  -nel·cy
co·lo·nial
co·lo·nial·ism
col·o·nist
col·o·ni·za·tion
col·o·nize
  -nized, -niz·ing
col·on·nade
col·o·ny
  -nies
col·o·phon

col·or
col·or·ation
col·or·a·tu·ra
col·or-blind
col·ored
col·or·fast
col·or·ful
col·or guard
col·or·less
co·los·sal
  -sal·ly
col·os·se·um
co·los·sus
  -si (pl)
col·umn
  -umned
co·lum·nar
col·um·nist
co·ma (insensibility;
  cf. *comma*)
co·ma·tose
com·bat
  -bat·ed, -bat·ing
com·bat·ant
com·bat·ive
com·bi·na·tion
com·bine
  -bined, -bin·ing
com·bo
  -bos
com·bus·ti·ble
com·bus·tion
come back (v)
come·back (n)

58

com·e·di·an
co·me·di·enne (fem)
com·e·dy
  -dies
come·ly
  -li·ness
come on (v)
come-on (n)
co·mes·ti·ble
com·et
com·fit
com·fort
com·fort·able
com·fort·er
com·ic
com·i·cal
com·ing
co·mi·ty
  -ties
com·ma (punctua-
  tion; cf. *coma*)
com·mand (order;
  cf. *commend*)
com·man·dant
com·man·deer
com·mand·er
com·mand·ment
com·mand mod·ule
com·man·do
  -dos
com·mem·o·rate
  -rat·ed, -rat·ing
com·mem·o·ra·tion
com·mem·o·ra·tive

com·mence
  -menced,
  -menc·ing
com·mence·ment
com·mend (praise;
  cf. *command*)
  -mend·able
  -mend·ably
com·men·da·tion
com·men·da·to·ry
com·men·su·ra·ble
  -bly, -bil·i·ty
com·men·su·rate
  -rate·ly
com·ment
com·men·tary
  -tar·ies
com·men·tate
  -tat·ed, -tat·ing
com·men·ta·tor
com·merce
com·mer·cial
com·mer·cial·ism
com·mer·cial·ize
  -iza·tion
com·min·gle
com·mis·er·ate
  -at·ed, -at·ing
com·mis·er·a·tion
com·mis·sar
com·mis·sary
  -sar·ies
com·mis·sion
  -sioned, -sion·ing

com·mis·sion·aire
com·mis·sion·er
com·mit
  -mit·ted, -mit·ting
com·mit·ment
com·mit·tee
com·mit·tee·man
com·mit·tee·wom·an
com·mode
com·mo·di·ous
com·mod·i·ty
  -ties
com·mo·dore
com·mon
com·mon·al·ty
  -ties
com·mon·er
com·mon·place
com·mon sense
  -sen·si·ble
com·mon·wealth
com·mo·tion
com·mu·nal
com·mune
  -muned, -mun·ing
com·mu·ni·ca·ble
com·mu·ni·cant
com·mu·ni·cate
  -cat·ed, -cat·ing
com·mu·ni·ca·tion
com·mu·ni·ca·tive
com·mu·nion
com·mu·ni·qué
com·mu·nism

com·mu·nist
 -nis·tic
com·mu·ni·ty
 -ties
com·mu·ta·tion
com·mute
 -mut·ed,
 -mut·ing,
 -mut·able
com·mu·ter
com·pact
 -pact·ible,
 -pac·tor
com·pa·nies
com·pan·ion
com·pan·ion·able
com·pan·ion·ship
com·pan·ion·way
com·pa·ny
 -nied, -ny·ing
com·pa·ra·ble
com·par·a·tive
com·pare
 -pared, -par·ing
com·par·i·son
com·part·ment
com·pass
com·pas·sion
com·pas·sion·ate
com·pat·i·ble
 -bly, -bil·i·ty
com·pa·tri·ot
com·pel
 -pelled, -pel·ling,

-pel·la·ble
com·pen·di·ous
com·pen·di·um
 -di·ums or -dia (pl)
com·pen·sate
 -sat·ed, -sat·ing
com·pen·sa·tion
 -tive, -to·ry
com·pete
 -pet·ed, -pet·ing
com·pe·tence
com·pe·ten·cy
 -cies
com·pe·tent
com·pe·ti·tion
com·pet·i·tive
com·pet·i·tor
com·pi·la·tion
com·pile
 -piled, -pil·ing
com·pil·er
com·pla·cence
com·pla·cen·cy
 -cies
com·pla·cent (self-
 satisfied; cf.
 complaisant)
com·plain
com·plain·ant
com·plaint
com·plai·sance
com·plai·sant
 (obliging; cf.
 complacent)

com·ple·ment (full
 quantity; cf.
 compliment)
com·ple·men·tal
com·ple·men·ta·ry
 -ri·ly
com·plete
 -plet·ed, -plet·ing
com·ple·tion
com·plex
com·plex·ion
 -ion·al, -ioned
com·plex·i·ty
com·pli·ance
com·pli·ant
com·pli·cate
 -cat·ed, -cat·ing
com·pli·ca·tion
com·plic·i·ty
 -ties
com·pli·ment
 (flattery; cf.
 complement)
com·pli·men·ta·ry
com·ply
 -plied, -ply·ing
com·po·nent
com·port
com·port·ment
com·pose
 -posed, -pos·ing
composed
 -pos·ed·ly
com·pos·er

com·pos·ite
  -it·ed, -it·ing
com·po·si·tion
com·pos·i·tor
com·post
com·po·sure
com·pound
  -pound·able
com·pre·hend
  -hend·ible
com·pre·hen·si·ble
com·pre·hen·sion
com·pre·hen·sive
com·press
com·pressed
com·press·ible
  -ibil·i·ty
com·pres·sion
com·pres·sor
com·prise
  -prised, -pris·ing
com·pro·mise
  -mised, -mis·ing
comp·trol·ler
com·pul·sion
com·pul·so·ry
  -ri·ly
com·punc·tion
  -tious
com·put·able
  -abil·i·ty
com·pu·ta·tion
com·pute
  -put·ed, -put·ing

com·put·er
  -er·like
com·put·er·ize
  -ized, -iz·ing,
  -iz·able
com·rade
con·cat·e·nate
con·cave
con·cav·i·ty
  -ties
con·ceal
  -ceal·able
con·cede
  -ced·ed, -ced·ing,
  -ced·ed·ly
con·ceit
con·ceit·ed
con·ceiv·able
  -ably, -abil·i·ty
con·ceive
  -ceived, -ceiv·ing
con·cen·trate
  -trat·ed, -trat·ing,
  -tra·tor
con·cen·tra·tion
con·cen·tric
  -tri·cal·ly
con·cept
con·cep·tion
  -tion·al
con·cep·tu·al
  -al·i·ty, -al·ly
con·cern
con·cerned

con·cern·ing
con·cert
con·cer·ti·na
con·cert·mas·ter
con·cer·to
con·ces·sion
  -sion·al, -sion·ary
con·ces·sion·aire
conch
con·cierge
con·cil·i·ate
  -at·ed, -at·ing,
  -a·tion
con·cise
con·clave
con·clude
  -clud·ed, -clud·ing
con·clu·sion
con·clu·sive
con·coct
  -coc·tion
con·com·i·tant
con·cord
con·cor·dance
con·cor·dat
con·course
con·crete
  -cret·ed,
  -cret·ing,
  -crete·ly
con·cu·bine
con·cur
  -curred, -cur·ring
con·cur·rence

con·cur·rent
con·cus·sion
  -sive
con·demn
  -dem·na·ble,
  -dem·na·to·ry
con·dem·na·tion
con·den·sa·tion
  -tion·al
con·dense
  -densed,
  -dens·ing,
  -dens·able
con·dens·er
con·de·scend
con·de·scend·ing
  -scend·ing·ly
con·de·scen·sion
con·di·ment
con·di·tion
  -tioned,
  -tion·ing,
  -tion·able
con·di·tion·al
con·dole
  -doled, -dol·ing
con·do·lence
con·do·min·i·um
con·do·na·tion
con·done
con·dor
con·duce
con·du·cive
con·duct

con·duc·tion
con·duc·tor
  -to·ri·al
con·duit
con·fab·u·late
  -lat·ed, -lat·ing,
  -la·to·ry
con·fec·tion
con·fec·tion·er
con·fec·tion·ery
  -er·ies
con·fed·er·a·cy
  -er·a·cies, -er·al
con·fed·er·ate
  -at·ed, -at·ing,
  -a·tive
con·fed·er·a·tion
con·fer
  -ferred,
  -fer·ring,
  -fer·ra·ble
con·fer·ee
con·fer·ence
con·fess
  -fess·able
con·fessed·ly
con·fes·sion
  -sion·al·ly
con·fes·sion·al
con·fes·sor
con·fet·ti
con·fi·dant (friend;
  cf. *confident*)
con·fide

  -fid·ed, -fid·ing
con·fi·dence
con·fi·dent (sure; cf.
  confidant)
con·fi·den·tial
  -ti·al·i·ty
con·fig·ure
  -ured, -ur·ing
con·fine
  -fined, -fin·ing
con·fine·ment
con·firm
  -firm·abil·i·ty,
  -firm·able
con·fir·ma·tion
con·firmed
con·fis·cate
  -cat·ed, -cat·ing,
  -ca·tion
con·fla·gra·tion
con·flict
con·flu·ence
con·form
  -form·ist
con·form·able
con·for·ma·tion
con·for·mi·ty
  -ties
con·found
con·found·ed
con·fra·ter·ni·ty
con·front
con·fron·ta·tion
Con·fu·cian

con·fuse
-fused, -fus·ing,
-fus·ing·ly
con·fu·sion
con·geal
con·ge·nial
-nial·i·ty
con·gen·i·tal
con·gest
-ges·tion
con·glom·er·ate
-at·ed, -at·ing,
-a·tive
con·glom·er·a·tion
con·grat·u·late
-lat·ed, -lat·ing,
-la·to·ry
con·grat·u·la·tion
con·gre·gate
-gat·ed, -gat·ing
con·gre·ga·tion
con·gre·ga·tion·al
con·gress
-gres·sio·nal
con·gress·man
con·gress·wom·an
con·gru·ence
con·gru·ent
con·gru·ity
-ities
con·gru·ous
con·ic
con·i·cal
co·ni·fer

-nif·er·ous
con·jec·tur·al
con·jec·ture
-tured, -tur·ing,
-tur·er
con·ju·gal
con·ju·gate
-gat·ed, -gat·ing
con·ju·ga·tion
con·junc·tion
con·junc·ti·va
con·junc·ture
con·jure
-jured, -jur·ing
con·jur·er
con·nect
-nect·able,
-nec·tor
con·nec·tion
con·nec·tive
con·niv·ance
con·nive
-nived, -niv·ing
con·nois·seur
con·no·ta·tion
con·no·ta·tive
con·note
-not·ed, -not·ing
con·nu·bi·al
con·quer
-quered, -quer·ing,
-quer·or
con·quest
con·san·guin·e·ous

con·san·guin·i·ty
-ties
con·science
con·sci·en·tious
con·scious
con·scious·ness
con·script
con·scrip·tion
con·se·crate
-crat·ed, -crat·ing,
-cra·tor
con·se·cra·tion
con·sec·u·tive
-tive·ly
con·sen·sus
con·sent
con·se·quence
con·se·quent
con·se·quen·tial
con·se·quent·ly
con·ser·va·tion
con·ser·va·tism
con·ser·va·tive
con·ser·va·to·ry
con·serve
-served,
-serv·ing,
-serv·er
con·sid·er
-ered, -er·ing
con·sid·er·able
-ably
con·sid·er·ate
con·sid·er·a·tion

con·sign
  -sign·able,
  -sig·na·tion,
  -sign·or
con·sign·ee
con·sign·ment
con·sist
con·sis·ten·cy
  -cies
con·sis·tent
con·so·la·tion
con·sole
  -soled, -sol·ing,
  -sol·ing·ly
con·sol·i·date
  -dat·ed, -dat·ing
con·sol·i·da·tion
con·som·mé
con·so·nance
con·so·nant
con·sort
con·sor·tium
  -sor·tia (pl)
con·spec·tus
con·spic·u·ous
con·spir·a·cy
  -cies
con·spir·a·tor
con·spire
  -spired, -spir·ing
con·sta·ble
con·stab·u·lary
  -lar·ies
con·stan·cy

  -cies
con·stant
con·stel·la·tion
con·ster·na·tion
con·sti·pate
  -pat·ed, -pat·ing
con·stit·u·en·cy
  -cies
con·stit·u·ent
con·sti·tute
  -tut·ed, -tut·ing
con·sti·tu·tion
con·sti·tu·tion·al
con·sti·tu·tion·al·i·ty
con·sti·tu·tion·al·ly
con·strain
con·straint
con·strict
con·stric·tion
con·stric·tor
con·struct
  -struct·ible,
  -struc·tor
con·struc·tion
con·struc·tion·ist
con·struc·tive
con·strue
  -strued, -stru·ing,
  -stru·able
con·sul (govern-
  ment official; cf.
  council, counsel)
con·sul·ar
con·sul·ate

con·sult
con·sul·tant
con·sul·ta·tion
con·sul·ta·tive
con·sume
  -sumed, -sum·ing
con·sum·ed·ly
con·sum·er
con·sum·er·ism
con·sum·mate
  -mat·ed, -mat·ing
con·sum·ma·tion
con·sump·tion
con·sump·tive
con·tact
con·ta·gion
con·ta·gious
con·tain·er
con·tain·ment
con·tam·i·nant
con·tam·i·nate
  -nat·ed, -nat·ing
con·tam·i·na·tion
con·tem·plate
  -plat·ed, -plat·ing
con·tem·pla·tion
con·tem·pla·tive
con·tem·po·ra·ne·ous
con·tem·po·rary
  -rar·ies, -rar·i·ly
con·tempt
con·tempt·ible
con·temp·tu·ous
con·tend

con·tent
con·ten·tion
con·ten·tious
con·tent·ment
con·test
con·tes·tant
con·tes·ta·tion
con·text
-tex·tu·al
con·tex·ture
con·ti·gu·ity
-ities
con·tig·u·ous
con·ti·nence
con·ti·nent
con·ti·nen·tal
con·tin·gen·cy
-cies
con·tin·gent
con·tin·u·al
con·tin·u·ance
con·tin·u·a·tion
con·tin·ue
-tinu·ing, -tin·ued
con·ti·nu·ity
-ities
con·tin·u·ous
con·tin·u·um
-ua (pl)
con·tort
-tor·tion
con·tor·tion·ist
con·tour
con·tra·band

con·tra·bass
con·tra·cep·tion
con·tract
-tract·ibil·i·ty,
-tract·ible
con·trac·tion
con·trac·tor
con·tra·dict
-dict·able
con·tra·dic·tion
con·tra·dic·to·ry
-ries, -ri·ly
con·tra·dis·tinc·tion
con·tra·in·di·cate
con·tral·to
-tos
con·trap·tion
con·tra·pun·tal
con·trari·wise
con·trary
-trar·ies, -trari·ly,
-trari·ness
con·trast
-trast·able
con·tra·vene
-vened, -ven·ing,
-ven·er
con·tra·ven·tion
con·tre·temps
con·trib·ute
-ut·ed, -ut·ing,
-u·tor
con·tri·bu·tion
con·trib·u·to·ry

con·trite
con·tri·tion
con·triv·ance
con·trive
-trived, -triv·ing
con·trol
-trolled, -trol·ling,
-trol·la·bil·i·ty
con·trol·ler
con·tro·ver·sial
-sial·ly
con·tro·ver·sy
-sies
con·tro·vert
con·tu·ma·cy
con·tu·sion
-tuse
co·nun·drum
con·va·lesce
-lesced, -lesc·ing,
-les·cence
con·vec·tion
con·vene
-vened, -ven·ing
con·ve·nience
con·ve·nient
con·vent
con·ven·tion
con·ven·tion·al
con·ven·tion·al·i·ty
-ties
con·verge
-verged, -verg·ing
con·ver·gence

con·ver·sant
con·ver·sa·tion
  -tion·al
con·ver·sa·tion·al·ist
con·verse
  -versed, -ver·sing,
  -verse·ly
con·ver·sion
con·vert
con·vert·er
con·vert·ible
  -ibil·i·ty
con·vex
con·vex·i·ty
  -ties
con·vey
  -veyed, -vey·ing
con·vey·ance
con·vey·er
con·vict
con·vic·tion
con·vince
  -vinced, -vinc·ing,
  -vinc·ing·ly
con·viv·ial
  -i·al·i·ty, -ial·ly
con·vo·ca·tion
con·voke
  -voked, -vok·ing
con·vo·lute
  -lut·ed, -lut·ing
con·voy
con·vulse
  -vulsed, -vuls·ing

con·vul·sion
con·vul·sive
cook·ery
  -er·ies
cook·ie
  -ies
cook·out (n)
cool
  cool·ly (coldly; cf.
  collie, coolie)
cool·ant
cool·er
coo·lie (laborer; cf.
  collie, coolly)
coon·skin
co·op·er·ate
co·op·er·a·tion
co·op·er·a·tive
co-opt
co·or·di·nate
co·or·di·na·tor
cope
  coped, cop·ing
Co·per·ni·can
copi·er
co·pi·lot
co·pi·ous
cop·per
cop·per·head
cop·per·plate
cop·per·smith
cop·u·late
  -lat·ed, -lat·ing
copy

cop·ies, cop·ied,
  copy·ing
copy·cat
copy·hold·er
copy·ist
copy·read·er
copy·right
co·que·try
  -tries
co·quette
cor·al (pink; cf.
  choral, chorale,
  corral)
cord (string; cf.
  chord)
cord·age
cor·dial
cor·dial·i·ty
cord·ite
cor·don
cor·do·van
cor·du·roy
  -roys
core (center; cf.
  corps, corpse)
  cored, cor·ing,
  cor·er
co·re·spon·dent
  (legal term; cf.
  correspondent)
co·ri·an·der
Co·rin·thi·an
cork·age
cork·screw

cork·wood

cor·mo·rant

corn bor·er

corn bread

corn·cob

corn·crib

cor·nea

cor·ner

  -nered, -ner·ing

cor·ner·stone

cor·ner·wise

cor·net

  -net·ist

corn-fed

corn·field

corn·flakes

corn·flow·er

cor·nice

  -niced, -nic·ing

corn·meal

corn pone

corn·stalk

corn·starch

cor·nu·co·pia

co·rol·la

  -late

cor·ol·lary

  -lar·ies

co·ro·na

cor·o·nary

  -nar·ies

cor·o·na·tion

cor·o·ner

cor·o·net

cor·po·ral

cor·po·rate

cor·po·ra·tion

cor·po·ra·tive

cor·po·re·al

corps (group of people; cf. *core, corpse*)

corps (pl)

corpse (body; cf. *core, corps*)

cor·pu·lence

cor·pu·lent

cor·pus

  -po·ra (pl)

cor·pus·cle

  -cu·lar

cor·rade

  -rad·ed, -rad·ing,

  -ra·sive

cor·ral (animal pen; cf. *choral, chorale, coral*)

  -ralled, -ral·ling

cor·rect

  -rect·able

cor·rec·tion

cor·rec·tive

cor·re·late

  -lat·ed, -lat·ing,

  -lat·able

cor·re·la·tion

cor·rel·a·tive

cor·re·spond

cor·re·spon·dence

  (letters; cf. *correspondents*)

cor·re·spon·dent

  (writer of letters; cf. *corespondent*),

cor·re·spon·dents

  (writers of letters; cf. *correspondence*)

cor·ri·dor

cor·rob·o·rate

  -rat·ed, -rat·ing,

  -ra·tion

cor·rode

  -rod·ed, -rod·ing,

  -rod·ible

cor·ro·sion

cor·ro·sive

cor·ru·gate

  -gat·ed, -gat·ing

cor·ru·ga·tion

cor·rupt

  -rupt·er,

  -rupt·ibil·i·ty,

  -rupt·ible

cor·rup·tion

cor·sage

corse (corpse; cf. *coarse, course*)

cor·set

cor·tege

cor·tex

  -ti·ces or -tex·es (pl)

cor·ti·sone
co·run·dum
cor·us·cate
  -cat·ed, -cat·ing
cor·vette
cos·met·ic
cos·me·tol·o·gist
cos·me·tol·o·gy
cos·mic
  -mic·al
cos·mog·o·ny
  -mog·o·nies,
  -mo·gon·ic
cos·mol·o·gy
  -gies
cos·mo·naut
cos·mo·pol·i·tan
cos·mos
cos·sack
cost
cost-ef·fec·tive
cost·ly
  -li·er, -li·est
cost-plus
cos·tume
  -tum·ey, -tumed,
  -tum·ing
cos·tum·er
co·te·rie (close
  group; cf. *cautery*)
co·ter·mi·nous
co·til·lion
cot·tage
cot·ton

-toned, -ton·ing
cot·ton·tail
cot·ton·wood
cou·gar
could
cou·lomb
coun·cil (assembly;
  cf. *consul, counsel*)
coun·cil·lor
coun·cil·man
coun·cil·wom·an
coun·sel (advice; cf.
  consul, council)
  -sel·ing, -seled
coun·sel·or
count down (v)
count·down (n)
coun·te·nance
  -nanced, -nanc·ing
count·er
coun·ter·act
coun·ter·bal·ance
coun·ter·claim
coun·ter·clock·wise
coun·ter·feit
  -feit·er
coun·ter·ir·ri·tant
coun·ter·mand
coun·ter·march
coun·ter·mine
coun·ter·pane
coun·ter·part
coun·ter·point
coun·ter·pro·duc·tive

coun·ter·rev·o·lu·tion
  -tion·ary
coun·ter·sign
coun·ter·spy
coun·ter·top
coun·ter·weight
count·ess
count·ing·house
count·less
coun·try
  -tries
coun·try·man
coun·try·side
coun·try·wom·an
coun·ty
  -ties
coup d'état
  coups d'état (pl)
cou·pé or coupe
cou·ple
  -pled, -pling
cou·pler
cou·plet
cou·pling
cou·pon
cour·age
cou·ra·geous
cou·ri·er
course (way; cf.
  coarse, corse)
  coursed,
  cours·ing
cour·te·ous
cour·te·san

cour·te·sy
-sies
court·house
court·ier
court·ly
-li·er, -li·est,
-li·ness
court-mar·tial
courts-martial or
court-martials (pl),
court-mar·tialed
court·room
court·ship
court·yard
cous·in
cou·ture
cou·tu·ri·er
cov·e·nant
-nan·tal
cov·er
-ered, -er·ing,
-er·able
cov·er·age
cov·er·all (adj)
cov·er·all (n)
-alled
cov·er charge
cov·er·let
co·vert
cov·er·ture
cov·et
-et·able, -et·er
cov·et·ous
cov·ey

cov·eys
cow·ard (frightened;
cf. *cowered*)
cow·ard·ice
cow·ard·ly
-li·ness
cow·bell
cow·boy
cow·catch·er
cow·ered (crouched;
cf. *coward*)
cow·girl
cow·hand
cow·hide
cow·lick
cowl·ing
cow·pea
cow·pox
cow·punch·er
cow·slip
cox·comb
cox·swain
coy
coy·ote
coy·otes
co·zy
-zi·er, -zi·ly,
-zi·ness
crab ap·ple
crabbed
crab·grass
crack·brain
-brained
crack down (v)

crack·down (n)
crack·er
crack·er·jack
crack·le
-led, -ling
crack·pot
cra·dle
-dled, -dling
crafts·man
crafts·wom·an
crafty
craft·i·er,
craft·i·ly,
craft·i·ness
cram
crammed,
cram·ming
cran·ber·ry
cra·ni·al
cra·ni·um
-ni·ums or
-nia (pl)
crank·case
crank pin
crank·shaft
cranky
crank·i·er,
crank·i·est,
crank·i·ness
cran·ny
-nies
cra·ter
cra·vat
cra·ven

craw·fish

cray·on

cra·zy
-zi·er, -zi·est, -zi·ly

creak (sound; cf.
creek, crick)

cream·ery
-er·ies

cream·i·ness

cream puff

cre·ate
-at·ed, -at·ing

cre·ation

cre·ative

cre·ator

crea·ture

cre·dence

cre·den·tial
-tialed, -tial·ing

cre·den·za

cred·i·bil·i·ty

cred·i·ble (believable;
cf. *creditable,
credulous*) -bly

cred·it

cred·it·able
(estimable; cf.
*credible, credu-
lous*)
-ably, -abil·i·ty

cred·it card

cred·i·tor

cre·do
cre·dos

cred·u·lous
(gullible; cf.
*credible, credit-
able*)

creek (water; cf.
creak, crick)

creepy
creep·i·er,
creep·i·est,
creep·i·ness

cre·mate
-mat·ed, -mat·ing,
-ma·tion

cre·ma·to·ry
-ries

cre·ole

cre·o·sote
-sot·ed, -sot·ing

crepe

cre·pus·cu·lar

cre·scen·do
-dos or -does (pl)

cres·cent

crest·fall·en

cre·tin
-tin·ous

cre·tonne

cre·vasse

crev·ice

crew
crews (group; cf.
cruise, cruse)

crib
cribbed, crib·bing

crib·bage

crick (cramp; cf.
creak, creek)

crick·et
-et·er

cri·er

crim·i·nal
-nal·ly

crim·i·nal·i·ty

crim·i·nol·o·gy

crim·son

cringe
cringed, cring·ing

crin·kle
-kled, -kling, -kly

crin·o·line

crip·ple
-pled, -pling

cri·sis
cri·ses (pl)

criss·cross

cri·te·ria (pl)
-ri·on (sing)

crit·ic

crit·i·cal
-cal·i·ty

crit·i·cism

crit·i·cize
-cized, -ciz·ing,
-ciz·able

cri·tique
-tiqued, -tiqu·ing

cro·chet

crock·ery

croc·o·dile

cro·cus
-cus·es (pl)

crois·sant

croon·er

crop
cropped, crop·ping

cro·quet (game; cf.
croquette)

cro·quette (food; cf.
croquet)

cro·sier

cross·bar

cross·bow

cross·breed

cross-coun·try

cross·cut

cross-ex·am·ine

cross-eyed

cross-grained

cross hair

cross·hatch

cross·ing

cross·over

cross-ques·tion

cross-ref·er·ence

cross·road

cross sec·tion

cross-stitch

cross·walk

cross·wise

crotch·et

crotch·ety

crou·pi·er

crou·ton

crow·bar

cru·cial

cru·ci·ble

cru·ci·fix

cru·ci·fix·ion

cru·ci·form

cru·ci·fy
-fied, -fy·ing

cru·di·ty
-ties

cru·el
-el·er, -el·est, -el·ly

cru·el·ty

cru·et

cruise (sail; cf.
crews, cruse)
cruised, cruis·ing

cruis·er

crul·ler

crum·ble (break; cf.
crumple)
-bled, -bling

crum·pet

crum·ple (wrinkle;
cf. *crumble*)
-pled, -pling

crup·per

cru·sade
-sad·ed, -sad·ing,
-sad·er

cruse (small cup; cf.
crews, cruise)

crus·ta·ceous

crux
crux·es or cru·ces
(pl)

cry
cried, cry·ing,
cries

cryo·bi·ol·o·gy

cryo·gen

cryo·gen·ics

crypt

crypt·anal·y·sis

cryp·tic

cryp·to·gram

crys·tal

crys·tal·line

crys·tal·li·za·tion

crys·tal·lize
-lized, -liz·ing,
-liz·able

cu·bic

cu·bi·cal (adj)

cu·bi·cle (n)

cu·bit

cuck·old

cuck·oo
cuck·oos

cu·cum·ber

cud·dle
-dled, -dling

cud·gel
-geled, -gel·ing

cue (signal; cf.
queue)
cued, cu·ing

cui·sine
cul-de-sac
  culs-de-sac (pl)
cu·li·nary
cul·mi·nate
  -nat·ed, -nat·ing
cul·mi·na·tion
cul·pa·ble
  -bly, -bil·i·ty
cul·prit
cul·ti·vate
  -vat·ed, -vat·ing,
  -vat·able
cul·ti·va·tion
cul·ti·va·tor
cul·tur·al
cul·ture
  -tured, -tur·ing
cul·vert
cum·ber·some
cum lau·de
cum·mer·bund
cu·mu·la·tive
cu·mu·lus
cu·ne·i·form
cun·ning
cup·board
cu·pel
cup·ful
  -fuls
cu·pid·i·ty
  -ties
cu·po·la
cur·able

cu·ra·çao
cu·ra·re
cu·rate
cu·ra·tive
cu·ra·tor
  -to·ri·al
curb·stone
cur·dle
  -dled, -dling
cu·rette
  -rett·ed, -rett·ing
cur·few
cu·rio
  -ri·os (pl)
cu·ri·os·i·ty
  -ties
cu·ri·ous
curli·cue
  -cued, -cu·ing
cur·rant (berry; cf.
  current)
cur·ren·cy
cur·rent (prevalent;
  cf. *currant*)
  -rent·ly
cur·ric·u·lum
  -la (pl)
cur·ry
  -ried, -ry·ing
cur·ry·comb
cur·sive
cur·sor
cur·so·ry
  -ri·ly

cur·tail
  -tail·er
cur·tain
  -tained, -tain·ing
cur·tain call
cur·va·ture
curve
  curved, curv·ing
cur·vi·lin·ear
cush·ion
  -iony, -ioned,
  -ion·ing
cus·pi·dor
cus·tard
cus·to·di·al
cus·to·di·an
cus·to·dy
  -dies
cus·tom
cus·tom·ary
cus·tom·er
cus·tom·house
cus·tom·ize
  -ized, -iz·ing, -iz·er
cus·tom-made
cut-and-dry
cut·away
cut·back
cu·ti·cle
cut·lass
cut·lery
cut·let
cut off (v)
cut·off (n)

cut·out (n, adj)
cut-rate
cut·throat
cut·ting
cut up (v)
cut·up (n)
cut·wa·ter
cut·worm
cy·an·a·mide
cy·an·ic
cy·a·nide
cy·ano·gen
cy·a·no·sis
cy·ber·net·ics

cy·cla·mate
cy·cle
  -cled, -cling, -cler
cy·cli·cal
cy·cloid
cy·clone
cy·clo·pe·dia
cy·clops
  -clo·pes (pl)
cy·clo·ra·ma
cy·clo·tron
cyg·net
cyl·in·der
cy·lin·dri·cal

cym·bal (musical;
  cf. *symbol*)
cyn·ic
cyn·i·cal
cyn·i·cism
cy·no·sure
cy·press
cyst
cys·tic
czar
cza·ri·na
Czech

D

dab·ble
  -bled, -bling
da ca·po
dachs·hund
Da·cron
dac·tyl
daf·fo·dil
dag·ger
da·guerre·o·type
dahl·ia
dai·ly
  -lies
dain·ty
  -ties, -ti·est, -ti·ly

dairy (for milk; cf.
  diary)
  dair·ies
dairy·maid
dairy·man
da·is
dai·sy
  -sies
dai·sy wheel
dal·li·ance
dal·ma·tian
dam
  dammed
  (confined; cf.

damned),
  dam·ming
dam·age
  -aged, -ag·ing,
  -ag·er
dam·ask
dam·na·ble
dam·na·tion
damned (cursed; cf.
  dammed)
  damned·er,
  damned·est
damn·ing
Dam·o·cles

damp·en
  -ened, -en·ing
damp·er
dam·sel
dance
  danced, danc·ing,
  danc·er
dan·de·li·on
dan·druff
dan·ger
dan·ger·ous
dan·gle
  -gled, -gling, -gler
Dan·ish
  Dan·ish (pl)
dan·seuse
dare·dev·il
dark·en
  -ened, -en·ing,
  -en·er
dark horse
dar·kle
  -kled, -kling
dark·ness
dark·room
dar·ling
Dar·win·ian
dash·board
das·tard·ly
da·ta (pl)
  da·tum (sing)
da·ta base
date
  dat·ed, dat·ing,

dat·er
daugh·ter
daugh·ter-in-law
  daugh·ters-in-law
  (pl)
dau·phin
dav·en·port
da·vit
daw·dle
  -dled, -dling, -dler
days
day·bed
day·book
day·break
day-care
day·dream
day·flow·er
day·light
day·room
day school
day·star
day·time
day-to-day
daz·zle
  -zled, -zling, -zler
dea·con
dead·beat
dead·en
  -ened, -en·ing
dead·eye
dead·fall
dead·head
dead heat
dead·light

dead·line
dead·lock
dead·ly
  -li·er, -li·est,
  -li·ness
dead·weight
dead·wood
deaf-mute
deal
  dealt, deal·ing,
  deal·er
dear (beloved; cf.
  deer)
dearth
death·bed
death ben·e·fit
death·blow
death·less
death·ly
death's-head
death war·rant
death·watch
de·ba·cle
de·bark
  -bar·ka·tion
de·base
de·bat·able
de·bate
  -bat·ed, -bat·ing,
  -bat·er
de·bauch
de·bauch·ery
  -er·ies
de·ben·ture

de·bil·i·tate
-tat·ed, -tat·ing,
-ta·tion
de·bil·i·ty
-ties
deb·it (bookkeeping
entry; cf. *debt*)
deb·o·nair
de·bug
de·bris
de·bris (pl)
debt (obligation; cf.
debit)
debt·or
de·but
deb·u·tante
de·cade
dec·a·dence
dec·a·dent
de·caf·fein·at·ed
deca·gon
deca·logue
de·camp
de·cant
de·cant·er
de·cap·i·tate
-tat·ed, -tat·ing,
-ta·tion
de·cath·lon
de·cay
de·cease
de·ceased (dead; cf.
diseased)
de·ceased (pl)

de·ce·dent
de·ceit
de·ceit·ful
de·ceive
-ceived, -ceiv·ing,
-ceiv·ing·ly
De·cem·ber
de·cen·cy
-cies
de·cent (proper; cf.
descent, dissent)
de·cen·tral·ize
de·cep·tion
de·cep·tive
deci·bel
de·cide
-cid·ed, -cid·ing
de·cid·u·ous
dec·i·mal
dec·i·mate
-mat·ed, -mat·ing,
-ma·tion
deci·me·ter
de·ci·pher
de·ci·sion
de·ci·sive
deck chair
de·claim
-claim·er,
-cla·ma·tion
dec·la·ra·tion
de·clar·a·tive
de·clare
-clared, -clar·ing

de·clen·sion
dec·li·na·tion
de·cline
-clined, -clin·ing,
-clin·able
de·cliv·i·ty
-ties
dé·col·le·té
de·com·pose
-pos·able,
-po·si·tion
de·con·tam·i·nate
dec·o·rate
-rat·ed, -rat·ing
dec·o·ra·tion
dec·o·ra·tive
dec·o·ra·tor
dec·o·rous
de·co·rum
de·coy
de·crease
-creased,
-creas·ing
de·cree (law; cf.
degree)
-creed, -cree·ing,
-cre·er
de·crep·it
de·cre·scen·do
-dos
de·cry
ded·i·cate
-cat·ed, -cat·ing,
-ca·tor

ded·i·ca·tion
de·duce
  -duced, -duc·ing,
  -duc·ible
de·duc·tion
de·duc·tive
deep·en
  -ened, -en·ing
deep-root·ed
deep-seat·ed
deer (animal; cf.
  dear)
  deer (pl)
deer·hound
deer·skin
de-es·ca·late
  -la·tion
de·face
de fac·to
de·fal·cate
  -cat·ed, -cat·ing
de·fal·ca·tion
def·a·ma·tion
de·fame
  -famed, -fam·ing,
  -fam·er
de·fault
  -fault·er
de·feat
de·fect
de·fec·tion
de·fec·tive
de·fend
de·fen·dant

de·fense
  -fensed, -fens·ing
de·fen·si·ble
de·fen·sive
de·fer
  -ferred, -fer·ring
def·er·ence
  (respect; cf.
  difference)
def·er·en·tial
  (respectful; cf.
  differential)
de·fer·ment
de·fer·ra·ble
de·fi·ance
de·fi·ant
de·fi·cien·cy
  -cies
de·fi·cient
def·i·cit
de·file
  -filed, -fil·ing,
  -fil·er
de·fine
  -fined, -fin·ing,
  -fin·able
def·i·nite (clear; cf.
  definitive)
def·i·ni·tion
de·fin·i·tive (final;
  cf. *definite*)
de·flate
  -flat·ed, -flat·ing,
  -fla·tor

de·fla·tion
de·flect
de·flec·tion
de·fo·li·ant
de·fo·li·ate
de·fo·li·a·tion
  -li·a·tor
de·form
de·for·ma·tion
de·for·mi·ty
  -ties
de·fraud
de·fray
de·funct
de·fy
  -fies, -fied, -fy·ing
de·gen·er·a·cy
  -cies
de·gen·er·ate
de·gen·er·a·tion
deg·ra·da·tion
de·grade
de·gree (from
  college; cf. *decree*)
de·hu·mid·i·fy
de·hy·drate
de·i·fi·ca·tion
deign
de·i·ty
  -ties
de·ject·ed
de·jec·tion
de ju·re
deka·gram

Del·a·ware
  Del·a·ware (pl)
de·lay
de·lec·ta·ble
del·e·gate
  -gat·ed, -gat·ing,
  -ga·tor
del·e·ga·tion
de·lete
  -let·ed, -let·ing
del·e·te·ri·ous
de·le·tion
delft·ware
de·lib·er·ate
  -at·ed, -at·ing
de·lib·er·a·tion
  -tive, -tive·ness,
  -tive·ly
del·i·ca·cy
  -cies
del·i·cate
del·i·ca·tes·sen
de·li·cious
de·light
de·light·ful
de·lin·eate
  -eat·ed, -eat·ing,
  -ea·tor
de·lin·ea·tion
de·lin·quen·cy
  -cies
de·lin·quent
del·i·ques·cent
de·lir·i·ous

de·lir·i·um
de·liv·er
  -ered, -er·ing,
  -er·able
de·liv·er·ance
de·liv·er·y
  -er·ies
de·lude
  -lud·ed, -lud·ing,
  -lud·er
del·uge
  -uged, -ug·ing
de·lu·sion
de·luxe
delve
  delved, delv·ing,
  delv·er
de·mag·ne·tize
dem·a·gogue
de·mand
de·mar·cate
  -cat·ed, -cat·ing,
  -ca·tion
de·mean
  -meaned,
  -mean·ing
de·mean·or
de·ment·ed
de·men·tia
de·mer·it
demi·god
demi·john
de·mil·i·ta·rize
de·mise

demi·tasse
de·mo·bi·lize
de·moc·ra·cy
  -cies
dem·o·crat
dem·o·crat·ic
de·mo·graph·ic
de·mog·ra·phy
de·mol·ish
de·mo·li·tion
de·mon
de·mon·e·tize
  -ti·za·tion
de·mon·stra·ble
dem·on·strate
  -strat·ed, -strat·ing
dem·on·stra·tion
de·mon·stra·tive
de·mon·stra·tor
de·mor·al·ize
de·mount
  -mount·able
de·mur (delay; cf.
  demure)
  -murred,
  -mur·ring
de·mure (modest;
  cf. *demur*)
de·mur·rage
de·mur·rer
de·na·ture
  -tured, -tur·ing
de·ni·al
den·im

den·i·zen
de·nom·i·na·tion
de·nom·i·na·tor
de·note
de·noue·ment
de·nounce
　-nounced,
　-nounc·ing,
　-nounce·ment
den·si·ty
　-ties
den·tal
den·ti·frice
den·tist
den·tist·ry
den·ture
de·nude
　-nud·ed, -nud·ing
de·nun·ci·a·tion
　-tive, -to·ry
de·ny
　-nied, -ny·ing,
　-ny·ing·ly
de·odor·ant
de·odor·ize
de·part
de·part·ment
　-men·tal,
　-men·tal·ly
de·par·ture
de·pend·able
de·pen·den·cy
　-cies
de·pen·dent

de·pict
　-pic·ter, -pic·tion
de·pil·a·to·ry
　-ries
de·plane
de·plete
　-plet·ed, -plet·ing,
　-ple·tion
de·plor·able
de·plore
　-plored, -plor·ing,
　-plor·ing·ly
de·ploy
de·pop·u·late
de·port·able
de·por·ta·tion
de·port·ment
de·pose
　-posed, -pos·ing
de·pos·it
　-it·ed, -it·ing, -i·tor
de·pos·i·tary
　-tar·ies
de·po·si·tion
de·pos·i·to·ry
　-ries
de·pot
de·prave
　-praved, -prav·ing,
　-pra·va·tion
　(corruption; cf.
　deprivation)
de·prav·i·ty
dep·re·cate

　-cat·ed, -cat·ing,
　-ca·tion
dep·re·ca·to·ry
de·pre·ci·ate
　-at·ed, -at·ing,
　-a·tion
dep·re·date
　-dat·ed, -dat·ing,
　-da·tion
de·press
de·pressed
de·pres·sion
de·pri·va·tion (loss;
　cf. *depravation*)
de·prive
　-prived, -priv·ing
dep·u·ta·tion
de·pute
dep·u·tize
　-tized, -tiz·ing,
　-ti·za·tion
dep·u·ty
　-ties
de·rail
de·range
　-ranged, -rang·ing,
　-range·ment
de·reg·u·la·tion
der·e·lict
der·e·lic·tion
de·ride
　-rid·ed, -rid·ing,
　-rid·ing·ly
de·ri·sion

de·ri·sive
de·ri·so·ry
der·i·va·tion
de·riv·a·tive
de·rive
  -rived, -riv·ing
der·ma·tol·o·gy
  -tol·o·gist,
  -to·log·ic,
  -to·log·i·cal
de·rog·a·to·ry
der·rick
der·vish
de·scend
de·scen·dant
de·scent (going
  down; cf. *decent,*
  dissent)
de·scribe
  -scribed,
  -scrib·ing,
  -scrib·able
de·scrip·tion
de·scrip·tive
des·e·crate
  -crat·ed, -crat·ing,
  -crat·or
des·e·cra·tion
de·seg·re·gate
de·sen·si·tize
des·ert (n)(dry
  country; cf.
  dessert)
de·sert (v)(leave; cf.

dessert)
de·ser·tion
de·serve
  -served, -serv·ing,
  -serv·er
de·served·ly
des·ic·cate
  -cated, -cat·ing,
  -ca·tion
de·sid·er·a·ta (pl)
  -tum (sing)
de·sign
des·ig·nate
  -nat·ed, -nat·ing,
  -na·tor
des·ig·na·tion
des·ig·nee
de·sign·er
de·sir·abil·i·ty
  -ties
de·sir·able
de·sire
  -sired, -sir·ing
de·sir·ous
de·sist
desk·top
  pub·lish·ing
des·o·late
  -lat·ed, -lat·ing,
  -lat·er
des·o·la·tion
de·spair
des·per·a·do
  -does (pl)

des·per·ate
  (hopeless; cf.
  disparate)
des·per·a·tion
des·pi·ca·ble
de·spise
  -spised, -spis·ing,
  -spis·er
de·spite
  -spit·ed, -spit·ing
de·spoil
de·spond
de·spon·den·cy
de·spon·dent
des·pot
des·pot·ic
des·po·tism
des·sert (food; cf.
  desert)
des·sert·spoon
des·ti·na·tion
des·tine
  -tined, -tin·ing
des·ti·ny
  -nies
des·ti·tute
des·ti·tu·tion
de·stroy
de·struc·ti·ble
de·struc·tion
de·struc·tive
de·sue·tude
des·ul·to·ry
de·tach

de·tach·ment
de·tail
de·tain
de·tect
  -tect·abil·i·ty,
  -tect·able
de·tec·tion
de·tec·tive
de·tec·tor
de·ten·tion
de·ter
  -terred, -ter·ring,
  -ter·ment
de·ter·gent
de·te·ri·o·rate
  -rat·ed, -rat·ing,
  -ra·tive
de·te·ri·o·ra·tion
de·ter·min·able
de·ter·mi·nant
de·ter·mi·nate
de·ter·mi·na·tion
de·ter·mine
  -mined, -min·ing
de·ter·min·ism
de·ter·rent
de·test
de·test·able
de·tes·ta·tion
de·throne
det·i·nue
det·o·nate
  -nat·ed, -nat·ing,
  -na·tive

det·o·na·tion
det·o·na·tor
de·tract
de·trac·tion
det·ri·ment
det·ri·men·tal
deutsche mark
dev·as·tate
  -tat·ed, -tat·ing,
  -ta·tion
de·vel·op
de·vel·op·er
de·vel·op·ing
de·vel·op·ment
de·vi·ate
  -at·ed, -at·ing,
  -a·tor
de·vi·a·tion
de·vice
  (n)(invention; cf.
  devise)
dev·il·fish
dev·il·ish
dev·il·ment
de·vi·ous
de·vise (v)(invent;
  cf. *device*)
  -vised, -vis·ing,
  -vis·er
de·void
de·volve
  -volved, -volv·ing,
  -volv·ment
de·vote

-vot·ed, -vot·ing
dev·o·tee
de·vo·tion
de·vo·tion·al
de·vour
de·vout
dew·ber·ry
dew·drop
dew point
dewy
  dew·i·er,
  dew·i·est,
  dew·i·ness
dex·ter·i·ty
  -ties
dex·ter·ous
dex·trose
di·a·be·tes
di·a·bet·ic
di·a·bol·ic
di·a·bol·i·cal
di·ab·o·lism
di·a·crit·i·cal
di·a·dem
di·aer·e·sis
  -aer·e·ses (pl),
  -ae·ret·ic
di·ag·nose
  -nosed, -nos·ing,
  -nos·able
di·ag·no·sis
  -ses (pl)
di·ag·nos·tic
di·ag·o·nal

di·a·gram
  -gramed,
  -gram·ing
di·a·gram·mat·ic
di·al
  -aled, -al·ing, -al·er
di·a·lect
di·a·lec·tic
di·a·lec·ti·cal
di·a·logue
  -logued, -logu·ing
di·al·y·sis
  -al·y·ses (pl),
  -a·lyt·ic
di·am·e·ter
di·a·met·ric
di·a·mond
di·a·per
  -pered, -per·ing
di·aph·a·nous
di·a·phragm
di·ar·rhea
di·a·ry (journal; cf.
  dairy)
  -ries
dia·ton·ic
di·a·tribe
di·chot·o·my
  -mies
Dic·ta·phone
dic·tate
  -tat·ed, -tat·ing
dic·ta·tion
dic·ta·tor

dic·ta·to·ri·al
dic·tion
dic·tio·nary
  -nar·ies
dic·tum
  dic·ta (pl)
di·dac·tic
die (expire; cf. *dye*)
  died (perished; cf.
  dyed), dy·ing
  (expiring; cf.
  dyeing)
die-hard (adj)
die-hard (n)
di·elec·tric
di·er·e·sis
die·sel
die·sink·er
di·et
di·etary
  -etar·ies
di·etet·ic
di·etet·ics
di·eti·tian
dif·fer
  -fered, -fer·ing
dif·fer·ence
  (unlikeness; cf.
  deference)
  -enced, -enc·ing
dif·fer·ent
dif·fer·en·tial
  (change; cf.
  deferential)

dif·fer·en·ti·ate
  -ti·at·ed, -ti·at·ing,
  -tia·ble
dif·fer·en·ti·a·tion
dif·fi·cult
dif·fi·cul·ty
  -ties
dif·fi·dence
dif·fi·dent
dif·frac·tion
dif·fuse
  -fused, -fus·ing
dif·fu·sion
di·gest
di·gest·ible
di·ges·tion
di·ges·tive
dig·it
dig·i·tal·is
dig·ni·fy
  -fied, -fy·ing
dig·ni·tary
  -tar·ies
dig·ni·ty
  -ties
di·gress
di·gres·sion
di·lap·i·date
  -dat·ed, -dat·ing,
  -da·tion
di·la·ta·tion
di·late
  -lat·ed, -lat·ing,
  -lat·able

di·la·tion
dil·a·to·ry
  -to·ri·ly, -to·ri·ness
di·lem·ma
dil·et·tante
dil·i·gence
dil·i·gent
di·lute
  -lut·ed, -lut·ing,
  -lut·er
di·lu·tion
di·men·sion
  -sioned, -sion·ing
di·min·ish
dim·i·nu·tion
di·min·u·tive
dim·i·ty
dim·mer
dim·ple
  -pled, -pling
dim·wit (n)
dim-wit·ted (adj)
di·nar (coin; cf.
  diner)
din·er (eater; cf.
  dinar)
di·nette
din·ghy (boat; cf.
  dingy)
  din·ghies (pl)
din·gy (dull; cf.
  dinghy)
  -gi·er, -gi·est
din·ner

din·ner jack·et
din·ner·ware
di·no·saur
di·oc·e·san
di·o·cese
  -ces·es (pl)
di·ode
di·o·ra·ma
diph·the·ria
diph·thong
di·plo·ma
  -mas
di·plo·ma·cy
dip·lo·mat
dip·lo·mat·ic
dip·per
dip·so·ma·nia
di·rect
di·rec·tion
di·rec·tive
di·rect·ly
di·rec·tor
di·rec·tor·ate
di·rec·to·ry
  -ries
dirge
di·ri·gi·ble
dirndl
dirty
  dirt·i·er, dirt·i·est,
  dirt·i·ness
dis·abil·i·ty
dis·able
  -abled, -abling,

  -able·ment
dis·abuse
dis·ad·van·tage
dis·ad·van·ta·geous
dis·af·fect·ed
dis·agree
dis·agree·able
dis·agree·ment
dis·al·low
  -low·ance
dis·ap·pear
dis·ap·pear·ance
dis·ap·point
dis·ap·point·ment
dis·ap·pro·ba·tion
dis·ap·prov·al
dis·ap·prove
dis·arm
  -ar·ma·ment,
  -arm·er
dis·ar·range
dis·ar·ray
dis·ar·tic·u·late
dis·as·sem·ble (take
  apart; cf.
  dissemble)
dis·as·so·ci·ate
di·sas·ter
di·sas·trous
dis·avow
  -avow·able,
  -avow·al
dis·band
dis·bar

dis·be·lief
dis·be·lieve
  -liev·er
dis·burse (pay out;
  cf. *disperse*)
  -bursed, -burs·ing,
  -burs·er
dis·burse·ment
disc
dis·card
dis·cern
  -cern·er,
  -cern·ible,
  -cern·ibly
dis·cern·ment
dis·charge
dis·ci·ple
dis·ci·pli·nar·i·an
dis·ci·plin·ary
dis·ci·pline
  -plined, -plin·ing,
  -plin·er
dis·claim
dis·claim·er
dis·close
dis·clo·sure
dis·co
  dis·cos
dis·cog·ra·phy
  -cog·ra·phies,
  -co·graph·i·cal
dis·col·or
dis·col·or·ation
dis·com·fit (balk; cf.

discomfort)
dis·com·fi·ture
dis·com·fort
  (uneasiness; cf.
  discomfit)
dis·com·pose
  -po·sure
dis·con·cert
dis·con·nect
dis·con·so·late
dis·con·tent
  -tent·ment
dis·con·tinu·ance
dis·con·tin·ue
dis·con·tin·u·ous
dis·cord
dis·cor·dance
dis·cor·dant
dis·co·theque
dis·count
dis·cour·age
  -aged, -ag·ing,
  -ag·ing·ly
dis·cour·age·ment
dis·course
  -coursed,
  -cours·ing,
  -cours·er
dis·cour·te·ous
dis·cour·te·sy
dis·cov·er
  -cov·ered,
  -cov·er·ing,
  -cov·er·able

dis·cov·ery
  -er·ies
dis·cred·it
dis·cred·it·able
dis·creet (prudent;
  cf. *discrete*)
dis·crep·an·cy
  -cies
dis·crete (separate;
  cf. *discreet*)
dis·cre·tion
dis·cre·tion·ary
dis·crim·i·nate
  -nat·ed, -nat·ing
dis·crim·i·na·tion
dis·crim·i·na·to·ry
dis·cur·sive
dis·cus (athletic
  term; cf. *discuss*)
  -cus·es (pl)
dis·cuss (talk about;
  cf. *discus*)
dis·cus·sion
dis·dain
dis·dain·ful
dis·ease
  dis·eased (ill; cf.
  deceased)
dis·em·bar·rass
dis·em·bow·el
dis·en·chant
  -chant·ing,
  -chant·ing·ly,
  -chant·ment

dis·en·gage
dis·en·tan·gle
dis·fa·vor
dis·fig·ure
　-ure·ment
dis·gorge
dis·grace
dis·grace·ful
dis·grun·tle
　-grun·tled,
　-grun·ting,
　-grun·tle·ment
dis·guise
　-guised, -guis·ing,
　-guis·er
dis·gust
dis·ha·bille
dis·har·mon·ic
dish·cloth
dis·heart·en
di·shev·el
　-eled, -el·ing
dis·hon·est
dis·hon·or
dis·hon·or·able
dish·pan
dish·rag
dish·wash·er
dish·wa·ter
dis·il·lu·sion
　-sioned, -sion·ing,
　-sion·ment
dis·in·cen·tive
dis·in·cli·na·tion

dis·in·fect
　-fec·tion
dis·in·fec·tant
dis·in·gen·u·ous
dis·in·her·it
dis·in·te·grate
dis·in·ter·est·ed
dis·join
dis·junc·tion
dis·junc·tive
disk
dis·kette
dis·like
dis·lo·cate
dis·lo·ca·tion
dis·lodge
dis·loy·al
dis·loy·al·ty
dis·mal
dis·man·tle
　-tled, -tling,
　-tle·ment
dis·may
　-mayed, -may·ing,
　-may·ing·ly
dis·mem·ber
　-bered, -ber·ing,
　-ber·ment
dis·miss
dis·miss·al
dis·mount
dis·obe·di·ence
dis·obe·di·ent
dis·obey

dis·oblige
dis·or·der
dis·or·dered
dis·or·der·ly
dis·or·ga·nize
　-ni·za·tion
dis·own
dis·par·age
　-aged, -ag·ing,
　-age·ment
dis·pa·rate
　(different; cf.
　desperate)
　-pa·rate·ly,
　-pa·rate·ness,
　-par·i·ty
dis·pas·sion·ate
dis·patch
dis·pel
　-pelled, -pel·ling
dis·pen·sa·ry
　-ries
dis·pen·sa·tion
dis·pense
　-pensed, -pens·ing
dis·pers·al
dis·perse (scatter;
　cf. *disburse*)
　-persed, -pers·ing,
　-pers·er
dis·per·sion
dispir·it
dis·place
dis·place·ment

dis·play
dis·please
dis·plea·sure
dis·pos·able
dis·pos·al
dis·pose
  -posed, -pos·ing,
  -pos·er
dis·po·si·tion
dis·pos·sess
dis·proof
dis·pro·por·tion
dis·pro·por·tion·ate
dis·prove
dis·pu·tant
dis·pu·ta·tion
dis·pu·ta·tious
dis·pute
  -put·ed, -put·ing,
  -put·er
dis·qual·i·fi·ca·tion
dis·qual·i·fy
dis·re·gard
dis·re·pair
dis·rep·u·ta·ble
dis·re·pute
dis·re·spect
  -spect·ful,
  -spect·ful·ly,
  -spect·ful·ness
dis·robe
dis·rupt
  -rupt·er, -rup·tive,
  -rup·tion

dis·sat·is·fac·tion
dis·sat·is·fied
dis·sect
dis·sec·tion
dis·sem·ble
  (disguise; cf.
  disassemble)
  -sem·bled,
  -sem·bling,
  -sem·bler
dis·sem·i·nate
  -nat·ed, -nat·ing,
  -na·tion
dis·sen·sion
dis·sent (disagree-
  ment; cf. *decent,*
  descent)
dis·sent·er
dis·ser·ta·tion
dis·ser·vice
dis·si·dence
dis·si·dent
dis·sim·i·lar
  -lar·i·ty, -lar·ly
dis·sim·u·late
  -lat·ed, -lat·ing,
  -la·tion
dis·si·pate
  -pat·ed, -pat·ing
dis·si·pa·tion
dis·so·ci·ate
  -at·ed, -at·ing
dis·so·ci·a·tion
dis·sol·u·ble

dis·so·lute
dis·so·lu·tion
dis·solve
dis·so·nance
dis·so·nant
dis·suade
  -suad·ed,
  -suad·ing,
  -suad·er
dis·sua·sion
dis·taff
  dis·taffs (pl)
dis·tance
  -tanced, -tanc·ing
dis·tant
dis·taste
dis·taste·ful
dis·tem·per
dis·tend
dis·ten·sion
dis·till
  -tilled, -till·ing
dis·til·late
dis·til·la·tion
dis·till·er
dis·till·ery
  -er·ies
dis·tinct
dis·tinc·tion
dis·tinc·tive
  -tive·ly, -tive·ness
dis·tin·guish
dis·tort
dis·tor·tion

dis·tract
dis·trac·tion
dis·traught
dis·tress
dis·trib·ute
  -ut·ed, -ut·ing,
  -u·tee
dis·tri·bu·tion
dis·trib·u·tor
dis·trict
dis·trust
dis·trust·ful
dis·turb
dis·tur·bance
dis·union
dis·use
dit·to
  dit·tos
di·ur·nal
di·va
  di·vas
di·van
div·er
di·verge
  -verged, -verg·ing
di·ver·gence
di·ver·gent
di·vers (various; cf.
  diverse)
di·verse (different;
  cf. *divers*)
di·ver·si·fy
  -fied, -fy·ing,
  -fi·ca·tion

di·ver·sion
di·ver·si·ty
  -ties
di·vert
di·vest
di·vide
  -vid·ed, -vid·ing,
  -vid·able
div·i·dend
div·i·na·tion
di·vine
  -vin·er, -vin·est,
  -vine·ly
di·vin·i·ty
  -ties
di·vi·sion
di·vorce
  -vorced, -vorc·ing,
  -vorce·ment
div·ot
di·vulge
  -vulged, -vulg·ing,
  -vul·gence
diz·zy
  -zi·er, -zi·est, -zi·ly
doc·ile
  doc·ile·ly,
  do·cil·i·ty
dock·et
dock·hand
dock·side
dock·yard
doc·tor
  -tor·al, -tored

doc·tor·ate
doc·trin·al
doc·trine
doc·u·ment
doc·u·men·ta·ry
doc·u·men·ta·tion
dodge
  dodged, dodg·ing
doe (deer; cf. *dough*)
  does
do·er
doe·skin
dog·catch·er
dog-eared
dog·fight
dog·ged
  -ged·ly, -ged·ness
dog·ger·el
dog·house
dog·ma
  dog·mas
dog·mat·ic
  -i·cal, -i·cal·ly
dog·ma·tism
do-good·er
dog pad·dle (n)
dog-pad·dle (v)
dog tag
dog·watch
dog·wood
doi·ly
  -lies
dol·ce
dol·drums

dole
  doled, dol·ing
dol·lar
dol·man (cloak; cf.
  dolmen)
  dol·mans
dol·men (monument;
  cf. *dolman*)
do·lor
do·lor·ous
  -ous·ly, -ous·ness
dol·phin
do·main
do·mes·tic
  -ti·cal·ly
do·mes·ti·cate
  -cat·ed, -cat·ing,
  -ca·tion
do·mes·tic·i·ty
do·mi·cile
  -ciled, -cil·ing
dom·i·nance
dom·i·nant
dom·i·nate
  -nat·ed, -nat·ing
dom·i·na·tion
dom·i·neer
dom·i·neer·ing
  -ing·ly
Do·min·i·can
do·min·ion
dom·i·no
  -noes
do·nate

-nat·ed, -nat·ing
do·na·tion
done (finished; cf.
  dun)
don·key
do·nor
don't (do not)
dooms·day
door·bell
door·keep·er
door·knob
door·mat
door·sill
door·stop
door·way
dor·mant
dor·mer
dor·mi·to·ry
  -ries
dor·mouse
dor·sal
dos·age
dos·sier
dot·age
dot·ard
dote
  dot·ed, dot·ing
dou·ble
  -bled, -bling
dou·ble-deal·ing
dou·ble-deck·er
dou·ble-faced
dou·ble-park
dou·ble-quick

dou·blet
dou·ble take
dou·ble-talk (n)
dou·ble-think
dou·ble time (n)
dou·ble-time (v)
doubt·ful
doubt·less
dough (bread; cf.
  doe)
dough·boy
dough·nut
doused
  doused, dous·ing
dove·tail
dow·a·ger
dowdy
  dowd·i·er,
  dowd·i·est,
  dowd·i·ness
dow·el
  -eled, -el·ing
dow·er
down-and-out
down·beat
down·cast
down·fall
down·grade
down·heart·ed
down·hill
down·pour
down·range
down·right
down·spout

Down's syndrome
down·stage
down·stairs
down·state
down·stream
down·stroke
down·swing
down·time
down-to-earth
down·town
down·trend
down·trod·den
down·turn
down·ward
down·wind
downy
  down·i·er,
  down·i·est
dow·ry
  -ries
dox·ol·o·gy
  -gies
doz·en
drab
  drab·ber,
  drab·best
drach·ma
  drach·mas
dra·co·ni·an
draft (draw; cf.
  draught, drought)
  draft·able,
  draft·er
drafts·man

drag
  dragged,
  drag·ging
drag·line
drag·net
drag·on
drag·on·fly
dra·goon
drain·age
drain·pipe
dra·mat·ic
dra·ma·tist
dra·ma·tize
  -tized, -tiz·ing
drap·ery
  -er·ies
dras·tic
  -ti·cal·ly
draught (drink; cf.
  draft, drought)
draw·bar
draw·ee
draw·er
dray·age
dread·ful
dream·land
dreamy
  dream·i·er,
  dream·i·est,
  dream·i·ly
drea·ry
  -ri·er, -ri·est
dress·er
dress·mak·er

drib·ble
  -bled, -bling
drift·wood
drill
drill·mas·ter
drill press
drink·able
drip
  dripped,
  drip·ping
drip-dry
drive
  driv·ing, driv·able
drive-in
driv·er
drive·way
driz·zle
  -zled, -zling
drom·e·dary
drop
  dropped,
  drop·ping
drop in (v)
drop-in (n)
drop-kick (v)
drop·kick (n)
drop leaf
drop·light
drop out (v)
drop·out (n)
drop·per
drop·sy
drought (dryness;
  cf. *draft, draught*)

drowsy
  drows·i·er,
  drows·i·est,
  drows·i·ly
drudg·ery
drug
  drugged,
  drug·ging
drug·gist
drug·store
drum
  drummed,
  drum·ming
drum·beat
drum·mer
drum·roll
drum·stick
drunk·ard
drunk·en
dry
  dries, dried, dri·er,
  dri·est
dry cell
dry-clean (v)
dry clean·ing
dry dock (n)
dry-dock (v)
dry rot (n)
dry-rot (v)
dry run
du·al (twofold; cf.
  duel)
du·bi·ous
du·cal

-cal·ly
duch·ess
duchy
  duch·ies
duck·ling
dud·geon
due
du·el (combat; cf.
  dual)
du·et
dug·out
duke
  duke·dom
dul·cet
dul·ci·mer
dull·ard
dumb·bell
dumb·wait·er
dum·my
  -mies, -mied,
  -my·ing
dump
dump·ling
dun (demand for
  payment; cf. *done*)
  dunned, dun·ning
dun·ga·ree
dun·geon
duo·dec·i·mal
du·o·de·num
du·plex
du·pli·cate
  -cat·ed, -cat·ing
du·pli·ca·tion

du·pli·ca·tor
du·plic·i·ty
du·ra·ble
  -bil·i·ty
dur·ing
dusky
  dusk·i·er,
  dusk·i·est
dust·bin
dust bowl
dust·cov·er
dust mop
dust·pan
dust storm
dusty
  dust·i·er,
  dust·i·est,
  dust·i·ly
Dutch ov·en
Dutch treat
du·te·ous
du·ti·able
du·ti·ful
du·ty
  -ties
dwell·ing
dwin·dle
  -dled, -dling
dye (color; cf. *die*)
  dyed (colored; cf.
  died), dye·ing
  (coloring; cf.
  dying)
dy·nam·ic

dy·na·mite
 -mit·ed, -mit·ing
dy·na·mo
 -mos
dy·na·mom·e·ter
dy·nast

dy·nas·ty
dys·en·tery
 -ter·ies (pl)
dys·func·tion
dys·lex·ia
 -lex·ic

dys·pep·sia
dys·pep·tic
dys·pho·ria
dys·tro·phy
 -phies

E

ea·ger
ea·gle
ear·ache
ear·drop
ear·drum
ear·ly
 -li·er, -li·est
ear·mark
earn (gain; cf. *urn*)
ear·nest
earn·ings
ear·phone
ear·ring
ear·shot
ear·split·ting
earth·born
earth·bound
earth·en·ware
earth·ly
 -li·ness
earth·quake
earth·ward

earth·wards
earth·work
earth·worm
ear·wax
ear·wig
ea·sel
ease·ment
eas·i·ly
east·bound
Eas·ter
east·ern
East·ern·er
east·ward
easy·go·ing
eat·able
eaves
ebb
eb·o·ny
 -nies
ebul·lient
eb·ul·li·tion
ec·cen·tric

ec·cen·tric·i·ty
 -ties
ec·cle·si·as·ti·cal
ech·e·lon
echo
 ech·oes
éclair
eclec·tic
eclipse
 eclipsed,
 eclips·ing
ecol·o·gy
 -gies, -gist
eco·nom·ic
eco·nom·i·cal
 -i·cal·ly
econ·o·mist
econ·o·mize
econ·o·my
 -mies
eco·sys·tem
ec·sta·sy

ec·stat·ic
ec·u·men·i·cal
ec·ze·ma
ed·dy
-dies, -died,
-dy·ing
edel·weiss
ede·ma
edge·ways
edg·ing
ed·i·ble
-bil·i·ty
edict
ed·i·fi·ca·tion
ed·i·fice
ed·i·fy
-fied, -fy·ing
ed·it
edi·tion (printing;
cf. *addition*)
ed·i·tor
ed·i·to·ri·al
ed·i·to·ri·al·ize
-ized, -iz·ing
ed·u·ca·ble
ed·u·cate
-cat·ed, -cat·ing
ed·u·ca·tion
ed·u·ca·tive
ed·u·ca·tor
ef·face
-faced, -fac·ing,
-face·ment
ef·fect (result; cf.

affect)
ef·fec·tive
-tive·ly,
-tive·ness
ef·fec·tu·al
ef·fec·tu·ate
-at·ed, -at·ing
ef·fem·i·nate
ef·fer·vesce
-vesced, -vesc·ing
ef·fete
ef·fi·ca·cious
ef·fi·ca·cy
-cies
ef·fi·cien·cy
-cies
ef·fi·cient
ef·fi·gy
-gies
ef·flo·res·cence
-cent
ef·flu·ent (flowing
out; cf. *affluent*)
ef·flu·vi·um
-via (pl)
ef·fort
ef·front·ery
ef·fu·sion
ef·fu·sive
egg·head
egg·nog
egg·plant
ego
egos

ego·cen·tric
ego·ism
ego·ist
ego·tism
egre·gious
egress
ei·der
eight
eighteen
-teenth
eighth
eighths
eighty
eight·ies,
eight·i·eth
ei·ther
ejac·u·late
-lat·ed, -lat·ing
ejac·u·la·tion
eject
elab·o·rate
-rat·ed, -rat·ing
élan
elapse (pass; cf. *lapse*)
elapsed, elaps·ing
elas·tic
elas·tic·i·ty
ela·tion
el·bow·room
el·der
el·der·ber·ry
el·dest
elect
elec·tion

elec·tive

elec·tor

elec·tor·al

elec·tor·ate

elec·tric

elec·tri·cal

elec·tri·cian

elec·tric·i·ty

elec·tri·fi·ca·tion

elec·tri·fy
  -fied, -fy·ing

elec·tro·cute
  -cut·ed, -cut·ing,
  -cu·tion

elec·trode

elec·trol·y·sis

elec·tro·lyte

elec·tro·mag·net

elec·tro·me·chan·i·cal

elec·tron

elec·tron·ic

elec·tron·ic mail

elec·tro·plate

elec·tro·scope

elec·tro·ther·mal
  -mal·ly

elec·tro·type

el·e·gance

el·e·gant

ele·gi·ac

el·e·gy
  -gies

el·e·ment

el·e·men·tal

el·e·men·ta·ry

el·e·phant

el·e·phan·tine

el·e·vate
  -vat·ed, -vat·ing

el·e·va·tor

elev·en
  -enth

elf
  elves (pl)

elic·it (draw out; cf.
  illicit)

el·i·gi·bil·i·ty

el·i·gi·ble (quali-
  fied; cf. *illegible,
  ineligible*)

elim·i·nate
  -nat·ed, -nat·ing

eli·sion

elite

elix·ir

Eliz·a·be·than

el·lipse

el·lip·sis
  -ses (pl)

el·lip·tic

el·o·cu·tion

elon·gate
  -gat·ed, -gat·ing

elon·ga·tion

elope
  eloped, elop·ing

el·o·quence

el·o·quent

else·where

elu·ci·date
  -dat·ed, -dat·ing,
  -da·tion

elude (escape; cf.
  allude)
  elud·ed, elud·ing

elu·sive (evasive; cf.
  illusive)

ema·ci·ate
  -at·ed, -at·ing

em·a·nate
  -nat·ed, -nat·ing

em·a·na·tion

eman·ci·pate
  -pat·ed, -pat·ing

eman·ci·pa·tion

emas·cu·late
  -lat·ed, -lat·ing

em·balm

em·bank·ment

em·bar·go
  -goes

em·bar·rass

em·bar·rass·ment

em·bas·sy
  -sies

em·bed
  -bed·ded,
  -bed·ding

em·bel·lish

em·bez·zle
  -zled, -zling,
  -zle·ment

em·bit·ter
em·bla·zon
  -zoned, -zon·ing
em·blem
em·blem·at·ic
em·bodi·ment
em·body
  -bod·ied,
  -body·ing
em·bold·en
em·bo·lism
em·boss
em·brace
  -braced, -brac·ing
em·bra·sure
em·broi·dery
  -der·ies
em·broil
em·bryo
  -bry·os
em·bry·on·ic
emend (correct; cf.
  amend)
emen·da·tion
em·er·ald
emerge
  emerged,
  emerg·ing
emer·gence
emer·gen·cy
  -cies
emer·gent
emer·i·tus
  -i·ti (pl)

em·i·grant
  (outgoing; cf.
  immigrant)
em·i·grate
  -grat·ed, -grat·ing
émi·gré
em·i·nence
em·i·nent (promi-
  nent; cf. *imma-
  nent, imminent*)
emir
em·is·sary
  -sar·ies
emis·sion
emit
  emit·ted,
  emit·ting
emol·lient
emol·u·ment
emo·tion
emo·tion·al
em·per·or
em·pha·sis
  -pha·ses (pl)
em·pha·size
  -sized, -siz·ing
em·phat·ic
em·phy·se·ma
em·pire
em·pir·ic
em·pir·i·cal
em·ploy
  -ploy·er
em·ploy·able

-abil·i·ty
em·ploy·ee
em·ploy·ment
em·po·ri·um
  -ri·ums
em·pow·er
em·press (n)(female
  ruler; cf. *impress*)
emp·ty
  -ties, -tied, -ti·ness
emp·ty-head·ed
em·py·re·an
emu
em·u·late
  -lat·ed, -lat·ing
em·u·la·tion
emul·si·fy
  -fied, -fy·ing,
  -fi·able
emul·sion
en·able
  -abled, -abling
en·act
en·act·ment
enam·el
  -eled, -eling
enam·el·ware
en·am·or
  -ored, -or·ing
en·camp·ment
en·caus·tic
en·ceph·a·lo·gram
en·chant·ing
en·chant·ment

en·chant·ress
en·chi·la·da
en·cir·cle
en·clave
en·close
en·clo·sure
en·co·mi·um
  -mi·ums
en·com·pass
en·core
  -cored, -cor·ing
en·coun·ter
  -tered, -ter·ing
en·cour·age
  -aged, -ag·ing
en·cour·age·ment
en·croach
  -croach·ment
en·cum·ber
  -bered, -ber·ing
en·cum·brance
en·cyc·li·cal
en·cy·clo·pe·dia
en·dan·ger
  -gered, -ger·ing
en·dear
en·dear·ment
en·deav·or
  -ored, -or·ing
en·dem·ic
end·ing
en·dive
end·less
end·line

end·long
end·most
end·note
en·do·crine gland
en·dor·phin
en·dorse
  -dorsed, -dors·ing
en·dorse·ment
en·dow
en·dow·ment
end prod·uct
end ta·ble
en·dur·able
en·dur·ance
en·dure
  -dured, -dur·ing
end·ways
en·e·ma
en·e·my
  -mies
en·er·get·ic
en·er·gize
  -gized, -giz·ing
en·er·giz·er
en·er·gy
  -gies
en·er·vate
  -vat·ed, -vat·ing
en·fee·ble
  -bled, -bling
en·fold
en·force
  -force·able,
  -force·ment

en·fran·chise
  -chised, -chis·ing,
  -chise·ment
en·gage
  -gaged, -gag·ing
en·gage·ment
en·gen·der
  -dered, -der·ing
en·gine
en·gi·neer
en·gi·neer·ing
En·glish
En·glish·man
En·glish·wom·an
en·graft
en·grave
  -graved,
  -grav·ing,
  -grav·er
en·gross
en·gross·ing
en·gross·ment
en·gulf
en·hance
  -hanced,
  -hanc·ing,
  -hance·ment
enig·ma
enig·mat·ic
en·join
en·joy
  -joy·able,
  -joy·ably
en·joy·ment

en·large
  -larged, -larg·ing
en·large·ment
en·light·en
  -ened, -en·ing
en·light·en·ment
en·list
  -list·ee, -list·ment
en·liv·en
en·mi·ty
  -ties
en·nui
enor·mi·ty
  -ties
enor·mous
enough
en·rage
en·rap·ture
  -tured, -tur·ing
en·rich
  -rich·ment
en·robe
en·roll
  -rolled, -roll·ee
en·roll·ment
en route
en·sconce
  -sconced,
  -sconc·ing
en·sem·ble
en·shrine
en·shroud
en·sign
en·slave

-slave·ment
en·snare
en·sue
  -sued, -su·ing
en·sure
  -sured, -sur·ing
en·tail
  -tail·ment
en·tan·gle
en·tan·gle·ment
en·ter
  -ter·ing
en·tered
en·ter·prise
en·ter·pris·ing
en·ter·tain
  -tain·er
en·ter·tain·ment
en·thrall
  -thralled,
  -thrall·ing
en·throne
en·thuse
  -thused, -thus·ing
en·thu·si·asm
en·thu·si·ast
en·thu·si·as·tic
  -ti·cal·ly
en·tice
  -ticed, -tic·ing,
  -tice·ment
en·tire
en·tire·ty
  -ties

en·ti·tle
  -tling
en·ti·tled
en·ti·ty
  -ties
en·tomb
en·tomb·ment
en·to·mol·o·gy
  (insects; cf.
  etymology)
en·tou·rage
en·trails
en·train
en·trance
  -tranced,
  -tranc·ing
en·trant
en·trap
  -trap·ment
en·treat
en·treaty
  -treat·ies
en·tree
en·tre·pre·neur
  -neur·ial,
  -neur·ship
en·try
  -tries
en·try·way
en·twine
enu·mer·ate
  -at·ed, -at·ing,
  -a·tion
enu·mer·a·tor

en·un·ci·ate
  -at·ed, -at·ing,
  -a·tion
en·vel·op (v)
  -op·ment
en·ve·lope (n)
en·ven·om
en·vi·able
  -ably
en·vi·ous
en·vi·ron
en·vi·ron·ment
en·vi·ron·men·tal
en·vis·age
  -aged, -ag·ing
en·vi·sion
en·voy
en·vy
  -vies
en·zyme
ep·au·let
ephem·er·al
ep·ic (poem; cf.
  epoch)
  ep·i·cal
ep·i·cure
ep·i·cu·re·an
ep·i·dem·ic
ep·i·der·mal
epi·der·mis
ep·i·gram (witty
  saying; cf.
  epigraph, epitaph,
  epithet)

ep·i·graph (motto;
  cf. *epigram,*
  epitaph, epithet)
ep·i·graph·ic
ep·i·lep·sy
  -sies
ep·i·lep·tic
ep·i·logue
epiph·a·ny
  -nies
epis·co·pal
Epis·co·pa·lian
ep·i·sode
ep·i·sod·ic
ep·i·sod·i·cal
epis·tle
epis·to·lary
  -lar·ies
ep·i·taph (inscrip-
  tion; cf. *epigram,*
  epigraph, epithet)
ep·i·thet (curse; cf.
  epigram,
  epigraph, epitaph)
epit·o·me
epit·o·mize
  -mized, -miz·ing
ep·och (era; cf. *epic*)
ep·och·al
ep·oxy
  -ox·ied, -oxy·ing
equa·ble
  equa·bil·i·ty
equal

equaled,
  equal·ing
equal·i·ty
equal·ize
  -ized, -iz·ing
equal·iz·er
equal·ly
equa·nim·i·ty
equa·tion
equa·tor
equa·to·ri·al
eques·tri·an
equi·an·gu·lar
equi·dis·tant
equi·lat·er·al
equi·lib·ri·um
  -ri·ums
equi·nox
equip
  equipped,
  equip·ping
equip·ment
eq·ui·ta·ble
eq·ui·ty
  -ties
equiv·a·lence
equiv·a·lent
equiv·o·cal
equiv·o·cate
  -cat·ed, -cat·ing
era
erad·i·cate
  -cated, -cat·ing,
  -ca·tion

erase
  erased, eras·ing,
  eras·able (can be
  erased; cf.
  irascible)
eras·er
era·sure
erect
erec·tion
er·go·nom·ics
  -nom·i·cal·ly
er·mine
  -mines
ero·sion
ero·sive
erot·ic
err
er·rand
er·rant
er·ra·ta (pl)
  -tum (sing)
er·rat·ic
er·ro·ne·ous
er·ror
erst·while
er·u·dite
er·u·di·tion
erupt (break out; cf.
  irrupt)
  erupt·ible
erup·tion
es·ca·late
  -lat·ed, -lat·ing,
  -la·tion

es·ca·la·tor
es·ca·pade
es·cape
  -caped, -cap·ing,
  -cap·er
es·cape·ment
es·cap·ism
es·ca·role
es·cheat
es·chew
es·cort
es·cri·toire
es·crow
Es·ki·mo
  -mo (pl)
esoph·a·gus
  -gi (pl)
es·o·ter·ic
es·pe·cial
es·pe·cial·ly
Es·pe·ran·to
es·pi·o·nage
es·pla·nade
es·pous·al
es·pouse
  -poused,
  -pous·ing, -pous·er
espres·so
  -sos
es·prit
es·py
  -pied, -py·ing
es·quire
es·say (try; cf. *assay*)

es·say·ist
es·sence
es·sen·tial
es·sen·ti·al·i·ty
  -ties
es·tab·lish
  -lished
es·tab·lish·ment
es·tate
es·teem
es·ti·ma·ble
es·ti·mate
  -mated, -mat·ing,
  -ma·tive
es·ti·ma·tion
es·top
  -topped, -top·ping
es·top·pel
es·trange
  -tranged,
  -trang·ing,
  -trange·ment
es·tu·ary
  -ar·ies
et cet·era
etch·ing
eter·nal
eter·ni·ty
  -ties
ether
ethe·re·al
  -al·i·ty, -al·ize
eth·i·cal
eth·ics

Ethi·o·pi·an
eth·nic
eth·yl
eth·yl·ene
et·i·quette
et·y·mol·o·gy (words;
   cf. *entomology*)
   -mol·o·gies,
   -mo·log·i·cal,
   -mo·log·i·cal·ly
eu·chre
   -chred, -chring
eu·clid·e·an
eu·lo·gize
   -gized, -giz·ing,
   -giz·er
eu·lo·gy
   -gies, -gis·tic
eu·phe·mism
   -mis·tic,
   -mis·ti·cal·ly
eu·pho·ni·ous
eu·pho·ny
   -pho·nies,
   -phon·ic
Eu·ro·pe·an
eu·tro·phi·ca·tion
evac·u·ate
   -at·ed, -at·ing,
   -a·tive
evac·u·a·tion
evade
   evad·ed, evad·ing,
   evad·er

eval·u·ate
   -a·tion, -at·ed,
   -at·ing
ev·a·nes·cence
evan·gel·i·cal
evan·ge·lism
evan·ge·list
evan·ge·lize
   -lized, -liz·ing,
   -li·za·tion
evap·o·rate
   -rat·ed, -rat·ing,
   -ra·tion
eva·sion
eva·sive
even
   evened, even·er
even·hand·ed
eve·ning (n)(time)
even·ing (v)
   (smoothing)
even·song
event
event·ful
even·tide
even·tu·al
even·tu·al·i·ty
   -ties
even·tu·al·ly
even·tu·ate
   -at·ed, -at·ing
ev·er·green
ev·er·last·ing
ev·er·more

ev·ery·body
ev·ery·day
ev·ery·place
ev·ery·thing
ev·ery·where
evict
   evic·tion, evic·tor
ev·i·dence
   -denced,
   -denc·ing
ev·i·dent
ev·i·den·tial
ev·i·den·tia·ry
evince
   evinced,
   evinc·ing,
   evinc·ible
evis·cer·ate
   -at·ed, -at·ing,
   -a·tion
evo·ca·ble
evo·ca·tion
   -ca·tor
evoc·a·tive
evoke
   evoked, evok·ing
evo·lu·tion
   -tion·ary,
   -tion·ari·ly,
   -tion·ism
evolve
   evolved,
   evolv·ing,
   evolv·able

ewe (sheep; cf. *yew,*
 you)
ex·ac·er·bate
 -bat·ed, -bat·ing,
 -ba·tion
ex·act
ex·act·ing
ex·ac·ti·tude
ex·act·ly
ex·ag·ger·ate
 -at·ed, -at·ing,
 -a·tion
ex·alt
ex·al·ta·tion
ex·am·i·na·tion
ex·am·ine
 -ined, -in·ing,
 -in·er
ex·am·ple
 -pled, -pling
ex·as·per·ate
 -at·ed, -at·ing,
 -at·ing·ly
ex·as·per·a·tion
ex·ca·vate
 -vat·ed, -vat·ing
ex·ca·va·tion
ex·ca·va·tor
ex·ceed (surpass; cf.
 accede)
ex·ceed·ing
ex·cel
 -celled, -cel·ling
ex·cel·lence

ex·cel·len·cy
ex·cel·lent
ex·cel·si·or
ex·cept (exclude; cf.
 accept)
ex·cep·tion
ex·cep·tion·al
ex·cerpt
ex·cess (surplus; cf.
 access)
ex·ces·sive
ex·change
 -changed,
 -chang·ing,
 -change·abil·i·ty
ex·che·quer
ex·cis·able
ex·cise
 -cised, -cis·ing
ex·cit·able
 -able·ness,
 -abil·i·ty
ex·ci·ta·tion
ex·cite
 -cit·ed, -cit·ing,
 -cit·ed·ly
ex·cite·ment
ex·claim
ex·cla·ma·tion
ex·clam·a·to·ry
ex·clude
 -clud·ed,
 -clud·ing, -clud·er
ex·clu·sion

ex·clu·sive
ex·com·mu·ni·cate
ex·com·mu·ni·ca·tion
ex·co·ri·ate
 -at·ed, -at·ing,
 -a·tion
ex·crete
 -cret·ed, -cret·ing,
 -cret·er
ex·cre·tion
ex·cru·ci·ate
 -at·ed, -at·ing
ex·cul·pate
 -pat·ed, -pat·ing,
 -pa·tion
ex·cul·pa·to·ry
ex·cur·sion
ex·cur·sive
ex·cuse
 -cused, -cus·ing,
 -cus·able
ex·e·cra·tion
ex·e·cute
 -cut·ed, -cut·ing
ex·e·cu·tion
ex·e·cu·tion·er
ex·ec·u·tive
ex·ec·u·tor
ex·ec·u·trix (fem)
 -tri·ces (pl)
ex·e·ge·sis
 -ge·ses (pl)
ex·em·plar
ex·em·pla·ry

ex·em·pli·fi·ca·tion
ex·em·pli·fy
  -fied, -fy·ing
ex·empt
ex·emp·tion
ex·er·cise (exertion;
  cf. *exorcise*)
  -cised, -cis·ing,
  -cis·able
ex·ert (exercise; cf.
  exsert)
ex·er·tion
ex·e·unt
ex·hal·ant
ex·ha·la·tion
ex·hale
  -haled, -hal·ing
ex·haust
  -haust·er,
  -haust·ible
ex·haus·tion
ex·haus·tive
ex·hib·it
  -i·tive, -i·to·ry,
  -i·tor
ex·hi·bi·tion
ex·hi·bi·tion·er
ex·hil·a·rate
  -rat·ed, -rat·ing,
  -rat·ing·ly
ex·hil·a·ra·tion
ex·hil·a·ra·tive
ex·hort
ex·hume

  -humed,
  -hum·ing,
  -hu·ma·tion
ex·i·gen·cy
  -cies
ex·ile
  -iled, -il·ing
ex·it
ex·ist
ex·ists
ex·is·tence
ex·is·tent
ex·is·ten·tial·ism
ex·it
ex·o·dus
ex·on·er·ate
  -at·ed, -at·ing,
  -a·tion
ex·or·bi·tant
ex·or·cise (expel; cf.
  exercise)
  -cised, -cis·ing
ex·o·ter·ic
ex·ot·ic
ex·pand
ex·panse
ex·pan·si·ble
ex·pan·sion
ex·pan·sive
ex par·te
ex·pa·ti·ate
  -at·ed, -at·ing
ex·pa·tri·ate
  -at·ed, -at·ing,

  -a·tion
ex·pect
ex·pec·tan·cy
  -cies
ex·pec·tant
ex·pec·ta·tion
ex·pec·to·rant
ex·pec·to·rate
  -rat·ed, -rat·ing,
  -ra·tion
ex·pe·di·en·cy
  -en·cies, -en·tial
ex·pe·di·ent
  -ent·ly
ex·pe·dite
  -dit·ed, -dit·ing
ex·pe·di·tion
ex·pe·di·tion·ary
ex·pe·di·tious
ex·pel
  -pelled, -pel·ling,
  -pel·la·ble
ex·pend·able
ex·pen·di·ture
ex·pense
  -penses, -pensed,
  -pen·sing
ex·pen·sive
ex·pe·ri·ence
  -enced, -enc·ing
ex·per·i·ment
ex·per·i·men·tal
ex·pert
  -pert·ly, -pert·ness

ex·pi·ate
-at·ed, -at·ing,
-a·ble
ex·pi·a·tion
ex·pi·a·to·ry
ex·pi·ra·tion
ex·pire
-pired, -pir·ing
ex·plain
-plain·able,
-plain·er
ex·pla·na·tion
ex·plan·a·to·ry
ex·ple·tive
ex·pli·ca·ble
ex·plic·it
ex·plode
-plod·ed,
-plod·ing, -plod·er
ex·ploit
ex·ploi·ta·tion
ex·plo·ra·tion
ex·plor·a·to·ry
ex·plore
-plored, -plor·ing
ex·plor·er
ex·plo·sion
ex·plo·sive
ex·po·nent
ex·port
-port·able,
-port·abil·i·ty
ex·por·ta·tion
ex·port·er

ex·pose (v)
-posed, -pos·ing,
-pos·er
ex·po·sé (n)
ex·po·si·tion
ex·pos·i·to·ry
ex post fac·to
ex·pos·tu·la·tion
ex·po·sure
ex·pound
ex·press
-press·er,
-press·ible
ex·pres·sion
ex·pres·sive
ex·press·ly
ex·press·way
ex·pul·sion
-pul·sive
ex·punge
-punged,
-pung·ing,
-pung·er
ex·pur·gate
-gated, -gat·ing,
-ga·tion
ex·pur·ga·to·ry
ex·qui·site
ex·sert (protrude; cf.
exert)
ex·sert·ed
ex·tant (existing; cf.
extent)
ex·tem·po·ra·ne·ous

ex·tem·po·rary
ex·tem·po·re
ex·tem·po·rize
-rized, -riz·ing,
-riz·er
ex·tend
ex·ten·si·ble
ex·ten·sion
ex·ten·sive
ex·tent (degree; cf.
extant)
ex·ten·u·ate
-at·ed, -at·ing,
-a·to·ry
ex·ten·u·a·tion
ex·te·ri·or
ex·ter·mi·nate
-nat·ed, -nat·ing,
-na·tion
ex·ter·mi·na·to·ry
ex·ter·nal
ex·ter·nal·ize
-ized, -iz·ing
ex·tinct
ex·tinc·tion
ex·tin·guish
-guish·able,
-guish·er
ex·tir·pate
-pat·ed, -pat·ing,
-pa·tion
ex·tol
-tolled, -tol·ling,
-tol·ler

ex·tort
ex·tor·tion
ex·tra
ex·tract
  -tract·abil·i·ty,
  -tract·able
ex·trac·tion
ex·trac·tive
ex·trac·tor
ex·tra·cur·ric·u·lar
ex·tra·dit·able
ex·tra·dite
  -dit·ed, -dit·ing
ex·tra·di·tion
ex·tral·i·ty
ex·tra·mar·i·tal
ex·tra·mu·ral
ex·tra·ne·ous
ex·traor·di·nary
  -nar·i·ly,
  -nari·ness
ex·trap·o·late
  -lated, -lat·ing,
  -la·tion

ex·tra·sen·so·ry
ex·trav·a·gance
ex·trav·a·gant
ex·trav·a·gan·za
ex·trav·a·sate
  -sat·ed, -sat·ing
ex·treme
ex·treme·ly
ex·trem·i·ty
  -ties
ex·tri·cate
  -cat·ed, -cat·ing,
  -ca·tion
ex·trin·sic
ex·tro·vert
ex·trude
  -trud·ed, -trud·ing,
  -trud·er
ex·tru·sion
ex·u·ber·ance
ex·u·ber·ant
ex·ude
  -ud·ed, -ud·ing
ex·ult

ex·ul·ta·tion
eye·ball
eye·brow
eyed
eye·drop·per
eye·ful
eye·glass
eye·hole
eye·lash
eye·let
eye·lid
eye·open·er
eye·piece
eye·sight
eye·sore
eye·spot
eye·strain
eye·tooth
eye·wash
eye·wink
eye·wit·ness
ey·rie (var. of *aerie*)

F

fa·ble
  -bled, -bling, -bler
fab·ric
fab·ri·cate

  -cat·ed, -cat·ing,
  -ca·tor
fab·ri·ca·tion
fab·u·lous

fa·cade
face·down
face-lift·ing
fac·er

fac·et (of diamond;
  cf. *faucet*)
fa·ce·tious
face-to-face
fa·cial
fac·ile
fa·cil·i·tate
  -tat·ed, -tat·ing,
  -ta·tor
fa·cil·i·ty
  -ties
fac·ing
fac·sim·i·le
fact find·er
fac·tion
  -tion·al,
  -tion·al·ism,
  -tion·al·ly
fac·tious (partisan;
  cf. *factitious,*
  fictitious)
fac·ti·tious
  (artificial; cf.
  factious,
  fictitious)
fac·tor
  -tored, -tor·ing,
  -tor·able
fac·to·ri·al
fac·to·ry
  -ries
fac·tu·al
fac·ul·ta·tive
fac·ul·ty

-ties
fad
fade
  fad·ed, fad·ing,
  fad·er
fag·ot
Fahr·en·heit
fail-safe
fail·ure
faint (weak; cf. *feint*)
  faint·ish, faint·ly
faint·heart·ed
fair (just; cf. *fare*)
fair·ground
fair·ly
fair-mind·ed
fair play
fair-spo·ken
fair trade (n)
fair-trade (v)
fair·way
fair-weath·er (adj)
fairy
  fairies, fairy·like
fairy·land
fairy tale (n)
fairy-tale (adj)
faith·ful
  -ful (pl), -ful·ly,
  -ful·ness
faith·less
fake
  faked, fak·ing,
  fak·er

fak·ir
fal·con
fal·la·cious
fal·la·cy
  -cies
fal·li·bil·i·ty
fal·li·ble
fall·ing-out
  fallings-out (pl)
fall out (v)
fall·out (n)
fal·low
false·hood
false
  false·ly,
  false·ness, fals·er
fal·set·to
  -tos
fal·si·fy
  -fied, -fy·ing,
  -fi·ca·tion
fal·si·ty
  -ties
fal·ter
  -tered, -ter·ing,
  -ter·er
fa·mil·iar
fa·mil·iar·i·ty
  -ties
fa·mil·iar·ize
  -ized, -iz·ing,
  -iza·tion
fam·i·ly
  -lies

fam·ine
fam·ish
fa·mous
fa·nat·ic
  -i·cal, -i·cal·ly
fa·nat·i·cism
fan·ci·ful
fan·cy
  -cies, -cied, -cy·ing
fan·cy-free
fan·cy·work
fan·fare
fan·tail
fan·ta·sia
fan·ta·size
  -sized, -siz·ing,
  -siz·er
fan·tas·tic
  -ti·cal, -ti·cal·ly
fan·ta·sy
  -sies, -sied, -sy·ing
far·a·day
far·a·way
farce
  farced, farc·ing
far·ci·cal
fare (price; cf. *fair*)
  fared, far·ing
fare·well
far·fetched
fa·ri·na
farm·er
farm·hand
farm·house

farm·ing
farm·land
farm·stead
farm·yard
far-off
far-out
far-reach·ing
far·row
far·see·ing
far·sight·ed
far·ther (at greater
  distance; cf.
  further)
far·ther·most
far·thest
far·thing
fas·cia
  -ci·ae (pl)
fas·ci·nate
  -nat·ed, -nat·ing
fas·ci·na·tion
fas·ci·na·tor
fas·cism
fash·ion
  -ioned, -ion·ing
fash·ion·able
fas·ten·ing
fas·tid·i·ous
fast·ness
fa·tal·i·ty
  -ties
fa·tal·ly
fate (destiny; cf. *fete*)
  fat·ed, fat·ing

fate·ful
fa·ther
  -ther·hood,
  -ther·less, -thered
fa·ther-in-law
  fa·thers-in-law (pl)
fa·ther·land
fa·ther·like
fa·ther·ly
fath·om
fath·om·able
fath·om·less
fa·tigue
  -tigued, -tigu·ing
fat·ten
  -tened, -ten·ing,
  -ten·ed
fat·ty
  -ti·er, -ti·est,
  -ti·ness
fa·tu·ity
fat·u·ous
fau·cet (for water; cf.
  facet)
fault·less
faulty
  fault·i·er,
  fault·i·ly,
  fault·i·ness
faun (deity; cf.
  fawn)
faux pas
  faux pas (pl)
fa·vor·able

fa·vored
fa·vor·ite
fa·vor·it·ism
fawn (deer; cf. *faun*)
faze
   fazed, faz·ing
fe·al·ty
fear·ful
fear·less
fear·some
fea·si·ble
   -bly, -bil·i·ty
feat (deed; cf. *feet*)
feath·er·bed·ding
feath·er·stitch
feath·er·weight
feath·ery
fea·ture
   -tured, -tur·ing,
   -ture·less
Feb·ru·ary
fe·cund
   -cun·di·ty
fed·er·al·ism
fed·er·al·ist
fed·er·al·iza·tion
fed·er·al·ize
   -ized, -iz·ing
fed·er·ate
   -at·ed, -at·ing
fed·er·a·tion
fee·ble
   -bler, -blest,
   -ble·ness

fee·ble·mind·ed
feed·back
feed·er
feed·stuff
feel·er
feel·ing
feet (pl. of *foot*; cf.
   feat)
feign
feigned
feint (trick; cf. *faint*)
feld·spar
fe·lic·i·tate
   -tat·ed, -tat·ing,
   -ta·tion
fe·lic·i·ty
   -ties
fe·line
fel·low
fel·low·ship
fel·on
fe·lo·ni·ous
fel·o·ny
   -nies
fe·male
fem·i·nine
fem·i·nin·i·ty
fem·i·nism
fe·mur
   fe·murs (pl)
fence
   fenced, fenc·ing,
   fenc·er
fend·er

fer·ment
   -able
fer·men·ta·tion
fe·ro·cious
fe·roc·i·ty
fer·ret
fer·ri·age
Fer·ris wheel
fer·rous
fer·ry·boat
fer·tile
fer·til·i·ty
fer·til·iza·tion
fer·til·ize
   -ized, -iz·ing,
   -iz·able
fer·til·iz·er
fer·vent
fer·vid
fer·vor
fes·ter
   -tered, -ter·ing
fes·ti·val
fes·tive
fes·tiv·i·ty
   -ties
fes·toon
fetch·ing
   -ing·ly
fete (festival; cf.
   fate)
fet·ed, fet·ing
fe·tish
fet·lock

fet·ter
fet·tle
fe·tus
feu·dal·ism
feu·dal·ize
  -ized, -iz·ing
feu·da·to·ry
feud·ist
fe·ver
  -vered, -ver·ing
fe·ver·ish
fey
fi·an·cé (masc)
fi·an·cée (fem)
fi·as·co
  -coes
fi·at
fi·ber·board
fi·ber·glass
fi·ber-op·tic (adj)
fi·ber op·tics (n)
fi·brous
fib·u·la
  -lae (pl)
fiche (microfilm; cf.
  fish)
  fiche (pl)
fick·le
fic·tion
  -tion·al, -tion·al·ly
fic·ti·tious
  (imaginary; cf.
  factious,
  factitious)

fid·dle
  -dled, -dling,
  -dler
fid·dle·stick
fi·del·i·ty
  -ties
fidg·ety
fi·du·cia·ry
  -ries
field
field day
field·er
field glass
field goal
field house
fiend
fierce
  fierc·er, fierc·est,
  fierce·ly
fi·ery
fi·es·ta
fif·teen
  -teenth
fifth
  fifths
fif·ty
  -ties, -ti·eth
fif·ty-fif·ty
fig·ment
fig·u·ra·tive
fig·ure
fig·ure·head
fig·u·rine
fil·a·ment

fil·bert
file
  fil·ing
filed
fil·ial
fil·i·bus·ter
  -tered, -ter·ing,
  -ter·er
fil·i·gree
  -greed, -gree·ing
fil·ing
Fil·i·pi·no
  Fil·i·pi·nos (pl)
fill·er
  fill·ers
fil·let
fill·ing
film·strip
fil·ter (strainer; cf.
  philter)
  -tered, -ter·ing
filthy
  filth·i·er,
  filth·i·est,
  filth·i·ly
fil·tra·tion
fi·nal
  -nal·ly
fi·na·le
fi·nal·ist
fi·nal·i·ty
  -ties
fi·nal·ize
  -ized, -iz·ing

fi·nance
-nanced, -nanc·ing
fi·nan·cial
fi·nan·cier
find·er
find·ing
fine
fined, fin·er,
fin·est
fine·ly
fine·ness
fin·ery
-er·ies
fi·nesse
-nessed, -ness·ing
fine-tune
fin·ger
-gered, -ger·ing
fin·ger bowl
fin·ger·print
fin·ger·tip
fin·icky
fi·nis
fin·ish
fin·ished
fi·nite
fir (tree; cf. *fur*)
fire·arm
fire·ball
fire·boat
fire·box
fire·break
fire·bug
fire·crack·er

fire-eat·er
fire fight·er
fire·fly
fire·house
fire·light
fire·man
fire·place
fire·plug
fire·pow·er
fire·proof
fire·side
fire tow·er
fire·trap
fire·wood
fir·ing
fir·kin
firm
firm·ly, firm·ness
first
first·born
first class (n)
first-class (adj, adv)
first·hand
first-rate
fis·cal (financial; cf.
physical)
fish (aquatic animal;
cf. *fiche*)
fish·er
fish·er·man
fish·ery
-er·ies
fish·hook
fish·ing

fish stick
fish·tail
fishy
fish·i·er, fish·i·est
fis·sion
-sioned, -sion·ing
fis·sion·able
fis·sure
-sured, -sur·ing
fit
fit·ted, fit·ting,
fit·ness
fit·ful
five·fold
fix·ate
-at·ed, -at·ing
fix·a·tion
fix·a·tive
fixed
fix·ing
fix·ture
fiz·zle
-zled, -zling
flab·ber·gast
flab·by
-bi·er, -bi·est,
-bi·ly
flac·cid
fla·con
flag·ging
flag·pole
fla·gran·cy
fla·grant
flag·ship

flag·staff
flag·stone
flail
flair (aptitude; cf.
  flare)
flaky
  flak·i·er,
  flak·i·est,
  flak·i·ness
flam·boy·ant
flame·out
flame·proof
fla·min·go
  -gos
flam·ma·ble
flan·nel
flap
  flapped, flap·ping
flap·jack
flap·per
flare (torch; cf. *flair*)
  flared, flar·ing
flare-up
flash·back
flash·board
flash·bulb
flash card
flash flood
flash·ing
flash·light
flash point
flashy
  flash·i·er,
  flash·i·est,

flash·i·ly
flat·bed
flat·boat
flat·car
flat·iron
flat·ten
  -tened, -ten·ing,
  -ten·er
flat·ter
  -ter·er, -ter·ing·ly
flat·tery
  -ter·ies
flat·top
flat·ware
flat·work
flaunt
fla·vor·ful
fla·vor
  -vored, -vor·ing
flax·seed
flaxy
  flax·i·er, flax·i·est
flea (insect; cf. *flee*)
flea·bite
flea-bit·ten
fledg·ling
flee (escape; cf. *flea*)
  fled, flee·ing
fleece
flesh
flesh·i·ness
flesh·ly
fleshy
  flesh·i·er,

flesh·i·est
flew (did fly; cf. *flu*,
  flue)
flex·i·ble
  -bly, -bil·i·ty
flex·time
flick·er
  -ered, -er·ing
fli·er
flight at·ten·dant
flight deck
flight pay
flight plan
flim·flam
  -flammed,
  -flam·ming,
  -flam·mer
flim·sy
  -si·er, -si·est,
  -si·ly
flint glass
flinty
  flint·i·er,
  flint·i·est,
  flint·i·ly
flip
  flipped, flip·ping
flip-flop
flip·pan·cy
  -cies
flip·pant
flip·per
flip side
flir·ta·tious

flit·ter
float·ing
floe (ice; cf. *flow*)
flood·gate
flood·light
flood·wa·ter
floor·board
floor·ing
floor lamp
floor·walk·er
flop·py
  -pies, -pi·er, -pi·ly
flop·py disk
flo·ral
flo·res·cence
flo·res·cent
flo·ri·cul·ture
flor·id
flo·ta·tion
flo·til·la
flot·sam
flounce
  flounced, flouncy,
  flounc·ing
floun·der
  -der (pl), -dered,
  -der·ing
flour (bread; cf.
  flower)
flour·ish
flow (of water; cf.
  floe)
flow·chart
flow·er (blossom; cf.

flour)
flow·er·pot
flow·ery
flown
flu (influenza; cf.
  flew, flue)
fluc·tu·ate
  -at·ed, -at·ing,
  -a·tion
flue (chimney; cf.
  flew, flu)
flu·en·cy
flu·ent
fluffy
  fluff·i·er,
  fluff·i·est,
  fluff·i·ness
flu·id
flu·id·ex·tract
flu·id·i·ty
flu·id·ounce
flu·o·res·cent
flu·o·ri·date
  -dat·ed, -dat·ing,
  -da·tion
flu·o·ride
flu·o·rine
flu·o·ro·scope
flur·ry
  -ries, -ried, -ry·ing
flut·ter
flux
fly·by
  fly·bys (pl)

fly-by-night
fly·catch·er
fly·er
fly·ing
fly·wheel
foamy
  foam·i·er,
  foam·i·est,
  foam·i·ness
fo·cal
fo·cal·ize
  -ized, -iz·ing,
  -iza·tion
fo·cus (sing)
fo·ci (pl)
fo·cus
  -cused, -cus·ing,
  -cus·able
fod·der
fog·bound
fog·gy (weather; cf.
  fogy)
  -gi·er, -gi·est,
  -gi·ness
fog·horn
fo·gy (person; cf.
  foggy)
  -gies, -gy·ish,
  -gy·ism
fold·er
fo·liage
fo·li·ate
fo·li·at·ed
fo·li·a·tion

fo·lio
  -li·os
folk·lore
folksy
  folks·i·er,
  folks·i·est
folk·tale
folk·way
fol·li·cle
fol·low
fol·low·er
fol·low·ing
fol·low through (v)
fol·low-through (n)
fol·low up (v)
fol·low-up (n, adj)
fol·ly
  -lies
fon·dant
fon·dle
  -dled, -dling, -dler
fond·ly
fond·ness
fon·due
font
fool·ery
  -er·ies
fool·har·dy
  -har·di·ly,
  -har·di·ness
fool·ish
fool·proof
fools·cap
foot·ball

foot·bath
foot·board
foot·bridge
foot·can·dle
foot·ed
foot·fall
foot fault (n)
foot·fault (v)
foot·gear
foot·hill
foot·hold
foot·ing
foot·lights
foot·lock·er
foot·loose
foot·mark
foot·note
foot·path
foot·print
foot·race
foot·rest
foot·sore
foot·step
foot·stool
foot·way
foot·wear
foot·work
for (function word;
  cf. *fore*)
for·age
  -aged, -ag·ing,
  -ag·er
for·ay
for·bear (be patient;

cf. *forebear*)
  -borne, -bear·ing,
  -bear·er
for·bear·ance
for·bid
  -bade, -bid·den,
  -bid·ding
forced
force·ful
for·ceps
  -ceps (pl)
  -ceps·like
forc·ible
fore (front; cf. *for*)
fore·arm
fore·bear (ancestor;
  cf. *forbear*)
fore·bode
fore·bod·ing
fore·cast
  -cast·ing,
  -cast·able, -cast·er
fore·close
fore·clo·sure
fore·fa·ther
fore·fin·ger
fore·foot
fore·front
fore·go
  -went, -gone,
  -go·ing
fore·ground
fore·hand
fore·hand·ed

fore·head
for·eign
for·eign·er
fore·judge
fore·lock
fore·man
fore·mast
fore·most
fore·name
fore·noon
fo·ren·sic
fore·or·dain
fore·part
fore·quar·ter
fore·run
  -ran, -run,
  -run·ning
fore·run·ner
fore·see
  -saw, -seen,
  -see·ing
fore·shad·ow
fore·short·en
fore·sight
for·est
  -est·al, -est·ed,
  -es·ta·tion
fore·stall
for·est·er
for·est·ry
fore·tell
  -told, -tell·ing,
  -tell·er
fore·thought

for·ev·er
fore·warn
fore·word (preface;
  cf. *forward*)
for·feit
for·fei·ture
forg·er
forg·ery
  -er·ies
for·get
  -got, -got·ten,
  -get·ting
for·get·ful
for·get-me-not
for·give·ness
for·giv·ing
for·go
  -went, -gone,
  -go·ing
for·lorn
form
for·mal
  -mal·ly (ceremoni-
  ally; cf. *formerly*),
  -mal·ness
form·al·de·hyde
for·mal·i·ty
  -ties
for·mal·ize
  -ized, -iz·ing,
  -iza·tion
for·mat
  -mat·ted,
  -mat·ting

for·ma·tion
for·ma·tive
for·mer (adj)
form·er (n)
for·mer·ly (previ-
  ously; cf.
  formally)
for·mi·da·ble
form·less
for·mu·la
  -las
for·mu·la·rize
  -rized, -ris·ing,
  -ri·za·tion
for·mu·late
  -lat·ed, -lat·ing,
  -la·tor
for·mu·la·tion
for·sake
  -sook, -saken,
  -sak·ing
for·swear
  -swore, -sworn,
  -swear·ing
for·syth·ia
fort (stronghold; cf.
  forte)
forte (talent; cf. *fort*)
forth (forward; cf.
  fourth)
forth·com·ing
forth·right
forth·with
for·ti·fi·ca·tion

for·ti·fi·er
for·ti·fy
  -fied, -fy·ing
for·tis·si·mo
  -mos
for·ti·tude
fort·night
FOR·TRAN
for·tress
for·tu·itous
for·tu·ity
  -ities
for·tu·nate
for·tune
  -tuned, -tun·ing
for·tune-tell·er
for·ty
  -ties, -ti·eth
for·ty-nin·er
fo·rum
  fo·rums
for·ward (ahead; cf.
  foreword)
  -ward·ly,
  -ward·ness
for·ward·er
for·ward·ing
for·wards
fos·sil
fos·sil·if·er·ous
fos·ter
  -tered, -ter·ing,
  -ter·er
foul (bad; cf. *fowl*)

foul·mouthed
foun·da·tion
found·er (n)
  -der·ing, -dered
foun·der (v)
found·ling
found·ry
  -ries
foun·tain
foun·tain·head
four·score
four·some
four·teen
  -teenth
fourth (next after
  third; cf. *forth*)
  fourths, fourth·ly
fowl (poultry; cf.
  foul)
  fowl (pl), fowl·er
fox·hole
fox·hound
fox ter·ri·er
fox-trot
foy·er
fra·cas
  -cas·es (pl)
frac·tion
frac·tion·al
frac·tious
frac·ture
  -tured, -tur·ing
frag·ile
  fra·gil·i·ty

frag·ment
frag·men·tar·y
fra·grance
fra·grant
frail·ty
  -ties
frame-up
frame·work
fram·ing
franc (money; cf.
  frank)
fran·chise
  -chised, -chis·ing
Fran·cis·can
frank (candid; cf.
  franc)
frank·furt·er
frank·in·cense
frank·ly
fran·tic
fra·ter·nal
fra·ter·ni·ty
  -ties
frat·er·nize
  -niz·ed, -niz·ing,
  -ni·za·tion
fraud·u·lence
fraud·u·lent
freak·ish
freck·le
  -led, -ling
free·board
free·born
free·dom

free-for-all
free·hand
free·hold
free lance (n)
free-lance (adj, v)
free·stand·ing
free·stone
free·style
free·think·er
free·way
freeze (from cold; cf.
  frieze)
  froze, fro·zen,
  freez·ing
freeze-dry
freez·er
freight
freight·er
fre·net·ic
fren·zy
  -zies, -zied,
  -zy·ing
Fre·on
fre·quen·cy
  -cies
fre·quent
fresh
  fresh·ly,
  fresh·ness
fres·co
  fres·coes
fresh·en
  -ened, -en·ing,
  -en·er

fresh·wa·ter
fret·ful
fret·work
fri·ar
fric·as·see
  -seed, -see·ing
fric·tion
fric·tion·al
Fri·day
friend
  friend·less,
  friend·less·ness
friend·ly
  -li·er, -li·est,
  -li·ness
friend·ship
frieze (ornament; cf.
  freeze)
frig·ate
fright
fright·en
  -ened, -en·ing,
  -en·ing·ly
fright·ful
frig·id
fri·gid·i·ty
frip·pery
  -per·ies
frit·ter
fri·vol·i·ty
  -ties
friv·o·lous
frog·man
frol·ic

-icked, -ick·ing
frol·ic·some
front·age
fron·tal
fron·tier
fron·tiers·man
fron·tis·piece
front·less
front man
front mat·ter
frost·bite
  -bit, -bit·ing,
  -bit·ten
frost·ing
froze
fro·zen
fru·gal
  -gal·i·ty, -gal·ly
fruit
fruit·cake
fruit·ful
fru·ition
fruit·less
frus·trate
  -trat·ed, -trat·ing
frus·tra·tion
fud·dy-dud·dy
  -dies
fu·el
  -eled, -el·ing
fu·el cell
fu·gi·tive
ful·crum
  -crums

ful·fill
-filled, -fill·ing,
-fill·ment
full
full·ness
full·back
full-blood·ed
full-bod·ied
full dress (n)
full-dress (adj)
full-fledged
full-scale
full-size
full time (n)
full-time (adj)
ful·ly
fum·ble
-bled, -bling, -bler
fu·mi·gate
-gat·ed, -gat·ing,
-ga·tion
func·tion
-tioned, -tion·ing
func·tion·al
fun·da·men·tal
-tal·ly
fun·da·men·tal·ism
fund-rais·ing
fu·ner·al (burial; cf.

funereal)
fu·ner·ary
fu·ne·re·al (solemn;
cf. *funeral*)
fun·gi·cide
fun·gous (adj)
fun·gus (n)(sing)
fun·gi (pl)
fu·nic·u·lar
fun·nel
-neled, -nel·ing
fun·ny
-ni·er, -ni·est,
-ni·ly
fur (hair; cf. *fir*)
furred, fur·ring
fur·be·low
fur·bish
fu·ri·ous
fur·long
fur·lough
fur·nace
fur·nish
fur·ni·ture
fu·ror
fur·ri·er
fur·ring
fur·row
fur·ry (with fur; cf.

fury)
-ri·er, -ri·est
fur·ther (in
addition; cf.
farther)
-thered, -ther·ing,
-ther·er
fur·ther·ance
fur·ther·more
fur·ther·most
fur·thest
fur·tive
fu·ry (rage; cf. *furry*)
-ries
fu·se·lage
fus·ible
fu·sion
fussy
fuss·i·er,
fuss·i·est,
fuss·i·ness
fu·tile
fu·til·i·ty
fu·ture
fu·tu·ri·ty
fuzzy
fuzz·i·er,
fuzz·i·est,
fuzz·i·ness

G

ga·ble
gad·about
gad·fly
gad·get
Gael·ic
gaffe
gai·ety
  -eties
gain
  gain·er
gain·ful
gait (manner of
  walking; cf. *gate*)
gal·axy
  -ax·ies
gal·lant
gal·lant·ry
  -ries
gal·le·on
gal·le·ria
gal·lery
  -ler·ies
gal·ley
  -leys
gal·lon
gal·lop
gal·lop·ing
gal·lows
  -lows (pl)

gall·stone
gal·va·nize
  -nized, -niz·ing,
  -ni·za·tion
gam·bit
gam·ble (bet; cf.
  gambol)
  -bled, -bling,
  -bler
gam·bol (play; cf.
  gamble)
  -boled, -bol·ing
gam·brel
game·keep·er
games·man·ship
gan·gli·on
  -glia (pl)
gang·plank
gan·grene
gang·ster
gant·let
ga·rage
  -raged, -rag·ing
gar·bage
gar·den
  -den·ed, -den·ing,
  -den·er
gar·de·nia
gar·gle

  -gled, -gling
gar·goyle
gar·land
gar·lic
gar·ment
gar·ner
  -nered, -ner·ing
gar·net
gar·nish
gar·nish·ee
  -eed, -ee·ing
gar·nish·ment
gar·ri·son
  -soned, -son·ing
gar·ru·li·ty
gar·ru·lous
gar·ter
gas·eous
gas·ket
gas·light
gas·o·hol
gas·o·line
gas·sy
  -si·er, -si·est,
  -si·ness
gas·tight
gas·tric
gas·tri·tis
gas·tro·in·tes·ti·nal

gas·tron·o·my
  -tro·nom·ic,
  -tro·nom·i·cal,
  -tro·nom·i·cal·ly
gate (door; cf. *gait*)
  gat·ed, gat·ing
gate·way
gau·dy
  gaud·i·er,
  gaud·i·est,
  gaud·i·ness
gauge
  gauged, gaug·ing,
  gauge·able
gaunt·let
gauze
gav·el
  -eled, -el·ing
gay·ness
ga·ze·bo
  -bos
ga·zelle
  -zelles
ga·zette
  -zett·ed, -zett·ing
gear·ing
gear·shift
gel·a·tin
ge·lat·i·nous
gen·darme
gen·der
  -dered, -der·ing
ge·ne·al·o·gy
  -al·o·gies,

  -a·log·i·cal,
  -a·log·i·cal·ly
gen·er·al
gen·er·al·i·ty
  -ties
gen·er·al·iza·tion
gen·er·al·ize
  -ized, -iz·ing,
  -iz·able
gen·er·al·ly
gen·er·al·ship
gen·er·ate
  -at·ed, -at·ing
gen·er·a·tion
gen·er·a·tive
gen·er·a·tor
ge·ner·ic
gen·er·os·i·ty
  -ties
gen·er·ous
gen·e·sis
  -e·ses (pl)
ge·net·ic
ge·nial
  -nial·i·ty, -nial·ly
gen·i·tal
gen·i·tive
ge·nius (greatly
  gifted; cf. *genus*)
  -nius·es (pl)
genre
gen·teel
gen·tile
gen·til·i·ty

  -ties
gen·tle
  gen·tler, gen·tlest,
  gent·ly
gen·tle·ness
gen·try
  -tries
gen·u·flect
  -flec·tion
gen·u·ine
ge·nus (classifica-
  tion; cf. *genius*)
  gen·era (pl)
ge·og·ra·pher
geo·graph·ic
ge·og·ra·phy
  -phies
geo·log·ic
ge·ol·o·gy
  -gies, -gist
ge·om·e·ter
geo·met·ric
geo·me·tri·cian
ge·om·e·try
  -tries
geo·ther·mal
ge·ra·ni·um
ge·ri·at·rics
Ger·man
ger·mane
ger·mi·cide
ger·mi·nate
  -nat·ed, -nat·ing,
  -na·tion

germ·proof
ger·ry·man·der
-dered, -der·ing
ger·und
ge·stalt
ge·sta·po
-pos
ges·tate
-tat·ed, -tat·ing
ges·ta·tion
ges·tic·u·late
-lat·ed, -lat·ing,
-la·tory
ges·tic·u·la·tion
ges·ture
-tured, -tur·ing
get
got, get·ting
get·away (n)
get-to·geth·er (n)
get up (v)
get·up (n)
gey·ser
ghast·ly
-li·er, -li·est,
-li·ness
gher·kin
ghet·to
-tos
ghost·ly
-li·er, -li·est,
-li·ness
ghoul (demon; cf.
goal)

gi·ant
gib·ber·ish
gibe (taunt; cf. *jibe,
jib*)
gibed, gib·ing
Gi·bral·tar
gid·dy
-di·er, -di·est,
-di·ness
gi·gan·tic
gig·gle
-gled, -gling
gig·o·lo
-los
gild (decorate with
gold; cf. *guild*)
gild·ed, gild·ing
gilt (gold-colored; cf.
guilt)
gilt-edged
gim·let
gim·mick
gin·ger
-gered, -ger·ing
gin·ger ale
gin·ger·bread
gin·ger·ly
ging·ham
gink·go
-goes
gin·seng
gi·raffe
-raffes
gird·er

gir·dle
-dled, -dling
girl·ish
girth
gist (essence; cf.
jest)
give-and-take
giv·en
give up
giz·zard
gla·cial
-cial·ly
gla·cier (ice; cf.
glazier)
glad
glad·ly, glad·ness
glad·den
-dened, -den·ing
glad·i·a·tor
glad·i·o·lus
-o·li (pl)
glam·or·ize
-ized, -iz·ing,
-iza·tion
glam·or·ous
glam·our
glance
glanced,
glanc·ing
glan·du·lar
glar·ing
glas·nost
glass·ine
glass·ware

glassy
glass·i·er,
glass·i·ness
glaze
glazed, glaz·ing,
glaz·er
gla·zier (glass-
worker; cf. *glacier*)
glean·ings
glee·ful
glid·er
glim·mer
-mered, -mer·ing
glimpse
glimpsed,
glimps·ing
glis·ten
-tened, -ten·ing
glit·ter
gloam·ing
glob·al
-al·ly
globe
glob·u·lar
glock·en·spiel
gloomy
gloom·i·er,
gloom·i·ly,
gloom·i·ness
glo·ri·fy
-fied, -fy·ing,
-fi·ca·tion
glo·ri·ous
glo·ry

glos·sa·ry
-ries
glossy
gloss·i·er,
gloss·i·est,
gloss·i·ness
glow·er
glow·worm
glu·cose
glue
glu·ey, glued,
glu·ing
glu·ten
-ten·ous
glut·ton
glut·ton·ous
glut·tony
-ton·ies
glyc·er·in
gnarl
gnarled
gnash
gnat
gnaw
gneiss
gnome
gnu (animal; cf.
knew, new)
gnu (pl)
go
goes, went, go·ing,
gone
go-ahead
goal (objective; cf.

ghoul)
goal·post
gob·ble
-bled, -bling
gob·bler
gob·let
gob·lin
go-cart
god·child
god·daugh·ter
god·dess
god·fa·ther
god·less
god·like
god·ly
-li·er, -li·est,
-li·ness
god·moth·er
god·par·ent
god·send
god·son
go-get·ter
gog·gle
-gled, -gling
goi·ter
gold·brick
gold·en
gold·en·rod
gold-filled
gold·fish
gold·smith
golf
Go·li·ath
gon·do·la

gon·do·lier
goo
  goo·ey
good-bye or
  good-by
good-heart·ed
good-hu·mored
good·ly
  -li·er, -li·est
good-na·tured
good·ness
good-tem·pered
good·will
goo·gol
goose·ber·ry
goose·flesh
goose·neck
go·pher
gorge
  gorged, gorg·ing,
  gorg·er
gor·geous
Gor·gon·zo·la
go·ril·la (animal; cf.
  guerrilla)
gos·pel
gos·sa·mer
gos·sip
Goth·ic
gou·lash
gourd
gour·met
gout
gov·ern

-ern·able
gov·er·nance
gov·ern·ess
gov·ern·ment
  -men·tal,
  -men·tal·ize,
  -men·tal·ly
gov·er·nor
gov·er·nor·ship
grab
  grabbed,
  grab·bing,
  grab·ber
grace·ful
grace·less
gra·cious
gra·da·tion
gra·di·ent
grad·u·al
grad·u·ate
  -at·ed, -at·ing
grad·u·a·tion
graf·fi·ti (pl)
  -to (sing), -tist
gram·mar
  -mar·i·an
gram·mat·i·cal
gram·o·phone
gra·na·ry
  -ries
grand·child
grand·daugh·ter
gran·deur
grand·fa·ther

gran·di·ose
gran·di·o·so
grand·moth·er
grand·son
grand·stand
grang·er
gran·ite
gran·ite·ware
grant·ee
grant-in-aid
  grants-in-aid (pl)
gran·u·lar
gran·u·late
  -lat·ed, -lat·ing
gran·u·la·tion
grape·fruit
grape·vine
graph·ic
graph·ite
grap·nel
grap·ple
  -pled, -pling, -pler
grasp
grassy
  grass·i·er
grate (irritate; cf.
  great)
  grat·ed, grat·ing,
  grat·er
grate·ful
grat·i·fi·ca·tion
grat·i·fy
  -fied, -fy·ing
grat·ing

119

gra·tis
grat·i·tude
gra·tu·itous
gra·tu·ity
  -ities
grav·el
  -eled, -el·ing
grave·stone
grave·yard
grav·i·tate
  -tat·ed, -tat·ing,
  -ta·tive
grav·i·ta·tion
grav·i·ty
  -ties
gra·vy
  -vies
gray·beard
gray·ish
grease
  greased, greas·ing
greas·er
grease·wood
greasy
  greas·i·er,
  greas·i·ness
great (large; cf.
  grate)
greedy
  greed·i·er,
  greed·i·est,
  greed·i·ness
green·back
green·ery

-er·ies
green-eyed
green·horn
green·house
green·ing
greet·ing
gre·gar·i·ous
Gre·go·ri·an
grem·lin
gre·nade
gren·a·dier
gren·a·dine
grey·hound
grid·dle
grid·iron
griev·ance
griev·ous
grif·fin
grill (broil; cf, *grille*)
grille (grating; cf.
  grill)
grill·work
gri·mace
grin
  grinned,
  grin·ning,
  grin·ning·ly
grind·stone
grip (grasp; cf. *gripe*,
  grippe)
  gripped,
  grip·ping, grip·per
gripe (complain; cf.
  grip, grippe)

grippe (sickness; cf.
  grip, gripe)
gris·ly (ghastly; cf.
  gristly, grizzly)
  -li·er, -li·est,
  -li·ness
gris·tle
gris·tly (full of
  gristle; cf. *grisly,
  grizzly*)
  -tli·er, -tli·est,
  -tli·ness
grist·mill
grit
  grit·ted, grit·ting
grit·ty
  -ti·er, -ti·est,
  -ti·ness
griz·zle
  -zled, -zling
griz·zly (bear; cf.
  grisly, gristly)
  -zli·est, -zli·est
groan (moan; cf.
  grown)
gro·cery
  -cer·ies
grog·gy
  -gi·er, -gi·est,
  -gi·ness
groove (rut; cf.
  grove)
  grooved,
  groov·ing

gross
gross·ly,
gross·ness
gro·tesque
ground·hog
ground·less
ground·ling
ground·wa·ter
ground·work
grove (trees; cf.
groove)
grov·el
-eled, -el·ing
grow
grow·ing, grow·er
growl·er
grown (matured; cf.
groan)
growth
grub
grubbed,
grub·bing
grub·stake
grudge
grudg·ing,
grudg·ing·ly
gru·el
gru·el·ing
grue·some
grum·ble
-bled, -bling, -bler
grumpy
grump·i·er,
grump·i·est,

grump·i·ness
guar·an·tee (n,
v)(secure; cf.
guaranty)
-teed, -tee·ing
guar·an·tor
guar·an·ty (n, v)
(a pledge; cf.
guarantee)
-ties, -tied, -ty·ing
guard·house
guard·ian
-ian·ship
guards·man
gu·ber·na·to·ri·al
guern·sey
-seys
guer·ril·la (soldier;
cf. *gorilla*)
guess
guess·ti·mate
guess·work
guest
guid·ance
guide·line
guild (association;
cf. *gild*)
guil·lo·tine
guilt (deserving
blame; cf. *gilt*)
guilt·less
guilty
guilt·i·er,
guilt·i·est,

guilt·i·ness
guin·ea
gui·tar
gull·ible
-ibly, -ibil·i·ty
gul·ly
-lies, -lied, -ly·ing
gum·drop
gum·my
-mi·er, -mi·est,
-mi·ness
gump·tion
gun·boat
gun·fire
gun·man
gun·nery
gun·pow·der
gun·shot
gun·wale
gup·py
-pies
gur·gle
-gled, -gling
gush·er
gus·to
-toes
gut·ter
gut·tur·al
guz·zle
-zled, -zling, -zler
gym·na·si·um
-si·ums
gym·nast
gym·nas·tic

gy·ne·col·o·gy
gyp·sum
gyp·sy
  -sies, -sied, -sy·ing

gy·rate
  -rat·ed, -rat·ing,
  -ra·tor
gy·ra·tion

gy·ro·com·pass
gy·ro·scope
gy·ro·sta·bi·liz·er

ha·be·as cor·pus
hab·er·dash·er
ha·bil·i·tate
  -tat·ed, -tat·ing
hab·it
hab·it·able
ha·bi·tant
hab·i·tat
hab·i·ta·tion
ha·bit·u·al
ha·bit·u·ate
  -at·ed, -at·ing
ha·ci·en·da
hack·er
hack·ney
  -neys, -neyed,
  -ney·ing
hack·saw
had·dock
hag·gard
hag·gle
  -gled, -gling
hail (ice; cf. *hale*)
hail·stone

hail·storm
hair (fur; cf. *hare*)
hair·brush
hair·cut
hair·dress·er
hair·line
hair·piece
hair·pin
hair·rais·ing
hairy
  hair·i·er,
  hair·i·ness
Hai·tian
hale (healthy; cf.
  hail)
  haled, hal·ing
half
  halves (pl)
half-and-half
half·back
half broth·er
half·heart·ed
half hour
half-moon

half note
half-pint
half sis·ter
half step
half·time
half-truth
half·way
hal·i·but
hall (room; cf. *haul*)
hal·le·lu·jah
hall·mark
hal·low
Hal·low·een
hal·lu·ci·nate
  -nat·ed, -nat·ing
hal·lu·ci·na·tion
hal·lu·ci·na·to·ry
hal·lu·ci·no·gen
  -gen·ic
hall·way
hal·ter
halve (v)(divide in
  half; cf. *have*)
  halved, halv·ing

ham·burg·er
ham·let
ham·mer
  -mered, -mer·ing
ham·mock
ham·per
  -pered, -per·ing
ham·ster
ham·string
  -strung
hand·bag
hand·ball
hand·bill
hand·book
hand·cuff
hand·ed·ness
hand·ful
  -fuls
hand·gun
hand·i·cap
  -cap·ping
hand·i·capped
hand·i·craft
hand·i·ly
hand·i·work
hand·ker·chief
  -chiefs
han·dle
  -dled, -dling
han·dle·bar
han·dler
hand·made
hand-me-down
hand·out

hand·rail
hand·saw
hand·shake
hand·some
  -some·ly
hands-on
hand·stand
hand·wo·ven
hand·write
  -wrote, -writ·ten
han·gar (shed; cf.
  hanger)
hang·er (for clothes;
  cf. *hangar*)
hang·ing
hang·nail
hang out (v)
hang·out (n)
han·ky-pan·ky
hap·haz·ard
hap·less
hap·pen
  -pened, -pen·ing
hap·pen·stance
hap·pi·ly
hap·pi·ness
hap·py
  -pi·er, -pi·est
hap·py-go-lucky
ha·rangue
  -rangued,
  -rangu·ing
ha·rass
har·bin·ger

har·bor
  -bored, -bor·ing
har·bor·age
hard-and-fast
hard·back
hard-boiled
hard copy
hard·cov·er
hard·en
  -ened, -en·ing
hard·fist·ed
hard·head·ed
hard·heart·ed
hard·ly
hard·ness
hard-nosed
hard-of-hear·ing
hard-pressed
hard·ship
hard·top
hard·ware
hard·wood
hard·work·ing
har·dy
  -di·er, -di·est,
  -di·ness
hare (rabbit; cf. *hair*)
  hares
hare·brained
hare·lip
har·em
har·le·quin
harm·ful
harm·less

har·mon·ic
har·mon·i·ca
har·mo·ni·ous
har·mo·nize
   -nized, -niz·ing
har·mo·ny
   -nies
har·ness
har·poon
harp·si·chord
har·ri·er
har·row
har·ry
   -ried, -ry·ing
hart (deer; cf. *heart*)
har·vest
has-been (n)
ha·sen·pfef·fer
hash·ish
hash mark
has·sle
   -sled, -sling
has·ten
   -tened, -ten·ing
hast·i·ly
hasty
   hast·i·er, hast·i·est,
   hast·i·ness
hatch·ery
   -er·ies
hatch·et
hatch·ing
hate·ful
ha·tred

hat·ter
haugh·ty
   -ti·er, -ti·est
haul (pull; cf. *hall*)
haunt
have (possess; cf.
   halve)
ha·ven
have-not (n)
hav·oc
Ha·wai·ian
haw·thorn
hay fe·ver
hay·rack
hay·seed
haz·ard
haz·ard·ous
haze
   hazed, haz·ing
ha·zel
hazy
   haz·i·er, haz·i·est,
   haz·i·ness
H-bomb
head·ache
head·band
head·cheese
head cold
head·first
head·hunt·er
head·ing
head·less
head·light
head·line

head·lock
head·long
head-on (adj)
head·phone
head·quar·ters
head·rest
head·room
head·set
head·strong
head·wait·er
head·way
head wind
heal (cure; cf. *heel*)
health
health·ful
healthy
   health·i·er,
   health·i·est
hear (listen; cf. *here*)
   heard (past tense
   of *hear*, cf. *herd*),
   hear·ing
hear·ken
   -kened, -ken·ing
hear·say
heart (in body; cf.
   hart)
heart·ache
heart·beat
heart·break
heart·bro·ken
heart·burn
heart·en
   -ened, -en·ing

heart·felt
hearth
hearth·stone
heart·i·ly
heart·land
heart·less
heart·sick
heart·warm·ing
hearty
  heart·i·er,
  heart·i·est
heat·er
hea·then
heath·er
heave
  heaved, heav·ing
heav·en
heav·en·ly
heav·en·ward
heavi·ly
heavy
  heavi·er, heavi·est
heavy-du·ty
heavy-foot·ed
heavy-hand·ed
heavy·heart·ed
heavy·weight
He·brew
hec·tic
hec·to·me·ter
hedge·hog
hedge·row
heed·ful
heed·less

heel (of foot; cf.
  heal)
heif·er
height
height·en
  -ened, -en·ing
hei·nous
heir (inheritor; cf.
  air)
heir·ess (fem)
heir·loom
he·li·cop·ter
he·lio·graph
he·lio·trope
he·li·pad
he·li·port
he·li·um
hel·lion
hel·met
helms·man
help·er
help·ful
help·less
help·mate
hel·ter-skel·ter
hemi·sphere
  -spher·ic
hem·line
hem·lock
he·mo·glo·bin
he·mo·phil·ia
hem·or·rhage
  -rhaged, -rhag·ing
hem·or·rhoid

hem·stitch
hence·forth
hence·for·ward
hep·a·ti·tis
hep·ta·gon
her·ald
he·ral·dic
her·ald·ry
  -ries
herb·age
herb·al
her·bi·cide
her·biv·o·rous
Her·cu·le·an
herd (group of
  animals; cf. *heard*)
herd·er
here (place; cf. *hear*)
here·abouts
here·af·ter
here·by
he·red·i·tary
he·red·i·ty
here·in
here·in·af·ter
here·in·be·fore
here·on
her·e·sy
  -sies
her·e·tic
he·ret·i·cal
here·to·fore
here·with
her·i·ta·ble

her·i·tage
her·mit
her·mit·age
her·nia
he·ro
  -roes
he·ro·ic
her·o·in (drug; cf. *heroine*)
her·o·ine (woman; cf. *heroin*)
her·o·ism
her·on
her·ring
her·ring·bone
her·self
hes·i·tan·cy
  -cies
hes·i·tant
hes·i·tate
  -tated, -tat·ing, -tat·ing·ly
hes·i·ta·tion
het·er·o·ge·ne·ity
het·er·o·ge·neous
hew (chop; cf. *hue*)
  hewed, hew·ing
hexa·dec·i·mal
hexa·gon
hex·ag·o·nal
hey·day
hi·a·tus
hi·ber·nate
  -nat·ed, -nat·ing,

-na·tion
hi·bis·cus
hic·cup
hick·o·ry
  -ries
hid·den
hide·away
hid·eous
hide·out
hi·er·arch
hi·er·ar·chi·cal
hi·er·ar·chy
  -chies
hi·ero·glyph·ic
high·ball
high chair
high-class
high fi·del·i·ty
high-grade
high·land
high·light
  -light·ed,
  -light·ing
high·ness
high-pitched
high-pres·sure
high-rise
high school
high-strung
high tech·nol·o·gy
high-ten·sion
high-test
high·way
hi·jack

hi·lar·i·ous
hi·lar·i·ty
hill·bil·ly
  -lies
hill·side
hilly
  hill·i·er, hill·i·est
him (pronoun; cf. *hymn*)
Hi·ma·la·yan
him·self
hin·der (v)
  -dered, -der·ing
hin·drance
hind·sight
Hin·du
hinge
  hinged, hing·ing
hin·ter·land
hip·bone
hip·pie
  -pies
hip·po·pot·a·mus
  -mus·es (pl)
hire
  hired, hir·ing
His·pan·ic
his·ta·mine
his·to·ri·an
his·tor·ic
his·tor·i·cal
his·to·ry
  -ries
his·tri·on·ic

hit
  hit·ting, hit·less
hit-and-miss
hit-and-run
hitch·hike
hith·er
hith·er·to
hoard (amass; cf.
  horde)
hoard·ing
hoarse (voice; cf.
  horse)
  hoars·er, hoars·est
hoax
hob·ble
  -bled, -bling
hob·by·horse
hob·gob·lin
hob·nob
  -nobbed,
  -nob·bing
ho·bo
  -boes
hock·ey
ho·cus-po·cus
hodge·podge
hoe
  hoed, hoe·ing
hoe·down
hog
  hogs, hogged,
  hog·ging
hog·wash
hold·er

hold·fast
hold·ing
hold over (v)
hold·over (n)
hold up (v)
hold·up (n)
hole (cavity; cf.
  whole)
hol·ey (full of holes;
  cf. *holly, holy,
  wholly*)
hol·i·day
ho·li·ness
hol·lan·daise sauce
hol·low
  -low·er, -low·est
hol·ly (shrub; cf.
  *holey, holy,
  wholly*)
ho·lo·caust
ho·lo·graph
hol·ster
ho·ly (sacred; cf.
  *holey, holly,
  wholly*)
  -li·er, -li·est
hom·age
hom·burg
home·body
home·com·ing
home·grown
home·land
home·less
home·like

home·ly (plain; cf.
  homey)
  -li·er, -li·est,
  -li·ness
home·made
home plate
home·room
home rule
home run
home·sick
home·site
home·spun
home·stead
home·stretch
home·town
home·ward
home·work
hom·ey (homelike;
  cf. *homely*)
  hom·ey·ness,
  hom·i·er,
  hom·i·est
ho·mi·cide
hom·i·ly
  -lies
ho·mo·ge·ne·ity
ho·mo·ge·neous
  (alike; cf.
  homogenous)
ho·mog·e·nize
  -nized, -niz·ing
ho·mog·e·nous (from
  same source; cf.
  homogeneous)

127

ho·mol·o·gous
hom·onym
ho·mo·phone
hon·est
hon·es·ty
  -ties
hon·ey
hon·ey·bee
hon·ey·comb
hon·ey·dew
hon·ey·moon
hon·ey·suck·le
hon·ky-tonk
hon·or
  -ored, -or·ing
hon·or·able
hon·o·rar·i·um
  -ia (pl)
hon·or·ary
hood·ed
hood·lum
hood·wink
hoof·er
hook up (v)
hook·up (n)
hook·worm
hooky
Hoo·sier
hope
  hoped, hop·ing
hope·ful
  -ful·ly
hope·less
hop·per

hop·scotch
horde (crowd; cf. *hoard*)
hore·hound
ho·ri·zon
hor·i·zon·tal
hor·mone
hor·net
horn·pipe
horny
horo·scope
hor·ri·ble
hor·rid
hor·ri·fy
  -fied, -fy·ing
hor·ror
hors d'oeuvre
  hors d'oeuvres (pl)
horse (animal; cf. *hoarse*)
horse·back
horse·fly
horse·hair
horse·play
horse·pow·er
horse·rad·ish
horse·shoe
hor·ti·cul·ture
  -tur·al
ho·siery
hos·pice
hos·pi·ta·ble
hos·pi·tal

hos·pi·tal·i·ty
  -ties
hos·pi·tal·ize
  -ized, -iz·ing
hos·tage
hos·tel·ry
  -ries
host·ess
hos·tile
hos·til·i·ty
  -ties
hos·tess
hos·tler
hot
  hot·ter, hot·test
hot air
hot·bed
hot-blood·ed
hot dog
ho·tel
hot·head
hot·house
hot plate
hot rod
hot·shot
hot tub
hot-wire
hour (60 minutes; cf. *our*)
hour·glass
hour-long
hour·ly
house
  housed, hous·ing

house·break
  -broke, -broken,
  -break·ing
house·clean
house·dress
house·hold
house·keep·er
house·lights
house·moth·er
house·plant
house sit·ter
house·wares
house·warm·ing
house·wife
  -wives (pl)
house·work
hov·el
hov·er
how·ev·er
how·it·zer
howl·er
how·so·ev·er
how-to
hua·ra·che
hub·bub
huck·le·ber·ry
huck·ster
hud·dle
  -dled, -dling
hue (color; cf. *hew*)
huffy
  huff·i·er,
  huff·i·est,
  huff·i·ness

huge
  hug·er, hug·est
hu·man
hu·mane
hu·man·ism
hu·man·i·tar·i·an
hu·man·i·ty
  -ties
hu·man·ize
  -ized, -iz·ing
hu·man·kind
hu·man·ly
hum·ble
  -ble·ness, -bly,
  -bled
hum·bug
hum·drum
hu·mer·us (bone; cf.
  humorous)
  hu·mer·i (pl)
hu·mid
hu·mid·i·fi·er
hu·mid·i·fy
  -fied, -fy·ing
hu·mid·i·ty
  -ties
hu·mi·dor
hu·mil·i·ate
  -at·ed, -at·ing,
  -a·tion
hu·mil·i·ty
hum·ming·bird
hu·mor
  -mored, -mor·ing

hu·mor·ist
hu·mor·ous (funny;
  cf. *humerus*)
hump·back
hunch·back
hun·dred
  hun·dredth
hun·dred·weight
Hun·gar·i·an
hun·ger
  -gered, -ger·ing
hun·gry
  -gri·er, gri·est,
  -gri·ly
hunt·er
hunts·man
hur·dle
  -dled, -dling, -dler
Hu·ron
hur·rah
hur·ri·cane
hur·ry
  -ried, -ry·ing
hurt
hus·band
hus·band·ry
hus·ky
  -ki·er, -ki·est
hus·tle
  -tled, -tling
hy·a·cinth
hy·brid
hy·dran·gea
hy·drant

hy·drate
  -drat·ed, -drat·ing
hy·drau·lic
hy·dro·car·bon
hy·dro·chlo·ric acid
hy·dro·chlo·ride
hy·dro·dy·nam·ics
hy·dro·elec·tric
hy·dro·gen
hy·drol·o·gy
hy·dro·ly·sis
hy·drom·e·ter
hy·dro·pho·bia
hy·dro·plane
hy·dro·pon·ics
hy·dro·scope
hy·dro·stat·ic
hy·drous
hy·e·na
hy·giene
  -gien·ic, -gien·ist

hymn (song; cf. *him*)
hym·nal
hym·nol·o·gy
hy·per·bo·la (curve;
  cf. *hyperbole*)
hy·per·bo·le
  (exaggeration; cf.
  hyperbola)
hy·per·crit·i·cal
  (overcritical; cf.
  hypocritical)
hy·per·sen·si·tive
hy·per·ten·sion
hy·phen
hy·phen·ate
  -at·ed, -at·ing
hyp·no·sis
hyp·not·ic
hyp·no·tism
  -tist
hyp·no·tize

  -tized, -tiz·ing
hy·po·chon·dria
hy·po·chon·dri·ac
hy·poc·ri·sy
hyp·o·crite
hyp·o·crit·i·cal
  (deceitful; cf.
  hypercritical)
hy·po·der·mal
hy·po·der·mic
hy·po·der·mis
hy·pot·e·nuse
hy·poth·e·cate
  -cat·ed, -cat·ing
hy·poth·e·sis (sing)
  -e·ses (pl)
hy·po·thet·i·cal
  -cal·ly
hys·te·ria
  -ter·ic, -ter·i·cal
hys·ter·ics

I

Ibe·ri·an
ibis (bird)
  ibis (pl)
ice
  iced, ic·ing
ice age
ice bag

ice·berg
ice·bound
ice-cold
ice cream
ice floe
ice pick
ice wa·ter

ici·cle
ic·ing
icon
icy
  ic·i·er, ic·i·est,
  ic·i·ness
idea

ide·al (perfect; cf.
  idle, idol, idyll)
ide·al·ism
ide·al·ist
ide·al·is·tic
ide·al·ize
  -ized, -iz·ing
ide·al·ly
iden·ti·cal
iden·ti·fi·ca·tion
iden·ti·fy
  -fied, -fy·ing,
  -fi·able
ide·ol·o·gy
  -gies
id·i·o·cy
  -cies
id·i·om
id·i·om·at·ic
id·io·syn·cra·sy
  -sies
id·i·ot
id·i·ot·ic
idle (inactive; cf.
  ideal, idol, idyll)
  idle·ness, idly,
  idling
idol (object of
  worship; cf. *ideal,
  idle, idyll*)
idol·a·trous
idol·a·try
  -tries
idol·ize

idyll (of rustic life;
  cf. *ideal, idle, idol*)
idyl·lic
if·fy
ig·loo
  -loos
ig·ne·ous
ig·nite
  -nit·ed, -nit·ing,
  -nit·able
ig·ni·tion
ig·no·ble
ig·no·min·i·ous
ig·no·mi·ny
  -nies
ig·no·ra·mus
  -mus·es
ig·no·rance
ig·no·rant
ig·nore
  -nored, -nor·ing
igua·na
il·e·um (intestine;
  cf. *ilium*)
  il·ea (pl)
il·i·um (pelvic bone;
  cf. *ileum*)
  il·ia (pl)
ilk
ill-ad·vised
ill-bred
il·le·gal
  -gal·i·ty, -gal·ly

il·leg·i·ble (unread-
  able; cf. *eligible,
  ineligible*)
  -bly, -bil·i·ty
il·le·git·i·ma·cy
il·le·git·i·mate
ill-fat·ed
ill-fa·vored
il·lib·er·al
il·lic·it (unlawful; cf.
  elicit)
il·lim·it·able
il·lit·er·a·cy
  -cies
il·lit·er·ate
  -ate·ly, -ate·ness
ill-man·nered
ill-na·tured
ill·ness
il·log·i·cal
ill-starred
ill-treat
il·lu·mi·nate
  -nat·ed, -nat·ing
il·lu·mi·na·tion
il·lu·mi·na·tive
il·lu·mine
  -mined, -min·ing
il·lu·sion
il·lu·sive (mislead-
  ing; cf. *elusive*)
  -sive·ly,
  -sive·ness
il·lu·so·ry

il·lus·trate
-trat·ed, -trat·ing,
-tra·tor
il·lus·tra·tion
il·lus·tra·tive
il·lus·tri·ous
ill will
im·age
-aged, -ag·ing,
-ag·er
im·ag·ery
-er·ies
imag·in·able
imag·i·nary
imag·i·na·tion
imag·i·na·tive
imag·ine
-ined, -in·ing
im·bal·ance
im·be·cile
im·be·cil·i·ty
im·bibe
-bibed, -bib·ing
im·bri·cate
-cat·ed, -cat·ing
im·bue
-bued, -bu·ing
im·i·ta·ble
im·i·tate
-tat·ed, -tat·ing,
-ta·tor
im·i·ta·tion
im·i·ta·tive
im·mac·u·late

im·ma·nent (within
the mind; cf.
eminent,
imminent)
im·ma·te·ri·al
im·ma·ture
im·mea·sur·able
im·me·di·a·cy
-cies
im·me·di·ate
im·me·di·ate·ly
im·me·mo·ri·al
im·mense
im·men·si·ty
-ties
im·merge
-merged,
-merg·ing,
-mer·gence
im·merse
-mersed,
-mers·ing
im·mer·sion
im·mi·grant
(incoming; cf.
emigrant)
im·mi·grate
-grat·ed, -grat·ing,
-gra·tion
im·mi·nence
im·mi·nent
(impending; cf.
eminent,
immanent)

im·mo·bile
im·mo·bi·lize
-li·za·tion, -liz·er
im·mod·er·ate
-ate·ly, -ate·ness,
-a·tion
im·mod·est
im·mo·late
-lat·ed, -lat·ing,
-la·tor
im·mor·al
im·mor·al·i·ty
im·mor·tal
im·mor·tal·i·ty
im·mor·tal·ize
-ized, -iz·ing
im·mov·able
im·mune
im·mu·ni·ty
-ties
im·mu·nize
-nized, -niz·ing,
-ni·za·tion
im·mu·nol·o·gy
im·mu·ta·ble
-ble·ness, -bil·i·ty
im·pact
im·pair
-pair·er,
-pair·ment
im·pal·pa·ble
im·pan·el
im·par·i·ty
im·part

im·par·tial
  -tial·i·ty, -tial·ly
im·par·ti·ble
im·pass·able
  (cannot be passed;
  cf. *impassible*)
im·passe
im·pas·si·ble
  (incapable of pain;
  cf. *impassable*)
im·pas·sion
  -sioned, -sion·ing
im·pas·sive
im·pa·tience
im·pa·tient
im·peach
  -peach·able,
  -peach·ment
im·pec·ca·ble
  -bly, -bil·i·ty
im·pe·cu·nious
im·pede
  -ped·ed, -ped·ing,
  -ped·er
im·ped·i·ment
im·ped·i·men·ta
im·pel
  -pelled, -pel·ling
im·pend
im·pen·e·tra·bil·i·ty
im·pen·e·tra·ble
im·per·a·tive
  -tive·ly, -tive·ness
im·per·cep·ti·ble

im·per·fect
  -fect·ly, -fect·ness
im·per·fec·tion
im·pe·ri·al
  -al·ly
im·pe·ri·al·ism
  -al·ist, -al·is·tic
im·per·il
  -iled, -il·ing,
  -il·ment
im·pe·ri·ous
im·per·ish·able
im·per·ma·nence
im·per·me·able
im·per·son·al
im·per·son·ate
  -at·ed, -at·ing,
  -ator
im·per·ti·nence
im·per·ti·nen·cy
  -cies
im·per·ti·nent
im·per·turb·able
  -ably, -abil·i·ty
im·per·vi·ous
im·pe·ti·go
im·pet·u·os·i·ty
  -ties
im·pet·u·ous
im·pe·tus
im·pi·ety
  -eties
im·pinge
  -pinged,

  -ping·ing,
  -pinge·ment
im·pi·ous
imp·ish
im·pla·ca·ble
im·plant
im·plau·si·ble
  -bil·i·ty
im·ple·ment
  -men·ta·tion
im·pli·cate
  -cat·ed, -cat·ing
im·pli·ca·tion
im·plic·it
im·plore
  -plored,
  -plor·ing,
  -plor·ing·ly
im·plo·sion
im·ply
  -plied, -ply·ing
im·po·lite
im·pol·i·tic
im·pon·der·a·ble
im·port
  -port·er
im·por·tance
im·por·tant
im·por·ta·tion
im·por·tu·nate
im·por·tune
  -tuned, -tun·ing
im·por·tu·ni·ty
  -ties

im·pose
-posed, -pos·ing,
-pos·er
im·po·si·tion
im·pos·si·bil·i·ty
im·pos·si·ble
im·pos·tor (pre-
tender; cf.
imposture)
im·pos·ture (fraud;
cf. *impostor*)
im·po·tence
im·po·tent
im·pound
im·pov·er·ish
im·prac·ti·ca·ble
-bly, -bil·i·ty
im·prac·ti·cal
im·pre·ca·tion
im·preg·na·ble
im·preg·nate
-nat·ed, -nat·ing
im·pre·sa·rio
-ri·os
im·press (influence;
cf. *empress*)
im·press·ible
im·pres·sion
im·pres·sion·able
im·pres·sive
im·pri·mis
im·print
im·pris·on
-on·ment

im·prob·a·ble
im·promp·tu
im·prop·er
im·pro·pri·ety
-eties
im·prov·able
im·prove
-proved,
-prov·ing
im·prove·ment
im·prov·i·dence
im·prov·i·dent
im·pro·vi·sa·tion
im·pro·vise
-vised, -vis·ing,
-vis·er
im·pru·dence
im·pru·dent
im·pu·dence
im·pu·dent
im·pugn
im·pulse
im·pul·sion
im·pul·sive
im·pu·ni·ty
im·pure
im·pu·ri·ty
-ties
im·pu·ta·tion
im·pute
-put·ed, -put·ing,
-put·able
in·abil·i·ty
in·ac·ces·si·ble

-bly, -bil·i·ty
in·ac·cu·ra·cy
-cies
in·ac·cu·rate
in·ac·tion
in·ac·tive
-tive·ly, -tiv·i·ty
in·ad·e·qua·cy
-cies
in·ad·e·quate
in·ad·mis·si·ble
in·ad·ver·tence
in·ad·ver·tent
in·ad·vis·able
in·alien·able
in·al·ter·able
inane
inane·ly,
inane·ness
in·an·i·mate
in·ap·peas·able
in·ap·pli·ca·ble
in·ap·po·site
in·ap·pre·cia·ble
in·ap·pre·cia·tive
in·ap·pro·pri·ate
in·apt
in·ar·tic·u·late
in·ar·tis·tic
in·as·much as
in·at·ten·tion
in·at·ten·tive
in·au·di·ble
in·au·gu·ral

in·au·gu·rate
  -rat·ed, -rat·ing
in·au·gu·ra·tion
in·aus·pi·cious
in·born
in·bound
in·bred
in·cal·cu·la·ble
in·ca·les·cence
in·can·desce
  -desced, -desc·ing
in·can·des·cence
in·can·des·cent
in·can·ta·tion
in·ca·pa·ble
  -bly, -bil·i·ty
in·ca·pac·i·tate
  -tat·ed, -tat·ing
in·ca·pac·i·ty
  -ties
in·car·cer·ate
  -at·ed, -at·ing,
  -a·tion
in·car·na·tion
in·cen·di·ary
  -ar·ies
in·cense
  -censed, -cens·ing
in·cen·tive
in·cep·tion
in·ces·sant
in·cest
in·ces·tu·ous
in·cho·ate

in·ci·dence
in·ci·dent
in·ci·den·tal
in·ci·den·tal·ly
in·cin·er·ate
  -at·ed, -at·ing,
  -a·tion
in·cin·er·a·tor
in·cip·i·ent
in·cise
  -cised, -cis·ing
in·ci·sion
in·ci·sive
  -sive·ly,
  -sive·ness
in·ci·sor
in·ci·ta·tion
in·cite (stir up; cf.
  insight)
  -cit·ed, -cit·ing,
  -cite·ment
in·clem·en·cy
in·clem·ent
in·cli·na·tion
in·cline
  -clined, -clin·ing
in·clude
in·clud·ed
-clud·ing
in·clu·sion
in·clu·sive
in·cog·ni·to
in·co·her·ence
in·co·her·ent

in·com·bus·ti·ble
in·come
in·com·ing
in·com·men·su·rate
in·com·mu·ni·ca·ble
in·com·pa·ra·ble
in·com·pat·i·bil·i·ty
  -ties
in·com·pat·i·ble
in·com·pe·tence
in·com·pe·tent
in·com·plete
in·com·pre·hen·si·ble
in·com·press·ible
in·com·put·able
in·con·ceiv·able
in·con·clu·sive
in·con·gru·ity
  -ities
in·con·gru·ous
in·con·se·quent
in·con·se·quen·tial
in·con·sid·er·able
in·con·sid·er·ate
in·con·sis·ten·cy
in·con·sis·tent
in·con·sol·able
in·con·spic·u·ous
in·con·stant
in·con·test·able
in·con·tro·vert·ible
in·con·ve·nience
in·con·ve·nient
in·con·vert·ible

in·cor·po·rate
-rat·ing, -ra·tion
in·cor·po·rat·ed
in·cor·po·re·al
in·cor·rect
in·cor·ri·gi·ble
-ble·ness, -bly,
-bil·i·ty
in·cor·rupt
in·cor·rupt·ible
in·crease
-creased,
-creas·ing,
-creas·able
in·creas·ing·ly
in·cred·i·ble
(unbelievable; cf.
incredulous)
-i·ble·ness, -i·bly,
-ibil·i·ty
in·cre·du·li·ty
in·cred·u·lous
(unbelieving; cf.
incredible)
in·cre·ment
-men·tal,
-men·tal·ly
in·crim·i·nate
-nat·ed, -nat·ing
in·crus·ta·tion
in·cu·bate
-bat·ed, -bat·ing
in·cu·ba·tion
in·cu·ba·tor

in·cul·cate
in·cum·ben·cy
-cies
in·cum·bent
in·cur
-curred, -cur·ring
in·cur·able
in·cur·sion
in·cur·vate
-vat·ed, -vat·ing,
-va·ture
in·debt·ed·ness
in·de·cen·cy
in·de·cent
in·de·ci·pher·able
in·de·ci·sion
in·de·ci·sive
in·de·co·rous
in·de·co·rum
in·deed
in·de·fat·i·ga·ble
in·de·fen·si·ble
in·de·fin·able
in·def·i·nite
in·del·i·ble
in·del·i·ca·cy
in·del·i·cate
in·dem·ni·fi·ca·tion
in·dem·ni·fy
-fied, -fy·ing, -fi·er
in·dem·ni·ty
-ties
in·dent
in·den·ta·tion

in·den·tion
in·den·ture
-tured, -tur·ing
in·de·pen·dence
in·de·pen·dent
in·de·scrib·able
in·de·struc·ti·ble
in·de·ter·min·able
in·de·ter·mi·nate
-nate·ly,
-nate·ness,
-na·tion
in·dex
in·dex·es or
in·di·ces (pl),
in·dex·er
in·dex·ing
In·dia
In·di·an
in·di·cate
-cat·ed, -cat·ing
in·di·ca·tion
in·dic·a·tive
in·di·ca·tor
in·dict (charge with
a crime; cf. *indite*)
in·dict·able
in·dict·ment
in·dif·fer·ence
in·dif·fer·ent
in·di·gence
in·dig·e·nous
(native to; cf.
indigent)

in·di·gent (poor; cf. *indigenous*)
in·di·gest·ible
in·di·ges·tion
in·dig·nant
in·dig·na·tion
in·dig·ni·ty
-ties
in·di·go
-gos
in·di·rect
-rect·ly, -rect·ness
in·di·rec·tion
in·dis·cern·ible
in·dis·creet (using poor judgment; cf. *indiscrete*)
in·dis·crete (not separate; cf. *indiscreet*)
in·dis·cre·tion
in·dis·crim·i·nate
in·dis·crim·i·na·tion
in·dis·pens·able
in·dis·posed
in·dis·po·si·tion
in·dis·put·able
in·dis·sol·u·ble
in·dis·tinct
in·dis·tin·guish·able
in·dite (write; cf. *indict*)
-dit·ed, -dit·ing
in·di·vid·u·al

in·di·vid·u·al·ism
in·di·vid·u·al·ist
in·di·vid·u·al·i·ty
-ties
in·di·vid·u·al·ize
-ized, -iz·ing, -iza·tion
in·di·vis·i·ble
In·do-Chi·nese
in·doc·tri·nate
-nat·ed, -nat·ing, -na·tion
in·do·lence
in·do·lent
in·dom·i·ta·ble
in·door
in·drawn
in·du·bi·ta·ble
in·duce
-duced, -duc·ing, -duc·ible
in·duce·ment
in·duct
in·duc·tion
in·duc·tive
in·duc·tor
in·dulge
-dulged, -dulg·ing, -dulg·er
in·dul·gence
-genced, -genc·ing
in·dul·gent

in·du·rate
in·dus·tri·al
in·dus·tri·al·ism
in·dus·tri·al·ist
in·dus·tri·al·ize
-ized, -iz·ing, -iza·tion
in·dus·tri·ous
in·dus·try
ine·bri·ate
-at·ed, -at·ing, -a·tion
in·ebri·ety
in·ed·i·ble
in·ef·fa·ble
in·ef·fec·tive
in·ef·fec·tu·al
in·ef·fi·ca·cious
in·ef·fi·ca·cy
in·ef·fi·cien·cy
-cies
in·ef·fi·cient
in·el·e·gance
in·el·e·gant
in·el·i·gi·ble (not qualified; cf. *eligible, illegible*), -bil·i·ty
in·el·o·quent
in·ept
-ep·ti·tude, -ept·ly, -ept·ness
in·equal·i·ty
in·eq·ui·ta·ble

137

in·eq·ui·ty
(unfairness; cf.
iniquity)
in·erad·i·ca·ble
in·ert
in·er·tia
in·es·cap·able
-ably
in·es·sen·tial
in·es·ti·ma·ble
in·ev·i·ta·ble
-ble·ness, -bly,
-bil·i·ty
in·ex·act
-ac·ti·tude, -act·ly,
-act·ness
in·ex·cus·able
in·ex·haust·ible
-ible·ness, -ibly,
-ibil·i·ty
in·ex·o·ra·ble
in·ex·pe·di·ent
in·ex·pen·sive
in·ex·pe·ri·ence
in·ex·pert
in·ex·pi·a·ble
in·ex·plain·able
in·ex·pli·ca·ble
in·ex·plic·it
in·ex·press·ible
in·ex·pres·sive
in·ex·pug·na·ble
in·ex·tin·guish·able
in·ex·tri·ca·ble

in·fal·li·ble
-bly, -bil·i·ty
in·fa·mous
in·fa·my
-mies
in·fan·cy
-cies
in·fant
in·fan·tile
in·fan·try
-tries
in·fat·u·ate
-at·ed, -at·ing,
-a·tion
in·fect
in·fec·tion
in·fec·tious
in·fec·tive
in·fe·lic·i·tous
in·fe·lic·i·ty
-ties
in·fer
-ferred, -fer·ring,
-fer·able
in·fer·ence
in·fer·en·tial
in·fe·ri·or
-or·i·ty
in·fer·nal
in·fer·no
-nos
in·fest
-fes·ta·tion
in·fi·del

in·fi·del·i·ty
-ties
in·field
in·fil·trate
-trat·ed, -trat·ing,
-tra·tion
in·fi·nite
in·fin·i·tes·i·mal
in·fin·i·tive
in·fin·i·ty
-ties
in·firm
in·fir·ma·ry
-ries
in·fir·mi·ty
-ties
in·flame
-flamed, -flam·ing
in·flam·ma·ble
in·flam·ma·tion
in·flam·ma·to·ry
in·flate
-flat·ed, -flat·ing
in·fla·tion
in·fla·tion·ary
in·flect
in·flec·tion
in·flex·i·ble
in·flict
in·flic·tion
in·flow
in·flu·ence
-enced, -enc·ing
in·flu·en·tial

in·flu·en·za
in·flux
in·form
in·for·mal
  -mal·i·ty, -mal·ly
in·for·mant
in·for·ma·tion
in·for·ma·tive
in·form·er
in·fract
  -frac·tion
in·fra·red
in·fra·struc·ture
in·fre·quent
in·fringe
  -fringed,
  -fring·ing
in·fringe·ment
in·fu·ri·ate
  -at·ed, -at·ing
in·fuse
  -fused, -fus·ing
in·fu·sion
in·ge·nious
  (inventive; cf.
  ingenuous)
in·ge·nue
in·ge·nu·ity
  -ties
in·gen·u·ous (candid;
  cf. *ingenious*)
in·glo·ri·ous
in·got
in·grained

in·grate
in·gra·ti·ate
  -at·ed, -at·ing,
  -a·tion
in·grat·i·tude
in·gre·di·ent
in·gress
in·grown
in·hab·it
in·hab·it·ant
in·hale
  -haled, -hal·ing
in·har·mo·ni·ous
in·her·ence
in·her·ent
in·her·it
in·her·i·tance
in·hib·it
in·hi·bi·tion
in·hib·i·tor
in·hos·pi·ta·ble
in-house
in·hu·man (lacking
  kindness; cf.
  inhumane)
in·hu·mane (not
  considerate; cf.
  inhuman)
in·hu·man·i·ty
  -ties
in·im·i·cal
in·im·i·ta·ble
in·iq·ui·tous
in·iq·ui·ty (wicked-

ness; cf. *inequity*)
  -ties
ini·tial
  -tialed, -tial·ing,
  -tial·ly
ini·ti·ate (v)
  -at·ed, -at·ing,
  -a·tor
ini·tia·tive
in·ject
in·jec·tion
in·ju·di·cious
in·junc·tion
in·jure
  -jured, -jur·ing
in·ju·ri·ous
in·ju·ry
  -ries
in·jus·tice
in·kling
in·laid
in·land
in·lay
in·let
in lo·co pa·ren·tis
in·mate
in·most
in·nate
in·ner
in·ning
inn·keep·er
in·no·cence
in·no·cent
in·noc·u·ous

in·no·vate
  -vat·ed, -vat·ing,
  -va·tor
in·no·va·tion
in·no·va·tive
in·nu·en·do
  -dos
in·nu·mer·a·ble
in·oc·u·late
  -lat·ed, -lat·ing
in·oc·u·la·tion
in·of·fen·sive
in·op·er·a·ble
in·op·por·tune
in·or·di·nate
in·or·gan·ic
in·put
  -put·ted, -put·ting
in·quest
in·quire
  -quired, -quir·ing
in·qui·ry
  -ries
in·qui·si·tion
in·quis·i·tive
in·quis·i·tor
in·road
in·sane
in·san·i·tary
in·san·i·ty
  -ties
in·sa·tia·ble
in·scribe
in·scrip·tion

in·scru·ta·ble
in·sect
in·sec·ti·cide
in·se·cure
  -cur·i·ty
in·sen·sate
in·sen·si·ble
in·sen·si·tive
in·sep·a·ra·ble
in·sert
in·ser·tion
in·ser·vice (adj)
in·side
in·sid·i·ous
in·sight (under-
  standing; cf.
  incite)
in·sig·nia
in·sig·nif·i·cance
in·sig·nif·i·cant
in·sin·cere
in·sin·u·ate
  -at·ed, -at·ing
in·sin·u·a·tion
in·sip·id
in·sist
in·sis·tence
in·sis·tent
in·so·far
in·sole
in·so·lence
in·so·lent
in·sol·u·ble
in·sol·vent

  -ven·cy
in·som·nia
in·sou·ci·ance
in·spect
in·spec·tion
in·spec·tor
in·spi·ra·tion
in·spire
  -spired, -spir·ing,
  -spir·er
in·sta·bil·i·ty
in·stall
  -stalled, -stall·ing,
  -stall·er
in·stal·la·tion
in·stall·ment
in·stance
  -stanced,
  -stanc·ing
in·stan·ta·neous
in·stant·ly
in·stead
in·step
in·sti·gate
  -gat·ed, -gat·ing,
  -ga·tor
in·still
  -stilled, -still·ing
in·stinct
in·stinc·tive
in·sti·tute
  -tut·ed, -tut·ing
in·sti·tu·tion
  -tion·al, -tion·al·ly

in·struct
in·struc·tion
 -tion·al
in·struc·tive
in·struc·tor
in·stru·ment
in·stru·men·tal
in·stru·men·tal·i·ty
in·stru·men·ta·tion
in·sub·or·di·nate
 -nate·ly, -na·tion
in·suf·fer·able
in·suf·fi·cient
in·su·lar
in·su·late
 -lat·ed, -lat·ing
in·su·la·tion
in·su·la·tor
in·su·lin
in·sult
in·su·per·a·ble
in·sup·port·able
in·sup·press·ible
in·sur·able
 -abil·i·ty
in·sur·ance
in·sure
 -sured, -sur·ing
in·sur·er
in·sur·gent
in·sur·rec·tion
in·tact
in·ta·glio
 -glios

in·take
in·tan·gi·ble
in·te·ger
in·te·gral
in·te·grate
 -grat·ed, -grat·ing
in·te·gra·tion
in·teg·ri·ty
in·tel·lect
in·tel·lec·tu·al
 -al·i·ty, -al·ly,
 -al·ness
in·tel·li·gence
in·tel·li·gent
in·tel·li·gi·ble
 -ble·ness, -bly,
 -bil·i·ty
in·tem·per·ance
in·tem·per·ate
 -ate·ly, -ate·ness
in·tend
in·tend·ing
in·tense
 -tense·ly,
 -tense·ness
in·ten·si·fy
 -fied, -fy·ing,
 -fi·ca·tion
in·ten·si·ty
 -ties
in·ten·sive
 -sive·ly, -sive·ness
in·tent
 -tent·ness

in·ten·tion
in·ten·tion·al
 -al·i·ty, -al·ly
in·ter
 -terred, -ter·ring
in·ter·ac·tion
in·ter·ac·tive
in·ter·cede
 -ced·ed, -ced·ing
in·ter·cept
in·ter·cep·tor
in·ter·ces·sion
in·ter·change
in·ter·change·able
 -able·ness, -ably
in·ter·col·le·giate
in·ter·com
in·ter·com·mu·ni·ca·tion
in·ter·con·nect
 -nec·tion
in·ter·course
in·ter·de·nom·i·na·tion·al
in·ter·de·part·men·tal
 -tal·ly
in·ter·de·pen·dent
in·ter·dict
 -dic·tion, -dic·tive,
 -dic·to·ry
in·ter·dis·ci·plin·ary
in·ter·est
in·ter·face
in·ter·fere
 -fered, -fer·ing
in·ter·fer·ence

in·ter·im
in·te·ri·or
in·ter·ject
  -jec·tor, -jec·to·ry
in·ter·jec·tion
in·ter·lock
in·ter·loc·u·tor
in·ter·lope
  -lop·er
in·ter·lude
in·ter·mar·riage
in·ter·me·di·ary
  -ar·ies
in·ter·me·di·ate
  -ate·ly, -ate·ness
in·ter·ment
in·ter·mi·na·ble
  -ble·ness, -bly
in·ter·min·gle
in·ter·mis·sion
in·ter·mit
  -mit·ted, -mit·ting
in·ter·mit·tent
in·tern
  -tern·ship
in·ter·nal
in·ter·na·tion·al
in·ter·na·tion·al·ize
  -iza·tion
in·ter·nist
in·ter·per·son·al
in·ter·po·late
  (insert)
  -lat·ed, -lat·ing

in·ter·pose
  -posed, -pos·ing
in·ter·pret (trans-
  late; cf. *interrupt*)
in·ter·pre·ta·tion
in·ter·pret·er
in·ter·ra·cial
  -cial·ly
in·ter·re·late
  -la·tion,
  -la·tion·ship
in·ter·ro·gate
  -gat·ed, -gat·ing,
  -ga·tion
in·ter·rog·a·tive
  -tive·ly
in·ter·rupt (break
  into; cf. *interpret*)
  -rup·tion,
  -rup·tive
in·ter·sect
in·ter·sec·tion
in·ter·sperse
  -spersed,
  -spers·ing,
  -sper·sion
in·ter·state
  (between states;
  cf. *intrastate*)
in·ter·twine
in·ter·ur·ban
in·ter·val
in·ter·vene
  -vened, -ven·ing,

  -ven·tion
in·ter·view
  -view·er
in·tes·ti·nal
  -nal·ly
in·tes·tine
in·ti·ma·cy
in·ti·mate
  -mat·ed, -mat·ing,
  -mate·ly
in·tim·i·date
  -dat·ed, -dat·ing,
  -da·tion
in·tol·er·a·ble
  -a·bly, -a·bil·i·ty
in·tol·er·ance
in·tol·er·ant
in·to·na·tion
in·tone
  -toned, -ton·ing
in·tox·i·cant
in·tox·i·cate
  -cat·ed, -cat·ing
in·tra·mu·ral
in·tran·si·gent
in·tran·si·tive
  -tive·ly
in·tra·state (within
  the state; cf.
  interstate)
in·trep·id
  -trep·id·ly,
  -trep·id·ness
in·tri·ca·cy

in·tri·cate
-cate·ly,
-cate·ness
in·trigue
-trigued,
-trigu·ing
in·trin·sic
-si·cal·ly
in·tro·duce
-duced, -duc·ing,
-duc·er
in·tro·duc·tion
in·tro·duc·to·ry
in·tro·spect
-spec·tive·ly,
-spec·tive·ness
in·tro·vert
in·trude
-trud·ed, -trud·ing,
-trud·er
in·tru·sion
in·tu·ition
in·tu·itive
-tive·ly, -tive·ness
in·un·date
-dat·ed, -dat·ing,
-da·tion
in·ure
-ured, -ur·ing
in·vade
-vad·ed, -vad·ing,
-vad·er
in·val·id (adj)
in·va·lid (n)

in·val·i·date
-da·tion, -da·tor
in·val·id·i·ty
-ties
in·valu·able
-ably
in·vari·able
-ably, -abil·i·ty
in·va·sion
in·vent
-ven·tor,
-ven·tress
in·ven·tion
in·ven·tive
-tive·ness
in·ven·to·ry
in·ven·to·ries
in·verse
-verse·ly
in·ver·sion
in·vert
in·vest
in·ves·ti·gate
-ga·tion,
-ga·tion·al, -ga·tor
in·ves·ti·ture
in·vest·ment
in·vig·o·rate
-rat·ed, -rat·ing,
-ra·tion
in·vin·ci·ble
-ble·ness, -bly,
-bil·i·ty
in·vis·i·ble

-ble·ness, -bly,
-bil·i·ty
in·vi·ta·tion
in·vite
-vit·ed, -vit·ing
in·vo·ca·tion
in·voice
-voiced, -voic·ing
in·voke
-voked, -vok·ing
in·vol·un·tary
-tari·ly, -tari·ness
in·volve
-volve·ment
in·vul·ner·a·ble
-bly, -bil·i·ty
in·ward
io·dine
ion·o·sphere
io·ta
ip·so fac·to
iras·ci·ble (quick to
anger; cf.
erasable)
-ble·ness, -bly,
-bil·i·ty
irate
irate·ly, irate·ness
ir·i·des·cence
ir·i·des·cent
iron·clad
iron·ic
iron·i·cal·ly
iron·ing

iro·ny
  -nies
ir·ra·di·ate
  -at·ed, -at·ing
ir·ra·tio·nal
  -nal·ly
ir·rec·on·cil·able
  -ably, -abil·i·ty
ir·re·duc·ible
ir·re·fut·able
  -ably, -abil·i·ty
ir·reg·u·lar
  -lar·ly
ir·rel·e·vance
ir·rel·e·vant
ir·re·li·gious
ir·rep·a·ra·ble
  -bly
ir·re·press·ible
  -ibly, -ibil·i·ty
ir·re·proach·able
  -ably, -abil·i·ty
ir·re·sist·ible
  -ible·ness, -ibly
ir·re·spec·tive
ir·re·spon·si·ble
  -ble·ness, -bly
ir·re·triev·able
  -ably, -abil·i·ty

ir·rev·er·ent
ir·re·vers·ible
  -ibly, -ibil·i·ty
ir·re·vo·ca·ble
  -bly
ir·ri·gate
  -gat·ed, -gat·ing,
  -ga·tion
ir·ri·ta·bil·i·ty
ir·ri·ta·ble
  -ble·ness, -bly
ir·ri·tant
ir·ri·tate
  -tat·ed, -tat·ing,
  -tat·ing·ly
ir·ri·ta·tion
ir·rupt (break in; cf.
  erupt)
  -rup·tion
isin·glass
is·land
isle (small island; cf.
  aisle)
iso·bar
iso·late
  -lat·ed, -lat·ing
iso·la·tion·ism
  -ist
iso·met·rics

isos·ce·les
iso·therm
iso·tope
Is·ra·el
Is·rae·li
is·sue
  -sued, -su·ing
isth·mus
ital·ic
ital·i·cize
  -cized, -ciz·ing
item
item·iza·tion
item·ize
  -ized, -iz·ing
itin·er·ant
itin·er·ary
  -ar·ies
itin·er·ate
its (possessive)
it's (it is or it has)
it·self
ivo·ry
  -ries
ivy
  ivies

J

jack·et
jack·ham·mer
jack-in-the-box
jack-in-the-pul·pit
   -pits
jack·knife
jack-of-all-trades
jack-o'-lan·tern
jack·pot
jack·rab·bit
jag·uar
jail·break
ja·lopy
   -lop·ies
jam (food; cf. *jamb*)
   jammed,
   jam·ming
jamb (of a door; cf.
   jam)
jam·bo·ree
jan·i·tor
   -to·rial
Jan·u·ary
ja·pan (varnish)
Jap·a·nese
   Jap·a·nese (pl)
jar
jar·gon
jas·mine

jas·per
jaun·dice
jav·e·lin
jaw·bone
jaw·break·er
jeal·ous
   -ous·ness
jeal·ou·sy
Je·ho·vah
jel·ly
   jel·lies, jel·lied,
   jel·lying
jel·ly·fish
jeop·ar·dize
   -dized, -diz·ing
jeop·ar·dy
jer·ky
   -i·er, -i·est
jest (joke; cf. *gist*)
Je·su·it
jet
   jet·ted, jet·ting
jet·ti·son
jet·ty
   -ties
jew·el
   -eled, -el·ing
jew·el·er
jew·el·ry

jib (sail; cf. *gibe*,
   jibe)
jibe (agree; cf. *gibe*,
   jib)
jig·gle
   -gled, -gling
jinx
jit·ter·bug
job
   jobbed, job·bing
job·ber
job·less
   -less·ness
job lot
jock·ey
   -eys, -eyed, -ey·ing
joc·u·lar
   -lar·i·ty
jog
   jogged, jog·ging
join·der
join·er
joint
   joint·ed·ly
join·ture
joke
   joked, jok·ing,
   jok·ing·ly
jok·er

jol·ly
  -li·er, -li·est
jon·quil
josh
jos·tle
jour·nal
jour·nal·ism
jour·nal·ist
jour·nal·is·tic
  -ti·cal·ly
jour·nal·ize
  -ized, -iz·ing
jour·ney
  -neys, -neyed,
  -ney·ing
jo·vial
jowl
joy·ful
  -ful·ly, -ful·ness
joy·ous
  -ous·ness
ju·bi·lant
ju·bi·la·tion
ju·bi·lee
judge
  judged, judg·ing
judg·ment

-men·tal,
  -men·tal·ly
ju·di·cial (of a judge;
  cf. *judicious*)
ju·di·cia·ry
ju·di·cious (of a
  judgment; cf.
  judicial)
ju·do
jug·ger·naut
jug·gle
  -gled, -gling
jug·u·lar
juice
  juiced, juic·ing
ju·lep
ju·li·enne
Ju·ly
jum·ble
  -bled, -bling
jum·bo
  -bos
jump·er
jump·ing jack
jump seat
junc·tion (joining;
  cf. *juncture*)

junc·ture (crisis; cf.
  junction)
June
jun·gle
ju·nior
ju·ni·per
jun·ket
junk·ie
  -ies
jun·ta
ju·ris·pru·dence
ju·rist
ju·ror
ju·ry
  -ries
jus·tice
jus·ti·fi·able
  -ably
jus·ti·fi·ca·tion
jus·ti·fi·er
jus·ti·fy
  -fied, -fy·ing, -fi·er
ju·ve·nile
jux·ta·pose
  -posed, -pos·ing

kaf·fee·klatsch
kai·ser
ka·lei·do·scope
ka·mi·ka·ze
kan·ga·roo
ka·pok
kar·at or car·at
(weight; cf. *caret*,
carrot)
ka·ra·te
kay·ak
keen
keen·ness,
keen·er
keep
kept, keep·ing
keep·sake
ken·nel
ker·nel (seed; cf.
colonel)
ker·o·sene
ketch·up (tomato
sauce; var. of
catsup)
key (to a door; cf.
quay)
keyed, key·less
key·board
key·hole

key·note
kha·ki
kick·back
kick off (v)
kick·off (n)
kid
kid·ded, kid·ding,
kid·ding·ly
kid·nap
-napped,
-nap·ping,
-nap·per
kid·ney
-neys
kill (slay; cf. *kiln*)
kill·er
kill·ing
kill·joy
kiln (oven; cf. *kill*)
ki·lo·byte
kilo·cy·cle
ki·lo·gram
ki·lo·me·ter
kilo·watt
ki·mo·no
-nos
kin·der·gar·ten
kind·heart·ed
kin·dle

-dled, -dling
kind·li·ness
kind·ness
kin·dred
ki·ne·sics
kin·es·the·sia
-thet·ic,
-thet·i·cal·ly
king·dom
king·fish
king·ly
king-size
kins·folk
kin·ship
ki·osk
kitch·en
kitch·en·ette
kitch·en·ware
kit·ten
ki·wi·fruit
knap·sack
knave (rogue; cf.
nave)
knav·ery
knead (dough; cf.
need)
knee·cap
knee-deep
knee-high

knew (did know; cf. *gnu, new*)
knick·knack
knife
knives (pl)
knight (title; cf. *night*)
knight·hood
knit
knit·ted, knit·ting, knit·ter

knock down (v)
knock·down (n, adj)
knock out (v)
knock·out (n)
knot (tied; cf. *not*)
knot·ted, knot·ting
knot·hole
know
knew, known, know·ing

know-how (n)
know-it-all
knowl·edge
knowl·edge·able
-able·ness, -ably
knuck·le
knuck·led, knuck·ling
ku·dos
kum·quat

la·bel
-beled, -bel·ing
la·bor
-bored, -bor·ing
lab·o·ra·to·ry
(science; cf. *lavatory*)
-ries
la·bor·er
la·bo·ri·ous
lab·y·rinth
lace
laced, lac·ing
lac·er·ate
-at·ed, -at·ing
lac·er·a·tion
lack·a·dai·si·cal

la·con·ic
-con·i·cal·ly
lac·quer
-quered, -quer·ing
la·crosse
lac·tate
-tat·ed, -tat·ing, -ta·tion
lad·der
lad·ing
lad·le
la·dy
-dies
la·dy·bug
la·dy·like
lag
lagged, lag·ging

la·goon
laid-back (adj)
lain (rested; cf. *lane*)
lais·sez-faire
la·ity
lamb·skin
lame (weak; cf. *lamé*)
lam·er, lam·est, lame·ness
la·mé (brocaded fabric; cf. *lame*)
la·ment
la·men·ta·ble
-bly
lam·en·ta·tion
lam·i·nate
-nat·ed, -nat·ing

lam·poon
lamp·post
lam·prey
land·fill
land·ing craft
land·la·dy
land·locked
land·lord
land·mark
land·own·er
land·scape
  -scaped, -scap·ing,
  -scap·er
land·slide
lane (path; cf. *lain*)
lan·guage
lan·guid
  -guid·ness
lan·guish
lanky
  lank·i·er, lank·i·est,
  lank·i·ness
lan·o·lin
lan·tern
lap
  lapped, lap·ping
lap·dog
la·pel
lap·i·dary
  -dar·ies
lapse (terminate; cf.
  elapse)
  lapsed, laps·ing
lar·ce·nous

lar·ce·ny
  -nies
lar·ghet·to
  -tos
lar·i·at
lark·spur
lar·va (sing)
  -vae (pl)
lar·yn·gi·tis
lar·ynx
la·sa·gna
las·civ·i·ous
  -ous·ness
la·ser
last min·ute
latch·key
latch·string
late
  lat·er (afterward;
  cf. *latter*), lat·est,
  late·ness
la·tent
lat·er·al
  -al·ly
lat·ish
lat·i·tude
lat·ter (subsequent;
  cf. *later*)
lat·tice
lat·tice·work
laud·able
lau·da·to·ry
laugh·able
  -ably

laugh·ing·stock
laugh·ter
launch
laun·der
  -dered, -der·ing
laun·der·ette
Laun·dro·mat
laun·dry
  -dries
lau·re·ate
lau·rel
lav·a·to·ry (for
  washing; cf.
  laboratory)
lav·en·der
  -dered, -der·ing
lav·ish
  -ish·ness
law-abid·ing
law·ful
  -ful·ly, -ful·ness
law·less
  -less·ness
law·mak·er
lawn mow·er
law·suit
law·yer
lax·a·tive
lax·ity
lay·away (n)
lay·er
lay·man
lay off (v)
lay·off (n)

lay out (v)
lay·out (n)
lay over (v)
lay·over (n)
lay·per·son
lay up (v)
lay-up (n)
lay·wom·an
lazy
  -zi·er, -zi·est, -zi·ly
lead (v)(guide)
lead (n)(metal; cf. *led*)
lead·en
lead·er
lead-in (n, adj)
lead off (v)
lead·off (n, adj)
lead time
lead up (v)
lead-up (n)
leaf
  leaves (pl)
leaf mold
league
leak·age
leak·proof
lean (thin; cf. *lien*)
lean-to
  lean-tos (pl)
leap
  leaped, leap·ing
leap year
learn
  learned, learn·ing,

learn·er
lease
  leased (past tense
  of *lease*; cf. *least*),
  leas·ing
least (smallest; cf.
  leased)
leath·er
  -ered, -er·ing
leath·er·neck
leave
  leav·ing
leav·en
  -ened, -en·ing
lec·tern
lec·tor
lec·ture
  -tured, -tur·ing,
  -tur·er
led (guided; cf. *lead*)
led·ger
lee·ward
lee·way
left-hand·ed
left·over
leg·a·cy
  -cies
le·gal
  -gal·ly
le·gal·ism
le·gal·i·ty
le·gal·ize
  -ized, -iz·ing
leg·end

leg·end·ary
  -en·dari·ly
leg·ging
leg·i·ble
  -bly, -bil·i·ty
le·gion
leg·is·late
  -lat·ed, -lat·ing
leg·is·la·tion
leg·is·la·tive
  -tive·ly
leg·is·la·tor
leg·is·la·ture
le·git·i·ma·cy
le·git·i·mate
  -mate·ly
leg·room
le·gume
leg·work
lei·sure
lei·sure·ly
lem·ming
lem·on·ade
le·mur
length
length·en
  -ened, -en·ing
lengthy
  length·i·er,
  length·i·ly,
  length·i·ness
le·nien·cy
le·nient
Le·nin·ism

len·til
leop·ard
le·o·tard
lep·re·chaun
lep·ro·sy
le·sion
les·see
less·en (decrease; cf.
   lesson)
   -ened, -en·ing
less·er
les·son (study; cf.
   lessen)
les·sor
let
   let or let·ted,
   let·ting
le·thal
le·thar·gic
   -gi·cal·ly
leth·ar·gy
let's (let us)
let·tered
let·ter·head
let·ter-per·fect
let·tuce
let up (v)
let·up (n)
leu·ke·mia
lev·ee (embank-
   ment; cf. *levy*)
   -eed, -ee·ing
lev·el
   -eled, -el·ing,

-el·ness
le·ver·age
le·vi·a·than
lev·i·ta·tion
lev·i·ty
levy (tax; cf. *levee*)
   lev·ies
lex·i·cog·ra·pher
li·a·bil·i·ty
   -ties
li·a·ble (obligated;
   cf. *libel*)
li·ai·son
li·ar
li·ba·tion
li·bel (defame; cf.
   liable)
   -beled, -bel·ing
li·bel·ous
lib·er·al
   -al·ly
lib·er·al·i·ty
   -ties
lib·er·al·ize
   -ized, -iz·ing,
   -iza·tion
lib·er·ate
   -at·ed, -at·ing,
   -a·tor
lib·er·a·tion
lib·er·ty
li·brar·i·an
li·brary
li·bret·to

li·cense
   -censed, -cens·ing,
   -cens·er
li·cen·tious
   -tious·ness
li·chen
lic·o·rice
lie (untruth; cf. *lye*)
lien (claim; cf. *lean*)
lieu
lieu·ten·an·cy
lieu·ten·ant
life
   lives (pl)
life·blood
life·boat
life·guard
life jack·et
life·less
   -less·ness
life·long
life·sav·er
life-size
life span
life·style
life·time
lift-off (n)
lig·a·ment
lig·a·ture
light·en
   -ened, -en·ing
   (becoming light;
   cf. *lightning*)
light·fast

light-fin·gered

light-head·ed

light·heart·ed

light·house

light·ning (electrical discharge; cf. *lightening*)

light pen

light·proof

lights-out

light·weight

light-year

lik·able
-able·ness, -abil·i·ty

like·li·hood

like·ly
like·li·er, like·li·est

like·ness

like·wise

li·lac

lil·li·pu·tian

lily-white

limb

lim·ber
-bered, -ber·ing

lim·bo
-bos

lime·light

lim·er·ick

lime·stone

lim·it
-it·less, -it·less·ly,

-it·less·ness

lim·i·ta·tion

lim·ou·sine

lim·pid

lin·age (number of lines; cf. *lineage*)

lin·eage (family; cf. *linage*)

lin·eal (ancestral line; cf. *linear*)

lin·ear (of lines; cf. *lineal*)

line·man

lin·en

line print·er

line up (v)

line·up (n)

lin·ger
-gered, -ger·ing

lin·ge·rie

lin·go
-goes

lin·guist

lin·i·ment

lin·ing

link·age

links (of chain; cf. *lynx*)

li·no·leum

Li·no·type

lin·seed

li·on·ess

li·on·heart·ed

lip-read

lip-read·ing

lip·stick

liq·ue·fac·tion

liq·ue·fy
-fied, -fy·ing, -fi·able

li·queur

liq·uid
-uid·i·ty, -uid·ly

liq·ui·date
-dat·ed, -dat·ing, -da·tion

li·quor

lis·ten
-tened, -ten·ing, -ten·er

list·less

list price

li·ter

lit·er·a·cy

lit·er·al

lit·er·al·ly

lit·er·ary

lit·er·ate

lit·er·a·ture

lithe

litho·graph
-gra·pher

li·thog·ra·phy

lit·i·gant

lit·i·gate
-gated, -gat·ing, -ga·tion

lit·ter

lit·ter·bag
lit·tle
-tler, -tlest
li·tur·gi·cal
lit·ur·gy
-gies
liv·able
live
lived, liv·ing
live-in (adj)
live·li·hood
live·long
live·ly
live·li·er,
live·li·est
live·stock
liv·id
liz·ard
lla·ma
load (burden; cf.
lode)
loan (for temporary
use; cf. lone)
loath·some
lob·by
-bies, -bied,
-by·ing
lob·ster
lo·cal (nearby; cf.
locale)
lo·cale (locality; cf.
local)
lo·cal·i·ty
-ties

lo·cal·ize
-ized, -iz·ing
lo·cate
-cat·ed, -cat·ing
lo·ca·tion
lock·jaw
lock·nut
lock out (v)
lock·out (n)
lock·smith
lock·step
lock·stitch
lock·up (n)
lo·co·mo·tion
lo·co·mo·tive
lo·cust
lo·cu·tion
lode (ore; cf. load)
lodge (n, v)(shelter;
cf. loge)
lodged, lodg·ing
log
logged, log·ging
log·a·rithm
loge (theater level;
cf. lodge)
log·ic
log·i·cal
-cal·ly, -cal·ness
lo·gis·tic
logo
log·os
loi·ter
lol·li·pop

lone (solitary; cf.
loan)
lone·li·ness
lone·ly
lone·some
long-dis·tance (adj,
adv)
lon·gev·i·ty
long·hand
long·horn
lon·gi·tude
lon·gi·tu·di·nal
long-range
long run
long·shore·man
long shot
long-suf·fer·ing
long suit
long-term
long-wind·ed
look·out (n)
loop
loop·hole
loose (adj, v)
(unattached; cf.
lose, loss)
loose·ly,
loose·ness, loosed
loose-leaf
loos·en
-ened, -en·ing
lop·sid·ed
lo·qua·cious
-cious·ness

lose (misplace; cf.
  loose, loss)
  lost, los·ing
loss (something lost;
  cf. *loose, lose*)
lo·tion
lot·tery
loud·mouthed
loud·speak·er
lounge
lou·ver
lov·able
  -able·ness, -ably
love·ly
  -li·er, -li·ness
love seat
love·sick
low-down (n)
low·down (adj)
low·er·case
  -cased, -cas·ing
low-key
  low-keyed
low-lev·el
low·ly
  low·li·ness
low-mind·ed
low-pres·sure
low-pro·file
low-ten·sion
lox
loy·al·ty

loz·enge
lu·bri·cant
lu·bri·cate
  -ca·tion
lu·cid
lu·cid·i·ty
lucky
  luck·i·ly
lu·cra·tive
lu·di·crous
lug
  lugged, lug·ging
lug·gage
lu·gu·bri·ous
luke·warm
lul·la·by
  -bies, -bied
lum·ba·go
lum·bar (adj)(nerve;
  cf. *lumber*)
lum·ber (n, v)(wood
  or to move
  heavily; cf.
  lumbar)
  -bered, -ber·ing
lum·ber·yard
lu·mi·nary
  -nar·ies
lu·mi·nous
lu·na·cy
  -cies
lu·nar

lu·na·tic
lun·cheon
lun·cheon·ette
lunch·room
lurch
lure
  lured, lur·ing
lu·rid
lus·cious
  -cious·ness
lus·ter
  -tered, -ter·ing
lust·ful
  -ful·ly, -ful·ness
lus·trous
lusty
lux·u·ri·ous
lux·u·ry
  -ries
ly·ce·um
lye (chemical; cf. *lie*)
ly·ing
lymph
lym·phat·ic
lynch
lynx (animal; cf.
  links)
  lynx (pl)
lyr·ic
lyr·i·cal
lyr·i·cism

ma·ca·bre
mac·ad·am
mac·ad·am·ize
  -ized, -iz·ing
mac·a·ro·ni
mac·a·roon
Ma·chi·a·vel·lian
ma·chine
ma·chine-read·able
ma·chin·ery
  -er·ies
ma·chin·ist
mack·er·el
mack·in·tosh
  (raincoat; cf.
  McIntosh)
mac·ro·cosm
mac·ro·eco·nom·ics
ma·cron
mad·am
mad·den
  -dened, -den·ing
made (did make; cf.
  maid)
made-up (adj)
mad·ness
mad·ri·gal
mag·a·zine
ma·gen·ta

mag·got
mag·ic
  -i·cal, -i·cal·ly
ma·gi·cian
mag·is·te·ri·al
mag·is·tra·cy
  -cies
mag·is·trate
Mag·na Char·ta
mag·na cum lau·de
mag·na·nim·i·ty
  -ties
mag·nan·i·mous
mag·nate (rich
  person; cf.
  magnet)
mag·ne·sia
mag·ne·sium
mag·net (attracts
  iron; cf. *magnate*)
mag·net·ic
mag·ne·tism
mag·ne·tite
mag·ne·tize
  -tized, -tiz·ing
mag·ni·fi·ca·tion
mag·nif·i·cence
mag·nif·i·cent
  (splendid; cf.

  munificent)
mag·nif·i·co
mag·ni·fi·er
mag·ni·fy
  -fied, -fy·ing
mag·ni·tude
mag·no·lia
mag·num
mag·pie
ma·ha·ra·ja
ma·hat·ma
ma·hog·a·ny
  -nies
maid (girl; cf. *made*)
maid·en
maid·en·ly
maid·en name
mail (letters; cf.
  male)
  mailed, mail·able,
  mail·abil·i·ty
mail·bag
mail·box
mail·er
mail or·der (n)
main (chief; cf.
  mane)
main·frame
main·land

main·ly
main·sail
main·spring
main·stay
main stem
main·stream
main·tain
main·te·nance
maize (corn; cf.
   maze)
ma·jes·tic
maj·es·ty
   -ties
ma·jor
   -jored, -jor·ing
ma·jor·do·mo
ma·jor·i·ty
   -ties
make-be·lieve
make·shift
make up (v)
make·up (n)
mak·ing
mal·ad·just·ment
mal·ad·min·is·tra·tion
mal·adroit
mal·a·dy
   -dies
mal·aise
mal·a·prop·ism
mal·ap·ro·pos
ma·lar·ia
Ma·lay
mal·con·tent

male (masculine; cf.
   mail)
male·dic·tion
ma·lev·o·lent
mal·fea·sance
mal·for·ma·tion
mal·formed
mal·func·tion
mal·ice
ma·li·cious
   (harmful)
ma·lign
ma·lig·nan·cy
   -cies
ma·lig·nant
ma·lig·ni·ty
ma·lin·ger
   -gered, -ger·ing
mal·lard
mal·lea·ble
mal·let
mal·nu·tri·tion
mal·odor
mal·odor·ous
mal·po·si·tion
mal·prac·tice
Mal·tese
malt·ose
mal·treat
mal·ver·sa·tion
mam·mal
mam·mon
mam·moth
man·a·cle

-cled, -cling
man·age
   -aged, -ag·ing
man·age·able
man·age·ment
man·ag·er
   -age·ri·al,
   -age·ri·al·ly
man·a·tee
man·da·mus
man·da·rin
man·da·tary (agent;
   cf. *mandatory*)
   -tar·ies
man·date
   -dat·ed, -dat·ing
man·da·to·ry
   (compelling; cf.
   mandatary)
   -ries
man·di·ble
man·do·lin
mane (hair; cf.
   main)
man-eat·er
ma·nège
ma·neu·ver
   -vered, -ver·ing,
   -ver·er
man·ga·nese
man·ger
man·gle
man·go
   -goes

man·grove
mangy
  mang·i·er,
  mang·i·est
man·han·dle
man·hat·tan
man·hood
man-hour
man·hunt
ma·nia
ma·ni·ac
ma·ni·a·cal
man·i·cure
  -cured, -cur·ing
man·i·cur·ist
man·i·fest
man·i·fes·ta·tion
man·i·fes·to
  -tos
man·i·fold
man·i·kin
ma·nila
ma·nip·u·late
  -lat·ed, -lat·ing,
  -la·tion
man·i·tou
man·kind
man·ly
  -li·er, -li·est,
  -li·ness
man-made
man·na
manned
man·ne·quin

man·ner (mode; cf.
  manor)
man·ner·ism
man·nish
man·ni·tol
man-of-war
  men-of-war (pl)
ma·nom·e·ter
man·or (estate; cf.
  manner)
man·pow·er
  (personnel
  available)
man·sion
man·slaugh·ter
man·slay·er
man·tel (shelf; cf.
  mantle)
man·tel·piece
man·til·la
man·tle (cloak; cf.
  mantel)
man·u·al
man·u·fac·ture
  -tur·ing, -tured
man·u·fac·tur·er
ma·nure
manu·script
many
many·fold
many-sid·ed
ma·ple
map·ping
mar·a·schi·no

-nos (pl)
mar·a·thon
ma·raud
mar·ble
  -bled, -bling
mar·ble·ize
  -ized, -iz·ing
March
mar·che·sa (fem)
  -che·se (pl)
mar·che·se (masc)
  -che·si (pl)
mar·chio·ness (fem)
Mar·di Gras
mar·ga·rine
mar·ga·ri·ta
mar·gin
mar·gin·al
mar·gi·na·lia
mar·grave
mari·gold
mari·jua·na
mar·i·nade
  -nad·ed, -nad·ing
ma·rine
mar·i·ner
mar·i·o·nette
mar·i·tal (marriage;
  cf. *martial*)
mar·i·time
mark down (v)
mark·down (n)
mar·ket
mar·ket·able

mar·ket·ing
mar·ket·place
marks·man
marks·wom·an
mark up (v)
mark·up (n)
mar·ma·lade
mar·mo·set
mar·mot
ma·roon
mar·quee (canopy)
mar·que·try
mar·riage
mar·row
mar·row·bone
mar·ry
  -ried, -ry·ing
mar·shal (officer; cf.
  martial)
  -shaled, -shal·ing
marsh·mal·low
marshy
  marsh·i·er,
  marsh·i·est
mar·su·pi·al
mar·ten (furbearing
  animal; cf. *martin*)
mar·tial (warlike; cf.
  marital, marshal)
  -tial·ly
mar·tian
mar·tin (bird; cf.
  marten)
mar·ti·net

mar·tyr
mar·tyr·dom
mar·vel
  -veled, -vel·ing
mar·vel·ous
mas·cot
mas·cu·line
  -line·ly, -lin·i·ty
mash·er
mask
ma·son
  -soned, -son·ing
Ma·son·ic
Ma·son·ite
ma·son·ry
  -ries
mas·quer·ade
  -ad·ed, -ad·ing
mas·sa·cre
  -sa·cred, -sa·cring
mas·sage
mas·seur (masc)
mas·seuse (fem)
mas·sif
mas·sive
mass media (pl)
  medium (sing)
mass-pro·duce
mas·ter
  -tered, -ter·ing
mas·ter·ful
mas·ter key
mas·ter·mind
mas·ter of

cer·e·mo·nies
mas·ter·piece
mas·ter plan
mas·ter ser·geant
mas·tery
mast·head
mas·ti·cate
  -cat·ed, -cat·ing
mas·tiff
mast·odon
mat·a·dor
match·book
match·less
match play
ma·te·ri·al
  (substance; cf.
  matériel)
  -al·ly, -al·ness
ma·te·ri·al·ism
  -ist, -is·tic
ma·te·ri·al·i·ty
  -ties
ma·te·ri·al·iza·tion
ma·te·ri·al·ize
  -ized, -iz·ing
ma·te·ria med·i·ca
ma·té·ri·el
  (equipment; cf.
  material)
ma·ter·nal
ma·ter·ni·ty
  -ties
math·e·mat·i·cal
math·e·ma·ti·cian

math·e·mat·ics
mat·i·nee
ma·tri·arch
ma·tri·ar·chy
-chies
ma·tri·cide
ma·tric·u·late
-lat·ed, -lat·ing
mat·ri·mo·nial
mat·ri·mo·ny
ma·trix
-tri·ces (pl)
ma·tron
ma·tron·ly
mat·ter
mat·ter-of-fact
mat·ting
mat·tock
mat·tress
mat·u·rate
-rat·ed, -rat·ing
mat·u·ra·tion
ma·ture
-tured
ma·tu·ri·ty
ma·tu·ti·nal
mat·zo
mat·zoth (pl)
maud·lin
mau·so·le·um
-leums
mauve
mav·er·ick
mawk·ish

max·im
max·i·mal
max·i·mize
-mized, -miz·ing,
-mi·za·tion
max·i·mum
may·be
May Day (May 1; cf.
Mayday)
May·day (signal; cf.
May Day)
may·flow·er
may·hem
may·on·naise
may·or
may·or·al·ty
may·pole
maze (puzzle; cf.
maize)
mazed, maz·ing
ma·zur·ka
mazy
Mc·In·tosh (apple;
cf. *mackintosh*)
mead·ow
mead·ow·lark
mea·ger
meal·time
mean (stingy; cf.
mien)
mean·ing,
mean·er,
mean·ness
me·an·der

-dered, -der·ing
mean·ing·less
mean·ly
mean·time
mean·while
mea·sles
mea·sly
mea·sure
-sured, -sur·ing,
-sur·able
mea·sure·less
mea·sure·ment
meat (food; cf. *meet*,
mete)
me·chan·ic
me·chan·i·cal
me·chan·ics
mech·a·nism
mech·a·nist
med·al (award; cf.
meddle)
med·al·ist
me·dal·lion
med·dle (interfere;
cf. *medal*)
-dled, -dling, -dler
med·dle·some
me·dia (pl)
me·di·um (sing)
me·di·al
me·di·an
me·di·ate
-at·ed, -at·ing
me·di·a·tion

me·di·a·tor
med·ic·aid
med·i·cal
medi·care
med·i·cate
 -cat·ed, -cat·ing
med·i·ca·tion
me·dic·i·nal
med·i·cine
me·di·eval
me·di·eval·ism
me·di·o·cre
me·di·oc·ri·ty
 -ties
med·i·tate
 -tat·ed, -tat·ing,
 -ta·tor
med·i·ta·tion
med·i·ta·tive
Med·i·ter·ra·nean
me·di·um (sing)
 me·dia (pl)
med·ley
 -leys
meet (encounter; cf.
 meat, mete)
meet·ing
meet·ing·house
mega·byte
mega·cy·cle
mega·phone
mel·an·cho·lia
mel·an·chol·ic
mel·an·choly

-chol·ies
mé·lange
mel·a·no·ma
me·lee
me·lio·rate
 -rat·ed, -rat·ing,
 -ra·tion
me·lio·rism
mel·lif·lu·ous
mel·low
me·lo·de·on
me·lod·ic
me·lo·di·ous
mel·o·dist
mel·o·dize
 -dized, -diz·ing
melo·dra·ma
melo·dra·mat·ic
mel·o·dy
 -dies
mel·on
mem·ber
mem·ber·ship
mem·brane
mem·bra·nous
me·men·to
 -tos
mem·oir
mem·o·ra·ble
mem·o·ran·dum
 (sing)
 -dums or -da (pl)
me·mo·ri·al
me·mo·ri·al·ist

me·mo·ri·al·ize
 -ized
mem·o·rize
 -rized, -riz·ing,
 -ri·za·tion
mem·o·ry
 -ries
men·ace
 -aced, -ac·ing,
 -ac·ing·ly
mé·nage
me·nag·er·ie
men·da·cious
men·dac·i·ty
 -ties
Men·de·lian
men·di·can·cy
men·di·cant
me·nial
men·in·gi·tis
 -git·i·des (pl)
Men·no·nite
men·stru·ate
men·tal
men·tal·i·ty
 -ties
men·thol
men·tion
 -tion·ing,
 -tion·able
men·tioned
men·tor
menu
mer·can·tile

mer·can·til·ism
mer·ce·nary
  -nar·ies
mer·cer·ize
  -ized, -iz·ing
mer·chan·dise
  -dised, -dis·ing,
  -dis·er
mer·chant
mer·chant·able
mer·chant·man
mer·ci·ful
mer·ci·less
mer·cu·ri·al
mer·cu·ric
mer·cu·rous
mer·cu·ry
  -ries
mer·cy
  -cies
mere·ly
merge
  merged, merg·ing
merg·er
me·rid·i·an
me·ringue
me·ri·no
  -nos
mer·it
mer·i·to·ri·ous
mer·maid
mer·ri·ment
merry
  -ri·er, -ri·est, -ri·ly

mer·ry-go-round
mer·ry·mak·ing
me·sa
mes·mer·ism
mes·mer·ize
me·so·mor·phic
mes·quite
mes·sage
  -saged, -sag·ing
mes·sen·ger
mes·si·ah
Messrs. (pl)
  Mr. (sing)
messy
  mess·i·er,
  mess·i·est
me·tab·o·lism
meta·car·pal
met·al (iron; cf.
    mettle)
  -aled, -al·ing
me·tal·lic
met·al·log·ra·phy
met·al·loid
met·al·lur·gy
  -gi·cal, -gist
met·al·work
meta·mor·phic
meta·mor·phism
meta·mor·phose
  -phosed, -phos·ing
meta·mor·pho·sis
  -pho·ses (pl)
met·a·phor

meta·phys·ic
meta·phys·i·cal
meta·phy·si·cian
meta·phys·ics
meta·tar·sal
meta·tar·sus
mete (measure; cf.
    meat, meet)
  met·ed, met·ing
me·te·or
me·te·or·ic
me·te·or·ite
me·te·or·oid
me·te·o·rol·o·gy
  -ro·log·ic,
  -ro·log·i·cal,
  -ro·log·i·cal·ly
me·ter
me·ter maid
meth·a·done
meth·ane
meth·od
me·thod·i·cal
meth·od·ist
meth·od·ize
  -ized, -iz·ing
meth·od·ol·o·gy
  -gies
me·tic·u·lous
met·ric
met·ri·cal
me·trol·o·gy
met·ro·nome
me·trop·o·lis

met·ro·pol·i·tan
met·tle (spirit; cf. *metal*)
met·tle·some
Mex·i·can
mez·za·nine
mez·zo-so·pra·no
mez·zo·tint
mi·as·ma
   -mas (pl), -mal, -mat·ic
mi·crobe
mi·cro·bi·ol·o·gy
mi·cro·com·put·er
mi·cro·cosm
mi·cro·fiche
   -fiche (pl)
mi·cro·film
mi·cro·form
mi·cro·graph
mi·crom·e·ter
mi·cron
mi·cro·or·gan·ism
mi·cro·phone
mi·cro·pro·ces·sor
mi·cro·scope
mi·cro·scop·ic
   -scop·i·cal·ly
mi·cro·sec·ond
mi·cro·wave
mid·air
mid·brain
mid·day
mid·dle

mid·dle-aged
mid·dle class (n)
mid·dle-class (adj)
mid·dle·man
mid·dle·weight
mid·dling
midg·et
mid·land
mid·life
mid·night
mid·riff
mid·ship·man
mid·size
mid·sum·mer
mid·term
mid·way
mid·week
mid·wife
mid·win·ter
mid·year
mien (bearing; cf. *mean*)
miff
might (strength; cf. *mite*)
might·i·ly
might·i·ness
mighty
   might·i·er,
   might·i·est
mi·gnon·ette
mi·graine
mi·grate
   -grat·ed, -grat·ing,

   -gra·tion
mi·gra·to·ry
mi·ka·do
mi·la·dy
mil·dew
mile·age
mile·post
mile·stone
mil·i·tance
mil·i·tan·cy
mil·i·tant
mil·i·ta·rism
   -rist, -ris·tic, -ris·ti·cal·ly
mil·i·ta·rize
   -rized, -riz·ing, -ri·za·tion
mil·i·tary
mil·i·tate
   -tat·ed, -tat·ing
mi·li·tia
milk glass
milk shake
milk snake
milk·weed
milky
   milk·i·er,
   milk·i·est,
   milk·i·ness
mill·age
mil·le·na·ry (1000th anniversary; cf. *millinery*)
   -ries

mil·len·ni·um
  -nia (pl)
mill·er
mil·let
mil·li·am·pere
mil·li·gram
mil·li·me·ter
mil·li·nery (hats; cf.
  millenary)
mill·ing
mil·lion
  mil·lionth
mil·lion·aire
mil·li·sec·ond
mil·li·volt
mil·li·watt
mill·pond
mill·race
mill·stone
mill·stream
mill wheel
mill·wright
mim·eo·graph
mi·me·sis
mi·met·ic
mim·ic
  -icked, -ick·ing
mim·ic·ry
  -ries
mi·mo·sa
min·a·ret
mi·na·to·ry
mince
  minced, minc·ing

mince·meat
mind (brain; cf.
  mined)
mind-bog·gling
mind·ful
mind read·er
mined (dug out; cf.
  mind)
mine
  min·er (mine
  worker; cf. *minor*)
min·er·al
min·er·al·ize
  -ized, -iz·ing
min·er·al·o·gy
  -al·og·i·cal,
  -al·o·gist
min·gle
  -gled, -gling
min·ia·ture
mini·com·put·er
mini·course
min·i·mal
min·i·mize
  -mized, -miz·ing
min·i·mum
  -i·ma (pl)
min·ing
min·ion
mini·state
min·is·ter (clergy-
  man; cf. *minster*)
  -tered, -ter·ing
min·is·te·ri·al

min·is·trant
min·is·tra·tion
min·is·try
  -tries
min·now
mi·nor (underage;
  cf. *miner*)
mi·nor·i·ty
min·ster (church; cf.
  minister)
min·strel
mint·age
min·u·end
min·u·et
mi·nus
mi·nus·cule
min·ute (n)(60
  seconds; cf.
  mi·nute)
mi·nute (adj)(very
  small; cf. *min·ute*)
min·ute hand
mi·nute·ly (in detail)
min·ute·man
mi·o·sis
  -ses (pl)
mir·a·cle
mi·rac·u·lous
mi·rage
mir·ror
mirth
  mirth·ful,
  mirth·ful·ly,
  mirth·ful·ness

mis·ad·ven·ture
mis·align
mis·al·li·ance
mis·an·thrope
mis·an·throp·ic
mis·an·thro·py
mis·ap·pre·hend
  -hen·sion
mis·ap·pro·pri·ate
mis·be·lief
mis·car·riage
mis·car·ry
mis·ce·ge·na·tion
mis·cel·la·nea
mis·cel·la·neous
mis·cel·la·ny
  -nies
mis·chance
mis·chief
mis·chie·vous
mis·com·mu·ni·ca·tion
mis·con·ceive
  -cep·tion
mis·con·duct
mis·con·strue
mis·cue
mis·deal
  -dealt, -dealing
mis·de·mean·or
mis·di·rect
mi·ser
mis·er·a·ble
mi·ser·ly
  -li·ness

mis·ery
  -er·ies
mis·fea·sance
mis·fire
mis·fit
mis·for·tune
mis·give
  -gave, -giv·en
mis·guide
mis·hap
mis·in·ter·pret
mis·join·der
mis·judge
mis·lay
  -laid, -lay·ing
mis·lead
  -led
mis·man·age
mis·no·mer
mi·sog·y·nist
mi·sol·o·gy
mis·place
mis·print
mis·pri·sion
mis·pro·nounce
mis·quote
mis·read
  -read, -read·ing
mis·rep·re·sent
  -sen·ta·tion,
  -sen·ta·tive
mis·rule
mis·sal (book; cf.
  missile, missive)

mis·sile (weapon; cf.
  missal, missive)
miss·ing
mis·sion
  -sioned,
  -sion·ing
mis·sion·ary
  -ar·ies
mis·sive (letter; cf.
  missal, missile)
mis·spell
mis·state
  -state·ment
mis·tak·able
mis·take
  -took, -tak·en,
  -tak·ing
mis·tle·toe
mis·tral
mis·treat
  -treat·ment
mis·tress
mis·tri·al
mis·trust
misty
mist·i·er,
mist·i·est,
mist·i·ness
mis·un·der·stand
  -stood, -stand·ing
mis·us·age
mis·use
mite (something
  tiny; cf. *might*)

164

mi·ter
 -tered, -ter·ing,
 -ter·er
mit·i·gate
 -gat·ed, -gat·ing
mit·ten
mit·ti·mus
mix·er
mix·ture
mix-up
mne·mon·ic (adj)
mne·mon·ics (n)
moan
moat (ditch; cf.
 mote)
mob
 mobbed,
 mob·bing
mo·bile
 -bil·i·ty
mo·bi·li·za·tion
mo·bi·lize
 -lized, -liz·ing
moc·ca·sin
mo·cha
mock·ery
 -er·ies
mock·ing·bird
mod·al (of a mode;
 cf. *model*)
 -al·ly
mo·dal·i·ty
 -ties
mode (fashion; cf.

mood)
mod·el (pattern; cf.
 modal)
 -eled, -el·ing
mo·dem
mod·er·ate
 -at·ed, -at·ing
mod·er·a·tor
mod·ern
mod·ern·ism
mod·ern·iza·tion
mod·ern·ize
 -ized, -iz·ing
mod·est
mod·es·ty
mo·di·cum
mod·i·fi·ca·tion
mod·i·fi·er
mod·i·fy
 -fied, -fy·ing
mod·ish
mod·u·lar
mod·u·late
 -lat·ed, -lat·ing,
 -la·tor
mod·u·la·tion
mod·ule
mod·u·lus
mo·dus ope·ran·di
mo·hair
Mo·hawk
moist
moist·en
 -ened, -en·ing

mois·ture
mo·lar
mo·las·ses
mold
moldy
 mold·i·er,
 mold·i·est
mo·lec·u·lar
mol·e·cule
mole·hill
mole·skin
mo·lest
 -les·ta·tion,
 -les·ter
mol·li·fy
 -fied, -fy·ing
mol·lusk
mol·ly·cod·dle
 -dled, -dling
mol·ten
mo·ment
mo·men·tari·ly
mo·men·tary
mo·ment·ly
mo·men·tous
mo·men·tum
mon·arch
mon·ar·chism
 -chist
mon·ar·chy
mon·as·tery
 -ter·ies
mo·nas·tic
Mon·day

mon·e·tary
mon·e·tize
  -tized, -tiz·ing
mon·ey
  mon·eys
mon·ey·bags
mon·eyed
mon·ey·lend·er
mon·ey-mak·er
mon·ey or·der
mon·ger
  -gered, -ger·ing
Mon·go·lian
mon·grel
mo·ni·tion
mon·i·tor
  -tor·ing, -tored
mon·i·to·ry
  -ries
monk·ery
  -er·ies
mon·key
  -keys, -keyed,
  -key·ing
mon·key wrench
mono·chro·mat·ic
mono·chrome
mon·o·cle
mo·nog·a·my
  -a·mous
mono·gram
  -grammed,
  -gram·ming
mono·graph

mono·lith
mono·logue
mo·nop·o·list
mo·nop·o·lis·tic
mo·nop·o·lize
  -lized, -liz·ing
mo·nop·o·ly
  -lies
mono·rail
mono·syl·lab·ic
mono·syl·la·ble
mono·tone
mo·not·o·nous
mo·not·o·ny
Mono·type
mon·ox·ide
mon·sieur
mon·si·gnor
  -gnors
mon·soon
mon·ster
mon·stros·i·ty
  -ties
mon·strous
mon·tage
  -taged, -tag·ing
month
month·ly
mon·u·ment
mon·u·men·tal
mood (feeling; cf.
  mode)
moody
  mood·i·er,

mood·i·est
moon·beam
moon·light
  -lighted,
  -light·ing, -light·er
moon·lit
moon·rise
moon·shine
moon·stone
moon·struck
moor·age
moor·ing
moose (large
  animal; cf. *mouse,*
  mousse)
  moose (pl)
mo·raine
mor·al (ethical; cf.
  morale)
mo·rale (attitude; cf.
  moral)
mor·al·ism
mor·al·ist
mo·ral·i·ty (virtue;
  cf. *mortality*)
  -ties
mor·al·ize
  -ized, -iz·ing,
  -iza·tion
mo·rass
mor·a·to·ri·um
Mo·ra·vi·an
mor·bid
mor·bid·i·ty

mor·dant (dyeing term; cf. *mordent*)

mor·dent (musical term; cf. *mordant*)

more or less

more·over

mo·res

Mor·mon

morn·ing (forenoon; cf. *mourning*)

mo·roc·co (leather)

mo·ron

-ron·ic

mo·rose

mor·phine

mor·phol·o·gy

mor·row

mor·sel

-seled, -sel·ing

mor·tal

mor·tal·i·ty (death rate; cf. *morality*)

mor·tar

mor·tar·board

mort·gage

mort·gag·ee

mort·gag·or

mor·ti·cian

mor·ti·fi·ca·tion

mor·ti·fy

-fied, -fy·ing

mor·tise

mor·tu·ary

-ar·ies

mo·sa·ic

Mo·ses

mo·sey

-seyed, -sey·ing

Mos·lem

mos·qui·to

-toes

moss·back

mote (speck; cf. *moat*)

mo·tel

moth·ball

moth-eat·en

moth·er

-ered, -er·ing

moth·er-in-law

moth·ers-in-law (pl)

moth·er·land

moth·er·ly

-li·ness

moth·er-of-pearl

moth·proof

mo·tif

mo·tion

-tioned, -tion·ing, -tion·less

mo·ti·vate

-vat·ed, -vat·ing

mo·ti·va·tion

mo·tive

mot·ley

mo·tor

mo·tor·bike

mo·tor·boat

mo·tor·cade

mo·tor·car

mo·tor·cy·cle

-cy·clist

mo·tor·drome

mo·tor·ist

mo·tor·ize

-ized, -iz·ing

mot·tle

-tled, -tling

mot·to

-toes

moun·tain

moun·tain·eer

moun·tain·ous

moun·tain·side

Mount·ie

mount·ing

mourn

mourn·er

mourn·ing (grieving; cf. *morning*)

mouse (small animal; cf. *moose*, *mousse*)

mice (pl), moused, mous·ing

mouse·trap

mousse (food; cf. *moose*, *mouse*)

mouth·ful

mouth·piece

mouth·wash
mou·ton
mov·able
move
  moved, mov·ing
move·ment
mov·ie
mow
  mowed, mow·ing
Mr.
  Messrs. (pl)
Mrs.
  Mes·dames (pl)
Ms.
  Mses. or Mss. (pl)
much
mu·ci·lage
muck·rake
mu·cous (adj)
mu·cus (n)
mud·dle
  -dled, -dling
mud·dy
  -died, -dy·ing,
  -di·ness
mud·guard
mud·sling·er
muf·fin
muf·fle
  -fled, -fling
muf·fler
muf·ti
mug
  mugged,

mug·ging
mug·ger
mu·lat·to
  -toes
mul·ber·ry
mul·ish
mull
mull·er
mul·ti·far·i·ous
mul·ti·form
mul·ti·lat·er·al
mul·ti·me·dia
mul·ti·mil·lion·aire
mul·ti·na·tion·al
mul·ti·ple
mul·ti·ple-choice
mul·ti·ple
  scle·ro·sis
mul·ti·plex
mul·ti·pli·cand
mul·ti·pli·ca·tion
mul·ti·plic·i·ty
  -ties
mul·ti·pli·er
mul·ti·ply
  -plied, -ply·ing
mul·ti·pro·cess·ing
mul·ti·pro·gram·ming
mul·ti·tude
mul·ti·tu·di·nous
mum·mi·fy
  -fied, -fy·ing
mum·my
  -mies

mun·dane
mu·nic·i·pal
mu·nic·i·pal·i·ty
mu·nif·i·cent
  (generous; cf.
  magnificent)
  -cence
mu·ni·tion
mu·ral
mur·der
  -dered, -der·ing
mur·der·er
mur·der·ous
murky
  murk·i·er,
  murk·i·est,
  murk·i·ly
mur·mur
mus·ca·tel
mus·cle (of body; cf.
  mussel, muzzle)
  -cled, -cling
mus·cle-bound
mus·cu·lar
mus·cu·lar
  dys·tro·phy
mus·cu·la·ture
muse
  mused, mus·ing
mu·se·um
mush·room
mushy
  mush·i·er,
  mush·i·est

mu·sic
mu·si·cal (about
   music; cf.
   musicale)
mu·si·cale (enter-
   tainment; cf.
   musical)
mu·si·cian
mus·ket
mus·ke·teer
musk·mel·on
musk-ox
musk·rat
musky
   musk·i·er,
   musk·i·est
Mus·lim (religion)
mus·lin (cloth)
mus·sel (shellfish;
   cf. *muscle, muzzle*)
must
mus·tache
mus·tang
mus·tard (plant; cf.
   mustered)

mus·ter
   -tered (assembled;
   cf. *mustard*),
   -ter·ing
musty
   must·i·er,
   must·i·est,
   must·i·ness
mu·ta·ble
mu·tant
mu·tate
   -tat·ed, -tat·ing
mu·ta·tion
mute
mu·ti·late
   -lat·ed, -lat·ing,
   -la·tion
mu·ti·neer
mu·ti·nous
mu·ti·ny
mut·ism
mut·ter
mut·ton
mu·tu·al
   -al·ly

mu·tu·al·ism
mu·tu·al·i·ty
muz·zle (mouth; cf.
   muscle, mussel)
   -zled, -zling
my·col·o·gy
my·o·pia
myr·i·ad
myrrh
my·self
mys·te·ri·ous
mys·tery
   -ter·ies
mys·tic
mys·ti·cal
mys·ti·cism
mys·ti·fi·ca·tion
mys·ti·fy
   -fied, -fy·ing
mys·tique
myth
myth·i·cal
myth·o·log·i·cal
my·thol·o·gy
   -gies

N

na·cho
   -chos
na·dir

nail
na·ive
na·ive·té

na·ked
name
   named, nam·ing

name·able
name·less
name·ly
name·plate
name·sake
nan·keen
nano·sec·ond
nap
  napped,
  nap·ping
na·palm
naph·tha
nap·kin
nar·cis·sism
nar·cis·sus
  -cis·si (pl)
nar·co·sis
  -co·ses (pl)
nar·cot·ic
nar·co·tize
  -tized, -tiz·ing
nar·rate
  -rat·ed, -rat·ing
nar·ra·tion
nar·ra·tive
nar·row
  -row·ly, -row·ness
nar·row-mind·ed
na·sal
  -sal·i·ty, -sal·ly
na·scent
nas·tur·tium
nas·ty
  -ti·er, -ti·est, -ti·ly

na·tal
na·tant
na·ta·to·ri·um
na·tion
na·tion·al
na·tion·al·ism
na·tion·al·i·ty
  -ties
na·tion·al·ize
  -ized, -iz·ing
na·tion·wide
na·tive
  -tive·ly, -tive·ness
na·tiv·ism
  -tiv·ist
na·tiv·i·ty
  -ties
nat·u·ral
nat·u·ral·ism
nat·u·ral·ist
nat·u·ral·is·tic
nat·u·ral·ize
  -ized, -iz·ing,
  -iza·tion
nat·u·ral·ly
na·ture
naugh·ty
  -ti·er, -ti·est, -ti·ly
nau·sea
nau·seous
nau·ti·cal
nau·ti·lus
Na·va·ho
na·val (of navy; cf.

navel)
nave (of church; cf.
  knave)
na·vel (of abdomen;
  cf. *naval*)
nav·i·ga·ble
nav·i·gate
  -gat·ed, -gat·ing
nav·i·ga·tion
nav·i·ga·tor
na·vy
  navies
na·vy yard
nay (no; cf. *née*,
  neigh)
Naz·a·rene
Na·zi
Ne·an·der·thal
Ne·a·pol·i·tan
near·by
near·ly
near·sight·ed
neat
  neat·ness
neb·u·la
  -las, -lar
neb·u·lize
  -lized, -liz·ing
neb·u·lous
nec·es·sar·i·ly
nec·es·sary
  -saries
ne·ces·si·tate
  -tat·ed, -tat·ing

ne·ces·si·ty
-ties
neck·er·chief
-chiefs
neck·lace
neck·line
neck·tie
nec·rop·sy
-sies
nec·tar
nec·tar·ine
née (born; cf. *nay*, *neigh*)
need (require; cf. *knead*)
need·ful
nee·dle
-dled, -dling
nee·dle·point
need·less
nee·dle·work
needy
need·i·er,
need·i·est
ne·far·i·ous
ne·gate
-gat·ed, -gat·ing
neg·a·tive
-tive·ly, -tive·ness
ne·glect
ne·glect·ful
neg·li·gee
neg·li·gence
neg·li·gent

neg·li·gi·ble
ne·go·tia·ble
-bil·i·ty
ne·go·ti·ate
-at·ed, -at·ing,
-a·tor
ne·go·ti·a·tion
Ne·gro
-groes, -groid
neigh (of horse; cf. *nay, née*)
neigh·bor
-bored, -bor·ing
neigh·bor·hood
neigh·bor·ly
nei·ther
nem·a·tode
nem·e·sis
-e·ses (pl)
neo·con·ser·va·tive
neo·phyte
neo·plasm
neph·ew
ne·phri·tis
-phrit·i·des (pl)
nep·o·tism
Nep·tune
nerve
nerved, nerv·ing
nerve·less
nerve-rack·ing
ner·vous
nervy
ne·science

nes·tle
-tled, -tling (v)
nest·ling (n)
neth·er·most
net·ting
net·tle
-tled, -tling
net·work
neu·ral
neu·ral·gia
neur·as·the·nia
neu·ri·tis
-rit·i·des (pl)
neu·rol·o·gist
neu·rol·o·gy
neu·ron
neu·ro·sis
-ro·ses (pl)
neu·rot·ic
neu·ter
neu·tral
-tral·ly
neu·tral·i·ty
neu·tral·iza·tion
neu·tral·ize
-ized, -iz·ing
neu·tron
nev·er
nev·er·the·less
new (recent; cf. *gnu*, *knew*)
new·ish, new·ness
new·born
new·com·er

new·el
new·ly
news·break
news·cast
news·let·ter
news·mag·a·zine
news·mon·ger
news·pa·per
news·print
news·reel
news·stand
news·wor·thy
  -wor·thi·ness
newsy
  news·i·er,
  news·i·est
New Year
next
next door (adv)
next-door (adj)
nib·ble
  -bled, -bling, -bler
nice·ty
  -ties
niche
  niched, nich·ing
nick
nick·el
  -eled, -el·ing
nick·el·if·er·ous
nick·el·ode·on
nick·name
nic·o·tine
niece

nig·gard
nig·gard·ly
night (darkness; cf.
  knight)
night·cap
night·clothes
night·club
night·fall
night·gown
night·hawk
night·in·gale
night·ly
night·mare
  -mar·ish
night·stick
night·time
night·walk·er
ni·hil·ism
  -ist, -is·tic
nim·ble
  -bler, -blest
nin·com·poop
  -poop·ery
nine·pin
nine·teen
  -teenth
nine·ty
  -ties, -ti·eth
ninth
  ninths
nip·per
nip·ple
ni·sei
  ni·sei (pl)

ni·trate
ni·tric
ni·tride
ni·tri·fi·ca·tion
ni·tri·fy
  -fied, -fy·ing
ni·trite
ni·tro·gen
ni·tro·glyc·er·in
ni·trous
nit·ty-grit·ty
no·bil·i·ty
no·ble
  -bler, -blest, -bly
no·body
  -bod·ies
noc·tur·nal
noc·turne
nod
  nod·ded, nod·ding
node
nod·u·lar
nod·ule
no-fault
noise
  noise·less
noisy
  nois·i·er,
  nois·i·est, nois·i·ly
no·mad
nom de plume
no·men·cla·ture
nom·i·nal
  -nal·ly

nom·i·nate
  -nat·ed, -nat·ing
nom·i·na·tion
nom·i·na·tive
nom·i·nee
non·bio·de·grad·able
non·cha·lant
non·com·bat·ant
non·com·mit·tal
non·con·duc·tor
non·con·form·ist
non·con·for·mi·ty
non·co·op·er·a·tion
non·de·script
non·en·ti·ty
non·es·sen·tial
none·the·less
non·ex·empt
non·ex·is·tent
non·fea·sance
non·fic·tion
non·im·pact
  print·er
non·in·ter·ven·tion
non·me·tal·lic
non·par·ti·san
non·prof·it
non·res·i·dent
non·re·sis·tant
non·re·stric·tive
non·re·turn·able
non·sched·uled
non·sense
  -sen·si·cal

non·skid
non·stan·dard
non·stop
non·sup·port
non·union
non·ver·bal
non·vi·o·lence
non·vi·o·lent
non·vot·ing
noo·dle
  -dled, -dling
noon·day
noon·tide
noon·time
nor·mal
  -mal·i·ty, -mal·ly
nor·mal·ize
  -ized, iz·ing,
  -iza·tion
nor·ma·tive
Norse
Norse·man
north·east
north·east·ern
north·er·ly
  -lies
north·ern
North·ern·er
north·land
north·ward
north·west
north·west·er·ly
north·west·ern
nose

nosed, nos·ing
nose·dive (n)
nose·gay
nose·piece
nose·wheel
no-show
nos·tal·gia
  -gic, -gi·cal·ly
nos·tril
nos·trum
not (negative; cf.
  knot)
no·ta·bil·i·ty
  -ties
no·ta·ble
no·ta·bly
no·ta·rize
  -rized, -riz·ing
no·ta·tion
note·book
not·ed
note·less
note·wor·thy
  -wor·thi·ly
noth·ing
noth·ing·ness
no·tice
  -ticed, -tic·ing
no·tice·able
  -tice·ably
no·ti·fi·ca·tion
no·ti·fy
  -fied, -fy·ing
no·tion

no·to·ri·ety
  -eties
no·to·ri·ous
not·with·stand·ing
nour·ish
nour·ish·ment
no·va·tion
nov·el
  -el·is·tic
nov·el·ette
nov·el·ist
nov·el·ize
  -ized, -iz·ing
no·vel·la
nov·el·ty
  -ties
No·vem·ber
no·ve·na
nov·ice
no·vi·tiate
No·vo·cain
now·a·days
no·way
no·where
no·win
nox·ious
noz·zle
nu·ance

nu·cle·ar
nu·cle·ate
  -at·ed, -at·ing,
  -ation
nu·cle·us
  nu·clei (pl)
nude
  nude·ly, nu·di·ty
nu·ga·to·ry
nug·get
nui·sance
nul·li·fi·ca·tion
nul·li·fi·er
nul·li·fy
  -fied, -fy·ing
num·ber
num·ber·less
nu·mer·al
nu·mer·ate
  -at·ed, -at·ing
nu·mer·a·tion
nu·mer·a·tor
nu·mer·i·cal
nu·mer·ol·o·gy
  -ol·o·gist
nu·mer·ous
nu·mis·mat·ics
  -ma·tist

num·skull
nun·nery
  -ner·ies
nup·tial
nurse·maid
nurs·ery
  -er·ies
nur·ture
  -tured, -tur·ing,
  -tur·er
nut·crack·er
nut·meg
nut·pick
nu·tri·ent
nu·tri·ment
nu·tri·tion
nu·tri·tion·ist
nu·tri·tious
  -tious·ly,
  -tious·ness
nut·shell
nut·ty
  nut·ti·er, nut·ti·est
nuz·zle
  -zled, -zling
ny·lon
nymph

oar (of a boat; cf. *or,*
    ore)
oar·lock
oars·man
oa·sis
    oa·ses (pl)
oat·cake
oath
oat·meal
ob·bli·ga·to
    -tos
ob·du·rate
obe·di·ence
obe·di·ent
obei·sance
obe·lisk
obese
obe·si·ty
obey
    obeyed, obey·ing
ob·fus·cate
    -cat·ed, -cat·ing,
    -ca·tion
obit·u·ary
    -ar·ies
ob·ject
ob·jec·tion
ob·jec·tion·able
ob·jec·tive

-tive·ly, -tive·ness,
    -tiv·i·ty
ob·jur·gate
    -gat·ed, -gat·ing,
    -ga·tion
ob·la·tion
ob·li·gate
    -gat·ed, -gat·ing
ob·li·ga·tion
oblig·a·to·ry
oblige
    obliged, oblig·ing
oblique
oblit·er·ate
    -at·ed, -at·ing
obliv·i·on
obliv·i·ous
ob·long
ob·nox·ious
oboe
    obo·ist
ob·scene
ob·scen·i·ty
    -ties
ob·scur·ant
ob·scure
    -scured, -scure·ly,
    -scure·ness
ob·scu·ri·ty

-ties
ob·se·qui·ous
ob·serv·able
ob·ser·vance
ob·ser·vant
ob·ser·va·tion
ob·ser·va·to·ry
    -ries
ob·serve
    -served, -serv·ing
ob·serv·er
ob·sess
ob·ses·sion
ob·ses·sive
ob·so·lesce
    -lesced, -lesc·ing
ob·so·les·cence
ob·so·les·cent
ob·so·lete
    -let·ed, -let·ing
ob·sta·cle
ob·stet·ric
ob·ste·tri·cian
ob·sti·na·cy
    -cies
ob·sti·nate
ob·strep·er·ous
ob·struct
ob·struc·tion

ob·tain
  -tain·able,
  -tain·abil·i·ty,
  -tain·ment
ob·trude
  -trud·ed, -trud·ing,
  -tru·sion
ob·tru·sive
ob·tuse
ob·verse
ob·vi·ate
  -at·ed, -at·ing,
  -a·tion
ob·vi·ous
oc·a·ri·na
oc·ca·sion
  -sioned, -sion·ing
oc·ca·sion·al
oc·ca·sion·al·ly
oc·ci·den·tal
  -tal·ly
oc·cip·i·tal
oc·clude
  -clud·ed,
  -clud·ing, -clu·sive
oc·clu·sion
oc·cult
oc·cult·ism
oc·cu·pan·cy
  -cies
oc·cu·pant
oc·cu·pa·tion
  -tion·al, -tion·al·ly
oc·cu·py

-pied, -py·ing,
  -pi·er
oc·cur
  -curred, -cur·ring
oc·cur·rence
ocean·go·ing
oce·an·ic
ocean·og·ra·phy
  -og·ra·pher,
  -o·graph·ic
oce·lot
o'clock
oc·ta·gon
  -tag·o·nal,
  -tag·o·nal·ly
oc·tane
oc·tave
oc·ta·vo
Oc·to·ber
oc·to·ge·nar·i·an
oc·to·pus
  -pus·es (pl)
oc·u·lar
oc·u·list
odd·i·ty
  -ties
ode (poem; cf. *owed*)
odi·ous
odi·um
odor
  odored, odor·less
odor·if·er·ous
odor·ize
  -ized, -iz·ing

od·ys·sey
  -seys
off·beat
off·cast
off-col·or
of·fend
  -fend·er
of·fense
of·fen·sive
of·fer
  -fer·ing
of·fered
of·fer·to·ry
  -ries
off·hand
off-hour
of·fice
of·fice·hold·er
of·fi·cer
of·fi·cial (autho-
  rized; cf. *officious*)
of·fi·cial·ism
of·fi·ci·ary
  -ar·ies
of·fi·ci·ate
  -at·ed, -at·ing,
  -a·tion
of·fi·cious (meddle-
  some; cf. *official*)
off·ing
off-key
off-lim·its
off-line
off-peak

off·print
off·sea·son
off·set
  -set, -set·ting
off·shore
off·side
off·spring
off·stage
off-the-rec·ord
off-white
off year
of·ten
of·ten·times
ohm
ohm·me·ter
oil·er
oil field
oil pan
oil·skin
oil slick
oil well
oily
  oil·i·er, oil·i·est,
  oil·i·ness
oint·ment
OK or okay
  OK'd or okayed,
  OK'ing or okay·ing
old·en
old-fash·ioned
old-line
old·ster
old-time (adj)
old-tim·er (n)

old-world (adj)
oleo·graph
oleo·mar·ga·rine
ol·fac·tion
ol·fac·to·ry
oli·gar·chy
  -chies
ol·ive
olym·pi·ad
Olym·pi·an
Olym·pic
Olym·pus
om·buds·man
om·elet
om·i·nous
  -nous·ness
omis·si·ble
omis·sion
omit
  omit·ted, omit·ting
om·ni·bus
om·ni·di·rec·tion·al
om·nip·o·tence
om·nip·o·tent
om·ni·pres·ent
om·ni·science
om·ni·scient
om·niv·o·rous
on-again, off-again
once-over (n)
on·col·o·gy
on·com·ing
one (single thing; cf.
  won)

one-lin·er
one·ness
one-on-one
oner·ous
one·self
one-sid·ed
one-time
one-to-one
one-up·man·ship
one-way (adj)
on·go·ing
on·ion
on·ion·skin
on-line
on·look·er
on·ly
on·rush
on·set
on·slaught
on·to
on·tog·e·ny
on·tol·o·gy
onus
on·ward
on·yx
oozy
  ooz·i·er, ooz·i·est
opac·i·ty
  -ties
opal·es·cent
opaque
open
  opened, open·ing,
  open·er

177

open air (n)
open-air (adj)
open-end (adj)
open·hand·ed
open·heart·ed
open-hearth
open house
open-mind·ed
open-mouthed
open·work
op·era
 -er·at·ic
op·er·a·ble
op·er·ate
 -at·ed
op·er·at·ing
op·er·a·tion
op·er·a·tion·al
op·er·a·tive
op·er·a·tor
op·er·et·ta
oph·thal·mol·o·gist
oph·thal·mol·o·gy
oph·thal·mo·scope
opi·ate
opin·ion
opin·ion·at·ed
opi·um
op·po·nent
op·por·tune
 -tune·ly,
 -tune·ness
op·por·tun·ism
 -tun·ist, -tu·nis·tic

op·por·tu·ni·ty
 -ties
op·pose
 -posed, -pos·ing,
 -pos·er
op·po·site
 -site·ly
op·po·si·tion
op·press
 -pres·sor
op·pres·sion
op·pres·sive
 -sive·ness
op·ti·cal
op·ti·cian
op·tics
op·ti·mal
 -mal·ly
op·ti·mism
 -mist, -mis·tic,
 -mis·ti·cal·ly
op·ti·mize
 -mized, -mizing
op·ti·mum
 -ma (pl)
op·tion
op·tion·al
 -al·ly
op·tom·e·trist
op·tom·e·try
 -to·met·ric
op·u·lence
op·u·lent
or (conjunction; cf.

 oar, ore)
or·a·cle
oral (spoken; cf.
 aural)
oral·ly
or·ange
or·ange·ade
orang·utan
ora·tion
or·a·tor
or·a·tor·i·cal
or·a·to·ry
 -ries
or·bit
 -bit·al
or·chard
or·ches·tra
or·ches·tral
or·ches·trate
 -trat·ed, -trat·ing,
 -tra·tor
or·ches·tra·tion
or·chid
or·dain
 -dain·ment
or·deal
or·der
 -dered, -dering
or·der·li·ness
or·der·ly
 -lies
or·di·nal
or·di·nance (law;
 cf. *ordnance*)

or·di·nary
    -nar·ies, -nari·ly,
    -nari·ness
or·di·nate
or·di·na·tion
ord·nance (muni-
    tions; cf.
    ordinance)
ore (mineral; cf. *oar*,
    or)
or·gan
or·gan·ic
    -i·cal·ly
or·gan·ism
or·gan·ist
or·ga·ni·za·tion
or·ga·nize
    -ga·nized,
    -ga·niz·ing,
    -gan·iz·able
or·gy
    -gies
ori·ent
ori·en·tal
ori·en·tal·ism
ori·en·tate
    -tat·ed, -tat·ing
ori·en·ta·tion
or·i·fice
or·i·gin
orig·i·nal
orig·i·nal·i·ty
orig·i·nate
    -nat·ed, -nat·ing,

    -na·tion, -na·tor
ori·ole
or·na·ment
or·na·men·tal
or·na·men·ta·tion
or·nate
or·ni·thol·o·gy
    -thol·o·gist,
    -tho·log·i·cal,
    -tho·log·i·cal·ly
or·phan
    -phaned,
    -phan·ing
or·phan·age
or·tho·dox
or·thog·ra·phy
or·tho·pe·dic
os·cil·late
    -lat·ed, -lat·ing
os·cil·la·tion
os·cil·la·tor
os·mo·sis
os·prey
os·si·fi·ca·tion
os·si·fy
    -fied, -fy·ing
os·ten·si·ble
os·ten·sive
    -sive·ly
os·ten·ta·tion
os·ten·ta·tious
os·teo·path
os·te·op·a·thy
    -teo·path·ic,

    -teo·path·i·cal·ly
os·teo·po·ro·sis
os·tra·cism
os·tra·cize
    -cized, -ciz·ing
os·trich
oth·er
oth·er·wise
ot·to·man
ought (should; cf.
    aught)
our (possessive; cf.
    hour)
our·self
our·selves
oust·er
out
out-and-out
out·bal·ance
out·bid
out·bound
out·break
out·burst
out·cast
out·class
out·come
out·cry
out·dat·ed
out·dis·tance
out·do
out·door (adj)
out·doors (n, adv)
out·er
out·er·most

out·field
out·fit
  -fit·ted, -fit·ting
out·fit·ter
out·flank
out·fox
out·go
  -goes
out·go·ing
out·grow
  -grew, -grown,
  -grow·ing
out·growth
out·guess
out·ing
out·land·ish
out·lay
  -laid, -lay·ing
out·let
out·line
out·live
out·look
out·ly·ing
out·ma·neu·ver
out·match
out·mode
  -mod·ed, -mod·ing
out·num·ber
out-of-date
out-of-door
out-of-the-way
out·pa·tient
out·point
out·post

out·pour·ing
out·put
  -put·ted
out·rage
  -raged, -rag·ing
out·ra·geous
out·reach
out·rid·er
out·rig·ger
out·right
out·run
  -ran, -run,
  -run·ning
out·sell
  -sold, -sell·ing
out·set
out·side
out·sid·er
out·skirt
out·smart
out·soar
out·speak
  -spoke, -spo·ken,
  -speak·ing
out·spread
  -spread,
  -spread·ing
out·stand·ing
out·stay
out·stretch
out·ward
out·ward·ly
out·wear
  -wore, -worn,

  -wear·ing
out·weigh
out·wit
out·work
oval
  oval·ness
ova·ry
  -ries
ova·tion
ov·en
over
over·abun·dance
over·achiev·er
over·all
over and over
over·arm
over·bal·ance
over·board
over·build
  -built, -build·ing
over·bur·den
over·cap·i·tal·ize
  -iza·tion
over·cast
  -cast, -cast·ing
over·charge
over·coat
over·come
  -came, -come,
  -com·ing
over·com·mit
over·do (too much;
  cf. *overdue*)
  -did, -do·ing, -does

over·dose
over·draft
over·draw
-drew, -drawn,
-draw·ing
over·due (past due;
cf. *overdo*)
over·flow
over·grow
-grew, -grown,
-grow·ing
over·hand
over·hang
-hung, -hang·ing
over·haul
over·head
over·hear
-heard, -hear·ing
over·heat
over·land
over·lay
-laid, -lay·ing
over·look
over·lord
over·ly
over·night
over·pass
over·pop·u·la·tion
over·pow·er
over·price
over·qual·i·fied
over·reach
over·ride
-rode, -rid·den,

-rid·ing
over·rule
over·run
-ran, -run,
-run·ning
over·seas
over·see
-saw, -seen,
-see·ing
over·seer
over·shad·ow
over·shoe
over·sight
over·size
over·sleep
-slept, -sleep·ing
over·spread
-spread,
-spread·ing
over·stay
over·step
over·sub·scribe
overt
overt·ness
over·take
-took, -tak·en,
-tak·ing
over-the-count·er
over·throw
-threw, -thrown,
-throw·ing
over·time
over·tone
over·ture

-tured, -tur·ing
over·turn
over·view
over·weigh
over·weight
over·whelm·ing
over·work
over·write
-wrote, -writ·ten
owe
owed (indebted;
cf. *ode*), ow·ing
owl·et
owl·ish
own
own·er,
own·er·ship
ox·al·ic ac·id
ox·bow
ox·ford
ox·heart
ox·i·da·tion
ox·ide
ox·i·dize
-dized, -diz·ing,
-diz·able
ox·tail
ox·tongue
ox·y·gen
ox·y·gen·ate
-at·ed, -at·ing
oys·ter
oys·ter bed
ozone

P

pace
  paced, pac·ing
pace·mak·er
pac·er
pachy·derm
pac·i·fi·er
pac·i·fist
pac·i·fy
  -fied, -fy·ing
pack·age
  -aged, -ag·ing
pack·age deal
pack·er
pack·et
pack·horse
pack·ing
pack·sad·dle
pact
pad
  pad·ded, pad·ding
pad·dle
  -dled, -dling
pad·dock
pad·lock
pa·dre
pa·gan
pa·gan·ism
pa·gan·ize
  -ized, -iz·ing

pag·eant
pag·eant·ry
pag·i·nate
  -nat·ed, -nat·ing
pag·i·na·tion
pa·go·da
paid
pail (bucket; cf. *pale*)
pain (hurt; cf. *pane*)
  pain·less
pain·ful
pain·kill·er
pains·tak·ing
paint·brush
paint·er
pair (two; cf. *pare,
  pear*)
pa·ja·mas
pal·ace
pal·at·able
pal·ate (roof of the
  mouth; cf. *palette,
  pallet*)
pa·la·tial
pale (white; cf. *pail*)
  pal·er, pal·est,
  pal·ing
pa·le·on·tol·o·gy
pal·ette (for paint;

cf. *palate, pallet*)
pal·i·mony
pal·i·sade
pall·bear·er
pal·let (couch; cf.
  palate, palette)
pal·lid
pal·lor
palm
pal·met·to
palm·ist·ry
pal·o·mi·no
pal·pa·ble
pal·pate (examine
  by touch; cf.
  palpitate)
pal·pi·tate (throb; cf.
  palpate)
pal·sy
  -sied, -sy·ing
pal·try (trivial; cf.
  poultry)
  -tri·er, -tri·est
pam·per
  -pered, -per·ing
pam·phlet
pan
  panned, pan·ning
pan·a·cea

Pan-Amer·i·can
pan·cake
pan·chro·mat·ic
pan·cre·as
pan·dem·ic
pan·de·mo·ni·um
pan·dow·dy
pane (of glass; cf.
  pain)
pan·el
  -eled, -el·ing
pan·el·ist
pan·han·dle
pan·ic
  -icked, -ick·ing
pan·ic-strick·en
pan·ora·ma
pan·sy
  -sies
pan·ta·loon
pan·the·on
pan·ther
pan·to·graph
pan·to·mime
  -mimed, -mim·ing
pan·try
pa·pa·cy
  -cies
pa·pal
pa·pa·raz·zi (pl)
  -raz·zo (sing)
pa·pa·ya
pa·per
pa·per·weight

pa·per·work
pa·pier-mâ·ché
pa·poose
pa·pri·ka
pa·py·rus
par·a·ble
pa·rab·o·la
para·chute
  -chut·ed, -chut·ing
pa·rade
par·a·digm
par·a·dise
par·a·dox·i·cal
par·af·fin
par·a·gon
para·graph
par·a·keet
para·lan·guage
para·le·gal
par·al·lel
par·al·lel·ism
par·al·lel·o·gram
pa·ral·y·sis
  -ses (pl)
par·a·lyt·ic
par·a·lyze
  -lyzed, -lyz·ing
para·med·ic
pa·ram·e·ter
par·a·mount
para·noia
para·noid
par·a·pet
par·a·pher·na·lia

para·phrase
  -phrased,
  -phras·ing
para·ple·gia
para·pro·fes·sion·al
par·a·site
para·sol
para·troop·er
par·boil
par·cel (bundle; cf.
  partial)
  -celed, -cel·ing
parch·ment
par·don
  -doned, -don·ing
par·don·able
par·don·er
pare (peel; cf. *pair,
  pear*)
  pared, par·ing
par·ent
pa·ren·tal
par·ent·age
pa·ren·the·sis
  -the·ses (pl),
  -thet·ic,
  -thet·i·cal·ly
par·ent·hood
pa·re·sis
par·fait
pa·ri·etal
pari-mu·tu·el
par·ish (church; cf.
  perish)

pa·rish·io·ner
par·i·ty
  -ties
park·way
par·lay (gamble)
par·lia·ment
par·lia·men·tar·i·an
par·lia·men·ta·ry
par·lor
pa·ro·chi·al
par·o·dy
  -dies
pa·role
  -roled, -rol·ing
par·ox·ysm
par·rot
par·si·mo·ni·ous
par·si·mo·ny
pars·ley
pars·nip
par·son
par·son·age
par·take
part·ed
par·tial (part; cf. *parcel*)
par·tial·i·ty
par·tic·i·pant
par·tic·i·pate
  -pat·ed, -pat·ing
par·tic·i·pa·tion
par·ti·ci·ple
par·ti·cle
par·tic·u·lar

par·tic·u·lar·i·ty
par·tic·u·lar·ize
  -ized, -iz·ing
par·tic·u·lar·ly
par·ti·san
par·ti·tion
part·ly
part·ner
part·ner·ship
par·tridge
part-time
par·tu·ri·tion
par·ty
  -ties, -tied, -ty·ing
pass
pass·able
pas·sage
pas·sage·way
pass·book
pas·sé
passed (of movement; cf. *past*)
pas·sen·ger
passe-par·tout
pass·er·by
  pass·ers·by (pl)
pass-fail
pas·si·ble
pass·ing
pas·sion
pas·sion·ate
pas·sive
pass·key
pass·port

pass·word
past (of time; cf. *passed*)
paste
  past·ed, past·ing
pas·tel
pas·tern
pas·teur·iza·tion
pas·teur·ize
  -ized, -iz·ing
pas·time
pas·tor
pas·to·ral
pas·to·ral·ism
pas·tor·ate
pas·tra·mi
past·ry
  -ries
pas·ture
  -tured, -tur·ing
pas·ty
  -ties
patch·work
pâ·té
pa·tent (adj)
pat·ent (n, v)
pa·ter·nal
pa·ter·nal·ism
pa·ter·ni·ty
pa·thet·ic
path·find·er
patho·log·i·cal
pa·thol·o·gy
  -gies

pa·thos
path·way
pa·tience
pa·tient
pa·tio
pa·tri·arch
pa·tri·ar·chy
  -chies
pa·tri·cian
pat·ri·mo·ny
pa·tri·ot
pa·tri·ot·ic
pa·tri·o·tism
pa·trol
  -trolled, -trol·ling
pa·tron
pa·tron·age
pa·tron·ize
  -ized, -iz·ing
pat·ter
pat·tern
pat·ty
  -ties
pau·ci·ty
paunch
pau·per
pause
pave
pa·vil·ion
paw
pawn·bro·ker
pay
  paid, pay·ing
pay·able

pay·check
pay·day
pay·ee
pay·load
pay·ment
pay off (v)
pay·off (n)
pay·roll
peace (calm; cf.
  piece)
peace·able
peace·ful
peace·mak·er
peace·time
peach
pea·cock
peak (top; cf. *peek,*
  pique)
peal (loud ringing;
  cf. *peel*)
pea·nut
pear (fruit; cf. *pair,*
  pare)
pearl
pear-shaped
peas·ant
peb·ble
pec·cant
pec·to·ral
pe·cu·liar
  -liar·ly
pe·cu·liar·i·ty
  -ties
pe·cu·ni·ary

ped·a·gog·ic
ped·a·gogue
ped·a·go·gy
ped·al (of a bicycle;
  cf. *peddle*)
  -aled, -al·ing
pe·dan·tic
ped·dle (sell; cf.
  pedal)
  -dled, -dling
ped·dler
ped·es·tal
pe·des·tri·an
pe·di·a·tri·cian
pe·di·at·rics
ped·i·cure
ped·i·gree
ped·i·ment
pe·dom·e·ter
peek (look; cf. *peak,*
  pique)
peel (pare; cf. *peal*)
peer (look; cf. *pier*)
peer·less
peeve
peg
  pegged, peg·ging
Peg·a·sus
pel·i·can
pel·let
pell-mell
pel·lu·cid
pelt
pel·vis

pen
  penned, pen·ning
pe·nal
pe·nal·ize
  -ized, -iz·ing
pen·al·ty
  -ties
pen·ance
pen·chant
pen·cil
  -ciled, -cil·ing
pen·dant
pen·dent
pend·ing
pen·du·lous
pen·du·lum
pen·e·tra·ble
  -bil·i·ty
pen·e·trate
  -trat·ed, -trat·ing
pen·e·tra·tion
pen·guin
pen·i·cil·lin
pen·in·su·la
pen·i·tence
pen·i·tent
pen·i·ten·tial
pen·i·ten·tia·ry
pen·knife
pen·man·ship
pen·nant
pen·ni·less
pen·ny
  -nies

pen·ny ante (n)
pen·ny-ante (adj)
pen·ny·weight
pe·nol·o·gy
pen·sion
  -sioned, -sion·ing
pen·sive
  -sive·ly,
  -sive·ness
pen·ta·gon
  -tag·o·nal
pen·tath·lon
Pen·te·cost
pent·house
pe·nult
pen·ul·ti·mate
pen·u·ry
pe·on
pe·o·ny
  -nies
peo·ple
  -pled, -pling
pep·per
  -pered, -per·ing
pep·per-and-salt
pep·per·corn
pep·per·mint
pep·pery
pep·sin
pep talk
per
per an·num
per·cale
per cap·i·ta

per·ceive
  -ceived, -ceiv·ing,
  -ceiv·able
per·cent
per·cent·age
per·cen·tile
per·cept
per·cep·ti·ble
per·cep·tion
per·cep·tive
per·cep·tu·al
Per·che·ron
per·co·late
  -lat·ed, -lat·ing
per·co·la·tor
per·cus·sion
per di·em
pe·remp·to·ry
pe·ren·ni·al
per·fect
per·fect·i·ble
per·fec·tion
per·fo·rate
  -rat·ed, -rat·ing
per·fo·ra·tion
per·form
  -form·er
per·for·mance
per·fume
  -fumed, -fum·ing
per·fum·er
per·func·to·ry
  -to·ri·ly
per·haps

per·il·ous
  -ous·ness
pe·rim·e·ter
pe·ri·od
pe·ri·od·ic
pe·ri·od·i·cal
  -cal·ly
pe·riph·er·al
pe·riph·er·y
  -er·ies
peri·scope
per·ish (die; cf.
  parish)
per·ish·able
  -abil·i·ty
peri·to·ni·tis
per·i·win·kle
per·jure
  -jured, -jur·ing
per·jur·er
per·ju·ry
per·ma·nence
per·ma·nen·cy
per·ma·nent
per·me·abil·i·ty
per·me·able
per·me·ate
  -at·ed, -at·ing
per·me·ation
per·mis·si·ble
per·mis·sion
per·mis·sive
  -sive·ness
per·mit

-mit·ted, -mit·ting
per·mu·ta·tion
per·ni·cious
  -cious·ness
per·ox·ide
per·pen·dic·u·lar
per·pe·trate
  -trat·ed, -trat·ing,
  -tra·tion
per·pet·u·al
  -al·ly
per·pet·u·ate
  -at·ed, -at·ing,
  -a·tion
per·pe·tu·ity
  -ities
per·plex
per·plex·i·ty
  -ties
per·qui·site
per se
per·se·cute (harass;
  cf. *prosecute*)
  -cut·ed, -cut·ing
per·se·cu·tion
per·se·ver·ance
per·se·vere
  -vered, -ver·ing,
  -ver·ing·ly
Per·sian
per·sim·mon
per·sist
per·sis·tence
per·sis·tent

per·son
per·son·able
per·son·age
per·son·al (not
  public; cf.
  personnel)
per·son·al·i·ty
  -ties
per·son·al·ize
per·son·al·ly
per·son·i·fi·ca·tion
per·son·i·fy
per·son·nel
  (employees; cf.
  personal)
per·spec·tive
  (appearance to the
  eye; cf. *prospec-
  tive*)
per·spi·ca·cious
per·spic·u·ous
per·spi·ra·tion
per·spire
  -spired, -spir·ing
per·suade
  -suad·ed,
  -suad·ing
per·sua·si·ble
per·sua·sion
per·sua·sive
  -sive·ness
per·tain
per·ti·na·cious
per·ti·nent

per·turb

pe·ruse
   -rused, -rus·ing,
   -rus·al

per·vade
   -vad·ed, -vad·ing

per·va·sive
   -sive·ness

per·verse
   -verse·ness,
   -ver·si·ty

per·ver·sion

per·ver·sive

per·vert

pes·si·mism
   -mist

pes·si·mis·tic

pes·ti·cide

pes·ti·lence

pes·ti·lent

pet
   pet·ted, pet·ting

pet·al

pe·tite (small)

pe·ti·tion
   -tioned, -tion·ing,
   -tion·er

pet·ri·fy
   -fied, -fy·ing

pe·tro·leum

pe·trol·o·gy

pet·ti·coat

pet·ty
   -ti·er, -ti·est,

-ti·ness

pet·u·lant

pe·tu·nia

pew·ter

pha·lanx
   -lanx·es (pl)

phan·tom

pha·raoh

phar·i·see

phar·ma·ceu·ti·cal

phar·ma·cist

phar·ma·cy
   -cies

phar·ynx

phase
   phased, phas·ing

phase out (v)

phase·out (n)

pheas·ant

phe·nom·e·nal

phe·nom·e·non
   -na (pl)

phi·lan·der
   -dered, -der·ing,
   -der·er

phil·an·throp·ic
   -i·cal·ly

phi·lan·thro·py
   -pies

phi·lat·e·list

phi·lat·e·ly
   phil·a·tel·ic

Phil·har·mon·ic

phi·lol·o·gy

phi·los·o·pher

philo·soph·i·cal
   -cal·ly

phi·los·o·phy
   -phies

phil·ter (drug; cf.
   filter)

phlegm

phleg·mat·ic

pho·bia

phoe·nix

pho·net·ic
   -net·i·cal

pho·nics

pho·no·graph

pho·ny

phos·phate

phos·pho·resce
   -resced, -resc·ing

phos·pho·res·cence

phos·pho·res·cent

phos·pho·ric

phos·pho·rous (adj)

phos·pho·rus (n)

pho·to·copy
   -cop·ier

pho·to·elec·tric

pho·to·en·grav·ing

pho·to·ge·nic
   -ni·cal·ly

pho·to·graph
   -tog·ra·pher

pho·to·graph·ic
   -i·cal·ly

pho·tog·ra·phy
phrase
  phrased,
  phras·ing
phrase·ol·o·gy
phre·nol·o·gy
  -gist
phys·ic (medicine;
  cf. *physique*,
  psychic)
phys·i·cal (of the
  body; cf. *fiscal*)
  -cal·ly, -cal·ness
phy·si·cian
phys·i·cist
phys·ics
phys·i·ol·o·gy
  -gist
phy·sique (of the
  body; cf. *physic*,
  psychic)
pi·a·nis·si·mo
pi·a·nist
pi·ano (n)
  pi·anos
pi·ca
pic·a·dor
pic·a·yune
  -yun·ish
pic·ca·lil·li
pic·co·lo
  -los
pick·er·el
pick·et

pick·le
  -led, -ling
pick·lock
pick·pock·et
pick up (v)
pick·up (n)
pic·nic
  -nicked, -nick·ing,
  -nick·er
pi·cot
pic·to·graph
pic·to·ri·al
  -al·ly
pic·ture
  -tured, -tur·ing
pic·tur·esque
  -esque·ly,
  -esque·ness
pid·gin (language;
  cf. *pigeon*)
piece (part; cf.
  peace)
  pieced, piec·ing
piece·meal
pie chart
pie·crust
pie·plant
pier (dock; cf. *peer*)
pierce
  pierced, pierc·ing
pi·ety
  -eties
pi·geon (bird; cf.
  pidgin)

pi·geon-toed
pig·gy·back
pig·ment
pig·men·ta·tion
pig·skin
pik·er
pi·laf
pi·las·ter
pile
  piled, pil·ing
pil·fer
  -fered, -fer·ing,
  -fer·age
pil·grim
pil·grim·age
  -aged, -ag·ing
pil·ing
pil·lage
  -laged, -lag·ing,
  -lag·er
pil·lar
pil·low
pil·low·case
pi·lot
pi·lot·house
pi·lot light
pi·men·to
  -tos
pim·ple
pin·afore
pin·cush·ion
pine
  pined, pin·ing
pine·ap·ple

189

pin·feath·er
pin·hole
pin·ion
pink·eye
pin·na·cle (highest
    point; cf. *pinochle*)
    -cled, -cling
pi·noch·le (card
    game; cf.
    pinnacle)
pin·point
pin·stripe
pin·up
pi·o·neer
pi·ous
pipe dream
pipe·line
pip·er
pipe wrench
pi·quant
pique (provoke; cf.
    peak, peek)
    piqued, piqu·ing
pi·ra·cy
    -cies
pi·ra·nha
pi·rate
    -rated, -rat·ing
pir·ou·ette
pis·ta·chio
pis·til (of plant; cf.
    pistol, pistole)
pis·tol (weapon; cf.
    pistil, pistole)

pis·tole (old coin; cf.
    pistil, pistol)
pis·ton
pitch
pitch-dark
pitch·er
pitch·fork
pit·e·ous
pit·fall
pithy
    pith·i·ly
piti·able
piti·ful
    -ful·ly, -ful·ness
piti·less
pit·tance
pi·tu·itary
pity
    pit·ied, pity·ing
piv·ot
piv·ot·al
piz·za
piz·ze·ria
piz·zi·ca·to
pla·ca·ble
plac·ard
pla·cate
    -cated, -cat·ing,
    -ca·tion
pla·ce·bo
    -bos
place·kick
place mat
place·ment

plac·id
pla·gia·rism
    -rist
pla·gia·rize
    -rized, -riz·ing
plague
    plagued,
    plagu·ing
plain (simple; cf.
    plane)
plain·clothes·man
plain·spo·ken
plain·tiff (complain-
    ant; cf. *plaintive*)
plain·tive (mourn-
    ful; cf. *plaintiff*)
    -tive·ly, -tive·ness
plait (fold; cf. *plat,
    plate, pleat*)
plan
    planned, plan·ning
plane (airplane; cf.
    plain)
plan·et
plan·e·tar·i·um
plan·e·tary
plank
plank·ton
plan·tain
plan·tar (of the sole;
    cf. *planter*)
plan·ta·tion
plant·er (farmer; cf.
    plantar)

plaque
plas·ter
  -tered, -ter·ing,
  -ter·er
plas·ter·board
plas·tic
plas·tic·i·ty
plat (map; cf. *plait,*
  plate, pleat)
plate (dish; cf. *plait,*
  plat, pleat)
pla·teau
plat·en
plat·form
plat·i·num
plat·i·tude
plat·i·tu·di·nous
pla·ton·ic
pla·toon
plat·ter
plau·dit
plau·si·bil·i·ty
  -ties
plau·si·ble
  -ble·ness, -bly
play back (v)
play·back (n)
play·er
play·ful
play·ground
play off (v)
play-off (n)
play·pen
play·suit

play·thing
play·wright
pla·za
plea
plead
  plead·ed,
  plead·ing,
  plead·able
pleas·ant
pleas·ant·ry
  -ries
please
  pleased, pleas·ing
plea·sur·able
plea·sure
pleat (arrange in
  pleats; cf. *plait,*
  plat, plate)
ple·be·ian
  -ian·ism
pleb·i·scite
pledge
  pledged,
  pledg·ing
plen·i·tude
plen·te·ous
plen·ti·ful
plen·ty
pleth·o·ra
pleu·ri·sy
pli·able
  -abil·i·ty
pli·ant
pli·ers

plod
  plod·ded,
  plod·ding,
  plod·der
plot
  plot·ted, plot·ting,
  plot·ter
plug
  plugged,
  plug·ging
plum (fruit; cf.
  plumb, plume)
plum·age
plumb (weight; cf.
  plum, plume)
plumb·er
plumb·ing
plumb line
plume (feather; cf.
  plum, plumb)
plum·met
plump·ness
plun·der
plunge
  plunged,
  plung·ing
plung·er
plu·ral
plu·ral·ism
  -is·tic
plu·ral·i·ty
  -ties
plu·ral·ize
  -ized, -iz·ing

191

plu·toc·ra·cy
-cies
plu·to·ni·um
ply·wood
pneu·mat·ic
pneu·mo·nia
pneu·mon·ic
poach·er
pock·et
-et·ful
pock·et·knife
pock·et-sized
po·di·a·try
-trist
po·di·um
po·em
po·esy
-esies
po·et
po·et·ic
po·et·ry
poi·gnan·cy
poi·gnant
poin·set·tia
point
point-blank
point·ed
point·er
point·less
poi·son
-soned, -son·ing
poi·son·ous
poi·son-pen (adj)
pok·er

po·lar
po·lar·i·ty
-ties
po·lar·iza·tion
po·lar·ize
-ized, -iz·ing
Po·lar·oid
pole (rod; cf. *poll*)
poled, pol·ing
po·lem·ic
po·lem·i·cal
pole vault (n)
pole-vault (v)
po·lice·man
po·lice·wom·an
pol·i·cy
-cies
pol·i·cy·hold·er
pol·ish
Pol·ish
po·lit·bu·ro
po·lite
-lit·er, -lit·est,
-lite·ness
pol·i·tic
po·lit·i·cal
-cal·ly
pol·i·ti·cian
pol·i·tics
pol·ka
poll (vote; cf. *pole*)
pol·len
pol·li·nate
-nat·ed, -nat·ing

poll tax
pol·lute
-lut·ed, -lut·ing,
-lut·er
pol·lu·tion
pol·ter·geist
poly·chro·mat·ic
poly·chrome
poly·eth·yl·ene
po·lyg·a·mous
po·lyg·a·my
-mist
poly·gon
poly·graph
poly·no·mi·al
pol·yp
poly·syl·lab·ic
poly·syl·la·ble
poly·tech·nic
poly·un·sat·u·rat·ed
pome·gran·ate
pom·mel
-meled, -mel·ing
pom·pa·dour
pom·pos·i·ty
-ties
pomp·ous
-ous·ness
pon·cho
pon·der
-dered, -der·ing
pon·der·a·ble
pon·der·ous
pon·tiff

pon·tif·i·cal
pon·tif·i·cate
pon·toon
po·ny
  -nies
poo·dle
pool·room
poor·ly
pop
  popped, pop·ping
pop·corn
pop·gun
pop·lar (tree; cf. *popular*)
pop·lin
pop·over
pop·py
  -pies
pop·u·lace (people; cf. *populous*)
pop·u·lar (widely liked; cf. *poplar*)
pop·u·lar·i·ty
pop·u·lar·ize
  -ized, -iz·ing, -iza·tion
pop·u·late
  -lat·ed, -lat·ing
pop·u·la·tion
pop·u·lous (thickly populated; cf. *populace*)
por·ce·lain
porch

por·cu·pine
pore (study; cf. *pour*)
  pored, por·ing
po·rous
por·poise
por·ridge
por·ta·ble
  -bly, -bil·i·ty
por·tage
  -taged, -tag·ing
por·tal
por·tend
por·tent
por·ten·tous
por·ter
por·ter·house
port·fo·lio
port·hole
por·ti·co
por·tion
  -tioned, -tion·ing
port·ly
  -li·er, -li·ness
por·trait
por·tray
por·tray·al
Por·tu·guese
po·si·tion
  -tioned, -tion·ing
pos·i·tive
  -tive·ly, -tive·ness
pos·i·tron
pos·se
pos·sess

-sess·or
pos·sessed
pos·ses·sion
pos·ses·sive
pos·si·bil·i·ty
  -ties
pos·si·ble
  -bly
post·age
post·al
post·box
post·card
post·date
post·doc·tor·al
post·er
pos·te·ri·or
pos·ter·i·ty
pos·tern
post·grad·u·ate
post·haste
post·hole
post·hu·mous
post·hyp·not·ic
post·lude
post·mark
post·mas·ter
post·mis·tress
post·mor·tem
post of·fice (n)
post·paid
post·par·tum
post·pone
  -poned, -pon·ing, -pone·ment

post·script
post·test
pos·tu·lant
pos·tu·late
  -lat·ed, -lat·ing
pos·ture
  -tured, -tur·ing
po·ta·ble
pot·ash
po·tas·si·um
po·ta·to
  -toes
pot·bel·ly
po·ten·cy
  -cies
po·tent
po·ten·tate
po·ten·tial
po·ten·ti·al·i·ty
pot·hole
po·tion
pot·luck
pot·pie
pot·pour·ri
pot·shot
pot·tage
pot·ter
pot·tery
  -ter·ies
pouch
poul·tice
  -ticed, -tic·ing
poul·try (fowl; cf.
  paltry)

pound·age
pour (rain; cf. *pore*)
  pour·able
poverty
pow·der
  -dered, -der·ing
pow·er·ful
pow·er·less
pow·er pack
prac·ti·ca·ble
  (feasible; cf.
  practical)
  -bly, -bil·i·ty
prac·ti·cal (useful;
  cf. *practicable*)
  -cal·i·ty, -cal·ness
prac·ti·cal·ly
prac·tice
prac·ti·cum
prac·ti·tio·ner
prag·mat·ic
prag·ma·tism
  -tist
prai·rie
praise
  praised, prais·ing
praise·wor·thy
pra·line
prank·ish
prat·tle
  -tled, -tling
pray (beseech; cf.
  prey)
prayer (address or

petition)
pray·er (one who
  prays)
preach
  preach·er
pre·am·ble
pre·can·cel
  -cel·la·tion
pre·car·i·ous
  -ous·ness
pre·cau·tion
  -tion·ary
pre·cede (go before;
  cf. *proceed*)
  -ced·ed, -ced·ing
pre·ce·dence
  (priority)
pre·ce·dent
pre·ced·ing
pre·cept
pre·cep·tive
pre·cep·tor
pre·ces·sion
  -sion·al
pre·cinct
pre·cious
prec·i·pice
pre·cip·i·tate
  -tat·ed, -tat·ing,
  -tate·ly
pre·cip·i·ta·tion
pre·cip·i·tous
pre·cise
pre·ci·sion

pre·clude
 -clud·ed, -clud·ing
pre·co·cious
 -cious·ness
pre·con·ceive
pre·con·cep·tion
pre·cook
pre·cur·sor
 -so·ry
pre·date
pred·a·tor
pred·a·to·ry
pre·de·cease
pre·de·ces·sor
pre·des·ti·na·tion
pre·des·tine
pre·de·ter·mine
pre·dic·a·ment
pred·i·cate
 -cat·ed, -cat·ing
pred·i·ca·tion
pre·dict
 -dict·able,
 -dict·abil·i·ty,
 -dic·tive
pre·dic·tion
pre·dis·pose
 -po·si·tion
pred·ni·sone
pre·dom·i·nance
pre·dom·i·nant
pre·dom·i·nate
pre·em·i·nence
pre·em·i·nent

pre·empt
pre·emp·tive
preen
pre·ex·ist
pre·fab·ri·cate
pref·ace
 -aced, -ac·ing
pref·a·to·ry
pre·fect
pre·fer
 -ferred, -fer·ring
pref·er·a·ble
pref·er·ence
pref·er·en·tial
pre·fix
pre·flight
preg·nan·cy
 -cies
preg·nant
pre·heat
pre·his·tor·ic
pre·judge
prej·u·dice
 -diced, -dic·ing
prej·u·di·cial
 -cial·ly, -cial·ness
prel·a·cy
prel·ate
pre·lim·i·nary
pre·lude
pre·ma·ture
 -ture·ly,
 -ture·ness,
 -tu·ri·ty

pre·med·i·tate
pre·med·i·ta·tion
pre·mier
prem·ise
pre·mi·um
pre·mo·ni·tion
pre·mon·i·to·ry
pre·na·tal
pre·oc·cu·pan·cy
pre·oc·cu·pa·tion
pre·oc·cu·pied
pre·oc·cu·py
pre·or·dain
 -dain·ment,
 -di·na·tion
prep·a·ra·tion
pre·par·a·tive
pre·pa·ra·to·ry
pre·pare
 -par·ing
prepared
pre·pared·ness
pre·pay
pre·pon·der·ance
pre·pon·der·ant
prep·o·si·tion
 -tion·al
pre·pos·sess
pre·pos·sess·ing
pre·pos·ses·sion
pre·pos·ter·ous
pre·re·cord
pre·reg·is·ter
pre·req·ui·site

pre·rog·a·tive
pres·age (n)
pre·sage (v)
Pres·by·te·ri·an
pre·school
pre·scribe (order as
   a remedy; cf.
   proscribe)
   -scribed, -scrib·ing
pre·scrip·tion
pre·scrip·tive
pres·ence (of mind;
   cf. *presents*)
pre·sent (v)
pres·ent (adj, n)
pre·sent·able
   -able·ness, -ably,
   -abil·i·ty
pre·sen·ta·tion
pres·ent-day
pre·sen·tee
pre·sen·ti·ment
   (foreboding; cf.
   presentment)
pres·ent·ly
pre·sent·ment
   (from grand jury;
   cf. *presentiment*)
pres·ents (gifts; cf.
   presence)
pre·serve
   pre·served,
   pre·serv·ing,
   pres·er·va·tion

pre·side
   -sid·ed, -sid·ing
pres·i·den·cy
pres·i·dent
   -den·tial,
   -den·tial·ly
press
press·ing
press·mark
press·room
press·run
pres·sure
pres·sur·ize
   -ized, -iz·ing,
   -iza·tion
pres·ti·dig·i·ta·tion
pres·tige
pres·ti·gious
pre·sum·able
pre·sume
   -sumed, -sum·ing
pre·sump·tion
pre·sump·tu·ous
pre·sup·pose
pre·tend
pre·tend·ed
pre·tense
pre·ten·sion
pre·ten·tious
pre·test
pre·text
pret·ty
   -ti·er, -ti·est, -ti·ly
pret·zel

pre·vail
pre·vail·ing
prev·a·lence
prev·a·lent
pre·var·i·cate
pre·vent
   -vent·able,
   -vent·abil·i·ty
pre·ven·tion
pre·ven·tive or
   pre·ven·ta·tive
pre·view
pre·vi·ous
   -ous·ly,
   -ous·ness
pre·vi·sion
   (foresight; cf.
   provision)
prey (victim; cf.
   pray)
price
   priced, pric·ing
price-cut·ter
price-fix·ing
price in·dex
price·less
price tag
prick·le
prick·ly
   -li·er, -li·est
pride
   prid·ed, prid·ing
priest
priest·hood

priest·ly
pri·ma·cy
pri·ma don·na
pri·ma fa·cie
pri·mar·i·ly
pri·ma·ry
  -ries
pri·mate
prim·er
prime time
pri·me·val
prim·i·tive
pri·mo·gen·i·ture
pri·mor·di·al
prim·rose
prince·ly
prin·cess
prin·ci·pal (chief;
  cf. *principle*)
  -pal·ly
prin·ci·pal·i·ty
prin·ci·ple (rule; cf.
  principal)
print·able
print·er
print·ing
print out (v)
print·out (n)
pri·or
pri·or·i·ty
  -ties
prism
pris·mat·ic
pris·on

pris·on·er
pris·tine
pri·va·cy
pri·vate
  -vate·ly, -vate·ness
pri·va·tion
priv·et
priv·i·lege
  -leged, -leg·ing
priv·i·ty
privy
prize
  prized, priz·ing
prob·a·bil·i·ty
prob·a·ble
prob·a·bly
pro·bate
  -bat·ed, -bat·ing
pro·ba·tion
  -tion·ary
pro·ba·tion·er
probe
  probed, prob·ing
prob·lem
prob·lem·at·ic
pro·bos·cis
  -cis·es (pl)
pro·ce·dur·al
pro·ce·dure
pro·ceed (move
  forward; cf.
  precede)
pro·ceed·ing
pro·cess

pro·ces·sion
pro·ces·sion·al
pro·ces·sor
pro·claim
proc·la·ma·tion
pro·cliv·i·ty
pro·cras·ti·nate
  -nat·ed, -nat·ing,
  -na·tion
pro·cre·ate
  -at·ed, -at·ing,
  -ation
proc·tor
proc·u·ra·tor
pro·cure
  -cured, -cur·ing,
  -cur·ance
prod·i·gal
pro·di·gious
prod·i·gy
  -gies
pro·duce
  -duced, -duc·ing,
  -duc·ible
pro·duc·er
prod·uct
pro·duc·tion
pro·duc·tive
pro·duc·tiv·i·ty
pro·fane
pro·fan·i·ty
  -ties
pro·fess
pro·fes·sion

pro·fes·sion·al
 -al·ly
pro·fes·sion·al·ism
pro·fes·sor
 -so·ri·al
pro·fes·sor·ship
prof·fer
 -fered, -fer·ing
pro·fi·cien·cy
pro·fi·cient
pro·file
 -filed, -fil·ing
prof·it (gain; cf.
 prophet)
prof·it·able
prof·i·teer
prof·li·gate
pro for·ma
pro·found
pro·fun·di·ty
pro·fuse
pro·fu·sion
prog·e·ny
 -nies
prog·no·sis
 -ses (pl)
prog·nos·tic
prog·nos·ti·cate
prog·nos·ti·ca·tion
pro·gram
 -grammed,
 -gram·ming,
 -gram·ma·ble
pro·gram·mat·ic

prog·ress (n)
pro·gress (v)
pro·gres·sion
pro·gres·sive
pro·hib·it
pro·hi·bi·tion·ist
pro·hib·i·tive
proj·ect (n)
pro·ject (v)
pro·jec·tile
pro·jec·tion·ist
pro·jec·tor
pro·le·tar·i·an
pro·le·tar·i·at
pro·lif·er·ate
 -at·ed, -at·ing
pro·lif·ic
pro·logue
pro·long
prom·e·nade
 -nad·ed, -nad·ing
prom·i·nence
prom·i·nent
pro·mis·cu·i·ty
pro·mis·cu·ous
prom·ise
 -ised, -is·ing
prom·is·so·ry
pro·mote
 -mot·ed, -mot·ing
pro·mot·er
pro·mo·tion
prompt
pro·mul·gate

 -gat·ed, -gat·ing,
 -ga·tion
pro·noun
pro·nounce
 -nounced,
 -nounc·ing,
 -nounc·able
pro·nounce·ment
pro·nun·ci·a·tion
proof·read·er
proof·room
pro·pa·gan·da
pro·pa·gan·dize
 -dized, -diz·ing
prop·a·gate
 -gat·ed, -gat·ing
prop·a·ga·tion
pro·pane
pro·pel
 -pelled, -pel·ling
pro·pel·lant
pro·pel·ler
pro·pen·si·ty
pro·per
prop·er·tied
prop·er·ty
 -ties
proph·e·cy (n)
 (prediction; cf.
 prophesy)-cies
proph·e·sy (v)
 (predict; cf.
 prophecy)
 -sied, -sy·ing

proph·et (predicts
    future; cf. *profit*)
pro·phet·ic
pro·phy·lac·tic
pro·pi·ti·ate
    -at·ed, -at·ing
pro·pi·tious
pro·po·nent
pro·por·tion
pro·por·tion·al
pro·por·tion·ate
pro·pos·al
pro·pose (state; cf.
    purpose)
    -pos·ing
pro·posed
prop·o·si·tion
    -tion·al
pro·pri·etary
pro·pri·etor
pro·pri·ety
    -eties
pro·pul·sion
pro·rate
    -rat·ed, -rat·ing
pro·sa·ic
pro·scribe (outlaw;
    cf. *prescribe*)
prose
pros·e·cute (legal
    trial; cf. *persecute*)
    -cut·ed, -cut·ing
pros·e·cu·tion
pros·e·cu·tor

pros·e·lyte
pros·pect
pro·spec·tive
    (expected; cf.
    perspective)
pro·spec·tus
pros·per
    -pered, -per·ing
pros·per·i·ty
pros·per·ous
pros·tate
pros·the·sis
pros·thet·ic
prosth·odon·tics
pros·ti·tute
    -tut·ed, -tut·ing
pros·trate
pro·tag·o·nist
pro·tect
    -tec·tive,
    -tec·tive·ly
pro·tec·tion
pro·tec·tion·ist
    -tion·ism
pro·tec·tor
pro·tec·tor·ate
pro·té·gé
pro·tein
pro tem
pro tem·po·re
pro·test
prot·es·tant
pro·tes·ta·tion
pro·to·col

pro·to·plasm
pro·to·type
pro·tract
pro·trac·tile
pro·trac·tion
pro·trac·tor
pro·trude
pro·tru·sion
pro·tru·sive
proud
prove
    proved, prov·ing,
    prov·able
prov·erb
pro·ver·bi·al
pro·vide
    -vid·ed, -vid·ing
prov·i·dence
prov·i·dent
prov·i·den·tial
pro·vid·er
prov·ince
pro·vin·cial
pro·vin·cial·ism
pro·vi·sion (act of
    providing; cf.
    prevision)
pro·vi·sion·al
pro·vi·so
prov·o·ca·tion
pro·voc·a·tive
pro·voke
    -voked, -vok·ing
prow·ess

prox·i·mal
prox·im·i·ty
prox·i·mo
proxy
  prox·ies
prude
pru·dence
pru·dent
pru·den·tial
prune
  pruned, prun·ing
pry
  pried, pry·ing
psalm
psalm·book
psalm·ist
pseu·do
pseud·onym
pso·ri·a·sis
psy·che·del·ic
psy·chi·a·try
  -chi·at·ric,
  -chi·a·trist
psy·chic (of the
  mind; cf. *physic*,
  physique)
psy·cho·anal·y·sis
  -an·a·lyst
psy·cho·an·a·lyze
psy·cho·log·i·cal
psy·chol·o·gy
  -gies, -gist
psy·cho·path
psy·cho·sis

-ses (pl)
psy·cho·so·mat·ic
psy·cho·ther·a·py
pu·ber·ty
pub·lic
pub·li·ca·tion
pub·li·cist
pub·lic·i·ty
pub·li·cize
  -cized, -ciz·ing
pub·lic·ly
pub·lish
  -lish·able
pub·lish·er
pud·ding
pud·dle
  -dled, -dling
pudgy
  pudg·i·er,
  pudg·i·ness
pueb·lo
  -los
puff
  puff·i·ness, puffy
pu·gi·lism
pug·na·cious
  -na·cious·ness,
  -nac·i·ty
pul·let
pul·ley
pull over (v)
pull·over (n, adj)
pul·mo·nary
pulp

pul·pit
pulp·wood
pul·sar
pul·sate
  -sat·ed, -sat·ing
pul·sa·tion
pulse
pul·ver·ize
  -ized, -iz·ing, -iz·er
pum·ice
pum·mel
  -meled, -mel·ing
pum·per·nick·el
pump·kin
punch
punch line
punc·tu·al
  -al·ly, -al·i·ty
punc·tu·ate
punc·tu·a·tion
punc·ture
  -tured, -tur·ing
pun·dit
pun·gen·cy
pun·gent
pun·ish
  -ish·able, -ish·er
pun·ish·ment
pu·ni·tive
pun·ster
punt·er
pu·ny
  -ni·er, -ni·est
pu·pil

pup·pet
pup·pet·ry
  -ries
pup·py
  -pies
pup tent
pur·chase
  -chased, -chas·ing,
  -chas·able
pu·ree
  -reed, -ree·ing
pure·ly
pur·ga·to·ry
  -ries
purge
  purged, purg·ing
pu·ri·fi·ca·tion
pu·ri·fy
  -fied, -fy·ing, -fi·er
pur·ist
pu·ri·tan
pu·ri·ty
pur·loin
pur·ple
pur·port
pur·pose (intention;
  cf. *propose*)
pur·pose·ly

purr
purse
purs·er
pur·su·ance
pur·su·ant
pur·sue
  -sued, -su·ing,
  -su·er
pur·suit
pur·vey·ance
pur·vey·or
pur·view
push
push but·ton (n)
push-but·ton (adj)
push·cart
push·ing
push·over (n)
push-pull (adj)
push-up (n)
pushy
  push·i·er,
  push·i·est,
  push·i·ness
pu·sil·lan·i·mous
pus·tu·lant
pus·tu·lar
pus·tule

put
  put, put·ting
put down (v)
put-down (n)
put off
put-on (adj, n)
pu·tre·fy
  -fied, -fy·ing
pu·trid
putt
put·ter
put·ty
  -ties
put up (v)
put-up (adj)
puz·zle
  -zled, -zling, -zler
puz·zle·ment
pyg·my
  -mies
py·or·rhea
pyr·a·mid
pyre
py·ro·ma·nia
  -ni·ac
py·ro·tech·nics
py·rox·y·lin
py·thon

Q

quack·ery
quad·ran·gle
  qua·dran·gu·lar
quad·rant
qua·drat·ic
qua·dren·ni·al
qua·dren·ni·um
quad·ri·ceps
quad·ri·lat·er·al
quad·ri·ple·gic
quad·ru·ped
qua·dru·ple
  -pled, -pling
qua·dru·plet
qua·dru·pli·cate
  -cat·ed, -cat·ing
quaff
quag·mire
quail
qual·i·fi·ca·tion
qual·i·fied
qual·i·fy
  -fied, -fy·ing
qual·i·ta·tive
qual·i·ty
  -ties
qualm
quan·da·ry
  -ries

quan·ti·fy
  -fied, -fy·ing
quan·ti·ta·tive
  -tive·ly, -tive·ness
quan·ti·ty
  -ties
quan·tum
  quan·ta (pl)
quar·an·tine
quar·rel
  -reled, -rel·ing
quar·rel·some
quar·ry
  -ries, -ried, -ry·ing
quar·ter
quar·ter·back
quar·ter·fi·nal
quar·ter·ly
quar·ter·mas·ter
quar·tet
quar·to
quarts (measures;
  cf. *quartz*)
quartz (mineral; cf.
  quarts)
qua·sar
qua·si
qua·si-ju·di·cial
qua·si-pub·lic

quay (wharf; cf. *key*)
quea·sy
  -si·er, -si·est,
  -si·ness
queen-size
queer
quer·u·lous
que·ry
  -ries, -ried,
  -ry·ing
ques·tion
ques·tion·able
  -ably
ques·tion·naire
queue (waiting line;
  cf. *cue*)
  queued, queu·ing
quib·ble
  -bled, -bling
quick·en
  -ened, -en·ing
quick-freeze (v)
  -froze, -fro·zen,
  -freez·ing
quick·ie
quick·sand
quick·sil·ver
quick-tem·pered
qui·es·cent

qui·et (silent; cf.
  quit, quite)
  -et·ness
qui·etude
qui·nine
quin·tes·sence
  quint·es·sen·tial
quin·tet
quin·tu·plet
quin·tu·pli·cate
  -cat·ed, -cat·ing
quip
  quipped,

quip·ping
quire (24 sheets; cf.
  choir)
quirk
  quirky,
  quirk·i·ness
quit (leave; cf. *quiet*,
  quite)
quit·claim
quite (completely;
  cf. *quiet, quit*)
quiv·er
  -ered, -er·ing

quix·ot·ic
quiz
  quizzed, quiz·zing
quiz·zi·cal
quo·rum
quo·ta
quot·able
quo·ta·tion
quote
  quot·ed, quot·ing
quo·tid·i·an
quo·tient

rab·bi
rab·bit
rab·ble
  -bled, -bling
rab·ble-rous·er
ra·bid
ra·bies
  -bies (pl)
rac·coon
race·horse
rac·er
race·track
ra·cial
rac·ing
rac·ism

-ist
rack·et
rack·e·teer
ra·con·teur
ra·dar
ra·dar·scope
ra·di·al
ra·di·ance
ra·di·ant
ra·di·ate
  -at·ed, -at·ing
ra·di·a·tion
ra·di·a·tor
rad·i·cal
rad·i·cal·ism

ra·dio
ra·dio·ac·tive
ra·dio·iso·tope
ra·di·ol·o·gy
ra·di·om·e·ter
  -e·try
ra·dio·sonde
ra·dio·ther·a·py
rad·ish
ra·di·um
ra·di·us
  ra·dii (pl)
ra·don
raf·fle
  -fled, -fling

raf·ter
rag·a·muf·fin
rag·ged (adj)
rag·ing
rag·lan
rag·time
rag·weed
rail·ing
rail·road
rail·way
rai·ment
rain (water; cf. *reign, rein*)
rain·bow
rain check
rain·coat
rain·drop
rain·fall
rain gauge
rain·mak·ing
rain·proof
rain·spout
rain·squall
rain·storm
rain·wa·ter
rain·wear
rainy
    rain·i·er, rain·i·est
raise (lift; cf. *rays, raze*)
    raised, rais·ing
rai·sin
rai·son d'être
ra·ja or ra·jah

rake
    raked, rak·ing
ral·ly
    -lied, -ly·ing
ram·ble
    -bled, -bling
ram·bler
ram·bunc·tious
ram·i·fi·ca·tion
ram·i·fy
    -fied, -fy·ing
ram·pant
ram·part
ram·rod
ram·shack·le
ranch·er
ran·cid
ran·cor
ran·cor·ous
ran·dom
ran·dom-ac·cess
    mem·o·ry
rangy
    rang·i·er,
    rang·i·est
ran·kle
    -kled, -kling
ran·sack
ran·som
rap (strike; cf. *wrap*)
    rapped (struck; cf. *rapt, wrapped*),
    rap·ping
rape

raped, rap·ing,
    rap·ist
rap·id
    -id·ness
rap·id-fire
ra·pid·i·ty
ra·pi·er
rap·ine
rap·pel
rap·port
rap·proche·ment
rapt (engrossed; cf. *rapped, wrapped*)
    rapt·ly, rapt·ness
rap·ture
    -tur·ous
rare·bit
rar·efac·tion
rar·efied
rar·efy
    -efied, -efy·ing
rare·ly
rar·i·ty
    -ties
ras·cal
rash
    rash·ness
rasp·ber·ry
ratch·et
rath·er
raths·kel·ler
rat·i·fy
    -fied, -fy·ing,
    -fi·ca·tion

rate
  rat·ed, rat·ing
ra·tio
ra·tion
  -tioned, -tion·ing
ra·tio·nal (reason-
  able; cf. *rationale*)
ra·tio·nale (basis; cf.
  rational)
ra·tio·nal·ize
  -ized, -iz·ing,
  -iza·tion
rat·tan
rat·tle
  -tled, -tling
rat·tle·snake
rat·trap
rau·cous
  -cous·ness
rav·age
  -aged, -ag·ing
rav·el
  -eled, -el·ing
ra·ven
rav·en·ous
ra·vine
rav·i·o·li
raw·hide
ray
rays (light beams; cf.
  raise, raze)
ray·on
raze (tear down; cf.
  raise, rays)

razed, raz·ing
ra·zor
ra·zor·back
re·act
re·ac·tion
re·ac·tion·ary
  -ar·ies
re·ac·tor
read·able
  -ably, -abil·i·ty
read·er·ship
read·i·ly
read-on·ly
  mem·o·ry
ready
  readi·er, readi·est
ready-made
ready-to-wear
re·al (true; cf. *reel*)
re·al es·tate
re·al·ism
  -ist, -is·tic,
  -is·ti·cal·ly
re·al·i·ty (real event;
  cf. *realty*)
  -ties
re·al·iza·tion
re·al·ize
  -ized, -iz·ing,
  -iz·able
re·al·ly
realm
Re·al·tor
re·al·ty (property; cf.

reality)
re·arm
  -ar·ma·ment
rea·son
  -soned, -son·ing
rea·son·able
  -ably
re·as·sur·ance
re·as·sure
re·bate
  -bat·ed, -bat·ing
reb·el (n)
re·bel (v)
  -belled, -bel·ling
re·bel·lion
re·bel·lious
re·birth
re·buff
re·buke
  -buked, -buk·ing
re·but
  -but·ted, -but·ting
re·but·tal
re·cal·ci·trant
re·call
  -call·able
re·cant
  -can·ta·tion
re·ca·pit·u·late
  -lat·ed, -lat·ing
re·ca·pit·u·la·tion
re·cap·ture
re·cede
  -ced·ed, -ced·ing

re·ceipt
re·ceiv·able
re·ceive
  -ceived, -ceiv·ing
re·ceiv·er·ship
re·cent
re·cep·ta·cle
re·cep·tion
re·cep·tion·ist
re·cep·tive
  -tiv·i·ty
re·cess
re·ces·sion
re·ces·sion·al
re·ces·sive
rec·i·pe
re·cip·i·ent
re·cip·ro·cal
  -cal·ly
re·cip·ro·cate
  -cat·ed, -cat·ing
re·cip·ro·ca·tion
rec·i·proc·i·ty
  -ties
re·cit·al
rec·i·ta·tion
re·cite
  -cit·ed, -cit·ing,
  -cit·er
reck·less
reck·on
  -oned, -on·ing
re·claim
rec·la·ma·tion

re·cline
  -clined, -clin·ing
re·cluse
  -clu·sive
rec·og·ni·tion
re·cog·ni·zance
rec·og·nize
  -nized, -niz·ing,
  -niz·able
re·coil
re·col·lect (collect
  again; cf. *recollect*)
rec·ol·lect (recall; cf.
  re-collect)
rec·om·mend
  -mended,
  -mend·ing,
  -mend·able
rec·om·men·da·tion
re·com·mit
  -mit·ment
rec·om·pense
  -pensed,
  -pens·ing
rec·on·cile
  -ciled, -cil·ing,
  -cile·ment
rec·on·cil·i·a·tion
  -cil·ia·to·ry
re·con·di·tion
re·con·firm
  -fir·ma·tion
re·con·nais·sance
re·con·noi·ter

  -noi·tered,
  -noi·ter·ing
re·con·sid·er
re·con·struc·tion
re·cord (v)
rec·ord (n)
re·coup
  -coup·able,
  -coup·ment
re·course
re·cov·er (cover
  again; cf. *recover*)
re·cov·er (regain; cf.
  re-cover)
  -ered, -er·ing
re·cov·ery
  -er·ies
rec·re·a·tion
re·crim·i·nate
  -nat·ed, -nat·ing,
  -na·tion
re·cruit
rect·an·gle
rect·an·gu·lar
rec·ti·fi·er
rec·ti·fy
  -fied, -fy·ing,
  -fi·ca·tion
rec·to·ry
  -ries
rec·tum
re·cu·per·ate
  -at·ed, -at·ing,
  -a·tion

re·cur
  -curred, -cur·ring,
  -cur·rence
re·cy·cle
red·bird
red-blood·ed
red-car·pet (adj)
Red Cross
re·dec·o·rate
re·deem
  -deem·able
re·deem·er
re·demp·tion
re·de·vel·op·ment
red-hand·ed (adj,
  adv)
red·head
re·dis·trib·ute
re·dis·trict
re·dou·ble
re·dress
re·duce
  -duced, -duc·ing,
  -duc·ible
re·duc·tion
re·dun·dan·cy
  -cies
re·dun·dant
red·wood
re·ed·u·cate
reek (smell; cf.
  wreck)
reel (spool; cf. *real*)
re·elect

re·em·ploy
re·en·act
re·en·trance
re·en·try
re·fer
  -fer·ring
ref·er·ee
  -eed, -ee·ing
ref·er·ence
  -enced, -enc·ing
ref·er·en·dum
re·ferred
re·fine
  -fined, -fin·ing
re·fine·ment
re·fin·ery
  -er·ies
re·flect
re·flec·tion
re·flec·tive
  -tive·ly, -tive·ness
re·flec·tor
re·flex
re·for·es·ta·tion
re·form
ref·or·ma·tion
re·for·ma·to·ry
  -ries
re·formed
re·frac·tion
re·frac·to·ry
  -ries
re·frain
re·fresh

re·fresh·ment
re·frig·er·ate
  -at·ed, -at·ing,
  -a·tion
re·frig·er·a·tor
ref·uge
  ref·uges, ref·ug·ing
ref·u·gee
re·fund
  -fund·able
re·fur·bish
re·fus·al
re·fuse (v)(reject)
  -fused, -fus·ing
ref·use (n)(garbage)
re·fute
  -fut·ed, -fut·ing,
  -fut·able
re·gain
re·gal
re·gale
  -galed, -gal·ing
re·gard
re·gard·less
re·gat·ta
re·gen·cy
  -cies
re·gen·er·ate
re·gen·er·a·tive
re·gent
reg·gae
re·gime
reg·i·men
re·gion

re·gion·al
reg·is·ter (enroll; cf. *registrar*)
  -tered, -ter·ing
reg·is·trar (record keeper; cf. *register*)
reg·is·tra·tion
reg·is·try
  -tries
re·gress
re·gres·sion
re·gres·sive
re·gret
  -gret·ted,
  -gret·ting, -gret·ful
re·gret·ta·ble
reg·u·lar
reg·u·lar·i·ty
  -ties
reg·u·late
  -lat·ed, -lat·ing,
  -la·to·ry
reg·u·la·tion
re·gur·gi·tate
  -tat·ed, -tat·ing
re·ha·bil·i·tate
  -tat·ed, -tat·ing
re·hears·al
re·hearse
  -hearsed,
  -hears·ing
reign (sovereignty; cf. *rain, rein*)
re·im·burse

  -bursed, -burs·ing,
  -burs·able
re·im·burse·ment
rein (of a horse; cf. *rain, reign*)
re·in·car·na·tion
rein·deer
re·in·force
re·in·force·ment
re·in·state
  -stat·ed, -stat·ing,
  -state·ment
re·in·sure
re·in·vest
re·is·sue
re·it·er·ate
  -at·ed, -at·ing,
  -a·tion
re·ject
re·jec·tion
re·joice
  -joiced, -joic·ing,
  -joic·ing·ly
re·join
re·ju·ve·nate
  -nat·ed, -nat·ing,
  -na·tion
re·lapse
  -lapsed, -laps·ing
re·late
  -lat·ed, -lat·ing
re·la·tion·ship
rel·a·tive
rel·a·tiv·i·ty

  -ties
re·lax
re·lax·ation
re·laxed
re·lay
  -layed, -lay·ing
re·lease
  -leased, -leas·ing
rel·e·gate
  -gat·ed, -gat·ing,
  -ga·tion
re·lent
re·lent·less
rel·e·vance
rel·e·vant
re·li·able
re·li·ance
re·li·ant
rel·ic
re·lief
re·lieve
  -lieved, -liev·ing,
  -liev·er
re·li·gion
re·li·gious
re·lin·quish
rel·ish
re·lo·cate
  -ca·tion
re·luc·tance
re·luc·tant
re·ly
  -lied, -ly·ing
re·main

re·main·der
-dered, -der·ing

re·mark

re·mark·able

re·me·di·al

rem·e·dy
-dies, -died,
-dy·ing

re·mem·ber
-bered, -ber·ing,
-ber·able

re·mem·brance

re·mind
-mind·er

rem·i·nisce
-nisced, -nisc·ing

rem·i·nis·cence

rem·i·nis·cent

re·mis·sion

re·mit·tance

re·mit·tent

rem·nant

re·mod·el

re·morse

re·mote
-mote·ly,
-mote·ness

re·mov·al

re·move
-moved, -mov·ing

re·mu·ner·ate
-at·ed, -at·ing,
-a·tor

re·mu·ner·a·tion

re·mu·ner·a·tive

re·nais·sance

ren·der
-dered, -der·ing,
-der·able

ren·dez·vous
ren·dez·vous (pl)

ren·di·tion

ren·e·gade

re·nege
-neged, -neg·ing,
-neg·er

re·ne·go·tia·ble

re·ne·go·ti·ate

re·new

re·new·able

re·new·al

re·nounce
-nounced,
-nounc·ing,
-nounce·ment

ren·o·vate
-vat·ed, -vat·ing,
-va·tion

re·nown

rent·al

re·nun·ci·a·tion

re·open

re·or·der

re·or·ga·ni·za·tion

re·pair

rep·a·ra·tion

re·pa·tri·ate
-at·ed, -at·ing,

-a·tion

re·pay
-paid, -pay·ing,
-pay·able

re·peal

re·peat

re·pel
-pelled, -pel·ling

re·pel·lent

re·pent

re·pen·tance

re·pen·tant

re·per·cus·sion

rep·er·toire

rep·er·to·ry
-ries

rep·e·ti·tion

rep·e·ti·tious

re·pet·i·tive
-tive·ly, -tive·ness

re·place
-place·able,
-plac·er

re·place·ment

re·plen·ish
-ish·able,
-ish·ment

re·plete

rep·li·ca

rep·li·cate
-cat·ed, -cat·ing

re·ply
-plies, -plied,
-ply·ing

re·port
re·port·er
re·pose
  -posed, -pos·ing
re·pos·i·to·ry
  -ries
re·pos·sess
  -sess·or
rep·re·hen·si·ble
rep·re·sent
  -sent·able, -sent·er
rep·re·sen·ta·tion
rep·re·sen·ta·tive
re·press
  -pres·sive
re·prieve
rep·ri·mand
re·print
re·pri·sal
re·proach
  -proach·ful,
  -proach·ful·ly,
  -proach·able
re·pro·duce
re·pro·duc·tion
re·pro·duc·tive
re·prog·ra·pher
re·pro·graph·ics
re·proof
re·prove
  -proved, -prov·ing,
  -prov·ing·ly
rep·tile
rep·til·ian

re·pub·lic
re·pub·li·can
re·pu·di·ate
  -at·ed, -at·ing
re·pu·di·a·tion
re·pug·nance
re·pug·nant
re·pulse
  -pulsed, -puls·ing
re·pul·sion
re·pul·sive
rep·u·ta·ble
rep·u·ta·tion
re·pute
  -put·ed, -put·ing
re·quest
re·qui·em
re·quire
  -quired, -quir·ing
re·quire·ment
req·ui·site
req·ui·si·tion
re·run
  -ran, -run·ning
re·sal·able
re·scind
res·cue
  -cued, -cu·ing,
  -cu·er
re·search
re·sem·blance
re·sem·ble
  -bled, -bling
re·sent

re·sent·ful
re·sent·ment
res·er·va·tion
re·serve
res·er·voir
re·shuf·fle
re·side
  -sid·ed, -sid·ing
res·i·dence (home;
  cf. *residents*)
res·i·den·cy
  -cies
res·i·den·tial
res·i·dents (those
  who reside; cf.
  residence)
re·sid·u·al
res·i·due
re·sign
res·ig·na·tion
re·sil·ience
re·sil·ient
res·in
re·sist
re·sis·tance
re·sis·tant
re·sis·tor
res·o·lu·tion
re·solve
  -solved, -solv·ing,
  -solv·able
res·o·nance
res·o·nant
re·sort

re·sound
re·source
re·source·ful
re·spect
re·spect·able
  -able·ness, -ably,
  -abil·i·ty
re·spect·ful
  -ful·ly (with
  deference; cf.
  respectively)
re·spec·tive
re·spec·tive·ly (in
  that order; cf.
  respectfully)
res·pi·ra·tion
  -ra·to·ry
res·pi·ra·tor
re·spite
re·splen·dent
re·spond
re·spon·dent
re·sponse
re·spon·si·bil·i·ty
  -ties
re·spon·si·ble
re·spon·sive
rest (repose; cf.
  wrest)
res·tau·rant
res·tau·ra·teur
rest home
res·ti·tu·tion
rest·less

res·to·ra·tion
re·store
  -stored, -stor·ing
re·strain
re·straint
re·strict
re·stric·tion
re·stric·tive
re·sult
re·sul·tant
re·sume (v)(begin
  again; cf. *résumé*)
  -sumed, -sum·ing
ré·su·mé
  (n)(summary; cf.
  resume)
re·sump·tion
re·sur·gence
res·ur·rect
res·ur·rec·tion
re·sus·ci·tate
  -tat·ed, -tat·ing,
  -ta·tion
re·tail
re·tail·er
re·tain
re·tain·er
re·tal·i·ate
  -at·ed, -at·ing,
  -a·tion
re·tal·i·a·to·ry
re·tar·da·tion
re·ten·tion
re·ten·tive

ret·i·cence
ret·i·cent
ret·i·na
re·tire
  -tired, -tir·ing
re·tire·ment
re·tool
re·touch
re·trace
re·tract
  -tract·able
re·trac·tion
re·treat
re·trench
ret·ri·bu·tion
re·trieve
  -trieved,
  -triev·ing,
  -triev·abil·i·ty
re·triev·er
ret·ro·ac·tive
ret·ro·gres·sion
ret·ro·spect
ret·ro·spec·tive
  -tive·ly
re·turn
re·turn·able
re·union
re·unite
re·us·able
re·use
re·veal (make
  known; cf. *revel*)
rev·eil·le

re·vel (celebrate; cf.
   reveal)
rev·e·la·tion
re·venge
   -venged,
   -veng·ing,
   -veng·er
rev·e·nue
re·ver·ber·ate
   -at·ed, -at·ing
re·ver·ber·a·tion
re·vere
   -vered, -ver·ing
rev·er·ence
rev·er·end
rev·er·ent
re·ver·sal
re·verse
   -versed, -vers·ing
re·vers·ible
re·vert
re·view (restudy; cf.
   revue)
re·view·er
re·vile
   -viled, -vil·ing
re·vise
   -vised, -vis·ing
re·vi·sion
re·vi·tal·ize
   -iz·ed, -iz·ing
re·viv·al
re·vive
   -vived, -viv·ing

re·vo·ca·ble
re·vo·ca·tion
re·voke
   -voked, -vok·ing
re·volt
rev·o·lu·tion
rev·o·lu·tion·ary
   -ar·ies
rev·o·lu·tion·ist
rev·o·lu·tion·ize
   -ized, -iz·ing
re·volve
re·volv·er
re·vue (theatrical
   performance; cf.
   review)
re·ward
re·wind
   -wound, -wind·ing
re·word
re·work
re·write
   -wrote, -writ·ten,
   -writ·ing
rhap·so·dy
   -dies
rheo·stat
rhet·o·ric
rhe·tor·i·cal
rheum (watery
   discharge; cf. *room*)
rheu·mat·ic
rheu·ma·tism
rhine·stone

rhi·ni·tis
rhi·noc·er·os
   -os·es (pl)
rho·do·den·dron
rhu·barb
rhyme
   rhymed, rhym·ing
rhythm
rhyth·mic
rib·bon
ric·er
rick·ets
rick·ety
ric·o·chet
   -cheted, -chet·ing
rid·dle
   -dled, -dling
rid·i·cule
   -culed, -cul·ing
ri·dic·u·lous
rif·fle (shuffle; cf.
   rifle)
   -fled, -fling
ri·fle (gun; cf. *riffle*)
   -fled, -fling
right (correct; cf.
   rite, write)
righ·teous
   -teous·ness
right·ful
right hand (n)
right-hand (adj)
right-of-way
   rights-of-way (pl)

rig·id

ri·gid·i·ty
  -ties

rig·or·ous

ring (a bell; cf. *wring*)

ring·mas·ter

ring·side

ring·worm

rinse

ri·ot·ous

rip·en
  -ened, -en·ing

rip off (v)

rip-off (n)

rip·ple
  -pled, -pling

rise
  rose, ris·en, ris·ing

risk

ris·qué

rite (ceremony; cf.
  right, write)

rit·u·al

ri·val
  -valed, -val·ing

ri·val·ry
  -ries

riv·er·bed

riv·er·boat

riv·et

road (highway; cf.
  rode, rowed)

road·block

road·way

road·work

rob
  robbed, rob·bing

rob·bery
  -ber·ies

rob·in

ro·bot

ro·bot·ics

ro·bust

rock bot·tom

rock·et

rode (did ride; cf.
  road, rowed)

ro·dent

ro·deo
  -de·os

rogue (scoundrel; cf.
  rouge)

role (part; cf. *roll*)

roll (turn over; cf.
  role)

roll call

roll·er coast·er

ro·maine

ro·mance
  -manced,
  -manc·ing

ro·man·tic

ro·man·ti·cism

rood (crucifix; cf.
  rude)

roof·top

rook·ery
  -er·ies

rook·ie

room (of a house; cf.
  rheum)

room·er (lodger; cf.
  rumor)

room·ful

room·mate

roost·er

root (of a tree; cf.
  rout, route)

root beer

ro·sa·ry
  -ries

ro·sette

rose·wood

ros·in

ros·ter

ros·trum

ro·ta·ry
  -ries

ro·tate
  -tat·ed, -tat·ing

ro·ta·tion

rote (memory; cf.
  wrote)

ro·tis·ser·ie

ro·tor

ro·tund

ro·tun·da

rouge (red coloring;
  cf. *rogue*)
  rouged, roug·ing

rough (rude; cf. *ruff*)
  rough·er, rough·est

213

rough·age

rough·en
-ened, -en·ing

rough·neck

rou·lette

round-the-clock

round-trip

rout (disperse; cf.
root, route)

route (highway; cf.
root, rout)
rout·ed, rout·ing

rou·tine

rou·tin·ize
-ized, -iz·ing

row

row·boat

row·dy
-di·er, -di·est,
-di·ness

rowed (did row; cf.
road, rode)

roy·al

roy·al·ist

roy·al·ty
-ties

rub
rubbed, rub·bing

rub·ber

rub·ber band

rub·ber·ize
-ized, -iz·ing

rub·ber stamp (n)

rub·ber-stamp (v, adj)

rub·bish

rub·ble

rub·down

ru·bel·la

ru·bric

ruck·us

rud·der

rud·dy

rude (rough; cf. *rood*)
rud·er, rud·est

ru·di·ment

ru·di·men·ta·ry

ruff (collar; cf. *rough*)

ruf·fi·an

ruf·fle
-fled, -fling

rug·ged
-ged·ness

ru·in·ous

rul·er

rum·ba

rum·ble
-bled, -bling

ru·mi·nant

rum·mage
-maged, -mag·ing

ru·mor (gossip; cf.
roomer)
-mored, -mor·ing

rum·ple
-pled, -pling

rum·pus

run away (v)

run·away (adj, n)

run down (v)

run-down (adj)

run·down (n)

rung (a bell; cf.
wrung)

run in (v)

run-in (n)

run·ner

run·ner-up
run·ners-up (pl)

run off (v)

run·off (n)

run on (v)

run-on (adj, n)

run over (v)

run-over (adj)

run·over (n)

run through (v)

run-through (n)

rup·ture
-tured, -tur·ing

ru·ral

rush hour

rus·set

rus·tic

rus·tle
-tled, -tling

rust·proof (adj)

ru·ta·ba·ga

ruth·less
-less·ness

rye (grain; cf. *wry*)

Sab·bath
sab·bat·i·cal
sa·ber
sa·ble
sab·o·tage
  -taged, -tag·ing
sab·o·teur
sac (pouch in
  animal; cf. *sack*)
sac·cha·rin (n)
sac·cha·rine (adj)
sack (bag; cf. *sac*)
sac·ra·ment
sac·ra·men·tal
sa·cred
sac·ri·fice
  -ficed, -fic·ing
sac·ri·fi·cial
sac·ri·lege
  -le·gious
sac·ro·sanct
sad·den
  -dened, -den·ing
sad·dle
  -dled, -dling
sa·dism
  -dist, -dis·tic
safe-de·pos·it box
safe·guard

safe·keep·ing
safe·ty
  -ties
saf·fron
sa·ga
sa·ga·cious
sa·gac·i·ty
sail (of a ship; cf.
  sale)
  sail·able
sail·boat
sail·cloth
sail·fish
sail·or
saint·ly
sal·able
  -abil·i·ty
sal·ad
sal·a·man·der
sa·la·mi
sal·a·ry
  -ries, -ried
sale (selling; cf. *sail*)
sales
sales·clerk
sales·per·son
sales·room
sa·lient
sa·line

sa·li·va
sal·i·vary
salm·on
sa·lon (shop; cf.
  saloon)
sa·loon (tavern; cf.
  salon)
sal·tine
salt·shak·er
salt·wa·ter (adj)
salty
  salt·i·er, salt·i·est
sal·u·tary
  -tari·ly, -tari·ness
sal·u·ta·tion
sa·lu·ta·to·ri·an
sa·lute
  -lut·ed, -lut·ing
sal·vage
  -vaged, -vag·ing,
  -vage·able
sal·va·tion
salve
Sa·mar·i·tan (n)
sa·mar·i·tan (adj)
same·ness
sam·pan
sam·ple
  -pled, -pling

215

sam·pler
sam·pling
san·a·to·ri·um
  -riums
sanc·ti·fi·ca·tion
sanc·ti·fy
  -fied, -fy·ing
sanc·ti·mo·nious
  -nious·ness
sanc·tion
  -tioned, -tion·ing
sanc·ti·ty
  -ties
sanc·tu·ary
  -ar·ies
sanc·tum
san·dal
san·dal·wood
sand·bag
sand·bank
sand·bar
sand·blast
sand·box
sand·lot
sand·pa·per
sand·pip·er
sand·stone
sand·storm
sand·wich
san·gui·nary
san·guine
  -guine·ly,
  -guine·ness,
  -guin·i·ty

san·i·tary
  -tari·ly
san·i·ta·tion
san·i·ty
sap·ling
sap·phire
sap·suck·er
sap·wood
sar·casm
sar·cas·tic
  -ti·cal·ly
sar·co·ma
  -mas
sar·dine
sar·don·ic
sar·gas·so
sa·rong
sar·sa·pa·ril·la
sar·to·ri·al
sas·sa·fras
sa·tan·ic
satch·el
sat·el·lite
sa·tia·ble
sa·tiate (adj)
sa·ti·ate (v)
  -at·ed, -at·ing
sat·in
sat·in·wood
sat·ire
sa·tir·ic
  -i·cal·ly
sat·is·fac·tion
sat·is·fac·to·ri·ly

sat·is·fac·to·ry
sat·is·fy
  -fied, -fy·ing
sat·u·rate
  -rat·ed, -rat·ing
sat·u·ra·tion
Sat·ur·day
sauce
sau·cer
sau·er·bra·ten
sau·er·kraut
sau·na
saun·ter
sau·sage
sau·té
  -téed, -té·ing
sau·ternes
sav·age
  -aged, -ag·ing,
  -age·ly
sa·van·na
sa·vant
sav·ior
sa·vory
sav·vy
saw·dust
saw·horse
saw·mill
sax·o·phone
say
  says, said, say·ing
say-so
scab·bard
scaf·fold

scald
scale
  scaled, scal·ing
scal·lion
scal·lop
scal·pel
scan
  scanned,
  scan·ning
scan·dal
scan·dal·ize
  -ized, -iz·ing
scan·dal·ous
Scan·di·na·vian
scan·ner
scanty
  scant·i·er,
  scant·i·est
scape·goat
scarce·ly
scar·ci·ty
  -ties
scare
  scared, scar·ing
scarf
  scarves or scarfs
  (pl)
scar·i·fy
  -fied, -fy·ing
scar·let
scath·ing
scat·ter
scav·en·ger
sce·nar·io

scene (locale; cf.
  seen)
scen·ery
  -er·ies
sce·nic
scent (odor; cf. *cent*,
  sent)
scep·ter
sched·ule
  -uled, -ul·ing
sche·mat·ic
scheme
  schemed,
  schem·ing
schism
schizo·phre·nia
schmaltz
schol·ar
schol·ar·ly
schol·ar·ship
scho·las·tic
school-age
school·bag
school board
school bus
school·child
school dis·trict
school·room
school·teach·er
school·work
schoo·ner
sci·at·i·ca
sci·ence
sci·en·tif·ic

-i·cal·ly
sci·en·tist
scin·til·la
scin·til·late
  -lat·ed, -lat·ing
sci·on
scis·sors
scle·ro·sis
score·board
score·card
score·keep·er
scorn·ful
scor·pi·on
scot-free
scoun·drel
scour
scourge
  scourged,
  scourg·ing
scout·mas·ter
scram·ble
  -bled, -bling
scrap·book
scratch
scrawl
screech
screen
  screen·able
screen·play
screw·ball
scrib·ble
  -bled, -bling
scrim·mage
  -maged, -mag·ing

scrim·shaw
script
scrip·tur·al
scrip·ture
scroll
scrounge
  scrounged,
  scroung·ing
scrub
  scrubbed,
  scrub·bing
scrump·tious
scru·ple
  -pled, -pling
scru·pu·lous
scru·ti·nize
  -nized, -niz·ing
scru·ti·ny
  -nies
scuf·fle
  -fled, -fling
scull (boat; cf. *skull*)
sculp·tor
sculp·tur·al
sculp·ture
  -tured, -tur·ing
scur·vy
scut·tle
  -tled, -tling
sea (ocean; cf. *see*)
sea·coast
sea·far·er
sea·food
sea gull

seal
  seal·ing (making
  secure; cf. *ceiling*)
sea-lane
seal·ant
seal·skin
seam (sewn; cf.
  seem)
  seam·less
sé·ance
sea·plane
sea·port
sear (burn; cf. *seer*)
search
  search·able,
  search·er,
  search·ing·ly
search·light
sea·shell
sea·shore
sea·sick
sea·son
  -soned, -son·ing
sea·son·able
sea·son·al
  -al·ly
seat belt
seat·ing
sea·wall
sea·ward
sea·wa·ter
sea·weed
sea·wor·thy
  -thi·ness

se·cant
se·cede
  -ced·ed, -ced·ing
se·ces·sion
se·clude
  -clud·ed, -clud·ing
se·clu·sion
seco·bar·bi·tal
sec·ond
sec·ond·ary
  -ari·ly
sec·ond class (n)
sec·ond-class (adj)
sec·ond-hand (adj)
sec·ond-rate (adj)
se·cre·cy
  -cies
se·cret
sec·re·tary
  -tar·ies, -tari·al
se·crete
  -cret·ed, -cret·ing
se·cre·tion
se·cre·tive
  -tive·ly, -tive·ness
sec·tar·i·an
sec·tion
sec·tor
  -tored, -tor·ing
sec·u·lar
sec·u·lar·ism
se·cure
  -cur·er, -cur·est,
  -cur·ing

se·cu·ri·ty
  -ties
se·dan
se·date
  -dat·ed, -dat·ing
se·da·tion
sed·a·tive
sed·en·tary
sed·i·ment
sed·i·men·ta·ry
se·di·tion
se·duce
  -duced, -duc·ing
se·duc·tion
se·duc·tive
  -tive·ness
see (perceive; cf.
  sea)
  saw, seen, see·ing,
  see·able
seed (of a plant; cf.
  cede)
seed·ling
seem (appear; cf.
  seam)
seem·ly
  -li·er, -li·est,
  -li·ness
seen (form of verb
  see; cf. *scene*)
seep·age
seer (prophet; cf.
  sear)
see·saw

see-through (adj)
seg·ment
seg·re·gate
seg·re·gat·ed
seg·re·ga·tion
seg·re·ga·tion·ist
se·gue
  -gued, -gue·ing
seis·mic
seis·mo·graph
seis·mom·e·ter
seize
  seized, seiz·ing
sei·zure
sel·dom
se·lect
se·lec·tion
se·lec·tive
self
  selves (pl)
self-ad·dressed
self-as·sured
self-cen·tered
self-com·posed
self-con·fi·dence
self-con·tained
self-con·trol
self-de·fense
self-de·struc·tion
self-
  de·ter·mi·na·tion
self-dis·ci·pline
self-ed·u·cat·ed
self-em·ployed

self-es·teem
self-ev·i·dent
self-ex·e·cut·ing
self-ex·plan·a·to·ry
self-ex·pres·sion
self-gov·ern·ment
self-help
self-im·age
self-in·crim·i·na·tion
self-in·dul·gence
self-in·sured
self-in·ter·est
self·ish
self-made
self-paced
self-pity
self-pos·sessed
self-pos·ses·sion
self-pres·er·va·tion
self-re·gard
self-re·li·ance
self-re·spect
self-sac·ri·fice
self·same
self-sat·is·fac·tion
self-start·er
self-suf·fi·cien·cy
self-suf·fi·cient
self-sup·port
self-taught
self-willed
self-wind·ing
sell·er (one who
  sells; cf. *cellar*)

sell out (v)
sell·out (n)
selt·zer
sel·vage
se·man·tic
sem·blance
se·mes·ter
semi·an·nu·al
semi·au·to·mat·ic
semi·au·ton·o·mous
semi·cir·cle
semi·civ·i·lized
semi·clas·si·cal
semi·co·lon
semi·con·duc·tor
semi·con·scious
semi·dark·ness
semi·fi·nal
semi·month·ly
sem·i·nar
sem·i·nary
  -nar·ies
semi·per·ma·nent
semi·pre·cious
semi·pri·vate
semi·pro·fes·sion·al
semi·skilled
semi·sweet
semi·trans·lu·cent
semi·trans·par·ent
semi·week·ly
semi·year·ly
sen·ate
sen·a·tor

sen·a·to·ri·al
send-off (n)
se·nile
se·nil·i·ty
se·nior
se·nior·i·ty
sen·sa·tion
sen·sa·tion·al
sense·less
sens·es (sensations;
  cf. *census*)
sen·si·bil·i·ty
  -ties
sen·si·ble
sen·si·tive
sen·si·tiv·i·ty
sen·si·tize
sen·sor (sensing
  device; cf. *censer,
  censor*)
sen·so·ry
sen·su·al
sen·su·ous
sent (dispatched; cf.
  cent, scent)
sen·tence
  -tenced, -tenc·ing
sen·ti·ment
sen·ti·men·tal
  -tal·ly
sen·ti·men·tal·ism
sen·ti·men·tal·i·ty
  -ties
sen·ti·nel

-neled, -nel·ing
sen·try
  -tries
sep·a·ra·ble
  -ble·ness, -bil·i·ty
sep·a·rate
sep·a·ra·tion
sep·a·rat·ist
Sep·tem·ber
sep·tic
sep·tu·a·ge·nar·i·an
se·quel
se·quence
  -quenced,
  -quenc·ing
se·quen·tial
  -tial·ly
se·ques·ter
  -tered, -ter·ing
se·quin
se·quoia
ser·e·nade
  -nad·ed, -nad·ing,
  -nad·er
ser·en·dip·i·ty
se·rene
se·ren·i·ty
serf (peasant; cf.
  surf)
serge (cloth; cf.
  surge)
ser·geant
se·ri·al (series; cf.
  cereal)

se·ri·al port
se·ri·al·ize
    -ized, -iz·ing,
    -iza·tion
se·ries (related
    group; cf. *serious,*
    serous)
se·ri·ous (grave; cf.
    series, serous)
se·ri·ous-mind·ed
ser·mon
se·rous (like serum;
    cf. *series, serious*)
ser·pent
ser·ra·tion
se·rum
ser·vant
serve
    served, serv·ing
ser·vice
    -viced, -vic·ing
ser·vice·able
ser·vile
ser·vi·tude
ses·a·me
ses·qui·cen·ten·ni·al
ses·sion (meeting;
    cf. *cession*)
set·back (n)
set·screw
set·tee
set·tle·ment
set·tling
set up (v)

set·up (n)
sev·en·teen
    -teenth
sev·enth
    -enths
sev·en·ty
    -ties, ti·eth
sev·er
    -ered, -er·ing
sev·er·al
sev·er·ance
se·vere
    -vere·ly,
    -vere·ness,
    -ver·i·ty
sew (stitch; cf. *so,*
    sow)
    sewed, sewn,
    sew·ing
sew·age
sew·er
sew·er·age
sex·a·ge·nar·i·an
sex·ism
    -ist
sex·tet
sex·ton
sex·u·al·i·ty
shab·by
    -bi·er, -bi·est,
    -bi·ness
shack·le
shade
    shad·ed, shad·ing

shad·ow
shad·owy
shake up (v)
shake-up (n)
shall
shal·lot
shal·low
sham
sham·ble
    -bled, -bling
shame
    shamed,
    sham·ing
shame·faced
shame·ful
shame·less
sham·poo
sham·rock
shang·hai
    -haied, -hai·ing
shan·ty
    -ties
shape·less
shape·ly
    -li·er, -li·est,
    -li·ness
share
    shared, shar·ing
shared log·ic
    sys·tem
shared re·source
    sys·tem
share·hold·er
shark·skin

sharp·en
  -ened, -en·ing,
  -en·er
sharp·er
sharp-eyed
sharp·shoot·er
sharp-sight·ed
sharp-tongued
sharp-wit·ted
shat·ter·proof
shawl
sheaf
shear (cut; cf. *sheer*)
  sheared, shorn,
  shear·ing
sheath (n)
  sheaths
sheathe (v)
  sheathed,
  sheath·ing
sheep·dog
sheep·herd·er
sheep·ish
sheep·skin
sheer (thin; cf. *shear*)
sheet met·al
shel·lac
  -lacked, -lack·ing
shell·fish
shell game
shell·proof
shell shock (n)
shell-shocked (adj)
shel·ter

-tered, -ter·ing
sher·bet
sher·iff
shield
shift·less
shim·mer
  -mered, -mer·ing
shim·my
  -mies, -mied,
  -my·ing
shine
shin·gle
  -gled, -gling
ship
  shipped, ship·ping
ship·mas·ter
ship·mate
ship·ment
ship·per
ship·wreck
ship·yard
shirr·ing
shirt·tail
shirt·waist
shish ke·bab
shiv·er
  -ered, -er·ing
shock·proof
shod
shoe
shoe·horn
shoe·lace
shoe·string
shone (gave light;

cf. *shown*)
shook-up
shoot (fire; cf. *chute*)
shop
  shopped,
  shop·ping
shop·lift·er
shop·per
shop·talk
shop·worn
shore·line
short·age
short·bread
short·cake
short·change
short cir·cuit (n)
short-cir·cuit (v)
short·com·ing
short·cut
short·en·ing
short·fall
short·hand·ed
short·horn
short-lived
short-range (adj)
short·sight·ed
short-spo·ken
short·stop
short-tem·pered
short-term
short-wind·ed
should
shoul·der
  -dered, -der·ing

shov·el
  -eled, -el·ing
show
  showed, shown,
  show·ing
show·er
shown (displayed;
  cf. *shone*)
show off (v)
show-off (n)
show·piece
show·place
show·room
showy
  showi·er,
  show·i·est,
  show·i·ness
shrap·nel
shred
  shred·der,
  shred·ding
shrewd
  shrewd·ness
shriek
shrimp
shrink·age
shriv·el
  -eled, -el·ing
shrub·bery
  -ber·ies
shud·der
  -dered, -der·ing
shuf·fle
  -fled, -fling

shut down (v)
shut·down (n)
shut in (v)
shut-in (adj, n)
shut off (v)
shut·off (n)
shut out (v)
shut·out (n)
shut·ter
shut·tle
  -tled, -tling
shy
  shi·er, shi·est,
  shy·ness
sib·ling
sick·en·ing
sick·le
sick leave
sick·ness
sick·room
side
  sid·ed, sid·ing
side·burns
side·line
side·show
side step (n)
side·step (v)
side·swipe
side·track
side·walk
side·wall
side·ways
si·dle
  -dled, -dling

siege
si·es·ta
sieve
  sieved, siev·ing
sigh
sight (vision; cf. *cite*,
  site)
sight·less
sight·ly
  sight·li·ness
sight-read (v)
sight-see·ing
sign
  sign·ee, sign·er
signed
sig·nal
  -naled, -nal·ing
sig·na·to·ry
sig·na·ture
sign·board
sig·net
sig·nif·i·cance
sig·nif·i·cant
sig·ni·fy
  -fied, -fy·ing
si·lage
si·lence
  -lenced,
  -lenc·ing
si·lenc·er
si·lent
sil·hou·ette
  -ett·ed, -ett·ing
sil·i·cate

sil·i·con (element; cf. *silicone*)

sil·i·cone (compound; cf. *silicon*)

silk·worm

silky

sil·ly
-li·er, -li·est

si·lo

sil·ver

sil·ver·ware

sil·very

sim·i·an

sim·i·lar

sim·i·lar·i·ty

sim·mer
-mered, -mer·ing

sim·ple
-pler, -plest

sim·plic·i·ty

sim·pli·fy
-fied, -fy·ing, -fi·ca·tion

sim·plism
-plis·tic

sim·ply

sim·u·lar

sim·u·late
-lat·ed, -lat·ing

sim·u·la·tion

si·mul·ta·neous

sin
sinned, sin·ning

since

sin·cere
-cer·er, -cer·est, -cere·ly

sin·cer·i·ty

sin·ew

sin·ewy

sin·ful
-ful·ly, -ful·ness

singe
singed, singe·ing

sin·gle

sin·gle-hand·ed
-ed·ness

sin·gle-mind·ed
-ed·ness

sin·gle-space (v)

sin·gle·ton

sin·gu·lar

sin·gu·lar·i·ty

sin·is·ter

sin·u·ous

si·nus

si·phon
-phoned, -phon·ing

si·ren

sir·loin

sis·ter-in-law
sis·ters-in-law (pl)

sit·com

sit-down (n)

site (place; cf. *cite*, *sight*)sit·ed, sit·ing

sit-in (n)

sit·u·ate
-at·ed, -at·ing

sit·u·a·tion

sit up (v)

sit-up (n)

six·teen
-teenth

sixth
sixths

six·ty
-ties, -ti·eth

size
sized, siz·ing

siz·able

siz·zle
-zled, -zling

skate·board

skat·er

skein

skel·e·ton

skep·tic

skep·ti·cal

skep·ti·cism

sketch

sketch·book

sketchy
sketch·i·er, sketch·i·est

skew·er

ski (blade for snow; cf. *sky*)
skis (pl. of *ski*; cf. *skies*), skied, ski·ing, ski·er

skid
skid·ded,
skid·ding
skilled
skill·ful
skim
skimmed,
skim·ming
skimpy
skin
skinned, skin·ning
skin·tight
skip
skipped, skip·ping
skir·mish
skull (bone of head;
cf. *scull*)
skunk
sky (atmosphere; cf.
ski)
skies (pl. of *sky*;
cf. *skis*)
sky blue (n)
sky·cap
sky·light
sky·line
sky·rock·et
sky·scrap·er
sky·ward
sky·way
slack·en
-ened, -en·ing
sla·lom
slam

slammed,
slam·ming
slan·der
-dered, -der·ing,
-der·ous·ly
slap
slapped, slap·ping
slap·stick
slaugh·ter
slav·ery
slav·ish
slay (kill; cf. *sleigh*)
slea·zy
-zi·er, -zi·est,
-zi·ness
sledge
sledge·ham·mer
sleep·er
sleep·less
sleep·walk·er
sleep·wear
sleepy
sleep·i·er,
sleep·i·est,
sleep·i·ness
sleeve
sleigh (winter
vehicle; cf. *slay*)
slen·der
sleuth
slide
slid·ing
slight
slim

slim·mer,
slim·mest
slime
sling·shot
slip
slipped, slip·ping
slip·case
slip·cov·er
slip·knot
slip-on (n)
slip-over (n)
slip·per
slip·pery
-peri·er, -peri·est,
-peri·ness
slip sheet (n)
slip-sheet (v)
slip·shod
slip up (v)
slip-up (n)
slith·er
sliv·er
sloe (fruit; cf. *slow*)
slo·gan
sloop
slope
sloped, slop·ing
slop·py
-pi·er, -pi·est,
-pi·ness
sloth·ful
slouch
slouchy
slouch·i·ness

slov·en·ly
slow (not fast; cf.
  sloe)
slow·down (n)
slow mo·tion (n)
slow-mo·tion (adj)
slow-wit·ted
sludge
slug
  slugged, slug·ging
slug·gish
slum
slum·ber
slush
small·pox
smart
  smart·ness
smash·up (n)
smat·ter·ing
smith·er·eens
smoke·house
smoke·less
smok·er
smok·ing room (n)
smok·ing-room
  (adj)
smoky
smol·der
  -dered, -der·ing
smooth
smor·gas·bord
smoth·er
  -ered, -er·ing
smudge

smudged,
  smudg·ing
smug·gle
  -gled, -gling
sna·fu
snag
  snagged,
  snag·ging
snail-paced
snake·skin
snap
  snapped,
  snap·ping
snap·drag·on
snap·shot
snare drum
sneak·er
sneer
sneeze
  sneezed,
  sneez·ing
snick·er
snide
  snide·ly,
  snide·ness
snip
  snipped, snip·ping
snip·py
  -pi·er, -pi·est
snob
snob·bery
  -ber·ies
snob·bish
  -bish·ness

snooze
snor·kel
snow·ball
snow·bank
snow·blow·er
snow·bound
snow·capped
snow·drift
snow·drop
snow·fall
snow·flake
snow·man
snow·mo·bile
snow·plow
snow·shoe
snow·storm
snow·suit
snowy
snub
  snubbed,
  snub·bing
snub-nosed
so (thus; cf. *sew*,
  sow)
soap·box
soap·suds
soapy
  soap·i·er,
  soap·i·ness
soar (rise aloft; cf.
  sore)
so·ber
  -bered, -ber·ing
so·bri·ety

so-called
soc·cer
so·cia·bil·i·ty
  -ties
so·cia·ble
  -ble·ness, -bly
so·cial
so·cial·ism
so·cial·ist
so·cial·ite
so·cial·ize
  -ized, -iz·ing
so·cial·ly
so·cial-mind·ed
so·ci·etal
so·ci·ety
  -et·ies
so·cio·eco·nom·ic
so·cio·log·i·cal
so·ci·ol·o·gy
  -gist
sock·et
so·da
sod·den
so·di·um
soft
  soft·ish, soft·ly,
  soft·ness
soft·ball
soft-boiled
soft copy
soft·en
  -ened, -en·ing
soft·heart·ed

soft soap (n)
soft-soap (v)
soft-spo·ken
soft·ware
soft·wood
sog·gy
  -gi·er, -gi·est,
  -gi·ness
soil
so·journ
so·lace
so·lar
sol·der
sol·dier
sold-out
sole (only; cf. *soul*)
so·le·cism
sole·ly
sol·emn
so·lem·ni·ty
  -ties
so·le·noid
so·lic·it
so·lic·i·ta·tion
so·lic·i·tor
so·lic·i·tous
so·lic·i·tude
sol·id
sol·i·dar·i·ty
so·lid·i·fy
  -fied, -fy·ing,
  -fi·ca·tion
so·lid·i·ty
  -ties

sol·id-state
so·lil·o·quy
  -quies
sol·i·taire
sol·i·tary
sol·i·tude
so·lo
sol·stice
sol·u·bil·i·ty
sol·u·ble
so·lu·tion
solv·able
  -abil·i·ty
solve
  solved, solv·ing
sol·ven·cy
sol·vent
som·ber
som·bre·ro
some (part; cf. *sum*)
some·body (pron)
some·day (adv)
some·how
some·one (pron)
some·place (adv)
som·er·sault
some·thing
some·time (adv)
some·what
some·where
som·nam·bu·lism
som·no·lent
son (child; cf. *sun*)
so·na·ta

song·bird
song·book
song·fest
song·writ·er
son-in-law
  sons-in-law (pl)
son·net
soothe
sooth·say·er
so·phis·ti·cate
so·phis·ti·cat·ed
so·phis·ti·ca·tion
soph·ist·ry
soph·o·more
so·pra·no
sor·cer·er
sor·cery
sor·did
sore (painful; cf.
  soar)
  sor·er, sor·est
sor·ghum
so·ror·i·ty
  -ties
sor·rel
sor·row
sor·row·ful
sor·ry
souf·flé
sought
soul (spirit; cf. *sole*)
soul-search·ing
sound·proof (adj, v)
soup du jour

source
sour·dough
south·bound
south·east
south·er·ly
south·ern
South·ern·er
south·land
south·paw
south pole
south·west
sou·ve·nir
sov·er·eign
sov·er·eign·ty
  -ties
so·vi·et
sow (n)(pig)
sow (v)(plant; cf.
  sew, so)sowed,
  sown, sow·ing
soy
soy·bean
space
  spaced, spac·ing
space-age
space·craft
space·flight
space shut·tle
space suit
spa·cious
  -cious·ness
spade·work
spa·ghet·ti
span·gle

span·iel
spare
  spared, spar·ing
spare·ribs
spar·kle
  -kled, -kling
spar·row
spas·mod·ic
spas·tic
spa·tial
spat·ter
spat·u·la
speak·er
spear
spear·mint
spe·cial
  -cial·ly, -cial·ness
spe·cial·ist
spe·cial·iza·tion
spe·cial·ize
  -ized, -iz·ing
spe·cial·ty
  -ties
spe·cie (coin; cf.
  species)
spe·cies (variety; cf.
  specie)
spe·cif·ic
  -i·cal·ly
spec·i·fi·ca·tion
spec·i·fy
  -fy·ing
spec·i·fied
spec·i·men

spec·ta·cle
spec·tac·u·lar
spec·ta·tor
spec·ter
spec·trum
  -tra (pl)
spec·u·late
spec·u·la·tion
spec·u·la·tive
spec·u·lum
speech
speech·less
speed·boat
speed·i·ly
speed lim·it
speed·om·e·ter
speed·up (n)
speed·way
spell
  spelled, spell·ing
spell·bind·er
spell·bound
spell check·er
spe·lunk·er
spent
sphag·num
sphere
sphinx
  sphinx·es (pl)
spice
  spiced, spic·ing
spicy
spi·der
spiel

spig·ot
spike
  spiked, spik·ing
spin·ach
spi·nal
spin·dle
  -dled, -dling
spine·less
spin·et
spin off (v)
spin-off (n)
spin·ster
spi·ral
  -raled, -ral·ing
spi·rea
spir·it
spir·it·ed
spir·i·tu·al
  -al·ly, -al·ness
spir·i·tu·al·ism
  -al·ist
spir·i·tu·al·i·ty
  -ties
spite·ful
splash·board
splash·down
splash guard
splen·did
  -did·ness
splen·dor
splice
  spliced, splic·ing
splin·ter
split

split·ting
split screen
split shift
splurge
spoil·age
spo·ken
spokes·per·son
spo·li·a·tion
sponge
  sponged, spong·ing
spongy
spon·sor
  -sored, -sor·ing
spon·ta·ne·ity
spon·ta·ne·ous
  -ous·ness
spoon-feed (v)
  spoon-fed,
  spoon-feed·ing
spoon·ful
  -fuls (pl)
spo·rad·ic
sports·cast
sports·man
sports·wear
sports·wom·an
sports·writ·er
spot
  spot·ted, spot·ting
spot-check (v)
spot·less
spot·light (n, v)
  -light·ed,
  -light·ing

sprawl
spread ea·gle (n)
spread-ea·gle (adj, v)
spread·sheet
spree
spright·ly
  -li·ness
spring·board
spring·time
sprin·kle
  -kler
sprin·kling
sprock·et
sprout
spruce
spu·mo·ni or
  spu·mo·ne
spur
  spurred,
  spur·ring
spu·ri·ous
spurn
spur-of-the-
  mo·ment
spurt
sput·nik
sput·ter
spy
  spied, spy·ing
squab
squab·ble
  -bled, -bling
squad·ron

squal·id
  -id·ness
squall
squa·lor
squan·der
  -dered, -der·ing
square
  squared,
  squar·ing
square root
squash
squat
  squat·ted,
  squat·ting
squawk
squeak
squea·mish
squee·gee
squeeze
  squeez·able,
  squeez·abil·i·ty
squir·rel
  -reled, -rel·ing
squirt
sta·bil·i·ty
  -ties
sta·bi·lize
  -lized, -liz·ing,
  -li·za·tion
sta·bi·liz·er
sta·ble
stac·ca·to
sta·di·um
  -dia (pl)

staff
stage fright
stage·hand
stag·ger
  -gered, -ger·ing
stag·nant
stag·nate
  -nat·ed, -nat·ing,
  -na·tion
staid (sedate; cf.
  stayed)
stain·less
stair (steps; cf. *stare*)
stair·case
stair·way
stair·well
stake (marker; cf.
  steak)
stake out (v)
stake·out (n)
sta·lac·tite (hangs
  down)
sta·lag·mite (stands
  up)
stale
stale·mate
stal·lion
stal·wart
sta·men
stam·i·na
stam·mer
  -mered, -mer·ing
stam·pede
stance

stanch
stan·chion
stand-alone
stan·dard
stan·dard-bear·er
  (n)
stan·dard·bred
stan·dard·ize
  -ized, -iz·ing,
  -iza·tion
stand by (v)
stand·by (n, adj,
  adv)
stand in (v)
stand-in (n)
stand off (v)
stand·off (adj, n)
stand out (v)
stand·out (n)
stand·point
stand·still
stand up (v)
stand-up (adj)
stan·za
sta·ple
star
  starred, star·ring
star·board
starchy
star·dom
star·dust
stare (look; cf. *stair*)
star·fish
star·gaz·er

star·let
star·light
star·ling
star·ry-eyed
star-span·gled
star·tle
  -tled, -tling
star·va·tion
starve
  starved, starv·ing
state·hood
state·house
state·less
state·ly
  -li·ness
state·ment
states·man
state·wide
stat·ic
sta·tion
  -tioned, -tion·ing
sta·tion·ary (fixed;
  cf. *stationery*)
sta·tio·nery (paper;
  cf. *stationary*)
sta·tis·tic
sta·tis·ti·cal
  -cal·ly
stat·is·ti·cian
stat·u·ary
  -ar·ies
stat·ue (sculpture;
  cf. *stature, statute*)
stat·u·esque

stat·u·ette
stat·ure (height; cf.
  statue, statute)
sta·tus
sta·tus quo
stat·ute (law; cf.
  statue, stature)
stat·u·to·ry
stay
stayed (past tense of
  stay; cf. *staid*),
  stay·ing
stead·fast
steady
  steadi·er,
  steadi·est,
  steadi·ly
steak (meat; cf.
  stake)
steal (rob; cf. *steel*)
stealth
steam·boat
steam·er
steam heat·ing
steam·ship
steel (metal; cf.
  steal)
steel·work
steel·yard
stee·ple
stee·ple·chase
stee·ple·jack
steer
stein

stem
  stemmed,
  stem·ming
stem·ware
sten·cil
  -ciled, -cil·ing
ste·nog·ra·pher
ste·nog·ra·phy
  steno·graph·ic
step (walk; cf.
  steppe)
step·child
step down (v)
step-down (n)
step·fa·ther
step in (v)
step-in (n)
step·lad·der
step·moth·er
step·par·ent
steppe (plain; cf.
  step)
step stool
step up (v)
step-up (adj, n)
ste·reo
ste·reo·scope
ste·reo·type
ster·ile
ste·ril·ize
  -ized, -iz·ing,
  -iza·tion
ster·ling
ster·num

stetho·scope
stew·ard
stick·ler
stick·pin
stick-to-it·ive·ness
stick up (v)
stick·up (n)
sticky
  stick·i·er,
  stick·i·est,
  stick·i·ness
stiff·en
sti·fle
  -fled, -fling
stig·ma (sing)
  stig·ma·ta (pl)
stig·ma·tize
  -tized, -tiz·ing
stile (fence; cf. *style*)
sti·let·to
  -tos
still·born
still life
stilt·ed
stim·u·lant
stim·u·late
  -lat·ed, -lat·ing,
  -la·tion
stim·u·lus (sing)
  -li (pl)
stin·gy
  -gi·er, -gi·est,
  -gi·ness
stink·weed

sti·pend
stip·u·late
  -lat·ed, -lat·ing
stip·u·la·tion
stir
  stirred, stir·ring
stir-fry (v)
stir·rup
stock·ade
stock·bro·ker
stock car
stock·hold·er
stock·ing
stock-in-trade (n)
stock·man
stock·pile (n, v)
stock·room
stock·yard
stodgy
  stodg·i·er,
  stodg·i·est,
  stodg·i·ness
sto·ic
stom·ach
stom·ach·ache
stone·cut·ter
stone-deaf
stone·ma·son
stone·ware
stone·work
stop
  stopped, stop·ping
stop-and-go
stop·light

stop·watch
stor·age
store
  stored, stor·ing,
  stor·able
store·house
store·keep·er
store·room
store·wide
stormy
  storm·i·er,
  storm·i·est,
  storm·i·ness
sto·ry
  -ries
sto·ry·tell·er
stout·heart·ed
  -ed·ness
stow·age
stow away (v)
stow·away (n)
strad·dle
  -dled, -dling,
  -dler
strag·gle
  -gled, -gling,
  -gler
straight (direct; cf.
  strait)
straight·edge
straight·en
  -ened, -en·ing
straight·for·ward
strain

strait (narrow; cf.
  straight)
strait·laced or
  straight·laced
strange
  strang·er,
  strang·est,
  strange·ly
stran·gle
  -gled, -gling, -gler
stran·gu·late
  -lated, -lat·ing
strap
  strapped,
  strap·ping
stra·te·gic
  -gi·cal, -gi·cal·ly
strat·e·gist
strat·e·gy
  -gies
strat·i·fy
  -fied, -fy·ing
strato·sphere
stra·tum
straw·ber·ry
stream
stream·lined
street·light
strength
strength·en
  -ened, -en·ing
stren·u·ous
  -ous·ness
strep·to·coc·cus

  -coc·ci (pl)
stress·ful
  -ful·ly
stretch
strict
stric·ture
stri·dent
strike out (v)
strike·out (n)
strike·over (n)
strin·gent
strip
  stripped,
  strip·ping,
  strip·pa·ble
strong·hold
struc·tur·al
  -al·ly
struc·ture
  -tured, -tur·ing
strug·gle
  -gled, -gling
strych·nine
stub
  stubbed,
  stub·bing
stub·born
  -born·ness
stuc·co
stu·dent
studies
stu·dio
stu·di·ous
  -ous·ness

study
  stud·ied,
  study·ing
stuff
stuffy
  stuff·i·er,
  stuff·i·est,
  stuff·i·ness
stu·pen·dous
stu·pid
  -pid·ness
stu·pid·i·ty
  -ties
stu·por
stur·dy
  -di·er, -di·est,
  -di·ness
stur·geon
stut·ter
  -ter·er
style (fashion; cf.
  stile)
  styled, styl·ing
style·book
styl·ist
styl·ize
  -ized, -iz·ing,
  -iza·tion
sty·lus
  -li (pl)
sty·mie
  -mied, -mie·ing
sua·sion
suave

sub·as·sem·bly
sub·av·er·age
sub·base·ment
sub·com·mit·tee
sub·con·scious
  -scious·ness
sub·con·tract
sub·con·trac·tor
sub·cu·ta·ne·ous
sub·di·vide
  -vid·er, -vi·sion
sub·due
  -dued, -du·ing
sub·head
sub·ject
sub·jec·tive
  -tive·ly, -tive·ness,
  -tiv·i·ty
sub·ju·gate
  -gat·ed, -gat·ing
sub·junc·tive
sub·lease
sub·let
  -let·ting
sub·lime
sub·lim·i·nal
sub·ma·rine
sub·merge
  -merged,
  -merg·ing,
  -mer·gence
sub·merse
  -mersed,
  -mers·ing,

  -mer·sion
sub·mers·ible
sub·mis·sion
sub·mis·sive
sub·mit
  -mit·ting, -mit·tal
sub·mit·ted
sub·nor·mal
  -mal·i·ty, -mal·ly
sub·or·di·nate
  -nat·ed, -nat·ing,
  -na·tion
sub·poe·na
  -naed, -na·ing
sub·ro·ga·tion
sub·scribe
  -scribed,
  -scrib·ing,
  -scrib·er
sub·script
sub·scrip·tion
sub·se·quent
sub·ser·vi·ence
sub·ser·vi·ent
sub·side
  -sid·ed, -sid·ing,
  -si·dence
sub·sid·i·ary
  -iar·ies
sub·si·dize
sub·si·dy
  -dies
sub·sist
sub·sis·tence

sub·stance
sub·stan·dard
sub·stan·tial
  -tial·ly
sub·stan·ti·ate
  -at·ed, -at·ing,
  -a·tion
sub·sti·tute
sub·sur·face
sub·ter·fuge
sub·ter·ra·nean
sub·ti·tle
sub·tle
sub·tle·ty
sub·tly
sub·to·tal
sub·tract
sub·trac·tion
sub·tra·hend
sub·trop·i·cal
sub·urb
  -ur·ban,
  -ur·ban·ite
sub·ur·bia
sub·ver·sion
  -ver·sion·ary,
  -ver·sive
sub·way
suc·ceed
suc·cess
suc·cess·ful
suc·ces·sion
suc·ces·sive
suc·ces·sor

suc·cinct
suc·cor (help; cf.
  sucker)
suc·co·tash
suc·cu·lent
suc·cumb
suck·er (fish; cf.
  succor)
suc·tion
sud·den
sue
  sued, su·ing
suede
su·et
suf·fer
  -fered, -fer·ing
suf·fice
suf·fi·cien·cy
suf·fi·cient
suf·fix
suf·fo·cate
  -cat·ed, -cat·ing,
  -ca·tion
suf·frage
sug·ar
sug·ar·cane
sug·ar·coat
sug·ar·plum
sug·gest
sug·ges·tion
sui·cid·al
sui·cide
suit (garment; cf.
  suite, sweet)

suit·able
  -able·ness, -ably,
  -abil·i·ty
suit·case
suite (group; cf. *suit,*
  sweet)
sul·fate
sul·fur
sulky
  sulk·i·ly,
  sulk·i·ness
sul·len
sul·tan
sul·try
  -tri·er, -tri·est,
  -tri·ness
sum (total; cf. *some*)
  summed,
  sum·ming
su·mac
sum·ma cum
  lau·de
sum·ma·rize
sum·ma·ry (brief
  account; cf.
  summery)
sum·ma·tion
sum·mer·time
sum·mery (like
  summer; cf.
  summary)
sum·mit
sum·mon
  -moned, -mon·ing

sump·tu·ous

sun (in the sky; cf. *son*)

sun·bath (n)

sun·bathe (v)

sun·beam

sun·burn

sun·dae (ice cream; cf. *Sunday*)

Sun·day (day of the week; cf. *sundae*)

sun·di·al

sun·down

sun·dries (n)

sun·dry (adj)

sun·flow·er

sun·glass·es

sunk·en

sun·lamp

sun·light

sun·lit

sun·ny
-ni·er, -ni·est, -ni·ly

sun·rise

sun·roof

sun·screen

sun·set

sun·shade

sun·shine

sun·spot

sun·stroke

sun·tan

sun·up

su·per·abun·dant

su·perb

su·per·ego

su·per·fi·cial

su·per·fi·ci·al·i·ty

su·per·flu·ous

su·per·hu·man

su·per·im·pose

su·per·in·tend

su·per·in·ten·dent

su·pe·ri·or

su·pe·ri·or·i·ty
-ties

su·per·la·tive

su·per·man

su·per·mar·ket

su·per·nat·u·ral

su·per·pow·er

su·per·script

su·per·sede
-sed·ed, -sed·ing

su·per·son·ic

su·per·sti·tion

su·per·sti·tious

su·per·struc·ture

su·per·vise
-vised, -vis·ing

su·per·vi·sion

su·per·vi·sor
-so·ry

su·per·wom·an

sup·per

sup·plant

sup·ple

sup·ple·ment

sup·ple·men·tal

sup·ple·men·ta·ry

sup·pli·cate
-cat·ed, -cat·ing, -ca·tion

sup·ply
-plies, -plied, -ply·ing, -pli·er

sup·port

sup·port·er

sup·pose
-posed, -pos·ing

sup·po·si·tion

sup·press
-ible

sup·pres·sion

su·prem·a·cist

su·prem·a·cy
-cies

su·preme

sur·charge

sure·fire

sure·foot·ed

sure·ly
(certainly; cf. *surly*)

sure·ty

surf (waves; cf. *serf*)

sur·face
-faced, -fac·ing

surf·board

sur·feit

surge (wave; cf. *serge*)

sur·geon

sur·gery

  -ger·ies

sur·gi·cal

sur·ly (sullen; cf.
  surely)

  -li·er, -li·est,

  -li·ness

sur·mise

  -mised, -mis·ing

sur·mount

  -mount·able

sur·name

sur·pass

sur·plice (garment;
  cf. *surplus*)

sur·plus (excess; cf.
  surplice)

sur·prise

  -prised, -pris·ing

sur·re·al·ism

sur·ren·der

  -dered, -der·ing

sur·rep·ti·tious

sur·ro·gate

sur·round

sur·tax

sur·veil·lance

sur·vey

  -veyed, -vey·ing

sur·vey·or

sur·viv·al

sur·vive

  -vived, -viv·ing,

  -vi·vor

sus·cep·ti·bil·i·ty

sus·cep·ti·ble

su·shi

sus·pect

sus·pend

sus·pense

sus·pen·sion

sus·pi·cion

sus·pi·cious

sus·tain

sus·te·nance

su·ture

  -tured, -tur·ing

svelte

swab

  swabbed,

  swab·bing

swal·low

swamp

swans·down

sward (grass; cf.
  sword)

swas·ti·ka

swatch

sweat·band

sweat·er

sweat·pants

sweat·shirt

sweaty

  sweat·i·er,

  sweat·i·est,

  sweat·i·ness

sweep·stakes

sweet (not sour; cf.
  suit, suite)

sweet·en

  -ened, -en·ing,

  -en·er

sweet·heart

sweet tooth

swel·ter

  -tered, -ter·ing

swerve

  swerved,

  swerv·ing

swim

  swim·ming,

  swim·mer

swim·ming·ly

swim·suit

swin·dle

  -dled, -dling,

  -dler

swing shift

switch·blade

switch·board

swiv·el

  -eled, -el·ing

swoon

swoop

sword (weapon; cf.
  sward)

sword·fish

syc·a·more

syl·lab·ic

syl·lab·i·cate

  -cat·ed, -cat·ing

syl·la·ble
syl·la·bus
 -bi (pl)
syl·lo·gism
sym·bi·o·sis
 -bi·ot·ic
sym·bol (emblem;
 cf. *cymbal*)
sym·bol·ic
 -bol·i·cal·ly
sym·bol·ism
sym·bol·ize
 -ized, -iz·ing,
 -iz·er
sym·met·ri·cal
sym·me·try
 -tries
sym·pa·thet·ic
sym·pa·thize
 -thized, -thiz·ing,
 -thiz·er

sym·pa·thy
 -thies
sym·phon·ic
sym·pho·ny
 -nies
sym·po·sium
symp·tom
syn·a·gogue
syn·chro·ni·za·tion
syn·chro·nize
 -nized, -niz·ing
syn·chro·nous
syn·co·pate
 -pat·ed, -pat·ing
syn·di·cate
 -cat·ed, -cat·ing,
 -ca·tion
syn·drome
syn·er·gism
syn·er·gy
syn·od

syn·onym
syn·on·y·mous
syn·op·sis
 -op·ses (pl)
syn·tax
syn·the·sis
 -the·ses (pl)
syn·the·size
 -sized, -siz·ing
syn·thet·ic
sy·ringe
syr·up
sys·tem
sys·tem·at·ic
 -at·i·cal·ly
sys·tem·atize
 -atized,
 -atiz·ing,
 -ati·za·tion

T

tab
 tabbed,
 tab·bing
Ta·bas·co
tab·er·na·cle
ta·ble
 -bled, -bling

tab·leau
 -leaux (pl)
ta·ble·spoon
tab·let
ta·ble·ware
tab·loid
ta·boo

tab·u·lar
tab·u·late
 -lat·ed, -lat·ing,
 -la·tion
tab·u·la·tor
ta·chis·to·scope
ta·chom·e·ter

tac·it
　-it·ness
tac·i·turn
tack·le
　-led, -ling
tac·o·nite
tact·ful
tac·tic
tac·ti·cal
tad·pole
taf·fe·ta
tag
　tagged, tag·ging
tag·board
tail (end; cf. *tale*)
tail·coat
tail·gate (n, v)
　-gat·ed, -gat·ing
tail·light
tai·lor
tail·piece
tail·spin
tail wind
taint
take off (v)
take·off (n)
take-out (adj)
take·out (n)
take over (v)
take·over (n)
talc
tale (story; cf. *tail*)
tal·ent
　-ent·ed, -ent·less

talk·ative
　-ative·ness
tal·low
tal·ly
　-lies
tal·on
ta·ma·le
tam·a·rack
tam·bou·rine
tam·per
　-pered, -per·ing,
　-per·proof
tam·pon
tan·a·ger
tan·dem
tan·gent
tan·ger·ine
tan·gi·ble
　-ble·ness, -bly,
　-bil·i·ty
tan·gle
　-gled, -gling
tank
　tank·ful
tan·ta·lize
　-lized, -liz·ing
tan·ta·mount
tap
　tapped, tap·ping
tape
　taped, tap·ing
ta·per (diminish; cf.
　tapir)
tape-re·cord (v)

tap·es·try
tape·worm
tap·i·o·ca
ta·pir (animal; cf.
　taper)
tap·root
tar·an·tel·la
ta·ran·tu·la
tar·dy
　-di·er, -di·est,
　-di·ness
tare (weight; cf. *tear*)
tar·get
tar·iff
tar·la·tan
tar·nish
tar·pau·lin
tar·pon
tar·ra·gon
tar·tan
tar·tar
task
task force
tas·sel
　-seled, -sel·ing
taste·ful
　-ful·ly, -ful·ness
tasty
　tast·i·ly, tast·i·ness
tat·ter·sall
tat·ting
tat·too
taught (instructed;
　cf. *taut*)

taunt
taut (tight; cf. *taught*)
tav·ern
taw·dry
tax
  tax·able
tax·a·tion
tax-ex·empt
taxi
  tax·ied, taxi·ing
taxi·cab
taxi·der·my
tax·pay·er
tea (a drink; cf. *tee*)
teach·able
teach·er
tea·cup
tea·ket·tle
teak·wood
team (in sports; cf. *teem*)
team·mate
team·ster
team·work
tear (rip; cf. *tare*)
tear (weep; cf. *tier*)
tear·drop
tear sheet
tea·spoon
tea·time
tech·ni·cal
  -cal·ly
tech·ni·cal·i·ty

tech·ni·cian
tech·nique
tech·no·log·i·cal
  -cal·ly
tech·nol·o·gy
  -gies
te·dious
  -dious·ness
tee (in golf; cf. *tea*)
teem (abound with; cf. *team*)
teen·age
teens
tee·ter
tee·to·tal·er
tele·cast
  -cast·ed, -cast·ing, -cast·er
tele·com·mu·ni·ca·tion
tele·con·fer·ence
  -enc·ing
tele·fac·sim·i·le
tele·gram
  -grammed, -gram·ming
tele·graph
tele·mar·ket·ing
te·lep·a·thy
tele·phone
te·le·pho·ny
tele·pho·to
tele·print·er
tele·pro·cess·ing
Tele·Promp·Ter

tele·scope
  -scoped, -scop·ing
tele·scop·ic
tele·text
tele·thon
Tele·type
tele·vise
  -vised, -vis·ing
tele·vi·sion
tell
  tell·ing
te·mer·i·ty
  -ties
tem·per
  -pered, -per·ing, -per·able
tem·per·a·ment
tem·per·ance
tem·per·ate
tem·per·a·ture
tem·pest
tem·pes·tu·ous
tem·plate
tem·ple
tem·po
  -pi (pl)
tem·po·ral
  -ral·ly
tem·po·rari·ly
tem·po·rary
  -rar·ies
tempt
temp·ta·tion
ten·a·ble

te·na·cious
te·nac·i·ty
ten·an·cy
ten·ant
  -ant·able
ten·den·cy
  -cies
ten·der
  -der·ness
ten·der·heart·ed
ten·der·ize
  -ized, -iz·ing,
  -iza·tion
ten·der·loin
ten·don
ten·dril
ten·e·ment
ten·nis
ten·or
ten·pin
ten·sile
ten·sion
  -sioned, -sion·ing
ten-speed
ten·ta·cle
ten·ta·tive
  -tive·ly, -tive·ness
tenth
  tenths
te·nu·ity
ten·u·ous
ten·ure
tep·id
te·qui·la

ter·mi·na·ble
ter·mi·nal
ter·mi·nate
  -nat·ed, -nat·ing
ter·mi·na·tion
ter·mi·nol·o·gy
ter·mite
tern (bird; cf. *turn*)
ter·race
  -raced, -rac·ing
ter·ra fir·ma
ter·rain
ter·ra·pin
ter·rar·i·um
  -ia (pl)
ter·raz·zo
ter·res·tri·al
  -al·ly
ter·ri·ble
  -ble·ness, -bly
ter·ri·er
ter·rif·ic
  -i·cal·ly
ter·ri·fy
  -fied, -fy·ing
ter·ri·to·ri·al
ter·ri·to·ry
  -ries
ter·ror
ter·ror·ism
  -ist
ter·ror·ize
  -ized, -iz·ing
terse

terse·ly, terse·ness
ter·tia·ry
  -ries
tes·ta·ment
test-drive
tes·ti·fy
  -fied, -fy·ing
tes·ti·mo·ni·al
tes·ti·mo·ny
  -nies
test tube (n)
test-tube (adj)
tet·a·nus
tête-à-tête
text
text·book
text ed·it·ing
tex·tile
tex·tu·al
tex·ture
  -tured, -tur·ing
than
thank
thank·ful
  -ful·ly, -ful·ness
thanks·giv·ing
the·ater
the·at·ri·cal
  -cal·ly
theft
their (possessive; cf.
  there, they're)
the·ism
theme

them·selves
then
thence·forth
theo·lo·gian
theo·log·i·cal
the·ol·o·gy
-gies
the·o·rem
the·o·ret·i·cal
the·o·rize
-rized, -riz·ing
the·o·ry
-ries
ther·a·peu·tic
ther·a·pist
ther·a·py
-pies
there (that place; cf.
their, they're)
there·by
there·fore
(consequently)
there·on
ther·mal
-mal·ly
ther·mo·dy·nam·ic
ther·mom·e·ter
ther·mo·stat
the·sau·rus
-sau·ri (pl)
these
the·sis
-ses (pl)
thes·pi·an

they're (they are; cf.
their, there)
thick·et
thick-skinned
thief
thieves (pl)
thiev·ish
thim·ble
thin
thin·ner,
thin·nest,
thin·nish
third class (n)
third-class (adj)
third world
thirst·i·ly
thirsty
thirst·i·er,
thirst·i·est,
thirst·i·ness
thir·teen
-teenth
thir·ty
-ties, -ti·eth
thith·er
tho·rac·ic
tho·rax
-rax·es (pl)
thorn
thorn·less,
thorn·like
thorny
thorn·i·er,
thorn·i·est,

thorn·i·ness
thor·ough (com-
plete; cf. *threw,
through*)
-ough·ness
thor·ough·bred
thor·ough·fare
though
thought
thought·ful
-ful·ness
thought-out
thou·sand
-sandth
thread·bare
thread·worm
threat·en
-ened, -en·ing,
-en·er
three·fold
three·score
three·some
thresh·old
threw (past tense of
throw; cf.
*thorough,
through*)
thrifty
thrift·i·er,
thrift·i·est,
thrift·i·ness
thrive
thrived, thriv·ing
throat

throe (effort; cf.
  throw)
throm·bo·sis
  -ses (pl)
throne (royal chair;
  cf. *thrown*)
throng
through (by means
  of; cf. *thorough*,
  threw)
through·out
through·put
throw (hurl; cf.
  throe)
  threw, thrown
  (hurled; cf. *throne*)
throw away (v)
throw·away (adj, n)
throw back (v)
throw·back (n)
thru·way
thumb·nail
thumb·print
thumb·screw
thumb·tack
thun·der·bolt
thun·der·head
thun·der·ous
thun·der·show·er
thun·der·storm
Thurs·day
thwart
thyme (spice; cf.
  time)

thy·mus
thy·roid
tib·ia
tic (twitching; cf.
  tick)
tick (of a clock; cf.
  tic)
tick·et
tick·le
  -led, -ling
tick·ler
tid·al
tide (ocean; cf. *tied*)
tide·mark
tide·wa·ter
ti·dy
  -di·er, -di·est, -di·ly
tie
  tied (past tense of
  tie; cf. *tide*), ty·ing
tie·break·er
tie·pin
tier (row; cf. *tear*)
ti·ger
tight·fist·ed
tight-lipped
tight-mouthed
tight·rope
tim·ber (wood; cf.
  timbre)
  -bered, -ber·ing
tim·ber·land
tim·ber·line
tim·bre (of the

voice; cf. *timber*)
time (duration; cf.
  thyme)
  timed, tim·ing
time-hon·ored
time-keep·er
time-lapse
time·less
time·ly
  -li·er, -li·est,
  -li·ness
time·piece
time-sav·ing
time-shar·ing
time sheet
time·ta·ble
time zone
tim·id
  tim·id·ly,
  ti·mid·i·ty
tim·o·thy
tinc·ture
  -tured, -tur·ing
tinge
  tinged, tinge·ing
tin·gle
  -gled, -gling
tin·sel
  -seled, -sel·ing
ti·ny
  -ni·er, -ni·est,
  -ni·ness
tip
  tipped, tip·ping

tip·ster
tip·toe
 -toed, -toe·ing
ti·rade
tire·some
 -some·ly,
 -some·ness
tis·sue
ti·tan
ti·tan·ic
tithe
 tithed, tith·ing
tit·il·late
 -lat·ed, -lat·ing
ti·tle
 -tled, -tling
ti·tle·hold·er
tit·mouse
tit·u·lar
to (preposition; cf.
 too, two)
toad·stool
toast
to·bac·co
to·bog·gan
to·day
toe (of foot; cf. *tow*)
 toed, toe·ing
toe·nail
tof·fee
to·ga
to·geth·er
tog·gle
 -gled, -gling

toi·let
to·ken
tol·er·a·ble
 -bly, -bil·i·ty
tol·er·ance
tol·er·ant
tol·er·ate
 -at·ed, -at·ing
tol·er·a·tion
toll·booth
toll bridge
toll call
toll·gate
toll road
tom·a·hawk
to·ma·to
 -toes
to·mor·row
ton·al
tone
 toned, ton·ing
tongue
tongue-tied
ton·ic
to·night
ton·sil
ton·sil·lec·to·my
ton·sil·li·tis
too (also; cf. *to, two*)
tool·box
tool·house
tool·mak·er
tool·room
tooth·ache

tooth·brush
tooth·paste
tooth·pick
top
 topped,
 top·ping
to·paz
top·coat
top·ic
top·i·cal
to·pog·ra·phy
top se·cret
top·side
top·soil
torch·bear·er
torch·light
to·re·ador
tor·ment
tor·men·tor
tor·na·do
 -does
tor·pe·do
 -does, -doed,
 -do·ing
torque
tor·rent
tor·ren·tial
 -tial·ly
tor·rid
tor·so
tor·ti·lla
tor·toise-shell
tor·tu·ous (winding;
 cf. *torturous*)

tor·ture
  -tured, -tur·ing,
  -tur·er
tor·tur·ous (painful;
  cf. *tortuous*)
to·tal
  -taled, -tal·ing
to·tal·i·tar·i·an
to·tal·i·ty
  -ties
to·tal·ly
to·tem
touch down (v)
touch·down (n)
tou·ché
touchy
tough
  tough·ness
tou·pee
tour·ism
tour·ist
tour·na·ment
tour·ney
  -neys, -neyed,
  -ney·ing
tour·ni·quet
tow (pull; cf. *toe*)
to·ward
tow·boat
tow·el
  -eled, -el·ing
tow·er
tow·line
town·ship

towns·peo·ple
tow·rope
tox·emia
tox·ic
  -ic·i·ty
tox·i·col·o·gy
trace
  traced, trac·ing,
  trace·able
tra·chea
  -che·ae (pl)
track (path; cf. *tract*)
  track·less
track·ing
tract (treatise; area;
  cf. *track*)
trac·tion
trac·tor
trade-in (n)
trade·mark
trade name
trade-off (n)
tra·di·tion
  -tion·al, -tion·al·ly,
  -tion·less
traf·fic
  -ficked, -fick·ing
trag·e·dy
  -dies
trag·ic
  -i·cal, -i·cal·ly
trail·er
  -er·ing
train·able

train·ee
trait
trai·tor
tra·jec·to·ry
  -ries
tram·ple
  -pled, -pling, -pler
tram·po·line
tran·quil
  -quil·ly
tran·quil·iz·er
tran·quil·li·ty
trans·act
trans·ac·tion
trans·at·lan·tic
tran·scend
tran·scen·dent
tran·scen·den·tal
tran·scen·den·tal·ism
trans·con·ti·nen·tal
tran·scribe
  -scribed, -scrib·ing
tran·script
tran·scrip·tion
trans·fer
  -ferred, -fer·ring,
  -fer·able
trans·fer·ence
trans·fig·ure
trans·fix
  -fix·ion
trans·form
trans·for·ma·tion
trans·form·er

trans·fuse
  -fused, -fus·ing
trans·gress
trans·gres·sion
tran·sient
tran·sis·tor
tran·sit
tran·si·tion
tran·si·tive
tran·si·to·ry
trans·late
  -lat·ed, -lat·ing,
  -la·tor
trans·la·tion
trans·lit·er·ate
trans·lu·cent
trans·mis·sion
trans·mit
  -mit·ted, -mit·ting,
  -mit·tal
trans·oce·an·ic
tran·som
trans·par·en·cy
  -cies
trans·par·ent
tran·spire
  -spired, -spir·ing
trans·plant
  -plant·able,
  -plan·ta·tion
trans·port
trans·por·ta·tion
trans·pose
  -posed, -pos·ing,

-pos·able
trans·po·si·tion
trans·verse
trap
  trapped, trap·ping
tra·peze
trau·ma
  -ma·ta (pl)
tra·vail (toil; cf.
  travel)
trav·el (journey; cf.
  travail)
  -eled, -el·ing
trav·el agent
trav·el·er
tra·verse
  -versed, -vers·ing,
  -vers·able
trav·es·ty
  -ties
treach·er·ous
treach·ery
  -er·ies
trea·dle
tread·mill
trea·son
trea·sure
trea·sur·er
trea·sury
treat
trea·tise
treat·ment
trea·ty
  -ties

tre·ble
tree fern
tree·top
tre·foil
trel·lis
trem·ble
tre·men·dous
  -dous·ness
trem·or
trem·u·lous
trench
tren·chan·cy
tren·chant
trep·i·da·tion
tres·pass
tres·tle
tri·ad
tri·al
tri·an·gle
tri·an·gu·lar
trib·al
  -al·ly
tribe
tri·bu·nal
tri·bune
trib·u·tary
  -tar·ies
trib·ute
trick·ery
trick·le
trick·ster
tri·col·or
tri·cy·cle
tri·dent

tri·en·ni·al
tri·fle
  -fled, -fling
tri·fo·cal
trig·ger
  -gered, -ger·ing
trig·o·nom·e·try
tril·lion
tril·li·um
tril·o·gy
  -gies
trin·ket
trip
  tripped,
  trip·ping
tri·ple
  -pled, -pling
trip·li·cate
  -cat·ed, -cat·ing,
  -ca·tion
tri·pod
tri·umph
  -um·phal
tri·um·phant
triv·et
triv·ia
triv·i·al
trol·ley
  -leys
trom·bone
  -bon·ist
troop (of soldiers; cf.
  troupe)
troop·ship

tro·phy
  -phies
trop·ic
trot
  trot·ted,
  trot·ting
trou·ba·dour
trou·ble
  -bled, -bling
trou·ble·shoot·er
trou·ble·some
  -some·ly,
  -some·ness
troupe (of actors; cf.
  troop)
trou·ser
trous·seau
  -seaux (pl)
trow·el
tru·an·cy
tru·ant
truck·load
truf·fle
tru·ism
  -is·tic
tru·ly
trum·pet
trum·pet·er
trun·cate
  -cat·ed, -cat·ing
trust·ee
  trust·eed,
  trust·ee·ing
trust·ee·ship

trust·ful
trust fund
trust·wor·thy
  -thi·ness
truth
  truths
truth·ful
try out (v)
try·out (n)
tryst
tset·se fly
tu·ba
tu·ber
tu·ber·cu·lar
tu·ber·cu·lin
tu·ber·cu·lo·sis
tu·bu·lar
Tu·dor
Tues·day
tug
  tugged,
  tug·ging
tu·ition
tu·lip
tu·lip·wood
tulle
tum·ble
  -bled, -bling
tum·bler
tum·ble·weed
tu·mor
  -mor·like
tu·mult
tu·mul·tu·ous

tu·na
tune
   tuned, tun·ing
tune·ful
tune-up
tung·sten
tu·nic
tun·nel
   -neled, -nel·ing
tur·ban (headdress;
   cf. *turbine*)
tur·bine (engine; cf.
   turban)
tur·bo·jet
tur·bu·lence
tur·bu·lent
tu·reen
tur·key
   -keys
tur·mer·ic
tur·moil
turn (rotate; cf. *tern*)
turn·about
turn around (v)
turn·around (n)
turn·around time
turn down (v)
turn·down (adj, n)
turn in (v)

turn-in (n)
tur·nip
turn·key
   -keys
turn off (v)
turn-off (n)
turn over (v)
turn·over (adj, n)
turn·pike
turn·stile
turn·ta·ble
tur·pen·tine
tur·quoise
tur·ret
tur·tle·dove
tur·tle·neck
tus·sle
   -sled, -sling
tu·te·lage
tu·tor
tu·to·ri·al
twelve
   twelfth
twen·ty
   -ties, -ti·eth
twice
twi·light
twitch
two (one and one; cf.

to, too)
two-piece (adj, n)
two-ply
ty·coon
ty·ing
type
   typed, typ·ing
type·cast
type·face
type·script
type·set·ter
type·write
type·writ·er
ty·phoid
ty·phoon
ty·phus
typ·i·cal
typ·i·fy
   -fied, -fy·ing
ty·pog·ra·pher
ty·po·graph·i·cal
ty·ran·ni·cal
tyr·an·nize
   -nized, -niz·ing
tyr·an·ny
   -nies
ty·rant
ty·ro

ubiq·ui·tous
ug·li·ness
ug·ly
  -li·er,
  -li·est
uku·le·le
ul·cer
ul·cer·ation
ul·cer·ous
ul·te·ri·or
ul·ti·mate
ul·ti·ma·tum
ul·tra·mod·ern
ul·tra·na·tion·al·ism
ul·tra·son·ic
ul·tra·vi·o·let
um·bil·i·cal
um·brage
um·brel·la
um·pire
un·abat·ed
un·able
un·abridged
un·ac·cept·able
un·ac·com·pa·nied
un·ac·count·able
un·ac·cus·tomed
un·adul·ter·at·ed
un·af·fect·ed

un·al·ter·able
un·am·big·u·ous
un-Amer·i·can
unan·i·mous
un·as·sum·ing
un·au·tho·rized
un·avail·able
un·avoid·able
un·aware
un·bal·anced
un·be·com·ing
un·be·liev·able
un·bend
un·bi·ased
un·but·ton
un·cer·tain
un·cer·tain·ty
un·char·i·ta·ble
un·civ·i·lized
un·cle
un·clean
un·com·fort·able
un·com·mit·ted
un·com·mu·ni·ca·tive
un·com·pli·men·ta·ry
un·com·pro·mis·ing
un·con·cerned
un·con·di·tion·al
un·con·quer·able

un·con·scio·na·ble
un·con·scious
un·con·trol·la·ble
un·con·ven·tion·al
un·con·vinc·ing
  -ing·ly
un·cor·rect·ed
unc·tion
un·de·ni·able
un·der·age
un·der·arm
un·der·brush
un·der·class·man
un·der·clothes
un·der·cov·er
un·der·cur·rent
un·der·de·vel·oped
un·der·dog
un·der·em·ploy·ment
un·der·go
un·der·grad·u·ate
un·der·ground
un·der·line
un·der·ly·ing
un·der·mine
un·der·neath
un·der·pass
un·der·priv·i·leged
un·der·rate

un·der·score
un·der·sell
un·der·shirt
un·der·side
un·der·signed
un·der·stand
un·der·stood
un·der·study
un·der·tak·er
un·der·tone
un·der·tow
un·der·val·ue
un·der·wa·ter
un·der way (adv)
un·der·way (adj)
un·der·wear
un·der·weight
un·der·went
un·der·world
un·der·write
un·de·sir·able
un·do (unfasten; cf. *undue*)
un·doubt·ed·ly
un·due (excessive; cf. *undo*)
un·du·la·tion
un·du·ly
un·earned
un·earth·ly
un·easy
  -eas·i·ness
un·em·ployed
un·en·cum·bered

un·equal
un·equiv·o·cal
un·err·ing
un·even
un·ex·pect·ed
un·fa·mil·iar
  -iar·i·ty
un·fa·vor·able
un·fore·seen
un·for·get·ta·ble
un·for·tu·nate
  -nate·ly
un·furl
un·gain·ly
uni·fi·ca·tion
uni·form
uni·for·mi·ty
  -ties
uni·fy
  -fied, -fy·ing
uni·lat·er·al
un·im·proved
un·in·hib·it·ed
un·in·sured
un·in·tel·li·gi·ble
union
union·ize
  -ized, -iz·ing
unique
  unique·ly,
  unique·ness
uni·sex
uni·son
unit

unite
Unit·ed States
uni·ty
  -ties
uni·ver·sal
uni·verse
uni·ver·si·ty
un·kind·ly
un·know·ing
un·known
un·law·ful
un·leash
un·less
un·let·tered
un·like·ly
un·lim·it·ed
un·manned
un·mind·ful
un·mit·i·gat·ed
un·named
un·nat·u·ral
un·nec·es·sary
un·nerve
  -nerv·ing·ly
un·ob·tru·sive
un·oc·cu·pied
un·or·tho·dox
un·paid
un·par·al·leled
un·pleas·ant
un·prec·e·dent·ed
un·prof·it·able
un·qual·i·fied
un·ques·tion·able

un·rav·el
un·re·al
un·rea·son·able
un·ru·ly
  -rul·i·ness
un·sat·is·fac·to·ry
  -ri·ly
un·sa·vory
un·scathed
un·scru·pu·lous
un·so·cia·ble
  -bil·i·ty
un·so·phis·ti·cat·ed
un·speak·able
un·think·able
un·ti·dy
  -di·ly, -di·ness
un·tie
un·til
un·time·ly
un·told
un·touch·able
un·truth·ful
un·used
un·usu·al
  -al·ly
un·want·ed
  (undesired; cf.
  unwonted)
un·war·rant·ed
un·wary
un·wieldy
  -wield·i·ly,
  -wield·i·ness

un·wont·ed
  (unaccustomed;
  cf. *unwanted*)
un·wor·thy
  -thi·ly, -thi·ness
un·writ·ten
up·bring·ing
up·com·ing
up·date
up·grade
up·heav·al
up·hill (adj, adv, n)
up·hold
  -held, -hold·ing
up·hol·ster
up·hol·stery
  -ster·ies
up·keep
up·land
up·lift
up·on
up·per
up·per class (n)
up·per-class (adj)
up·per·class·man
up·per·cut
up·per·most
up·right
up·ris·ing
up·roar·i·ous
up·root
up·set
  -set·ting
up·shot

up·stage
up·stairs
up·start
up·state (adj, adv, n)
up·stream
up·swing
up·tight
up-to-date
up·ward
ura·ni·um
ur·ban (of city; cf.
  urbane)
ur·bane (suave; cf.
  urban)
ur·ban·iza·tion
ur·chin
urge
  urged, urg·ing
ur·gen·cy
  -cies
ur·gent
uri·nary
urn (vase; cf. *earn*)
us·able
us·age
use
  used
us·ing
use·ful
use·ful·ness
use·less
us·er-friend·ly
ush·er
  -ered, -er·ing

usu·al
-al·ly
usu·rer
usu·ri·ous
usurp
usu·ry
-ries

uten·sil
uter·ine
util·i·tar·i·an
util·i·ty
-ties
uti·li·za·tion
uti·lize

-liz·ing
uti·lized
ut·most
uto·pia
ut·ter
ut·ter·ance

V

va·can·cy
-cies
va·cant
va·cate
-cat·ed, -cat·ing
va·ca·tion
-tioned,
-tion·ing,
-tion·er
vac·ci·nate
-nat·ed, -nat·ing
vac·ci·na·tion
vac·cine
vac·il·late
-lat·ed, -lat·ing
vac·il·la·tion
vac·u·um
vag·a·bond
va·gran·cy
-cies
va·grant

vague
vagu·er, vagu·est,
vague·ly,
vague·ness
vain (conceited; cf.
vane, vein)
va·lance (drapery;
cf. *valence*)
vale (valley; cf. *veil*)
vale·dic·to·ri·an
vale·dic·to·ry
-ries
va·lence (combining
power; cf.
valance)
val·en·tine
va·let
val·iant
val·id
va·lid·i·ty
val·i·date

-dat·ed, -dat·ing
val·i·da·tion
va·lise
val·ley
-leys
val·or
valu·able
val·u·a·tion
val·ue
valve
vam·pire
van·dal·ism
vane (weather; cf.
vain, vein)
van·guard
va·nil·la
van·ish
van·i·ty
-ties
van·quish
van·tage

va·por
-pored, -por·ing

va·por·ize
-ized, -iz·ing,
-iza·tion

va·por·iz·er

va·por·ous

vari·able
-abil·i·ty

vari·ance

vari·ant

vari·a·tion

var·i·cose

var·ied

var·ie·gate
-gat·ed, -gat·ing

var·ie·ga·tion

va·ri·ety

var·i·ous

var·nish

vary (diversify; cf.
very)
var·ied, vary·ing

vas·cu·lar

va·sec·to·my
-mies

Vas·e·line

Vat·i·can

vaude·ville
-vil·lian

vault

veg·e·ta·ble

veg·e·tar·i·an

veg·e·tate

-tat·ed, -tat·ing

veg·e·ta·tion

veg·e·ta·tive

ve·he·mence

ve·he·ment

ve·hi·cle

ve·hic·u·lar

veil (garment; cf.
vale)

vein (blood vessel;
cf. *vain, vane*)

ve·loc·i·ty
-ties

ve·lour

vel·vet

ven·det·ta

ven·dor

ve·neer

ven·er·a·ble

ven·er·ate
-at·ed, -at·ing

ven·er·a·tion

ven·geance

venge·ful
-ful·ly, -ful·ness

ven·i·son

ven·om·ous

ven·ti·late
-lat·ed, -lat·ing

ven·ti·la·tion

ven·ti·la·tor

ven·tri·cle

ven·tril·o·quism

ven·tril·o·quist

ven·ture
-tured, -tur·ing

ven·ture·some
-some·ly,
-some·ness

ven·ue

ve·ra·cious (truthful;
cf. *voracious*)

ve·rac·i·ty
-ties

ve·ran·da

ver·bal
-bal·ly

ver·bal·ism

ver·bal·ize
-ized, -iz·ing,
-iza·tion

ver·ba·tim

ver·biage

ver·bose
-bose·ly,
-bose·ness,
-bos·i·ty

ver·dict

verge
verged, verg·ing

ver·i·fi·ca·tion

ver·i·fy
-fied, -fy·ing

ver·mil·ion or
ver·mil·lion

ver·min
-min (pl)

ver·nac·u·lar

ver·nal
ver·sa·tile
ver·sa·til·i·ty
ver·si·fi·ca·tion
ver·si·fy
  -fied, -fy·ing
ver·sion
ver·sus
ver·te·bra
  -brae (pl)
ver·te·brate
ver·tex
  ver·ti·ces (pl)
ver·ti·cal
  -cal·ly, -cal·ness
very (extremely; cf.
  vary)
ves·i·cle
ves·per
ves·sel
ves·tige
vest·ment
vet·er·an
vet·er·i·nary
  -nar·ies
ve·to
  -toes
ve·toed
vex·a·tion
via
vi·a·ble
  -bil·i·ty
via·duct
vi·al (bottle; cf. *vile,*
  viol)

vi·brant
vi·brate
  -brat·ed, -brat·ing
vi·bra·tion
vi·bra·to
vi·bra·tor
vic·ar
vi·car·i·ous
vice (sin; cf. *vise*)
vice-chan·cel·lor
vice pres·i·dent
vice ver·sa
vi·chys·soise
vi·cin·i·ty
  -ties
vi·cious
vic·tim
vic·tim·ize
  -ized, -iz·ing
vic·tor
vic·to·ri·ous
vic·to·ry
  -ries
vi·cu·ña
vid·eo
vid·eo·cas·sette
vid·eo·con·fer·ence
vid·eo·disc or
  vid·eo·disk
vid·eo dis·play
  ter·mi·nal
vid·eo·phone
vid·eo·tape

vid·eo·tex
vie
  vied, vy·ing
view·point
vig·il
vig·i·lance
vig·i·lant
vig·i·lan·te
vi·gnette
vig·or·ous
vile (odious; cf. *vial,*
  viol)
vil·i·fy
  -fied, -fy·ing,
  -fi·er
vil·lage
vil·lain
vil·lain·ous
vin·ai·grette
vin·di·cate
  -cat·ed, -cat·ing
vin·di·ca·tion
vin·dic·a·tive
  (justifying; cf.
  vindictive)
vin·dic·tive
  (vengeful; cf.
  vindicative)
vin·e·gar
vine·yard
vin·tage
vi·ol (instrument; cf.
  vial, vile)
vi·o·la

vi·o·late
-lat·ed, -lat·ing
vi·o·lence
vi·o·lent
vi·o·let
vi·o·lin
vi·per
vir·gin
vir·ile
vi·ril·i·ty
vir·tu·al
vir·tu·al·ly
vir·tue
vir·tu·os·i·ty
-ties
vir·tu·o·so
vir·u·lent
vi·rus
vis·age
vis-à-vis
vis·count
vise (tool; cf. *vice*)
vis·i·bil·i·ty
vis·i·ble
-ble·ness, -bly
vi·sion
-sion·al, -sion·al·ly
vi·sion·ary
-ar·ies
vis·it
-it·ing
vis·i·ta·tion
vis·i·tor
vi·sor

vis·ta
vi·su·al
-al·ly
vi·su·al aid
vi·su·al·ize
-ized, -iz·ing
vi·ta
vi·tae (pl)
vi·tal
vi·tal·i·ty
-ties
vi·tal·ize
-ized, -iz·ing,
-iza·tion
vi·ta·min
vit·ri·ol
vi·va
vi·va·cious
viv·id
-id·ness, -id·ly
vi·vip·a·rous
vivi·sec·tion
vix·en
vo·cab·u·lary
-lar·ies
vo·cal
-cal·ly
vo·cal·ist
vo·cal·ize
-ized, -iz·ing,
-iza·tion
vo·ca·tion (career;
cf. *avocation*)
vo·ca·tion·al

-al·ly
vo·cif·er·ous
-ous·ness
vod·ka
voice
voiced, voic·ing
voice·less
voice mail
voice rec·og·ni·tion
void·able
vol·a·tile
-tile·ness, -til·i·ty
vol·can·ic
vol·ca·no
-noes
vo·li·tion
vol·ley
-leys, -leyed,
-ley·ing
vol·ley·ball
volt·age
vol·u·ble
vol·ume
-umed, -um·ing
vol·u·met·ric
vo·lu·mi·nous
vol·un·ta·rism
vol·un·tary
-tar·ies, -tari·ly,
-tari·ness
vol·un·teer
vol·un·teer·ism
vo·lup·tuous
vom·it

voo·doo
-doos
vo·ra·cious (greedy;
cf. *veracious*)
-cious·ness
vo·rac·i·ty
vor·tex
-ti·ces (pl)
vote
vot·ed, vot·ing
vo·tive

-tive·ly, -tive·ness
vouch
vouch·er
vow·el
voy·age
-aged, -ag·ing,
-ag·er
vul·ca·ni·za·tion
vul·ca·nize
-nized, -niz·ing,
-niz·er

vul·gar
vul·gar·ism
vul·gar·i·ty
-ties
vul·gar·iza·tion
vul·ner·a·ble
-ble·ness, -bly,
-bil·i·ty
vul·ture

wad
wad·ded, wad·ding
wad·dle
-dled, -dling
wa·fer
waf·fle
-fled, -fling
wag
wagged, wag·ging
wage
waged, wag·ing
wa·ger
-gered, -ger·ing
wag·on
waist (blouse; cf.
waste)
waist·line

wait (delay; cf.
weight)
wait·er
wait·ress
waive (abandon; cf.
wave)
waived, waiv·ing
waiv·er (abandon-
ment; cf. *waver*)
wake
waked, wak·ing
walk
walk·ie-talk·ie
walk-in (adj, n)
walk-on (n)
walk out (v)
walk·out (n)

walk·over (n)
walk-up (n, adj)
wal·let
wall·eye
wal·low
wall·pa·per (n, v)
wal·nut
wal·rus
waltz
wan·der
-dered, -der·ing
wan·der·lust
want (desire; cf.
wont, won't)
wan·ton
war
warred, war·ring

war·bler
war·den
ward·robe
ware (goods; cf.
  wear, where)
ware·house
war·fare
war·fa·rin
war·head
war-horse
warm·heart·ed
war·mon·ger
warmth
warm up (v)
warm-up (n)
warn·ing
warp
war·rant
war·rant·able
war·ran·tee (person;
  cf. *warranty*)
war·ran·tor
war·ran·ty
  (guarantee; cf.
  warrantee)
  -ties
war·rior
war·ship
war·time
wary
  wari·ly, wari·ness
wash·able
  -abil·i·ty
wash·cloth

wash out (v)
wash·out (n)
wasn't (was not)
was·sail
waste (needless
  destruction; cf.
  waist)
  wast·ed, wast·ing
waste·bas·ket
waste·ful
  -ful·ly, -ful·ness
waste·land
waste·pa·per
watch
watch·dog
watch·ful
watch out (v)
watch·tow·er
watch·word
wa·ter
wa·ter·borne
wa·ter·col·or
wa·ter·cress
wa·ter·fall
wa·ter·fowl
wa·ter·front
wa·ter·line
wa·ter·logged
wa·ter·mark
wa·ter·mel·on
wa·ter pipe
wa·ter po·lo
wa·ter·proof
wa·ter·re·pel·lent

wa·ter·re·sis·tant
wa·ter·shed
wa·ter·spout
wa·ter·tight
wa·ter·way
wa·ter·works
wa·tery
  -ter·i·ness
watt·age
wave (beckon; cf.
  waive)
  waved, wav·ing
wave·length
wa·ver (hesitate; cf.
  waiver)
  -vered, -ver·ing
wavy
  wav·i·er, wav·i·est,
  wav·i·ness
waxy
way (direction; cf.
  weigh)
way·lay
  -laid, -lay·ing
way·side
way·ward
weak (adj)(feeble; cf.
  week)
weak·en
  weak·ened,
  weak·en·ing
weak·heart·ed
weak·ling
weak-mind·ed

weak·ness

weal (state; welt; cf.
  *we'll, wheal,
  wheel*)

wealth

wealthy
  wealth·i·er,
  wealth·i·est,
  wealth·i·ness

weap·on

wear (clothes; cf.
  ware, where)

wear·able
  -abil·i·ty

wea·ri·less

wea·ri·some

wea·ry
  -ri·er, -ri·est, -ri·ly

wea·sel
  -seled, -sel·ing

weath·er (atmo-
  spheric condi-
  tions; cf. *whether*)

weath·er·ize
  -iza·tion

weath·er·proof

weav·er

web
  webbed, web·bing

wed
  wed·ded,
  wed·ding

we'd (we would)

wedge

wedged, wedg·ing

Wedg·wood

Wednes·day

week (n)(7 days; cf.
  weak)

week·day

week·end

wee·vil

weigh (ponder; cf.
  way)

weight (poundage;
  cf. *wait*)

weight·less
  -less·ness

weighty

weird

wel·come
  -comed, -com·ing,
  -come·ness

weld

wel·fare

wel·far·ism

well

we'll (we will; cf.
  *weal, wheal,
  wheel*)

well-be·ing

well-bred

well-con·di·tioned

well-de·fined

well-found·ed

well-groomed

well-ground·ed

well-han·dled

well·head

well-heeled

well-in·formed

well-known

well-mean·ing

well-off

well-read

well-round·ed

well-spo·ken

well-thought-of

well-timed

well-to-do

well-wish·er

well-worn

went

were

we're (we are)

weren't (were not)

were·wolf

west·bound

west·er·ly

west·ern

West·ern·er

west·ward

wet (moist; cf. *whet*)
  wet·ted, wet·ting

wet blan·ket (n)

wet·land

we've (we have)

whale
  whaled, whal·ing

whale·bone

wharf
  wharves (pl)

what·ev·er

what·so·ev·er

wheal (welt; cf. *weal, we'll, wheel*)

wheel (turn; cf. *weal, we'll, wheal*)

wheel·bar·row

wheel·chair

whence

when·ev·er

when·so·ev·er

where (in what place; cf. *ware, wear*)

where·as

where·by

where·fore

where·in

where·so·ev·er

where·up·on

wher·ev·er

where·with·al

whet (sharpen; cf. *wet*)

whet·ted, whet·ting

wheth·er (if; cf. *weather*)

whey

which (pronoun; cf. *witch*)

which·ev·er

which·so·ev·er

while (during; cf. *wile*)

whiled, whil·ing

whim·per

-pered, -per·ing

whim·si·cal

-cal·ly, -cal·ness

whine (cry; cf. *wine*)

whined, whin·ing

whip

whipped, whip·ping

whip·cord

whip·lash

whip·pet

whip·poor·will

whirl·pool

whirl·wind

whisk

whis·ker

whis·key

whis·per

-pered, -per·ing

whis·tle

-tled, -tling

whis·tler

white·cap

white-col·lar

white·fish

whit·en

-ened, -en·ing

white·out

white·wash

whith·er (where; cf. *wither*)

whit·low

whit·tle

-tled, -tling, -tler

who·ev·er

whole (entire; cf. *hole*)

whole·heart·ed

whole·sale

whole·some

whol·ly (entirely; cf. *holey, holly, holy*)

whom·ev·er

who's (who is; cf. *whose*)

whose (possessive of *who*; cf. *who's*)

why

wick·ed·ness

wick·er·work

wick·et

wide-an·gle (adj)

wide-awake (adj)

wid·en

wide·spread

wid·ow

wid·ow·er

width

wield

wie·ner

wife

wives (pl)

wild·cat

wil·der·ness

wild·fire

wild·life
wile (trick; cf. *while*)
 wiled, wil·ing
will·ful
will·pow·er
win
 win·ning,
 win·less,
 win·na·ble
wind
wind·blown
wind·break
wind·burn
wind·fall
wind·jam·mer
wind·mill
win·dow
win·dow·pane
win·dow-shop (v)
 win·dow-shop·per
 (n)
win·dow·sill
wind·pipe
wind·proof
wind·shield
wind·storm
wind·swept
wind up (v)
wind·up (adj, n)
wind·ward
wine (drink; cf.
 whine)
wine·glass
wine·grow·er

wine·press
wine·shop
wing
wing·span
wing·spread
win·ner
win·some
 -some·ly,
 -some·ness
win·ter
 -tered, -ter·ing
win·ter·ize
 -ized, -iz·ing
win·ter-kill (v)
win·try or win·tery
wire·less
wire·tap
wis·dom
wise
 wise·ly, wise·ness
wish·bone
wish·ful
wist·ful
 -ful·ly, -ful·ness
witch (hag; cf.
 which)
witch·craft
with
with·draw
with·draw·al
with·er (shrivel; cf.
 whither)
 -ered, -er·ing
with·hold

with·in
with·out
with·stand
 -stood
wit·ness
wit·ti·cism
wit·ting·ly
wit·ty
 -ti·ly, -ti·ness
wiz·ard
woe·be·gone
wolf·hound
wol·ver·ine
wom·an
 wom·en (pl)
wom·an·ly
 -li·ness
womb
won (did win; cf. *one*)
won·der
 -dered, -der·ing
won·der·ful
won·der·land
won·der·ment
won·drous
 -drous·ness
wont (custom; cf.
 want, won't)
won't (will not; cf.
 want, wont)
wood (lumber; cf.
 would)
wood carv·ing (n)
 wood-car·ver

wood·chuck
wood·cut·ter
wood·ed
wood·en
wood·land
wood·lot
wood·peck·er
wood·pile
wood·wind
wood·work
wool·en
wool·ly or wool·ie
  -lies
word
word·book
wordy
  word·i·er,
  word·i·est,
  word·i·ly
word-of-mouth (adj)
word pro·cess·ing
word pro·ces·sor
word wrap
work
  worked, work·ing
work·able
work·a·hol·ic
work·bas·ket
work·bench
work·book
work·day
work force
work load
work·man·like

work·man·ship
work out (v)
work·out (n)
work·room
work·shop
work·sta·tion
work·ta·ble
work·week
world·ly
  -li·ness
world·wide
worm·wood
worn-out
wor·ri·some
wor·ry
  -ries, -ried, -ry·ing
worse
wor·ship
  -shiped, ship·ing,
  -ship·er
worst
worth
worth·less
  -less·ness
worth·while (adj)
  -while·ness
wor·thy
  -thi·ly, -thi·ness
would (auxiliary
  verb; cf. *wood*)
wouldn't (would
  not)
wound
wran·gle

-gled, -gling
wrap (envelope; cf.
  rap)
wrapped (envel-
  oped; cf. *rapped*,
  rapt), wrap·ping
wrap·around
wrap·per
wrap up (v)
wrap-up (n)
wrath
wreath (n)
wreathe (v)
wreck (ruin; cf. *reek*)
wreck·age
wreck·er
wren
wrench
wrest (pull away; cf.
  rest)
wres·tle
  -tled, -tling
wretch·ed
  -ed·ness
wrig·gle
  -gled, -gling, -gly
wring (twist; cf.
  ring)
wrin·kle
  -kled, -kling
wrist
wrist·lock
wrist·watch
writ

W-X-Y write/yet

write (compose; cf.
  right, rite)
write in (v)
write-in (adj, n)
write off (v)
write-off (n)
write up (v)
write-up (n)
writhe

writhed, with·ing
writ·ing
writ·ten
wrong
  wronged,
  wrong·ing
wrong·do·er
wrong·do·ing
wrong·ful

-ful·ly, -ful·ness
wrote (did write; cf.
  rote)
wrought
wrung (twisted; cf.
  rung)
wry (perverse; cf. *rye*)

xe·non
xe·no·pho·bia
xe·rog·ra·phy

xe·ro·graph·ic
Xe·rox
X ray (n)

X-ray (adj, v)
xy·lo·phone

yacht
yak
yam
yank
Yan·kee
yard·age
yard·mas·ter
yard·stick
yar·mul·ke
yarn

yawl
yawn
year·book
year·ling
year·ly
yearn
yeast
yel·low
  -low·ish
yelp

yen
  yenned,
  yen·ning
yeo·men
ye·shi·va or
  ye·shi·vah
yes-man
yes·ter·day
yes·ter·year
yet

yew (tree; cf. *ewe, you*)
Yid·dish
yield
yip
  yipped, yip·ping
yo·del
  -deled, -del·ing
yo·ga
yo·gurt
yoke (harness; cf. *yolk*)
yo·kel

yolk (of egg; cf. *yoke*)
Yom Kip·pur
yon·der
yore (past time; cf. *your, you're*)
you (pronoun; cf. *ewe, yew*)
young
  young·ish, young·ness
young·ster
your (possessive of you; cf. *yore, you're*)

you're (you are; cf. *yore, your*)
your·self
  -selves (pl)
youth·ful
  -ful·ly, -ful·ness
yowl
yt·ter·bi·um
yt·tri·um
yule
yule·tide
yup·pie

Z

zag
  zagged, zag·ging
za·ny
  -nies, -ni·ly, -ni·ness
zeal
zeal·ot
zeal·ous
  -ous·ness
ze·bra
zeit·geist
ze·nith
zeph·yr
zep·pe·lin
ze·ro

  -ros
zest
zest·ful
  -ful·ly, -ful·ness
zig·zag
  -zagged, -zag·ging
zilch
zinc
zinc ox·ide
zin·nia
Zi·on·ism
  -ist
zip
  zipped, zip·ping
zip code

zip·per
zip·pered
zir·con
zir·co·ni·um
zith·er
zo·di·ac
zone
  zoned, zon·ing
zoo·log·i·cal
zo·ol·o·gy
zuc·chi·ni
Zu·lu
Zu·ni
zwie·back

?

Appendix

Spelling Tips

Understanding the following common families of spelling patterns may help to avoid many spelling errors.

The Final Consonant
When is a final consonant doubled?

1. When a word of one syllable (*skin*) ends in a single consonant (sk*i*n) preceded by a single vowel (sk*i*n), double the final consonant before a suffix that begins with a vowel (skinn*ing*) or before the suffix -*y* (skinn*y*).

beg	beggar	begged
star	starring	starry
swim	swimming	swimmer

Exception: When a one-syllable word ends in *y* preceded by a single vowel, do not double the *y* before a suffix beginning with a vowel.

pay	payee
joy	joyous
toy	toying

2. When a word of more than one syllable ends in a single consonant (prefe*r*) preceded by a single vowel (pref*e*r) and the accent falls on the last syllable of the root word (pre*fer*), double the final consonant before a suffix beginning with a vowel (preferr*ed*).

forbid	forbidden
occur	occurring
begin	beginning
allot	allotted

Exception: If the accent shifts to the first syllable of such a word when a suffix beginning with a vowel is added, do not double the final consonant.

> preferred *but* preferable
> transferred *but* transferee

When is a final consonant not doubled?

1. When a word of one syllable ends in a single consonant (sa*d*) preceded by a single vowel (s*a*d), do not double the final consonant before a suffix beginning with a consonant (sad*ly*).

glad	gladly
boy	boyhood
wit	witness

2. When a word of more than one syllable ends in a single consonant (cance*l*) preceded by a single vowel (canc*e*l) and the accent does not fall on the last syllable of the root word, do not double the final consonant before a suffix beginning with a vowel (cancel*ed*).

total	totaled	totaling
credit	credited	creditor
abandon	abandoned	abandoning
model	modeled	modeling

3. When a word of one or more syllables ends in a single consonant (stou*t*) preceded by more than one vowel (st*ou*t), do not double the final consonant before any suffix, whether it begins with a consonant (stout*ly*) or a vowel (stout*er*).

riot	riotous
equal	equaled
deceit	deceitful

Spelling Tips

4. When a word of one or more syllables ends with more than one consonant (ha*nd*), do not double the final consonant before any suffix.

cold	colder
warm	warmly
bless	blessed
sleigh	sleighing

The Final Silent *e*

1. Words ending in silent *e* usually drop the *e* before a suffix beginning with a vowel and before the suffix *y*.

accuse	accusing
able	ably
escalate	escalation
ease	easy
bandage	bandaging
ice	icy

2. Words ending in *ce* or *ge* usually retain the *e* before a suffix beginning with *a* or *o*.

knowledge	knowledgeable
exchange	exchangeable
advantage	advantageous
courage	courageous
service	serviceable
enforce	enforceable

3. Words ending in silent *e* usually retain the *e* before a suffix beginning with a consonant.

name	namely
sincere	sincerely
one	oneness
manage	management

4.   Words ending in *ie* change the *ie* to *y* before adding *ing*.

die   dying
lie   lying

The Final *y*

1.   Words ending in *y* preceded by a consonant change the *y* to *i* before any suffix except one beginning with *i*.

apply   applied *but* applying
reply   replied *but* replying
comply complied   complies *but* complying
imply   implied   implies *but* implying

2.   Words ending in *y* preceded by a vowel usually retain the *y* before any suffix.

pray   praying   prayed
lay   laying
employ   employable

Words with *ei* and *ie*.   Put *i* before *e* except after *c* or when sounded like *a* as in *neighbor* or *weigh*.

believe   friend   (*i* before *e*)
receive   conceive   (except after *c*)
vein   eight   their   (sounded as *a*)

Words Ending in *-cede*, *-ceed*, and *-sede*

1.   Only one word ends in *-sede*: supersede.
2.   Only three words end in *-ceed*: exceed, proceed, succeed.
3.   All other words ending with the syllable pronounced "seed" are spelled *-cede*: precede, accede, intercede.

*The Spelling Tips section is based on *The Gregg Reference Manual, Sixth Edition,* Sabin, William, pages 135-138.

Style for Writing Numbers

Number expression is an area of English style about which even the experts sometimes disagree. Basically, numbers may be expressed either as figures or as spelled words.

Decisions about the use of figures or words may depend on any of several factors. A number expressed in figures is readily recognized and quickly comprehended. A number expressed as spelled words, on the other hand, is less obvious. Figures are considered less formal than numbers as spelled words. The following guidelines explain the most-used ways of handling numbers in writing.

1. The Basic Number Rule

Most occurrences of numbers in written material can be covered by the following basic rule: the numbers one through ten are spelled, while numbers greater than ten are expressed in figures. Numbers used with units of measure should always be expressed in figures.

Within 20 days, six students will complete the program.

The speaker brought four handouts for each of the 66 people.

The room is 9 feet by 12 feet.

2. The First Word of a Sentence

A number used as the first word of a sentence should always be spelled.

Eighteen boxes of books arrived at the library.

Two horses were hitched to the carriage.

3. The Same Kind of Data

If one number in a list of related numbers is larger than ten, all numbers in that list should be expressed in figures.

Please send 4 pens, 9 markers, and 12 envelopes.

I bought two cups, five plates, and six glasses.

4. Two Numbers Together

Often when two numbers occur together in a sentence, one of the numbers is part of a compound expression modifying a noun. One of the numbers—usually the first one—should be spelled, and the other should be expressed in figures. The first number should be spelled unless its spelling will make an awkwardly long expression.

I need wallpaper to cover one 8-foot panel.

Please order 500 eight-page booklets.

If two numbers appear together in a sentence and both are expressed in the same style, use a comma to separate them.

On December 13, 428 students will graduate.

When the clock struck nine, four knocks sounded at the door.

Hyphenation of Compound Adjectives

Sometimes two or more words express a single meaning in modifying a noun. That expression, called a compound adjective, is hyphenated.

We need to keep an up-to-date calendar.

Long after winter ended, I found my long-lost mittens.

Abbreviations and Acronyms

Abbreviations

An abbreviation is a shortened form of a word or phrase. In some kinds of writing the use of abbreviations is appropriate. These include reports, statistical data, in-house documents and communications of an informal nature. However, in more formal kinds of writing, the use of most abbreviations should be avoided.

If a writer is doubtful about whether use of abbreviations is appropriate in a given situation, he or she should spell out the complete word or phrase. The very common abbreviations of people's titles, educational degrees, or times of day are always acceptable.

Many abbreviations—but not all—end with a period. If a period occurs within an abbreviation, no space appears after the period. The following list shows some common abbreviations:

Mr., Mrs., Ms., Dr., Sen., Rep., Fr., the Rev., Ph.D., M.S., MBA, B.S.Ed., B.S., B.B.A., a.m., p.m., etc. (and so on), i.e (that is), vs. (versus), et al. (and others), cf. (compare), e.g. (for example).

Some abbreviations are pronounced in their abbreviated form, letter by letter. These very common abbreviations are represented by all-capital letters with no punctuation. The following list shows examples of some of these abbreviations:

IBM (International Business Machines), IRS (Internal Revenue Service), FBI (Federal Bureau of Investigation), SEC (Securities and Exchange Commission), UN (United Nations), TV (television), S & L (savings and loan), GOP (Grand Old Party), SS (social security), CD (certificate of deposit), FTC (Federal

Trade Commission), IQ (Intelligence Quotient), ACLU (American Civil Liberties Union), CRT (cathode-ray tube), CPU (central processing unit), OCR (optical character reader).

Some abbreviations of this type have even replaced the names which they originally represented.

Acronyms

The abbreviations shown above are pronounced by individual alphabetic letter. An acronym, on the other hand, is a series of letters which is read as a word. It appears in all-capital letters with no spaces or punctuation, just as the above-listed abbreviations do, but an acronym is pronounceable. The following list shows some examples of acronyms:

SALT (Strategic Arms Limitation Talks), ZIP (Zone Improvement Program), HUD (Housing and Urban Development), IRA (Individual Retirement Act), CAD (computer-aided design), COBOL (Common Business-Oriented Language), ROM (read-only memory).

Acronyms sometimes use only the first letter of each word the acronym represents (SALT). At other times, the acronym may use more than one letter from one or more word (COBOL).

Troublesome Place Names

Troublesome Place Names

United States

Alabama
Anniston
Bessemer
Gadsden
Montgomery
Phenix City
Scottsboro
Talladega
Tallassee
Tuscaloosa

Alaska
Anchorage
Fairbanks
Juneau
Sitka
Valdez

Arizona
Flagstaff
Nogales
Phoenix
Scottsdale
Tempe
Tucson
Yuma

Arkansas
Arkadelphia
Blytheville
Little Rock
Paragould
Pine Bluff

California
Alameda
Anaheim
Berkeley
Cerritos
Chula Vista
El Cajon
Fresno
Inglewood
Littlerock
Los Angeles
Monterey
Oxnard
Pasadena
Pittsburg
Redding
Sacramento
San Bernardino
San Diego
San Francisco
Santa Cruz
Torrance
Van Nuys
Yucaipa

Colorado
Arvada
Denver
Durango
Englewood
Greeley
Northglenn
Pueblo
Salida

Connecticut
Bridgeport
Danbury
Greenwich
Hartford
Meriden
Naugatuck
Norwich
Southington
Stamford

Delaware
Bellfonte
Dover
Milford
Newark
Wilmington

Florida
Boca Raton
Fort Lauderdale
Gainesville
Hialeah
Kissimmee
Miami
Okeechobee
Orlando
Pensacola
Sarasota
Tallahassee

Georgia
Atlanta
Dahlonega
LaFayette

Macon
Savannah
Smyrna
Valdosta
Warner Robins

Hawaii
Hilo
Honolulu
Kailua
Kaneohe
Lahaina
Waikiki Beach
Waipahu

Idaho
Boise
Coeur d'Alene
Ketchum
Lewiston
Moscow
Nampa
Pocatello

Illinois
Alsip
Carbondale
Champaign
Chicago
Decatur
De Kalb
Des Plaines
Elgin
Joliet
Kankakee
Moline

Peoria
Schaumburg
Skokie
Springfield
Urbana
Waukegan
Wilmette

Indiana
Elkhart
Indianapolis
Kokomo
Lafayette
Muncie
Portage
Rensselaer
South Bend
Terre Haute
Valparaiso
Vincennes

Iowa
Bettendorf
Davenport
Des Moines
Dubuque
Humboldt
Indianola
Ottumwa
Sioux City

Kansas
Emporia
Leavenworth
Manhattan
Osawatomie

Pittsburg
Topeka
Wichita

Kentucky
Bowling Green
Covington
Frankfort
Lexington
Louisville
Owensboro
Paducah

Louisiana
Baton Rouge
Bogalusa
Houma
Lafayette
Natchitoches
New Orleans
Shreveport
Thibodaux

Maine
Augusta
Bangor
Biddeford
Brunswick
Kennebunkport
Presque Isle

Maryland
Annapolis
Baltimore
Bethesda
Chevy Chase

Troublesome Place Names

Frederick
Gaithersburg
Hagerstown

Massachusetts
Amherst
Andover
Boston
Cambridge
Dartmouth
Framingham
Holyoke
Ipswich
Methuen
Nantucket
Northampton
Shrewsbury
Tewksbury
Waltham
Wellesley
Worcester

Michigan
Ann Arbor
Berkley
Cheboygan
Dearborn
Detroit
Escanaba
Grosse Pointe
Kalamazoo
Lansing
Marquette
Menominee
Muskegon
Saginaw

Wyandotte
Ypsilanti

Minnesota
Bemidji
Brainerd
Duluth
Edina
Fairbault
Mankato
Minneapolis
St. Paul
Winona

Mississippi
Biloxi
Bogalusa
Jackson
Meridian
Natchez
Picayune
Tupelo
Vicksburg
Yazoo City

Missouri
Affton
Cape Girardeau
Florissant
Hannibal
Jefferson City
Joplin
Sedalia
Tuscumbia

Montana
Billings
Bozeman
Butte
Havre
Helena
Kalispell
Lewistown
Missoula

Nebraska
Bellevue
Kearney
Lincoln
North Platte
Ogallala
Omaha
Papillion

Nevada
Carson City
Elko
Las Vegas
Reno
Winnemucca

New Hampshire
Concord
Laconia
Manchester
Nashua
Portsmouth

New Jersey
Bayonne
Camden

Englewood
Hackensack
Hoboken
Lyndhurst
Montclair
Paramus
Passaic
Paterson
Perth Amboy
Secaucus
Trenton
Wyckoff

New Mexico
Alamogordo
Albuquerque
Gallup
Las Cruces
Roswell
Santa Fe
Tucumcari
Zuni

New York
Albany
Batavia
Binghamton
Buffalo
Elmira
Ithaca
Massapequa
New Rochelle
Ossining
Patterson
Peekskill
Plattsburgh

Poughkeepsie
Rochester
Schenectady
Syracuse
Tonawanda
Utica
Yonkers

North Carolina
Asheville
Cary
Charlotte
Durham
Fayetteville
Fuquay-Varina
Greensboro
Raleigh
Roxboro
Winston-Salem

North Dakota
Bismarck
Fargo
Grand Forks
Minot
Williston

Ohio
Ashtabula
Bellefontaine
Berea
Chillicothe
Cincinnati
Columbus
Cuyahoga Falls
Dayton

Elyria
Lorain
Massillon
Piqua
Sandusky
Steubenville
Toledo
Van Wert
Wooster
Xenia

Oklahoma
Ardmore
Chickasha
Enid
McAlester
Muskogee
Oklahoma City
Ponca City
Stillwater
Tulsa

Oregon
Coos Bay
Corvallis
Eugene
Klamath Falls
Milwaukie
Portland
Salem
Tillamook

Pennsylvania
Aliquippa
Altoona
Carlisle

Troublesome Place Names

Edinboro
Harrisburg
McKeesport
Philadelphia
Pittsburgh
Punxsutawney
Reading
Scranton
Wilkes-Barre

Puerto Rico
Aguadilla
Arecibo
Bayamón
Caguas
Mayagüez
Ponce
San Juan
Trujillo Alto

Rhode Island
Coventry
Narragansett
Pawtucket
Providence
Warwick
Woonsocket

South Carolina
Beaufort
Charleston
Columbia
Greenville
Myrtle Beach
Spartanburg
Sumter

South Dakota
Aberdeen
Belle Fourche
De Smet
Pierre

Tennessee
Chattanooga
Gallatin
Knoxville
Memphis
Murfreesboro
Nashville
Sewanee

Texas
Abilene
Amarillo
Austin
Corpus Christi
Dallas
Edinburg
El Paso
Galveston
Killeen
Laredo
Lubbock
Nacogdoches
San Antonio
Texarkana
Waco
Waxachachie

Utah
Ogden
Orem

Provo
Salt Lake City

Vermont
Brattleboro
Burlington
Montpelier
Winooski

Virginia
Alexandria
Charlottesville
Chesapeake
Fairfax
Lynchburg
Norfolk
Richmond
Roanoke
Suffolk

Washington
Bellevue
Edmonds
Kennewick
Olympia
Seattle
Spokane
Tacoma
Walla Walla
Yakima

West Virginia
Beckley
Charleston
Charles Town
Clarksburg

Troublesome Place Names

Follansbee
Huntington
McMechen
Weirton
Wheeling

Wisconsin
Beloit
Eau Claire
Fond du Lac
Green Bay
Kenosha
La Crosse
Madison
Manitowoc
Menomonie
Milwaukee
Neenah
Oshkosh
Racine
Sheboygan
Wausau
Wauwatosa

Wyoming
Casper
Cheyenne
Gillette
Laramie

Canada

Alberta
Calgary
Edmonton
Lethbridge

Medicine Hat
Red Deer

British Columbia
Chilliwhack
Kamloops
Penticton
Vancouver
Victoria

Manitoba
Dauphin
Portage la Prairie
Selkirk
Thompson
Winnipeg

New Brunswick
Campbellton
Chatham
Dieppe
Edmundston
Fredericton
Moncton

Newfoundland
Bonavista
Corner Brook
St. John's
Stephenville

Nova Scotia
Dartmouth
Glace Bay
Halifax
New Glasgow

Truro

Ontario
Ajax
Etobicoke
Guelph
Kitchener
Mississauga
Ottawa
Sault Ste. Marie
Sudbury
Toronto
Windsor

Prince Edward Island
Charlottetown
Montague
St. Eleanors

Quebec
Brossard
Charlesbourg
Châteauguay
Gaspé
Gatineau
Joliette
LaSalle
Longueuil
Montreal
Quebec
Trois-Rivières

Saskatchewan
Esterhazy
Humboldt

Troublesome Place Names

Lloydminster
Moose Jaw
Regina
Saskatoon

Mexico
Acapulco
Aguascalientes
Chihuahua
Ciudad Juárez
Cuernavaca
Ensenada
Guadalajara
Hermosillo
Mexico City
Monterrey
Oaxaca
Tampico
Taxco
Tijuana
Veracruz
Villahermosa
Zacatecas